THE CORPORATE ADDRESS BOOK

THE CORPORATE ADDRESS BOOK

*How to Reach the
1,000 Most Important
Companies in the U.S.*

MICHAEL LEVINE

A Perigee Book

G. P. Putnam's Sons
Publishers Since 1838
200 Madison Avenue
New York, NY 10016

Library of Congress Cataloging-in-Publication Data

Levine, Michael.
    The corporate address book.

    "A Perigee book."
    Includes index.
    1. Corporations—United States—
Directories.
I. Title.
HG4057.A288   1987   338.7'4'02573   87-11162
ISBN 0-399-51384-1

Printed in the United States of America
1   2   3   4   5   6   7   8   9   10

To everyone who has ever kissed my forehead,
held my hand or whispered in my ear,
"Keep going," this book is dedicated.
—Michael Levine
July 1987

ACKNOWLEDGMENTS

The idea of *The Corporate Address Book: How to Reach the 1,000 Most Important Companies in the U.S.* grew out of the phenomenal success of my first book, *The Address Book: How to Reach Anyone Who's Anyone.*

So again I find myself in great debt to the following people. To each my love and thanks.

Bart Andrews, a brilliant literary agent, who has become one of my dearest friends.

Sherry Robb, Bart's partner and a merchandising wiz second to none.

The rest of the Andrews & Robb Literary Agency, including Robert Drake and Curtis Hayes.

Judy Linden, my editor at Putnam, who was constantly supportive and always available, truthful and loving.

The Putnam's team: Gene Brissie, Marilyn Ducksworth, Phyllis Grann, Suzanne Herz, Eleanor Holdridge, Janis Vallely and Neil Sigman. I would be hard pressed to find a group of professionals more committed to higher standards of excellence.

My father, Arthur Levine, whose lessons as a loving father I will try to emulate when it is my turn to be a parent.

My office family, who put up with me more waking hours than anyone else: Michelle Bega, Diana Chitow, Cary Goldberg, David Hill, Jennifer Johnston, Carl Lee, Victoria Miller, Monique Moss, Mitchell Schneider, Jim Sliman, David Wayne and Julie Wheeler.

A salute to the following uniquely brilliant people who have greatly affected my thinking: William F. Buckley, Jr., Leo Buscaglia, Harold Kushner, Arthur Laffer, M. Scott Peck, and Tom Peters.

My special friends, many of whom have been in my life a long time and I hope will never leave: Rana Bendixen, Ken Bostic, Bill Calkins, Stella Goodman, Mike Greenwald, Monika Harrison, Richard Imprescia, Michael Klein, Lori Kleinman, Joanna Langfield, Carol Lanning, Richard Lawson, Marilyn Beck-Levine, Patty Levine, Karen L'Heureux, Nancy

Mager, John McKillop, Deborah Palan, Janice Prager, Ron Remis, Harry Sandler, Jerry Swartz, Josh Trabulus, Erline White and Bobby Yosten.

Dennis Prager, who makes the most compelling case for belief in God I have ever heard, and who challenged me to "think a second time."

A special thanks to Mark Dossa, my head of research, who helped me immensely in compiling this book.

—Michael Levine
July 1987

CONTENTS

FOREWORD
by Arthur Laffer, Ph.D.

As one of President Reagan's most important economic advisors, Arthur Laffer is considered among the most brilliant economists of our time. Dr. Laffer received a B.A. in Economics from Yale University in 1963, prior to which he also attended the University of Munich, Germany. He received an M.B.A. (1965) and a Ph.D. in Economics (1972) from Stanford University.

Part of what Michael Levine has accomplished by writing this book is obvious enough at even the most casual glance. Because Michael is one of the most plainspoken and straightforward people you're ever likely to meet (certainly he's one of the most plainspoken and straightforward people *I've* ever met), he's announced his purpose in no uncertain terms right on his title page. *The Corporate Address Book* is a "how-to" book—a book that tells you exactly how to go about reaching the 1,000 most important businesses in America.

But that's by no means all his book is. It is also a tool that could be of inestimable value to every businessman, every businesswoman and every consumer in America. If used to its full potential, it could even be a major factor in bringing about the economic revival of our country.

To explain why this is so, I must digress for a moment and talk about something that doesn't really exist outside the imaginations and mathematical models of economists—The Market. Markets exist, of course. There's the New York Stock Market, there's the Pacific Stock Exchange in Los Angeles and there's the Commodities Exchange in Chicago. There's J. C. Penney, there's Montgomery Ward and there's the supermarket where you buy your groceries. There's the corner newsstand and there's the neighborhood shoe repair shop. All these are markets, and there are millions of others like them operating all over our nation 24 hours a day. Markets, places where goods and services are bought and sold, are quite real.

The Market, on the other hand, is not real. It is merely an abstraction, a convenient fiction, a way of condensing into two simple words the incredibly complex, interconnected and interdependent system that emerges spontaneously as a result of all the millions upon millions of choices made minute by minute, hour by hour, day in and day out, by all the millions of entrepreneurs, manufacturers, service workers, financiers, traders and consumers who make up what we call The Economy.

11

The Market, operating according to the rules we call the Laws of Supply and Demand, has proved to be the most efficient engine for economic progress, the most effective means of steadily creating new wealth and improving the overall standard of living, that has ever been developed in human society.

And one of the chief reasons for The Market's superiority to all other known methods of arranging our economic affairs is its capacity for improving communication among those who want to do business with one another. No central planner could ever possibly tell you what specific goods and services will best satisfy the goals and purposes of society. Even if such a planner could somehow collect all the information he would need to make such a judgment, by the time he had assembled and collated it, things would have changed, and his information would be information about history, about the way The Market used to be but is no longer.

The Market itself, however, can easily tell you what goods and services will best satisfy the goals and purposes of society. At any given moment, any investor or manufacturer can learn a great deal about what goods and services are most in demand by merely comparing the market prices of those goods and services with the costs of producing them—by looking at the fabled "bottom line."

But informative as the bottom line is, there are other, more direct sources of information on which a businessman or businesswoman may draw—and will draw if he or she is wise. Which brings us back to the importance of this book. Though much may be learned about what consumers like and don't like from a look at the bottom line, even more may be learned from a look at their own expression of their opinions in personal letters.

And if ever there was a time when better communication between American business and American consumers was needed, that time is now. In recent decades, American business has declined sadly when it comes to pleasing the consumer. American shoppers now prefer imported cars, imported audio and video equipment and, to a steadily increasing extent, imported computers. The best new ideas no longer originate with American firms, as they once did, but with Japanese and German firms. The shelves of our bookstores are full of volumes hailing the innovator, the entrepreneur, as the last best hope of the once-proud American economy. Business consultants advise large established firms to find ways to encourage "entrepreneurship"—innovation from within their ranks—as the only alternative to stagnation and decline.

But how are such reforms as these to be accomplished if American businessmen and businesswomen and American consumers don't talk—and listen—to one another? Studies show that most consumers who do write to corporate executives do so because they want to complain, because they want to pay compliments or because they want to suggest new ideas. More consumers should write for such reasons. And what they write should be read.

12

If you are an American consumer and you are dissatisfied with American products, don't just turn to the Japanese. Let the American companies know what they're doing wrong—and what they're doing right. If you are an American businessman or businesswoman looking for new ideas—ways to develop new products or improve old ones—be aware that you can do far worse than to listen to the advice of your customers.

If America is to become innovative again, if it is to lead the world once more in excellence, in productivity and in creativity, it will be because individual Americans share their ideas, because they seize the initiative and communicate with one another—about what can be done, what should be done and what should be abandoned and left behind us. Michael Levine has provided the tool that can make all this possible. The rest, and the future of the American economy, is up to all the rest of us.

—Arthur Laffer, Ph.D.
July 1987

INTRODUCTION

When I first wrote the bestselling *The Address Book: How to Reach Anyone Who's Anyone* (Putnam/Perigee), several years ago, I assumed that the majority of people were buying it to obtain addresses of celebrities. Having been an autograph collector, I naturally assumed that most people were, like myself, more interested in a fan letter sourcebook than a consumer tool.

Time has taught me I was both right and wrong. The tremendous success of *The Address Book* did confirm the star-struck nature of the public. However, I greatly underestimated the desire of people to contact businesses. Hence this book.

Ninety-five percent of the consumer contact with businesses falls into three specific areas:

- Complaints and Compliments—While negative responses outweigh the positive ten to one, most people do contact businesses to complain or compliment.

- Ideas—Everything imaginable is suggested, from new products to improvements on current service.

- Jobs.

Since the first publication of *The Address Book,* I have spoken to hundreds of companies and people, received over 20,000 pieces of mail, and done scores of media interviews, all confirming two points. One, people have a lot to say, and two, businesses are very anxious to hear it.

Here are some professional tips on communicating your message more effectively.

Complaints and Compliments

Do remember that while most people write only when there is a problem, companies are anxious to hear the good as well. Don't hesitate to write when a person or business performs exceptionally well. Here are some suggestions for successful complaint letters:

- Include your name, address, and home and work phone numbers.

- Type your letter, if possible. If it is handwritten, be sure it is neat and legible.
- Make it brief and to the point. Include all pertinent facts (date of transaction, item involved, store and so forth) and what you believe would be a fair and just settlement of the problem. Attach documentation to support your case. Send copies, not originals.
- Remember, the person reading your letter is not personally responsible for your problem, but may be responsible for solving it. Therefore, avoid writing a sarcastic, threatening or angry letter. It may lessen your chances of getting the complaint resolved.
- Send copies of your letter to a lawyer, the Better Business Bureau, the Chamber of Commerce, consumer advocates and so forth. This technique carries a lot of weight and shows that you mean business.
- Keep copies of your letter and all related documents and information.

Sample Complaint Letter

Your address
City, state, ZIP Code
Date

Appropriate person
Company name
Street address
City, state, ZIP Code

Dear (appropriate name):

Specific background information.

State problem clearly and concisely.

Ask for satisfaction.

On (date), I purchased a (name of product with serial or model number). Upon taking it home and following the enclosed instructions for its use, I discovered that your product does not perform satisfactorily. Specifically, it does not (describe function) as I expected it would based on the advertising and packaging.

I would appreciate your (state the action you want). Enclosed you will find copies of my records (receipt, warranty, guarantee,

State time parameter.

Include phone numbers.

cancelled check and so forth) to verify the purchase. I look forward to your reply within (reasonable period of time) before seeking third-party assistance. You may contact me at the above address or by phone at (home and office numbers).

Thank you for your prompt resolution of this problem.

Sincerely,

Your name

Send copies of letter to all appropriate persons and organizations.

cc: Chamber of Commerce
Related associations
Dealer through whom product was purchased
Local media or consumer advocate

There are some national consumer organizations that may be of help to you in resolving your complaints:

American Consumers Assn.
332 S Michigan Avenue #1405
Chicago, IL 60604
James S. Tiernan, Executive Director
(312) 922-5250

Automotive Consumer Action Panel
c/o Natl. Automotive Dealers Assoc.
8400 Westpack Drive
McLean, VA 22101
Deborah M. Hopkins, Director
(703) 821-7144

Cemetery Consumer Service Council
Post Office Box 3574
Washington, DC 20007
Robert M. Fells, Director
(703) 379-6426

Consumer Exchange Club
Post Office Box 13708
Wauwatosa, WI 53213
Becky Thompson, Director

Consumer Federation of America
1424 16th Street NW #604
Washington, DC 20036
Stephen J. Brobeck, Executive Officer
(202) 387-6121

Consumer Information Center
General Services Administration
Washington, DC 20405

**Consumer Organization for the
Hearing Impaired**
Post Office Box 8188
10801 Rockville Pike
Rockville, MD 20852
William Paschall, Director

Consumers Union of the U.S.
256 Washington Street
Mount Vernon, NY 10553
Rhoda H. Karpatkin, Executive
Director
(914) 667-9400

Ideas

This is an area in which there are fewer accepted rules, so go for it!

Many major manufacturers won't consider a letter or prototype from an individual suggesting a new idea. The standard route is to request a submission form from the company. This usually contains a legal agreement that promises the company won't steal your idea. Usually, you have to wait two or three months for a reply.

There are two ways to gain an edge over thousands of other people proposing ideas. First, you need to make an impression on the company. If you have no previous success, consider approaching someone who does, a design firm, for instance, or a lawyer whose clients have worked with the manufacturers before. Of course, if you send your idea to a small, less-known company, a patent or copyright attorney is essential.

The second way to gain an edge is to take a more sophisticated approach when you write. Read articles about the company and ask for an annual report. Find out what direction the company is moving in and then decide how your idea fits in with its product strategy.

Companies are more likely to establish a relationship if you can discuss your product in terms of tooling (the amount and expense of engineering involved), sourcing (where the manufacturing can be done at an economical price) and profit potential.

Even though it may appear to be a difficult process from idea to completion, every major executive I spoke with encouraged new ideas from the public.

So go forth, be creative, break some rules and have fun.

Jobs

After speaking to several dozen of the nation's top personnel directors, I am convinced that people just don't spend enough time preparing their resumes or themselves for a job interview. A job interview is the time to sell your talents to a prospective employer. During the interview, your qualifications, appearance and general fitness will be judged by the employer for the job opening. This is your chance to convince him or her that you are the best one for the job.

This is also your chance to appraise the job, the employer and the firm. You will be able to decide if this company suits your career needs and interests and whether the employer is the type you want to work for.

Before the interview, you should prepare yourself well. Assemble all the papers that you need and have the information about yourself firmly in mind. Don't forget to take copies of your resume. Although you may have already submitted one, it's good to have an extra copy. If your work is the sort you can show in an interview, such as publications, procedures or artwork, take some along with you.

- Know what you have to offer—what education, training or work experience you have.
- Learn all that you can about the company—what does it do, its product or service and its hiring policies.
- Learn the area salary scale for the job you are applying for—don't sell yourself short, make sure the salary offered is competitive.

During the interview:

- Be pleasant and friendly but businesslike.
- Let the employer control the interview. Keep your answers short and to the point.
- Stress your qualifications but don't exaggerate.
- When discussing former employers, don't criticize.
- If the employer doesn't offer you a job, ask when you can call and find out his or her decision.
- Thank the employer for the interview and then follow up with a thank-you note.

Your resume is your marketing tool for selling yourself to a prospective employer. Since you want your resume to fit onto one page, you should use the "who, what, where, when, and why" formula and be concise and clear in your format and presentation. You should try to make your resume brief and appealing to the eye, so that the person scanning the page can pick out your best assets and work experience immediately. Employers read through many resumes for a single job and it is important that you make yours easy to understand.

Most resumes are organized in chronological order, starting with the latest job experience and working backward. This format is easy to follow and focuses on your career development. Since you list your responsibilities for each job, try not to repeat tasks in each job description. You only need to list inclusive years to designate employment dates, months are not necessary.

When writing your resume, don't include negative experiences, your salary history or expectations, personal data (marital status, height, weight and so forth) or evidence of long periods of unemployment. Make it look and sound as positive as you can.

Your resume is a reflection of your professionalism, and its appearance is very important. You should have it printed on quality paper using a good copying process such as laser or offset printing.

Have someone proofread it for you. Spelling mistakes on a resume could be the difference between getting an interview or not.

If you answer an ad through the mail, you should include a cover letter. This gives you the opportunity to briefly highlight your qualifications for the position you are seeking. The letter should include a statement of the position you are applying for and how you learned about it. You should also state why you are applying for the job and what qualifications you have. The closing paragraph should thank the reader for his or her consideration and ask for an interview.

Sample Resume

Mark S. Dossa
3399 Star Lane
Lafayette, CA 98765
(800) 283-2929

Education

September 1981–June 1983	Mt. Diablo Junior College. General education courses with an emphasis on business.
September 1983–May 1985	California State University. Bachelor of Arts in Journalism with option in Public Relations.

Experience

May 1986–February 1987	Park Public Relations Company. Assistant Publicist. Wrote press releases, arranged interviews for clients, involved in heavy media contact, performed general office duties.

August 1985–May 1986	*Sun Valley Times.* Reporter. Covered sporting events, conducted interviews with athletes, wrote column on sports trivia.
January 1983–June 1985	Lost Hills Country Club. Waiter. Developed customer relations, promoted sales, trained new employees.
Activities	Member, Public Relations Student Society of America; weightlifting; reading; skiing.
References	Available upon request.

Why These 1,000?

What makes a company one of the 1,000 most important in America? The companies listed in this book have a profound effect on our lives.

Important companies are generally big, but not always the biggest. For example, Mrs. Fields is probably not one of the 1,000 largest companies in America, but I felt its influence made it important to include.

I made my choices after consulting editors from some of the country's most important business publications, including *The Wall Street Journal, Forbes, Fortune, Business Week,* and *Barrons.*

As you examine the entries and review all of the subsidiaries and divisions that the main companies are responsible for, I think you'll find that these companies are extremely important to most Americans.

Success Stories

I am anxious to hear whether *The Corporate Address Book* has helped you. If as a consumer or businessperson you have found this book of service, please let us know. Your comments are extremely useful for future editions.

How to Use This Book

This book is organized for maximum efficiency to help you locate a specific company or group of leading firms within an industry.

There are 30 general categories in the book. Each of the 1,000 companies is listed under the category that best describes it. For example, the Ford Motor Company would be found in the automotive category, and McDonald's would be listed under foods.

The index lists every company in alphabetical order.

AEROSPACE

ALLIED-SIGNAL, INC.
Post Office Box 2245R
Morristown, NY 07960
(201) 455-2000
Primary Business: Aerospace products
Chairman of the Board: Michael D.
  Dingman
CEO: Michael D. Dingman
Vice-Chairman: Forrest N. Shumway
Senior Vice-President (Public Affairs):
  David G. Powell
Senior Vice-President (Human
  Resources): Edwin M. Halkyard
Sales : $10 billion
Net Worth: $3.3 billion
# of Employees: 114,500

Miscellaneous Facts: Incorporated in
  1985 in Delaware as successor to
  Allied Chemical Corp.

THE BOEING CO.
7755 E Marginal Ways
Seattle, WA 98108
(206) 655-2121
Primary Business: Maker of jet
  airplanes, missiles
CEO: T. A. Wilson
President: Frank A. Shrontz
Vice-Chairman: Malcolm T. Stamper
Senior Vice-President: Lionel D. Alford
Senior Vice-President: K. F. Holtby
Sales: $10.35 billion
Net Worth: $3.6 billion
# of Employees: 97,147

Subsidiary:
Boeing Computer Services, Inc.

Divisions:
Boeing Marine Systems
Boeing Military Airplane Co.
Boeing Aerospace Co.
Boeing Commercial Airplane Co.

Miscellaneous Facts: Incorporated in
  1934 in Delaware as Boeing Airplane
  Co. Present name adopted in 1961.

CESSNA AIRCRAFT CO.
5800 E Pawnee Road
Wichita, KS 67218
(316) 685-9111
Primary Business: Aviation products
Chairman of the Board: Russell W.
  Meyer, Jr.
CEO: Russell W. Meyer, Jr.
President: R. W. Van Sant
Senior Vice-President (Personnel): John
  E. Moore
Senior Vice-President (Marketing):
  Brian E. Barents
Sales: $690 million
Net Worth: $334 million
# of Employees: 8,645

Subsidiaries:
Cessna Disc Corp.
Cessna Finance Corp.
Cessna International Finance Corp.
United Hyraulics Corp.

Divisions:
Cessna Fluid Power Div.
Citation Marketing Div.
Conquest Marketing Div.
McCauley Accessories Div.

EX-CELL-O CORP.
2855 Coolidge
Troy, MI 48084
(313) 637-1000
Primary Business: Aerospace and
  automotive components
Chairman of the Board: E. Paul Casey
CEO: E. Paul Casey
President: E. Paul Casey
Vice-President (Human Resources): J.
  William Lenz
Vice-President (Communications): Terry
  W. Wilson
Vice-President and General Counsel:
  Alan D. MacDonald
Revenue: $1.14 billion
Net Worth: $494 million
# of Employees: 13,000

Subsidiaries:
Accurate Bushing Co.
Ace Industries, Inc.
Atlantic Aerospace, Inc.

Babco Industries, Inc.
Bryant Grinder Corp.
Cadillac Gage Co.

Divisions:
Aerospace Group
Airfoil Div.
Remex Cam Operations
Combat Vehicle Operations
Davidson Rubber Co.
McCord Gasket Corp.

FAIRCHILD INDUSTRIES, INC.
Post Office Box 10801
Washington Dulles Airport
Chantilly, VA 22021
(703) 478-5800
Primary Business: Commercial/industrial
 communications
Chairman of the Board: Emanuel
 Fthenakis
Executive Vice-President: James R.
 Wilson
Senior Vice-President
 (Communications): Philip Schneider
Director, Employee Relations: Frank J.
 Schmidt
Sales: $855 million
Net Worth: $208 million
# of Employees: 12,380

Subsidiaries:
Fairchild Aircraft Co.
VSI Corp.

Divisions:
Fairchild Industrial Products Co.
Fairchild Republic Co.
Fairchild Space Co.
Fairchild Control Systems Co.
Greer Hydraulics

GARRETT CORP.
9851 Sepulveda Boulevard
Los Angeles, CA 90009
(213) 776-1010
Primary Business: Aircraft air-
 conditioning and cabin pressurization
 systems
Chairman: Roy Ekrom
CEO: Roy Ekrom
President: J. A. Teske
Group Vice-President (Sales and
 Service): R. J. Wright

Vice-President and General Counsel: S.
 G. Hamilton
Manager, Public Relations: D. M.
 Franson
Sales: $1.97 billion
# of Employees: 23,000

GENERAL DYNAMICS CORP.
Pierre Laclede Center
St. Louis, MO 63105
(314) 889-8200
Primary Business: Aerospace products
Chairman of the Board: Stanley C. Pace
CEO: Stanley C. Pace
President: Oliver C. Boileau
Executive Vice-President: Richard E.
 Adams
Vice-President (Government Relations):
 Otto J. Glasser
Vice-President (Human Resources):
 Arch H. Rambeau
Sales: $8.2 billion
Net Worth: $1.34 billion
# of Employees: 103,300

Subsidiaries:
Cessna Aircraft Co.
Datagraphix, Inc.
Meterial Service Corp.
General Dynamics Services Co.

Divisions:
Convair Div.
Data Systems Div.
Electric Boat Div.
Electronics Div.
Fort Worth Div.
Space Systems Div.

Miscellaneous Facts: Incorporated in
 1952 in Delaware.

GRUMMAN CORP.
1111 Stewart Avenue
Bethpage, NY 11714
(516) 575-2464
Primary Business: Holding company,
 military aircraft
Chairman: John C. Bierwirth
CEO: John C. Bierwirth
President: George M. Skurla
Senior Vice-President (Corporate
 Service): Robert J. Myers
Vice-President (Community Relations):
 John J. Carroll

Vice-President and General Counsel:
Thomas L. Genovese
Revenue: $3.09 billion
Net Worth: $402 million
# of Employees: 32,000

Subsidiaries:
Grumman Aerospace Corp.
Grumman Allied
Grumman Credit Corp.
Grumman Data Systems

Divisions:
ADI Transportation
Grumman Data Systems Institute
Grumman International, Inc.
Grumman Ohio Corp.

Miscellaneous Facts: Incorporated in
1929 in New York as Grumman
Aircraft Engineering Corp. Present
name adopted in 1969.

GULFSTREAM AEROSPACE CORP.
Post Office Box 2201
Travis Field
Savannah, GA 31402
(912) 946-3000
Primary Business: Designs special-
purpose aircraft
Chairman of the Board: Allen E.
Paulson
CEO: Allen E. Paulson
President: Allen E. Paulson
Executive Vice-President: Albert H.
Glenn
Senior Vice-President: James L.
Bradbury
# of Employees: 3,800

Miscellaneous Facts: Subsidiary of
Chrysler Corp.

HONEYWELL, INC.
Honeywell Plaza
Minneapolis, MN 55408
(612) 870-5200
Primary Business: Aerospace and
defense systems
Chairman: Edson W. Spencer
Vice-Chairman: James J. Renier
Vice-President (Communications): Dean
B. Randall
Vice-President (Human Resources):
Fosten A. Boyle
Revenue: $6.75 billion

Net Worth: $2.6 billion
# of Employees: 94,100

Divisions:
Commercial Aviation Div.
Military Avionics Div.
Space and Strategic Avionics Div.
Defense Systems Div.
Underseas Systems Div.
Solid State Product Center
Communication Network Div.
Medical Electronics Div.
Honeywell Information Systems

Miscellaneous Facts: One of the world's
leading providers in process
automation and control.

JOHNSON CONTROLS, INC.
5757 N Green Bay Avenue
Milwaukee, WI 53209
(414) 228-1200
Primary Business: Builds automation
systems
Chairman of the Board: F. L. Brengel
Vice-Chairman: J. F. Daly
Executive Vice-President: William L.
Rootham
Public Relations Manager: D. M. Zutz
Sales: $1.8 billion
Net Worth: $765 million
# of Employees: 29,000

Subsidiaries:
Ferro Manufacturing Corp.
Hoover Universal, Inc.
Johnson Controls International, Inc.

LEAR SIEGLER, INC.
2850 Ocean Park Boulevard
Santa Monica, CA 90405
(213) 452-6000
Primary Business: Aerospace
Chairman of the Board: Robert T.
Campion
CEO: Robert T. Campion
President: Norman A. Barkeley
Vice-Chairman: K. Robert Hahn
Vice-President (Public Relations):
William M. O'Hern
Vice-President (Personnel): Carroll
Rosenberg
Sales: $2.4 billion
Net Worth: $642 million
# of Employees: 29,725

Subsidiaries:
Piper Aircraft Corp.
Standard Tool Co.

Divisions:
Smith & Wesson Div.
Burroughs Div.
Audiotone Div.
Bogen Div.
General Seating Div.
Peerless Div.

LITTON INDUSTRIES, INC.
360 N Crescent Drive
Beverly Hills, CA 90210
(213) 859-5000
Primary Business: Business machinery,
  office copiers
Chairman of the Board: Fred W.
  O'Green
CEO: Fred W. O'Green
President: Orion L. Hoch
Vice-President (Corporate
  Communications): F. James Carr
Senior Vice-President and General
  Counsel: Robert H. Lentz
Executive Vice-President: Joseph F.
  Caliguiri
Revenue: $4.6 billion
Net Worth: $2.1 billion
# of Employees: 66,000

Subsidiaries:
Aero Service Corp.
Applied Technology
Core Laboratories, Inc.
Litton Laser Systems
Itek Composition Systems
Kimball Systems, Inc.
Gardner Machine Co.
Landis Tool Co.
Twin City Tool
Litton Systems, Inc.

Miscellaneous Facts: Incorporated in
  1953 in Delaware as Electro Dynamics
  Corp. Present name adopted in 1953.

LOCKHEED CORP.
2555 Hollywood Way
Burbank, CA 91520
(818) 847-6121
Primary Business: Defense systems
Chairman: Lawrence O. Kitchen
CEO: Lawrence O. Kitchen

President: Robert A. Fuhrman
Vice-President (Human Resources):
  Louis J. Bernard
Vice-President (Corporate
  Communications): H. David Crowther
Vice-President (Marketing): Charles de
  Bedts
Sales: $9.11 billion
Net Worth: $1.5 billion
# of Employees: 87,300

Subsidiaries:
Avicom International, Inc.
Lockheed Aeromod, Inc.
Lockheed Support Systems
Murdock Engineering Co.
Cadam Inc.
Datacom Systems Corp.
Advanced Marine Systems
Lockport Marine, Inc.
Lockheed Electronics Co., Inc.
Lockheed Corp. International
Lockheed Finance Corp.

MCDONNELL DOUGLAS CORP.
Post Office Box 516
St. Louis, MO 63166
(314) 232-0232
Primary Business: Aerospace
Chairman: Sanford N. McDonnell
CEO: Sanford N. McDonnell
President: John F. McDonnell
Vice-President (Productivity): David C.
  Arnold
Vice-President (Personnel): James H.
  MacDonald
Vice-President (Communications):
  Gerald J. Meyer
Sales: $11.66 billion
Net Worth: $2.6 billion
# of Employees: 100,391

Subsidiaries:
McDonnell Douglas Helicopter Co.
McDonnell Douglas Realty Co.
McDonnell Douglas Finance Corp.
Telecheck Services, Inc.

Divisions:
Douglas Aircraft Co.
McDonnell Aircraft Co.
McDonnell Douglas Astronautics

MARTIN MARIETTA CORP.

6801 Rockledge Drive
Bethesda, MD 20817
(301) 897-6000
Primary Business: Aerospace, defense,
electronics specialties
Chairman: Laurence J. Adams
Senior Vice-President: Norman R.
Augustine
Vice-President (Communication
Systems): William P. Osborne
Vice-President (Personnel): Bobby F.
Leonard
Revenue: $4.41 billion
Net Worth: $1.7 billion
# of employees: 66,000

Subsidiaries:
Martin Marietta Energy Systems, Inc.
Chesapeake Park, Inc.
Martin Marietta Environmental Systems
Martin Marietta Ordnance Systems, Inc.
Orlando Central Park, Inc.

Miscellaneous Facts: Incorporated in
1961 in Maryland.

NORTHROP CORP.

1840 Century Park E
Los Angeles, CA 90067
(213) 553-6262
Primary Business: Aircraft and
electronic systems
Chairman: Thomas V. Jones
CEO: Thomas V. Jones
President: Frank W. Lynch
Senior Vice-President (Advanced
Projects): Welko E. Gasich
Senior Vice-President (Government
Relations): Stanley Ebner
Vice-President (Public Affairs): Les
Daly
Revenue: $5.10 billion
Net Worth: $899 million
# of Employees: 47,000

Divisions:
Northrop Defense Systems Div.
Electro-Mechanical Div.
Electronics Div.
Northrop Services, Inc.
Precision Products Div.
Wilcox Electric, Inc.
Aircraft Div.
Aircraft Services Div.
Advanced Systems Div.
Ventura Div.

PPG INDUSTRIES, INC.

One PPG Place
Pittsburgh, PA 15222
(412) 434-3131
Primary Business: Flat glass, auto and
aircraft glass
Chairman: Vincent A. Sarni
CEO: Vincent A. Sarni
President: Edward J. Slack
Vice-Chairman: Frank V. Breeze
Group Vice-President (Glass): Eugene
B. Moiser
Vice-President (Corporate
Communications): Francis B. O'Neil
Revenue: $4.24 billion
Net Worth: $1.7 billion
# of Employees: 38,000

Affiliates:
Arkansas Chemicals, Inc.
Pittsburgh Corning Corp.

RAYTHEON CO.

141 Spring Street
Lexington, MA 02173
(617) 862-6600
Primary Business: Microwave, power
Chairman: Thomas L. Phillips
CEO: Thomas L. Phillips
President: D. Brainerd Holmes
Vice-President (Public Relations):
Richard R. Mau
Vice-President (Manufacturing): John
R. Pasquariello
Revenue: $6 billion
Net Worth: $1.9 billion
# of Employees: 73,300

Subsidiaries:
Amana Refrigeration, Inc.
The Badger Co., Inc.
Beech Aircraft Corp.
Caloric Corp.
Glenwood Range Co.
Modern Maid Co.
Raytheon Service Co.
Sedco Systems, Inc.
Sorensen Co.
Speed Queen Co.
Switchcraft, Inc.

ROCKWELL INTERNATIONAL CORP.

600 Grant Street
Pittsburgh, PA 15219
(412) 565-2000

Primary Business: Aerospace
Chairman: Robert Anderson
CEO: Robert Anderson
President: Donald R. Beall
Senior Vice-President
  (Communications): Samuel Petok
Senior Vice-President (Government
  Relations): Bastian Hello
Revenue: $11.32 billion
Net Worth: $2.9 billion
# of Employees: 123,759

Operations:
Advanced Development Center
Allen-Bradley Co.
Automotive
Collins Air Transport Div.
North American Aircraft
Ricketdyne Div.
Satellite Systems Div.
Space Station Systems Div.
Space Transportation Systems Div.

Miscellaneous Facts: Incorporated in
  1928 in Delaware as North American
  Aviation. Present name adopted in
  1973.

ROHR INDUSTRIES
Post Office Box 878
Chula Vista, CA 92012
(619) 691-4111
Primary Business: Aircraft engine
  components manufacturer
Chairman of the Board: Harry W. Todd
CEO: Harry W. Todd
President: Harry W. Todd
Senior Vice-President: Paul E. Brunton
Director, Public Affairs: L. J. Peeples
Revenue: $613 million
# of Employees: 8,000

TELEDYNE, INC.
1901 Avenue of the Stars
Los Angeles, CA 90067
(213) 277-3311
Primary Business: Produces electronic
  and aviation control systems
Chairman: Henry E. Singleton
CEO: Henry E. Singleton
President: George A. Roberts
Vice-President: Wilson W. Sick, Jr.
Revenue: $3.49 billion
Net Worth: $1.57 billion
# of Employees: 45,000

Subsidiaries:
Teledyne Acoustic Research
Teledyne Adams
Teledyne Amco
Teledyne Big Beam
Teledyne CAE
Teledyne Casting Service
Teledyne CME
Teledyne Getz
Teledyne Hanau

TEXTRON, INC.
40 Westminster Street
Providence, RI 02903
(401) 421-2800
Primary Business: Aerospace/
  technology, helicopters, rocket
  engines
Chairman: Robert P. Straetz
CEO: B. F. Dolan
President: B. F. Dolan
Senior Vice-President (Human
  Resources): William F. Wayland
Vice-President (Corporate
  Communications): Raymond W.
  Caine, Jr.
Sales: $3.22 billion
Net Worth: $1.63 billion
# of Employees: 56,000

Subsidiaries:
Avco Corp.
The Paul Revere Corp.
Avco Aerostructures
Avco Systems Textron
Bell Aerospace Textron
Bell Helicopter Textron
HR Textron, Inc.

Divisions:
Camcar Div.
E-Z-Go Div.
Randall Div.

TODD SHIPYARDS CORP.
1 State Street Plaza
New York, NY 10004
(212) 668-4700
Primary Business: Shipbuilding
Chairman of the Board: John T.
  Gilbride
CEO: John T. Gilbride
President: Hans K. Schaefer
Senior Vice-President: Joseph H. Dugan
Vice-President: Clifford E. Jones

Revenue: $622.31 million
Net Worth: $115 million
# of Employees: 8,600

Subsidiaries:
The Aro Corp.
Aro International Corp.
Modernair Corp.

TRW, INC.
23555 Euclid Avenue
Cleveland, OH 44117
(216) 383-2121
Primary Business: Car and truck parts,
  spacecraft and propulsion products
Chairman: Ruben F. Mettler
CEO: Ruben F. Mettler
Vice-Chairman: Joseph T. Gorman
Vice-President (Defense Systems):
  James R. Burnett
Vice-President (Communications):
  Thomas J. Fay
Revenue: $6.06 billion
Net Worth: $1.72 billion
# of Employees: 93,524

Groups:
TRW Automotive Aftermarket Group
TRW Engine Components Group
TRW General Components Group
TRW Steering Components Group
TRW Controls and Fasteners Group
TRW Defense Systems Group
TRW Electronic Components Group
TRW Aircraft Group
TRW Industrial Products Group

TRW, Inc., Cutting Tools
TRW Energy Products Group
TRW Information Systems Group

Miscellaneous Facts: Incorporated in
  1916 in Ohio as The Steel Products
  Co. Present name adopted in 1965.

UNITED TECHNOLOGIES CORP.
United Technologies Building
Hartford, CT 06101
(203) 728-7000
Primary Business: Designs high-
  technology products
Chairman of the Board: Harry J. Gray
CEO: Robert F. Daniell
President: Robert F. Daniell
Senior Executive Vice-President: Hubert
  Faure
Senior Vice-President (Human
  Resources): Sidney F. McKenna
Sales: $14.9 billion
Net Worth: $4.4 billion
# of Employees: 184,800

Subsidiaries:
Alma Plastics Co.
Carrier Corp.
Elliott Co.
Essex Group, Inc.
Mostek Corp.
Norden Systems, Inc.
Otis Group

Miscellaneous Facts: Incorporated in
  1934 in Delaware.

APPAREL

ARIS GLOVES
417 Fifth Avenue
New York, NY 10016
(212) 532-8627
Primary Business: Ladies' and men's
   gloves manufacturer
Chairman of the Board: Lari Stanton
CEO: Lari Stanton
# of Employees: 197

Miscellaneous Facts: Subsidiary of Sara
   Lee Corp.

THE ARROW CO.
530 Fifth Avenue
New York, NY 10036
(212) 930-2900
Primary Business: Maker of men's
   apparel
President: Harris R. Hester

Miscellaneous Facts: Division of Cluett,
   Peabody & Co.

CALVIN KLEIN INDUSTRIES, INC.
1400 Broadway
New York, NY 10018
(212) 575-0800
Primary Business: Clothing
   manufacturer
Chairman of the Board: Barry K.
   Schwartz
Vice-Chairman: Calvin Klein
# of Employees: 1,600

Subsidiaries:
Puritan Fashions Corp.

CLUETT, PEABODY & CO., INC.
510 Fifth Avenue
New York, NY 10036
(212) 930-3000
Primary Business: Men's shirts,
   underwear, and other clothing
Chairman: Henry H. Henley, Jr.
CEO: Henry H. Henley, Jr.
President: Gordon E. Allen
Vice-President (Corporate Relations):
   Cochran B. Supplee
Vice-President (Personnel): D. Michael
   Roark

Revenue: $949.27 million
Net Worth: $245 million
# of Employees: 18,818

Subsidiaries:
Alatex Marketing
Duofold Inc.
Six Continents, Ltd.
Spring City Knitting Co.
Textest, Inc.

Divisions:
The Arrow Co.
CSM Div.
Ron Chereskin Menswear
Cluett YouthWear
Cosco
Dobie Originals
Halston for Men
Jet Sew, Inc.
RPM Fashions
Sunday's Sportswear Co.

DANSKIN, INC.
700 Fairfield Avenue
Stamford, CT 06902
(203) 356-8000
Primary Business: Women's tights
   manufacturer
Senior Vice-President: William F.
   Karnbach

Miscellaneous Facts: Subsidiary of
   Beatrice Companies, Inc.

FRUIT OF THE LOOM, INC.
One Fruit of the Loom Drive
Bowling Green, KY 42102
(502) 781-6400
Primary Business: Manufacturer of
   underwear
Executive Vice-President: David
   Dreschler
# of Emloyees: 300

Miscellaneous Facts: Subsidiary of Farley
   Industries.

GENESCO, INC.
Genesco Park
Nashville, TN 37202
(615) 367-7000

Primary Business: Hosiery, suits, shoes manufacturer
Chairman of the Board: Richard W. Hanselman
CEO: Richard W. Hanselman
President: Richard W. Hanselman
Executive Vice-President: Larry B. Shelton
Vice-President (Human Resources): Don H. Hartin
Revenue: $595 million
# of Employees: 12,000

HAGGAR CO.
6113 Lemmon Avenue
Dallas, TX 75209
(214) 352-8481
Primary Business: Maker of men's and boys' slacks
Chairman: Edmond R. Haggar
President: Joseph M. Haggar, Jr.
Honorary Chairman: Joseph M. Haggar, Sr.
Sales: $220 million
# of Employees: 6,500

INTERCO, INC.
Ten Broadway
Post Office Box 8777
St. Louis, MO 63102
(314) 863-1100
Primary Business: Apparel manufacturing
Chairman: Harvey Saligman
CEO: Harvey Saligman
President: Harry M. Krogh
Vice-Chairman: Ronald L. Aylward
Senior Vice-President: Eugene F. Smith
Sales: $2.62 billion
Net Worth: $1.11 billion
# of Employees: 50,000

Subsidiaries:
Abe Schrader Corp.
Big Yank Corp.
The Biltwell Co., Inc.
Cowden Manufacturing Co.
Ethan Allen, Inc.
The Florsheim Shoe Co.
International Hat Co.
Londontown Corp.
Queen Casuals, Inc.
Stuffed Shirt, Inc.

Miscellaneous Facts: Incorporated in 1921 in Delaware as International Shoe Co. Present name adopted in 1966.

JANTZEN, INC.
Post Office Box 3001
Portland, OR 97208
(503) 238-5000
Primary Business: Men's and women's clothing
CEO: Jerome M. Pool
President: Jerome M. Pool
Vice-President (Sales, Men's Division): Dennis Maloney
Vice-President (Sales, Misses Division): Doug Gibson
Director of Public Relations: A. McArthur
Sales Range: $150–$175 million
# of Employees: 4,000

JOCKEY INTERNATIONAL, INC.
2300 60th Street
Kenosha, WI 53140
(414) 658-8111
Primary Business: Maker of men's, boys' and ladies' underwear
Chairman: Donna Wolf Steigerwaldt
CEO: Donna Wolf Steigerwaldt
President: Howard D. Cooley
Vice-President (General Sales): Arthur F. DeCesaro, Jr.
Vice-President (Human Resources): John H. Casey
# of Employees: 1,500

Miscellaneous Facts: Founded in 1876 by Samuel T. Cooper. The classic brief was the first underwear ever packaged and sold in a self-selection fixture. Former professional baseball player Jim Palmer is the company spokesperson.

KELLWOOD CO.
600 Kellwood Parkway
St. Louis, MO 63107
(314) 576-3100
Primary Business: Men's, women's and children's apparel
Chairman of the Board: Fred W. Wenzel
CEO: William J. McKenna

President: William J. McKenna
Vice-President: Bud Berman
Vice-President: Joseph P. Collins
Sales: $588 million
# of Employees: 16,000

THE LEE APPAREL COMPANY, INC.
9001 W 67th Street
Merriam, KS 66202
(913) 384-4000
Primary Business: Jean bottoms and
  tops
Chairman: L. R. Pugh
President: M. G. Winne
Vice-President (Sales): R. S. Mangini
Vice-President (Merchandising): R. S.
  Stel
Sales: $418 million
# of Employees: 10,100

L'EGGS PRODUCTS, INC.
Post Office Box 2495
Winston-Salem, NC 27102
(919) 768-9540
Primary Business: Ladies' hosiery
President: Walter Pilcher
Vice-President (Marketing): John Piazza
Vice-President (Employee Relations):
  Douglas Volz
# of Employees: 5,500

Miscellaneous Facts: Division of Sara
  Lee Corp.

LEVI STRAUSS & CO.
1155 Battery Street
San Francisco, CA 94111
(415) 544-6000
Primary Business: Men's, women's and
  children's apparel
Chairman: Peter E. Haas
CEO: Robert D. Haas
President: Robert D. Haas
Chairman, Executive Committee:
  Walter A. Haas, Jr.
Vice-President (Corporate Affairs): Rita
  M. Guiney
Vice-President (Human Resources):
  Donna Goya
Revenue: $2.51 billion
Net Worth: $807 million
# of Employees: 37,000

Subsidiaries:
Battery Street Enterprises, Inc.
Resistol Hats Div.
Levi Strauss Employee Purchase Plan
Levi Strauss International

Miscellaneous Facts: Subsidiary of Levi
  Strauss Assoc., Inc. One of the
  world's largest clothing
  manufacturers. Women make up 78
  percent of the work force.

LIZ CLAIBORNE, INC.
1441 Broadway
New York, NY 10018
(212) 354-4900
Primary Business: Design and market
  women's clothing
Co-Chairman: Arthur Ortenberg
Co-Chairman: Jerome A. Chazen
President: Elizabeth Claiborne
  Ortenberg
Vice-President (Sales, Misses): Fred
  Best
Vice-President (Sales, LizWear): Stuart
  Stiegel
Manager, Personnel: Jorge Fiqueredo
Sales: $391 million
Net Worth: $104 million
# of Employees: 1,700

Divisions:
Claiborne, Inc.
Dress Div.
Liz Kids Div.
LizWear Div.
Petites Div.
Sportswear Div.

MUNSINGWEAR, INC.
724 N First Street
Minneapolis, MN 55401
(612) 340-4700
Primary Business: Men's underwear and
  sleepwear
CEO: George K. Hansen
Vice-President (Administration): Robert
  G. Higginbotham
Division President (Men's and Boys'):
  Glen E. Pitts
Revenue: $114.65 million
Net Worth: $31.4 million
# of Employees: 3,543

Subsidiary:
Form-O-Uth, Inc.

OXFORD INDUSTRIES, INC.
222 Piedmont Avenue., NE
Atlanta, GA 30308
(404) 659-2424
Primary Business: Men's and women's
  apparel
Chairman of the Board: J. Hicks Lanier
President: J. Hicks Lanier
Group Vice-President: Knowlton J.
  O'Reilly
Group Vice-President: John M. Hall
Vice-President (Human Resources):
  Grady M. Jackson
Sales: $558 million
Net Worth: $143 million
# of Employees: 12,362

Divisions:
Dress Div.
Holbrook Shirt Co.
Lanier Clothes
Mercona Sport Div.
Oxford Collection
Oxford Separates
Oxford Shirts
Oxford Slacks Div.
Oxford Sportswear & Apparel

PHILLIPS-VAN HEUSEN CORP.
1290 Avenue of the Americas
New York, NY 10104
(212) 541-5200
Primary Business: Men's wear
Chairman of the Board: Seymour J.
  Phillips
CEO: Lawrence S. Phillips
President: Lawrence S. Phillips
Executive Vice-President: Robert F.
  Reilly
Vice-President: Brue J. Klatsky
Sales: $550 million
Net Worth: $150 million
# of Employees: 7,300

Subsidiaries:
Hamburger's/Kenned's
Harris & Frank
Joseph & Feiss Co.
Juster's
Somerset Knitting Mills

Divisions:
PVH Private Label Group
PVH Outlet Stores
PVH Somerset Co. Div.
Van Heusen Co.

VF CORP.
1047 N Park Road
Wyomissing, PA 19610
(215) 378-1151
Primary Business: Apparel for men,
  women and children
Chairman of the Board: L. R. Pugh
President: Robert E. Gregory
Vice-President: Larry J. Weidenheimer
Vice-President: Janet L. Peters
Revenue: $1.17 billion
# of Employees: 31,800

Shoes

CONVERSE, INC.
55 Fordham Road
Wilmington, MA 01887
(617) 657-5500
Primary Business: Athletic footwear
Chairman: Richard Loynd
President: John P. O'Neil
Vice-President (Sales): Riney Lochmann
Personnel Director: Don Wolcott
Sales: $265.60 million
Net Worth: $83 million
# of Employees: 3,500

ETONIC, INC.
147 Center Street
Brockton, MA 02402
(617) 583-9100
Primary Business: Manufactures running
  shoes
President: Stephen A. Tennen
# of Employees: 1,000

Miscellaneous Facts: Subsidiary of
  Colgate-Palmolive Co.

KIWI BRANDS, INC.
Route 662 N
Douglassville, PA 19518
(215) 385-3041
Primary Business: Shoe care and
  household cleaning products
President: Michael A. Burnett
Vice-President (Sales): Thomas G. Hill
Vice-President (Finance): Arthur J.
  DiFuria
Sales: $60 million
# of Employees: 305

Miscellaneous Facts: Subsidiary of Sara Lee Corp.

NIKE, INC.
3900 SW Murray Boulevard
Beaverton, OR 97005
(503) 641-6453
Chairman: Philip H. Knight
CEO: Philip H. Knight
President: Philip H. Knight
Vice-Chairman: William J. Bowerman
Executive Vice-President: Delbert J.
  Hayes
Sales: $920 million
Net Worth: $316 million
# of Employees: 3,600

Subsidiaries:
Nike International, Ltd.

U.S. SHOE CORP.
One Eastwood Drive
Cincinnati, OH 45227
(513) 527-7000
Primary Business: Men's and women's
  shoes
Chairman: Philip G. Barach
CEO: Philip G. Barach
President: Philip G. Barach
Executive Vice-President (Shoe Retail):
  Ralph O. Smith
Group Vice-President (Women's
  Footwear): Seymour Gladman
Director, Human Resources: Dale
  Kopinsk
Revenue: $1.92 billion
Net Worth: $477 million
# of Employees: 28,000

Divisions:
Calvin Klein Div.
Capezio Div.
Garolini Div.
Marx & Newman Div.
Mushrooms Div.
Pappagallo Div.
Precision Lenscrafters
Red Cross Shoe Div.
Selby Div.
Texas Boot Div.
August Max

Textiles

COLLINS & AIKMAN CORP.
210 Madison Avenue
New York, NY 10016
(212) 578-1200
Primary Business: Textile products
Chairman: Donald F. McCullough
CEO: Donald F. McCullough
President: Alfred S. Crimmins
Vice-President and General Counsel:
  Charles H. Scherer
Director, Corporate Relations: J. J.
  Rogan
Revenue: $1.04 billion
Net Worth: $289 million
# of Employees: 10,000

Divisions:
Automotive & Specialty Products Div.
Bath Fashion Div.
Decorative Fabrics Div.
Fashion Fabrics Div.

SPRINGS INDUSTRIES, INC.
205 N White Street
Fort Mill, SC 29715
(803) 547-2901
Primary Business: Cotton-synthetic
  blends
Chairman: Walter Y. Elisha
CEO: Walter Y. Elisha
President: W. Paul Tippett
Vice-President (Communications): J.
  Marshall Doswell
Senior Vice-President (Human
  Resources): J. Spratt White
President (Consumer Fashion): Murphy
  L. Fontenot
Revenue: $944.99 million
Net Worth: $441 million
# of Employees: 21,300

Subsidiaries:
M. Lowenstein Corp.
Clark-Schwebel Fiber Glass Corp.
Accel Plastic Products Group
Fiber Glass Reinforcements

Miscellaneous Facts: Markets products
  under the Springmaid label.

J. P. STEVENS & CO., INC.
1185 Avenue of the Americas
New York, NY 10036
(212) 930-2000
Primary Business: Textiles manufacturer
Chairman of the Board: Whitney
  Stevens
CEO: Whitney Stevens
President: Ward Burns
Vice-Chairman: David M. Tracy
Executive Vice-President (Human
  Resources): Thomas Durst
Sales: $1.6 billion
Net Worth: $501 million
# of Employees: 23,000

Subsidiaries:
Stevens Aviation, Inc.

**UNITED MERCHANTS &
  MANUFACTURERS, INC.**
1407 Broadway
New York, NY 10018
(212) 930-3900
Primary Business: Rayon, cotton, print
  cloth manufacturer
Chairman of the Board: Martin J.
  Schwab
CEO: Uzi Ruskin
President: Uzi Ruskin
Executive Vice-President: Tomas Furth
Executive Vice-President: Sidney O.
  Margolis

Revenue: $800 million
# of Employees: 8,500

WEST POINT-PEPPERELL, INC.
Post Office Box 71
West Point, GA 31833
(404) 645-4000
Primary Business: Apparel, household
  fabrics
Chairman: J. L. Lanier, Jr.
CEO: J. A. Lanier, Jr.
President: C. J. Kjorlien
Vice-President (Manufacturing): Charles
  Crowder
Vice-President (Personnel): Vance L.
  Cathey
Sales: $1.33 billion
Net Worth: $461 million
# of Employees: 20,461

Subsidiaries:
Cluett, Peabody & Co., Inc.

Divisions:
The Arrow Co.
CSM Div.
Cosco
Dobie Originals
Jet Sew, Inc.
Arrow Women's Wear
Newton Knitting Mills
RPM Fashions, Inc.

AUTOMOTIVE

AMERICAN MOTORS
27777 Franklin Road
Southfield, MI 48034
(313) 827-1000
Primary Business: Auto manufacturer
Chairman: W. Paul Tippett
CEO: Jose J.Dedeurwaerder
President: Jose J. Dedeurwaerder
Vice-President (Public Relations): Jerry
L. Sloan
Vice-President (Industrial Relations):
Richard A. Calmers
Vice-President (Marketing): Joseph E.
Cappy
Sales: $4.21 billion
Net Worth: $278 million
# of Employees: 21,900

Subsidiaries:
American Motors Leasing Corp.
American Motors Sales Corp.
American Motors Financial Corp.
American Motors Realty Corp.
Coleman Products
Jeep Corp.
Mercury Plastics Co.
Renault U.S.A., Inc.

Miscellaneous Facts: Started out as
Thomas B. Jeffery Co., in 1916
became Nash Motors, in 1936 became
Nash-Kelvinator, and in 1954
American Motors. Today, American
Motors markets its passenger cars and
Jeep vehicles in every state and in
more than 140 countries.

BUICK MOTOR DIV.
902 E Hamilton Avenue
Flint, MI 48505
(313) 766-5000
Primary Business: Automobiles
General Manager: Lloyd E. Reuss
General Sales Manager: Jimmy C.
Perkins
Personnel Director: Wilbur J. Rowland
Public Relations Director: Thomas L.
Pond
# of Employees: 19,700

Miscellaneous Facts: Div. of General
Motors Corp.

CADILLAC MOTOR CAR DIV.
2860 Clark Avenue
Detroit, MI 48232
(313) 554-5067
Primary Business: Automobile
manufacturer
General Manager: John O.
Grettenberger
General Sales Manager: L. B. Pryor
Personnel Manager: Patricia J. Michalek
Chief Engineer: Warren D. Hirschfield
Director, Public Relations: Sheri J.
Perelli
# of Employees: 870

Miscellaneous Facts: Div. of General
Motors Corp.

CHEVROLET MOTOR DIV.
30007 Van Dyke Avenue
Detroit, MI 48090
(313) 556-5000
Primary Business: Manufacturer of
automobiles and trucks
General Manager: Robert Burger
Director of Engineering: Donald Runkel
General Sales Manager: Robert Starr
Director, Public Relations: James J.
Williams

Miscellaneous Facts: Subsidiary of
General Motors Corp.

CHRYSLER CORP.
12000 Chrysler Drive
Highland Park, MI 48203
(313) 956-5252
Primary Business: Manufacturer of
automobiles, trucks and parts
Chairman of the Board: Lee A. Iacocca
Vice-Chairman: Gerald Greenwald
President: Harold K. Sperlich
Executive Vice-President: Bennett S.
Bidwell
Vice-President (Public Relations): Baron
K. Bates
Vice-President (Personnel): Glen White
Sales: $19.75 billion
Net Worth: $3.3 billion
# of Employees: 133,811

Subsidiaries:
Chrysler Financial Corp.
E. F. Hutton Credit Corp.
Gulfstream Aerospace Corp.

Divisions:
Components Business Products Div.
Amplex Div.
Automotive Sales Div.
Fleet Div.
Parts & Service Operations

Miscellaneous Facts: Chrysler car divisions are the fastest-growing in the U.S. automotive industry. Incorporated in 1925 in Delaware.

FORD MOTOR CO.
The American Road
Dearborn, MI 48126
(313) 322-3000
Primary Business: Automobiles, trucks, tractors
Chairman: Donald E. Peterson
President: Harold A. Poling
Vice-Chairman: William C. Ford
Vice-President (Sales): Louis E. Lataif
Vice-President (External Affairs): Allan D. Gilmour
Sales: $52.40 billion
Net Worth: $12.27 billion
# of Employees: 383,696

Subsidiaries:
American Renaissance Insurance Co.
Dearborn Capital Corp.
The Dearborn Inn Co.
Dearborn Marine, Inc.
Environ, Inc.
FN Venture Corp.
First Nationwide Financial Corp.
Ford Auto Club, Inc.
Ford Communications
American Road Equity Corp.
Ford Consumer Credit Co.
Ford Financial Services, Inc.
Ford Life Insurance Co.
Philco Finance Co.
Fordson Coal Co.
Ghia, Inc.
Humbolt Mining Co.
Sunglas Products Co.

Miscellaneous Facts: Founded by Henry Ford. Serves customers in nearly 150 countries. Is the second-largest manufacturing company in U.S.

FRUEHAUF CORP.
10900 Harper Avenue
Detroit, MI 48213
(313) 267-1000
Primary Business: Truck trailers, cargo containers
Chairman of the Board: Robert D. Rowan
President: Thomas J. Reghanti
Vice-President (Marketing): Charles P. Jacoby
Public Relations Manager: James A. Bianchi
Director of Personnel: James Tutorow
Revenue: $2.79 billion
Net Worth: $1.18 billion
# of Employees: 26,700

Subsidiaries:
Decatur Aluminum Co.
Fruehaur Finance Co.
The Mercer Co.
Fruehauf International Co.
Jacksonville Shipyards, Inc.

Divisions:
Freuhauf Div.
Government Services Div.
Hobbs Trailers
Liquid and Bulk Tank Div.

Miscellaneous Facts: Incorporated in 1918 in Michigan as Fruehauf Trailer Co. Present name adopted in 1963.

GENERAL MOTORS CORP.
3044 W Grand Boulevard
Detroit, MI 48202
(313) 248-6100
Primary Business: Automobiles, trucks, buses manufacturing
Chairman: Roger B. Smith
CEO: Roger B. Smith
President: F. James McDonald
Vice-President (Public Relations): John W. McNulty
Vice-President (Design): Irwin W. Rybicki
Vice-President (Customer Sales and Service): James G.Vorhes
Sales: $96.37 billion
Net Worth: $24.2 billion
# of Employees: 748,000

Subsidiaries:
Electronic Data Systems Corp.
GM Hughes Electronic Corp.

Delco Electronics Corp.
Hughes Aircraft Co.
General Motors Acceptance Corp.

Vehicle Groups:
Buick, Oldsmobile, Cadillac Group
Chevrolet-Pontiac Group
Truck & Bus Group
GMC Truck & Coach Operation

Miscellaneous Facts: Organized on September 16, 1908. Incorporated in 1916 in Delaware.

HARLEY-DAVIDSON MOTOR CO., INC.
3700 W Juneau Avenue
Milwaukee, WI 53208
(414) 342-4680
Primary Business: Maker of motorcycles and parts
Chairman: Vaughn L. Beals
CEO: Vaughn L. Beals
President: C. K. Thompson
Vice-President (Engineering): J. L. Bleustein
Vice-President (Manufacturing): T. Gelb
Sales: $280 million
# of Employees: 2,600

KAWASAKI MOTORS CORP., U.S.A.
9950 Jeronimo Road
Irvine, CA 92718
(714) 770-0400
Primary Business: Motorcycles, parts
President: M. Tazaki
Vice-President (Sales): Gary Johnson
Director, Communications: M. Vaughan
Personnel Director: J. Klein
Sales: $375 million
# of Employees: 400

Subsidiaries:
Kawasaki Motors Manufacturing Corp., U.S.A.

Miscellaneous Facts: Subsidiary of Kawasaki Heavy Motors Industries, Japan.

MACK TRUCKS, INC.
2100 Mack Boulevard
Allentown, PA 18103
(215) 439-3011
Primary Business: Trucks, parts and service

Chairman: A. W. Pelletier
CEO: J. B. Curcio
President: J. B. Curcio
Senior Vice-President (Sales): J. P. Rossetti
Senior Vice-President (Human Resources): William E. Walker
Sales: $2.01 billion
# of Employees: 14,300

Miscellaneous Facts: Founded in 1900 as Mack Brothers Motor Car Co. by John M., Augustus F., William C., Joseph S., and Charles W. Mack. Company introduced the first motorized hook and ladder fire truck in 1910. One of America's largest producers of heavy-duty diesel trucks.

MASERATI AUTOMOBILES, INC.
1501 Caton Avenue
Baltimore, MD 21227
(301) 646-3630
Primary Business: Import and sale of automobiles
President: George A. Garbutt
Treasurer: Gertrude J. Garbutt
General Sales Manager: Roy Baily
Secretary: Howard Chase
Sales: $50 million
# of Employees: 27

Subsidiaries:
Benelli/Moto Guzzi North America

MITSUBISHI MOTOR SALES OF AMERICA, INC.
10540 Talbert Avenue
Fountain Valley, CA 92708
(714) 963-7677
Primary Business: Distributes automobiles
Chairman of the Board: T. Nishina
CEO: Kazue Naganuma
Manager, Sales: Jeanne Hoover
Personnel Director: Norman M. Baker
# of Employees: 330

NAVISTAR INTERNATIONAL CORP.
401 N Michigan Avenue
Chicago, IL 60611
(312) 836-2000
Primary Business: Maker of medium and heavy-duty trucks

Chairman of the Board: Donald D. Lennox
CEO: Donald D. Lennox
President: Neil Springer
Vice-Chairman: James C. Cotting
Vice-President (Corporate Relations): Roxanne Decyk
Vice-President (Human Resources): Joseph V. Thompson
Sales: $3.5 billion
Net Worth: $301 million
# of Employees: 15,000

Subsidiaries:
Navistar Financial Corp.

Miscellaneous Facts: Incorporated in 1965 in Delaware as International Harvester Corp. Present name adopted in 1986.

OLDSMOBILE DIV.
920 Townsend Street
Lansing, MI 48933
(517) 377-5000
Primary Business: Automobiles and parts
General Manager: William W. Lane
General Sales Manager: Dave Lahti
Advertising Manager: Richard Billings
Director of Public Relations: Philip I. Workman
Director of Personnel: Michael Tierney
# of Employees: 16,000

Miscellaneous Facts: A division of General Motors Corp.

PACCAR, INC.
777 106th Avenue, NE
Bellevue, WA 98004
(206) 455-7400
Primary Business: Trucking
Chairman of the Board: Charles M. Pigott
President: Charles M. Pigott
Executive Vice-President: William N. Gross
Senior Vice-President: Jack A. Chantrey
Sales: $1.8 billion
Net Worth: $754 million
# of Employees: 8,317

Divisions:
Kenworth Truck Co. Div.
Paccar Parts Div.

Peterbuilt Motors Co. Div.
Wagner Mining Equipment Co. Div.

SAAB-SCANIA OF AMERICA, INC.
Post Office Box 697
Orange, CT 06477
(203) 795-5671
Primary Business: Automobiles, heavy-duty trucks
Chairman: P. Henry Meuller
President: Robert J. Sinclair
Vice-President (Sales and Marketing): Sten O. Helling
Public Relations Manager: Lennart Lonnegren
Personnel Manager: Patricia Agres
Revenue: $600 million
# of Employees: 600

SUBARU OF AMERICA, INC.
7040 Central Highway
Pennsauken, NJ 08109
(609) 488-8500
Primary Business: Imports and distributes automobiles and parts
CEO: Harvey H. Lamm
President: Harvey H. Lamm
Vice-President (Corporate Communications): Charles D. Mahin
Vice-President (Parts): Edward C. Schloth
Vice-President (Sales and Marketing): Eugene L. Egan
Sales: $1.17 billion
Net Worth: $266 million
# of Employees: 850

Subsidiaries:
Southeast Subaru, Inc.
Southwest Subaru, Inc.
Subaru Atlantic, Inc.
Subaru Financial Services, Inc.
Subaru of Northern California, Inc.
Subaru of Southern California

VOLKSWAGEN OF AMERICA, INC.
888 W Big Beaver
Troy, MI 48007
(313) 362-6000
Primary Business: Manufactures automobiles
Chairman: Carl H. Hahn
CEO: Noel Phillips

President: Noel Phillips
Executive Vice-President: Peter Weiher
Vice-President (Parts Div.): Ulrich
  Fahrun
Sales: $4.08 billion
# of Employees: 11,000

Subsidiaries:
Triumph Adler North America, Inc.

Miscellaneous Facts: Subsidiary of
  Volkswagen AG.

YUGO AMERICA, INC.
28 Park Way
Upper Saddle River, NJ 07458
(201) 825-4600
Primary Business: Importer of
  automobiles
Chairman of the Board: Malcolm N.
  Bricklin
CEO: Malcolm N. Bricklin
President: William E. Prior
Vice-Chairman: Ira V. Edelson
Vice-President (Human Resources):
  William Rogalin
Sales: $120 million
# of Employees: 174

Parts and Service

AAMCO TRANSMISSIONS, INC.
1 President Boulevard
Bala-Cynwyd, PA 19004
(215) 668-2900
Primary Business: Franchise sales, auto
  parts
Chairman of the Board: Robert Morgan
Executive Vice-President and General
  Manager: A. Bernstein
Vice-President: William Shnycer
Vice-President (Finance): Martin
  Shames
Vice-President (Personnel): Michael
  Haber
Sales: $45 million
# of Employees: 325

Miscellaneous Facts: Subsidiary of
  Aamco Industries, Ltd.

AC SPARK PLUG
1300 N Dort Highway
Flint, MI 48506
(313) 236-5000
Primary Business: Auto accessories
General Manager: John R. Wilson
General Sales Manager: Leonard F.
  Swoyer
Director, Public Relations: John V.
  Dinan, Jr.
Personnel Director: J. Houston
# of Employees: 15,000

Miscellaneous Facts: Subsidiary of
  General Motors Corp.

AUTOLITE DIV.
1600 N Union Street
Fostoria, OH 44830
(514) 446-2929
Primary Business: Spark plug
  manufacturer
General Manager: Mark W. Semeyn

Miscellaneous Facts: Division of Allied-
  Signal, Inc.

BRIGGS & STRATTON CORP.
12301 W Wirth Street
Wauwatosa, WI 53222
(414) 259-5333
Primary Business: Maker of gasoline and
  diesel engines
CEO: Frederick P. Stratton, Jr.
President: Frederick P. Stratton, Jr.
Executive Vice-President: Laverne J.
  Socks
Vice-President (Service): Charles L.
  Fricke
Vice-President (Sales): James F. Sullivan
Sales: $700 million
Net Worth: $283 million
# of Employees: 8,777

Subsidiaries:
Briggs & Stratton Export, Inc.

Miscellaneous Facts: Incorporated in
  1924 in Delaware.

THE BUDD CO.
3155 W Big Beaver Road
Box 2601
Troy, MI 48084
(313) 643-3500

Primary Business: Auto and truck body
components
CEO: James H. McNeal, Jr.
President: James H. McNeal, Jr.
Vice-President (Employee Relations):
Robert J. Wangbichler
Vice-President (Public Affairs): Paul O.
Sichert, Jr.
Sales: $1.04 billion
# of Employees: 14,000

Subsidiaries:
Freeway Truck Parts
Milford Fabricating Co.
Waupaca Foundry, Inc.
Woodings Verona Tool Works, Inc.

Miscellaneous Facts: Subsidiary of
Thyssen AG.

CHAMPION SPARK PLUG CO.
900 Upton Avenue
Toledo, OH 43607
(419) 535-2567
Primary Business: Spark plugs,
windshield wipers
Chairman of the Board: R. A.
Strahahan, Jr.
President: R. J. Brotse, Jr.
Vice-President (Sales): C. A. Schwalbe,
Jr.
Vice-President (Public Affairs): G. M.
Galster
Revenue: $816.50 million
Net Worth: $359 million
# of Employees: 12,600

Subsidiaries:
The Anderson Co. of Indiana
Baron Drawn Steel Corp.
DeVilbiss Electronics Corp.
Iowa Industries, Inc.
PB Marketing, Inc.
Westchester Industrial Park, Inc.

Miscellaneous Facts: Maker of Anco
wiper blades. Incorporated in 1938 in
Delaware.

CUMMINS ENGINE CO., INC.
Post Office Box 3005
Columbus, IN 47202
(812) 377-5451
Primary Business: High-speed diesel
engines
Chairman: Henry B. Schacht

CEO: Henry B.Schacht
President: James A. Henderson
Vice-Chairman: Richard B. Stoner
Vice-President (Public Relations): B.
Joseph White
Vice-President (Human Resources):
Harold B. Higgins
Sales: $2.32 billion
Net Worth: $649 million
# of Employees: 22,788

Subsidiaries:
Atlas Crankshaft Corp.
Cummins Americas, Inc.
Cummins Diesel Sales Corp.
Cummins Export Corp.
Cummins Great Lakes, Inc.
Cummins International Sales, Inc.
Cummins Northwest, Inc.
Cummins Puerto Rico, Inc.
Diesel Controls Technology, Inc.
Fleetguard, Inc.

Miscellaneous Facts: Incorporated in
1919 in Indiana.

DANA CORP.
Post Office Box 1000
Toledo, OH 43697
(419) 535-4500
Primary Business: Mobile fluid power
products, auto parts
Chairman: Gerald B. Mitchell
CEO: Gerald B. Mitchell
President: Gerald B. Mitchell
Executive Vice-President: Sidney C.
Howell
Vice-President (Public Affairs): Robert
A. Cowie
Vice-President and General Counsel:
Martin J. Strobel
Sales: $3.57 billion
Net Worth: $1.2 billion
# of Employees: 37.300

Subsidiaries:
Diamond Financial Holdings, Inc.
Potomac Leasing
Shannon Properties
Summey Building Systems
Hylant-McLean
Warner Electric Brake & Clutch Co.

Divisions:
Boston Industrial Products Div.
Controls Div.
Gresen Manufacturing Div.

Parish Div.
Racine Hydraulics Div.
Spicer Axle Div.
Beloit Div.

DONNELLY CORP.
414 E 40th Street
Holland, MI 49423
(616) 394-2200
Primary Business: Rear-view mirrors for
  automobiles
Chairman: John Fenlon Donnelly
President: John D. Baumgartner
Vice-President: James Knister
Vice-President: Brendan Moreland
Sales: $75 million
# of Employees: 1,000

FEDERAL-MOGAL
Post Office Box 1966
Detroit, MI 48231
(313) 354-7700
Primary Business: Auto replacement
  parts manufacturer
Chairman of the Board: Thomas F.
  Russell
CEO: Thomas F. Russell
President: William C. Adams
Senior Vice-President: Herbert H.
  Kietzer
Vice-President (Employee Relations):
  James M. Eastman
Revenue: $911 million
# of Employees: 14,000

GENUINE PARTS CO.
2999 Circle 75 Parkway
Atlanta, GA 30339
(404) 953-1700
Primary Business: Auto replacement
  parts
Chairman: Wilton Looney
CEO: Wilton Looney
President: W. C. Hatcher
Vice-Chairman: Earl Dolive
Senior Vice-President (Personnel):
  Louis Rice, Jr.
Executive Vice-President: Larry L.
  Prince
Revenue: $2.07 billion
Net Worth: $770 million
# of Employees: 13,000

Subsidiary:
Motion Industries, Inc.

GRAND AUTO, INC.
7200 Edgewater Drive
Oakland, CA 94621
(415) 568-6500
Primary Business: Auto accessories and
  parts
Chairman: Irving Krantzman
CEO: Irving Krantzman
President: Irving Krantzman
Senior Executive Vice-President: Max
  M. Brown
Executive Vice-President: John F.
  Goodsell
Vice-President (Merchandising): Robert
  Seymour
Sales: $167.28 million
Net Worth: $32 million
# of Employees: 2,155

Subsidiary:
Automotive Wholesalers, Inc.

MIDAS INTERNATIONAL CORP.
224 N Michigan Avenue
Chicago, IL 60601
(312) 565-7500
Primary Business: Mufflers and other
  auto parts
CEO: John R. Moore
President: John R. Moore
Vice-President and General Counsel:
  Robert M. Bailey
Vice-President (Franchise Operations):
  Russell J. Richards
Vice-President (Human Resources):
  Brian W. Burhoe
Sales: $298 million
# of Employees: 2,720

Miscellaneous Facts: Subsidiary of IC
  Industries, Inc. Company toll-free
  consumer telephone number is (800)
  821-8545.

SEALED POWER CORP.
100 Terrace Plaza
Muskegon, MI 49443
(616) 724-5011
Primary Business: Piston rings, filters
  manufacturer

Chairman of the Board: Robert D.
Tuttle
CEO: Robert D. Tuttle
President: Charles E. Johnson II
Group Vice-President: Charles H. Roth
Group Vice-President: Dale A. Johnson
Revenue: $500 million
# of Employees: 7,000

SHELLER-GLOBE CORP.
1505 Jefferson Avenue
Toledo, OH 43624
(419) 255-8840
Primary Business: Automotive parts and
accessories
Chairman: Chester Devenow
CEO: Chester Devenow
President: James A. Graham
Vice-Chairman: John R. Eastman
Vice-President (Human Resources):
John L. Bradley
Revenue: $816.42 million
Net Worth: $203 million
# of Employees: 12,000

Subsidiaries:
Northern Fibre Products Co.
Southern Fibre Products Co.
Victoreen, Inc.

SNAP-ON TOOLS CORP.
2801 80th Street
Kenosha, WI 53140
(414) 656-5200
Primary Business: Tool manufacturer
Chairman: William B. Rayburn
CEO: William B. Rayburn
President: William B. Rayburn
Director of Public Relations: Clarence J.
Niemi
Vice-President (National Sales): Michael
G. Hassett
Vice-President (Employee Relations):
Donald E. Lyons
Revenue: $540 million
Net Worth: $337 million
# of Employees: 6,045

Subsidiaries:
Snap-On Tools International, Ltd.
A.T.I. Industries, Inc.

SPARKOMATIC CORP.
Milford, PA 18337
(717) 296-6444

Primary Business: Auto accessories
President: Edward Anchel
Vice-President (Marketing): James D.
Pedranti
National Sales Manager: James Minarik
Sales: $50 million
# of Employees: 275

STP CORP.
5300 Broken Sound Boulevard, NW
Boca Raton, FL 33431
(305) 994-1000
Primary Business: Oil, gas and diesel
fuel treatment
CEO: Leo J. LeClair
President: Leo J. LeClair
Vice-President (Sales): Jerry Dannecker
Vice-President (Racing): Ralph Salvino
# of Employees: 260

Miscellaneous Facts: Subsidiary of Union
Carbide Corp.

SUNDSTRAND CORP.
4751 Harrison Avenue
Box 7003
Rockford, IL 61125
(815) 226-6000
Primary Business: Hydrostatic and
hydromechanical transmissions
Chairman: Evans W. Erikson
CEO: Evans W. Erikson
Vice-Chairman: Don R. O'Hare
Executive Vice-President: David
MacMorris
Vice-President and General Counsel:
Richard M. Schilling
Public Relations Director: Robert E.
Carlson
Sales: $1.04 billion
# of Employees: 15,200

Miscellaneous Facts: Incorporated in
1966 in Delaware to succeed
Sundstrand Co.

TENNECO AUTOMOTIVE
108 Wilmot Road
Deerfield, IL 60015
(312) 632-8871
Primary Business: Exhaust systems
CEO: James K. Ashford
President: James K. Ashford
Senior Vice-President: John P. Reilly

Vice-President (Sales): Paul R. Frank
Revenue: $900 million
# of Employees: 12,000

Tires and Rubber

ARMSTRONG RUBBER CO.
500 Sargent Drive
New Haven, CT 06511
(203) 784-2200
Primary Business: Tires and tubes,
 wheels
Chairman of the Board: James A. Walsh
CEO: James A. Walsh
President: Frank R. O'Keefe, Jr.
Vice-President (Personnel and Public
 Affairs): G. Robert Millar
Public Relations Director: Roby
 Raymond (Mrs.)
Revenue: $665.65 million
Net Worth: $208.72 million
# of Employees: 5,200

Subsidiaries:
Arco Wheel, Inc.
Armstrong Acceptance Co., Inc.
Armstrong Rubber Export, Ltd.
Richmond Converters, Inc.
S & A Truck Tire Sales and Service
 Corp.

Divisions:
Industrial Tire & Assembly Business
 Div.
Midwest Div.
Pacific Coast Div.
Special Products Div.
Textile Div.

Miscellaneous Facts: Incorporated in
 1940 in Connecticut.

BIG O TIRE DEALERS, INC.
6021 S Syracuse Way
Englewood, CO 80111
(303) 779-9991
Primary Business: Franchise sale of
 tires, wheels
Chairman: Norman L. Affleck
President: Norman L. Affleck
Vice-President (Finance): William H.
 Spencer
Vice-President (Administration): David
 Fredrick

Sales: $60-plus million
# of Employees: 300

COOPER TIRE & RUBBER CO.
Lima & Western Avenue
Findlay, OH 45840
(419) 423-1321
Primary Business: Manufactures tires
 and rubber products
Chairman of the Board: Edward E.
 Brewer
President: Ivan W. Gorr
Executive Vice-President: William T.
 Fitzgerald
Vice-President: Charles H. Bernhardt
Revenue: $555 million
# of Employees: 4,800

DUNLOP TIRE AND RUBBER CORP.
Post Office Box 1109
Buffalo, NY 14240
(716) 879-8258
Primary Business: Manufactures tires
Chairman of the Board: R. L. Clark
CEO: R. L. Clark
President: R. L. Clark
Vice-President: Ronald Palmer
Vice-President (Employee Relations):
 C. Roger Jones
Sales: $5 billion
# of Employees: 3,000

FIRESTONE TIRE & RUBBER CO.
1200 Firestone Parkway
Akron, OH 44317
(216) 379-7000
Primary Business: Tires, tubes and other
 rubber goods
Chairman: John J. Nevin
CEO: John J. Nevin
President: John J. Nevin
Vice-Chairman: Leon R. Brodeur
Vice-President and General Counsel:
 Thomas M. Forman
Vice-President (Human Resources):
 Donald L. Groniger
Sales: $4 billion
Net Worth: $1.16 billion
# of Employees: 59,900

Divisions:
The Fidesta Co.
Firestone Building Products Co.

Firestone Industrial Products Co.
Firestone Steel Products Co.
Firestone Textiles Co.
Firestone World Tire Group

Miscellaneous Facts: Founded by Harvey
S. Firestone in Akron, Ohio, in 1900.
Developed first commercial
demountable rim in 1907. Company
announced the development of the
first tubeless truck tire. Operates the
largest chain of automotive service
centers in the U.S. Company toll-free
consumer number is (800) 321-1252.

GENCORP, INC.
One General Street
Akron, OH 44329
(216) 798-3000
Primary Business: Maker of tires and
other rubber products
CEO: A. W. Reynolds
President: A. W. Reynolds
Vice-President (Communications):
Steven G. Ellis
Vice-President and General Counsel: C.
R. Ennis
Vice-President (Human Resources):
Robert Malcolm
Sales: $3.02 billion
Net Worth: $1.5 billion
# of Employees: 28,000

Subsidiaries:
DiversiTech General
General Tire, Inc.
Aerojet General
Chemical Construction Corp.
The General Tire Realty Co.
RKO General, Inc.

Radio and TV Stations:
KFRC (AM)
KHJ (AM)
WAXY (FM)
WOR (AM)
KHJ-TV
WHBQ-TV
WOR-TV

Miscellaneous Facts: Incorporated in
1915 in Ohio as General Rubber Mfg.
Co. Name changed in 1915 to General
Tire & Rubber Co. Present name
adopted in 1984.

THE B. F. GOODRICH CO.
500 S Main Street
Akron, OH 44318
(216) 374-2000
Primary Business: Tires and tubes,
industrial rubber products
manufacturing
Chairman: John D. Ong
CEO: John D. Ong
President: Patrick C. Ross
Vice-President (Human Resources):
Albin E. Ulle
Vice-President and General Counsel:
Jon V. Heider
Revenue: $3.44 billion
Net Worth: $711 million
# of Employees: 29,427

Divisions:
Aerospace & Defense Div.
Elastomers & Latex Div.
Geon Vinyl Div.
Industrial Products
Specialty Polymers & Chemicals Div.
Tires & Related Products
Tremco, Inc.

Miscellaneous Facts: Incorporated in
1912 in New York. Company was
founded by Dr. Benjamin F. Goodrich
in 1870.

THE GOODYEAR TIRE & RUBBER CO.
1144 E Market Street
Akron, OH 44316
(216) 796-2121
Primary Business: Tires, tubes
manufacturing
Chairman: Robert E. Mercer
CEO: Robert E. Mercer
Vice-Chairman: Ib Thomsen
Vice-President (Tire Sales and
Marketing): James W. Barnett
Vice-President (Public Relations):
William L. Newkirk
Revenue: $10.24 billion
Net Worth: $3.51 billion
# of Employees: 133,271

Subsidiaries:
Celeron Corp.
Cosmoflex, Inc.
Goodyear Aerospace Corp.
Goodyear Atomic Corp.
Goodyear Farms

Hose Couplings Mfg., Inc.
The Kelly-Springfield Tire Co.
Lee Tire & Rubber Co.
Motor Wheel Corp.
Reneer Films Corp.
Wingfoot Films Corp.

UNIROYAL, INC.
World Headquarters
Middlebury, CT 06762
(203) 573-2000
Primary Business: Tires and tubes,
 rubber goods
Chairman: Joseph P. Flannery
CEO: Joseph P. Flannery
President: Joseph P. Flannery
Group Vice-President (Tires): Sheldon
 R. Salzman
Vice-President (Human Resources):
 Ronald H. Hawkins
Director of Corporate Communications:
 Yanis Bibelnieks
Sales: $2.12 billion
Net Worth: $673 million
# of Employees: 20,600

Subsidiaries:
Synpol, Inc.
USCO Distribution Services, Inc.

Miscellaneous Facts: Company toll-free
 consumer number is (800) 521-9796.

Miscellaneous

ALLRIGHT AUTO PARKS, INC.
1919 Smith Street
Houston, TX 77002
(713) 222-2505

Primary Business: Operates parking lots
 and garages
Chairman of the Board: James Y. T.
 Tang
CEO: James Y. T. Tang
President: A. J. Layden
Public Relations Director: H. M.
 Sinclair
Sales: $120 million
# of Employees: 2,050

Miscellaneous Facts: Owns and operates
 58 subsidiaries across the U.S.

TOKHEIM CORP.
1602 Wabash Avenue
Post Office Box 360
Fort Wayne, IN 46801
(219) 423-2552
Primary Business: Gas service station
 dispensers, accessories
Chairman: Richard B. Doner
CEO: Richard B. Doner
President: Richard B. Doner
Group Vice-President: Raymond J.
 Simmons
Vice-President (Sales): David C. Rowan
Director, Human Resources: Myron L.
 Marsh
Sales: $157.52 million
Net Worth: $73 million
# of Employees: 1,970

Subsidiaries:
Tokheim International Sales, Inc.
Tokheim Investment Corp.

Miscellaneous Facts: Incorporated in
 1918 in Indiana as Tokheim Oil Tank
 & Pump Co. Present name adopted in
 1953.

BANKS

H. F. AHMANSON & CO.
3731 Wilshire Boulevard
Los Angeles, CA 90010
(213) 487-4277
Primary Business: Holding company, savings and loan
Chairman of the Board: William H Ahmanson
CEO: Richard H. Deihl
President: Richard H. Deihl
Vice-Chairman: Robert M. DeKruif
Senior Vice-President: Michael Brent
Revenue: $2.71 billion
# of Employees: 6,000

Subsidiaries:
Home Savings of America
Bankers National Life Insurance Co.
National American Life Insurance Co. of Calif.
Trans-Oceanic Life Insurance Co.
National American Insurance Co. of New York
National American Insurance Co.

ALLIED BANCSHARES, INC.
1000 Louisiana
Houston, TX 77002
(713) 224-6611
Primary Business: Holding company for banks
Chairman: Walter M. Mischer
CEO: Gerald H. Smith
President: D. Kent Anderson
Senior Vice-President (Human Resources): Thomas Y. Hamilton
Vice-President (Investments): Robert B. Conning
Revenue: $1.08 billion
Net Worth: $594 million
# of Employees: 3,614

Miscellaneous Facts: Operates 53 Allied Banks in the United States.

AMERICAN CONTINENTAL CORP.
2735 Camelback Road
Phoenix, AZ 85016
(602) 957-7170
Primary Business: Real estate, banking

Chairman of the Board: Charles H. Keating, Jr.
President: Charles H. Keating, Jr.
Vice-President: Judy J. Wischer
Vice-President: Larry Dannenfelt
Revenue: $682 million
# of Employees: 400

Subsidiaries:
First Lincoln Financial Corp.
Keating Homes, Inc.
Medema Homes of Utah, Inc.

BANKAMERICA CORP.
Bank of America Center
San Francisco, CA 94104
(415) 622-3456
Primary Business: Multibank holding company
Chairman: Leland S. Prussia
CEO: Tom Clausen
President: Tom Clausen
Vice-Chairman: Arthur V. Toupin
Senior Vice-President: Stephen McLin
Vice-President (Personnel): Robert N. Beck
Gross Operating Revenue: $13.30 billion
Net Worth: $5.1 billion
# of Employees: 88,810

Subsidiaries:
BA Cheque Corp.
BA Managistics
BankAmerica Realty Services, Inc.
BankAmerica Capital Corp.
BankAmerica World Trade Corp.
FinanceAmerica Thrift Corp.
The Charles Schwab Corp.
SeaFirst Corp.

BANKERS TRUST NEW YORK CORP.
280 Park Avenue
New York, NY 10017
(212) 250-2500
Primary Business: Bank holding company
Chairman: Alfred Brittain III
CEO: Alfred Brittain III
President: Charles S. Sanford, Jr.
Executive Vice-President and General Counsel: James J. Baechle

Executive Vice-President: Philip M.
  Hampton
Director of Personnel: Shelley Beers
Total Assets: $45.20 billion
Net Worth: $2.1 billion
# of Employees: 11,650

Subsidiaries:
BT Commercial Corp.
BT Equipment Leasing, Inc.
BT Futures Corp.
BT International Trading Corp.
Bankers Trust Co.
Bankers Trust Co. of Florida

BANK OF BOSTON CORP.
100 Federal Street
Boston, MA 02110
(617) 434-2200
Primary Business: Bank holding
  company
Chairman of the Board: William M.
  Brown
President: Ira Stepanian
Executive Vice-President: Alan L.
  McKinnon
Public Relations Manager: L. E.
  Wheeler
Assets: $28.2 billion
Net Worth: $1.5 billion
# of Employees: 20,000

Subsidiaries:
BancBoston Brokerage, Inc.
BancBoston Clearance, Inc.
Colonial Bancorp, Inc.
FNBC Realty Corp.
FSC Corp.

THE CHASE MANHATTAN CORP.
One Chase Manhattan Plaza
New York, NY 10005
(212) 552-2222
Primary Business: Multibank holding
  company
Chairman: Willard C. Butcher
CEO: Willard C. Butcher
President: Thomas G. Labrecque
Vice-Chairman: Robert R. Douglass
Executive Vice-President: A. Edward
  Allinson
Senior Vice-President and General
  Auditor: O. J. McGill
Gross Operating Earnings: $9.88 billion
Net Worth: $4 million
# of Emloyees: 37,800

Subsidiaries:
CMRCC, Inc.
Chase Commercial Corp.
Chase Home Mortgage Corp.
Chase Manhattan National Corp.
Chase International Investment Corp.
Chase Manhattan Capital Corp.
Chase Manhattan Service Corp.

CHEMICAL NEW YORK CORP.
277 Park Avenue
New York, NY 10172
(212) 310-6161
Primary Business: Bank holding
  company
Chairman: Walter V. Shipley
President: Robert J. Callander
President: Thomas S. Johnson
President: Robert I. Lipp
Executive Vice-President (Personnel):
  Patrick J. Scollard
Gross Operating Earnings: $8.86 billion
Net Worth: $2.5 billion
# of Employees: 20,000

Subsidiaries:
Alexander, Scriver & Assoc., Inc.
Bach Holding Corp.
Chem Advertising, Inc.
Chemical Bank
Chemical Mortgage Co.
Chemical Realty Corp.

CITICORP
399 Park Avenue
New York, NY 10022
(212) 559-1000
Primary Business: Holding company,
  banks
Chairman: John S. Reed
Vice-Chairman: Hans H. Angermueller
Vice-Chairman: James D. Farley
Senior Vice-President and General
  Counsel: Patrick J. Mulhern
Chief Auditor: Daniel T. Jacobsen
Vice-President (Personnel): Pamela
  Slaherty
Net Income: $890 million
Net Worth: $6.4 billion
# of Employees: 71,000

Subsidiaries:
Citibank N.A.
Citicorp Diners Club, Inc.
Citicorp Acceptance Co., Inc.
Citicorp Business Credit, Inc.

Citicorp Homeowners, Inc.
Citicorp Capital Investors, Ltd.

Miscellaneous Facts: Makes more money than any other bank in the country.

CONTINENTAL ILLINOIS CORP.
231 S LaSalle Street
Chicago, IL 60697
(312) 828-2345
Primary Business: Bank holding company
Chairman: John E. Swearingen
CEO: John E. Swearingen
Executive Vice-President and General Counsel: Richard S. Brennan
Senior Vice-President (Personal Banking): Joel J. Crabtree
Senior Vice-President (Corporate Affairs): John V. Egan, Jr.
Senior Vice-President and Auditor: Karl T. Barthelmess, Jr.
Gross Operating Earnings: $4.09 billion
# of Employees: 9,618

Subsidiary:
Continental Bank International

FINANCIAL CORP. OF AMERICA
18401 Von Karman Avenue
Irvine, CA 92715
(714) 553-6900
Primary Business: Holding company, savings and loan
Chairman: William Popejoy
CEO: William Popejoy
President: William Popejoy
Executive Vice-President–Chief Lending Officer: Michael A. Durkin
Executive Vice-President and General Counsel: Donald E. Rover
Senior Vice-President: William E. Griscom
Revenue: $3.30 billion
Net Worth: $229 million
# of Employees: 5,318

Subsidiary:
American Savings & Loan

FIRST CHICAGO CORP.
One First National Plaza
Chicago, IL 60670
(312) 732-4000

Primary Business: Bank holding company
Chairman of the Board: Barry F. Sullivan
CEO: Barry F. Sullivan
President: Richard L. Thomas
Personnel Director: S. C. Diamond
Assets: $38.89 billion
Net Worth: $2 billion
# of Employees: 14,276

Subsidiaries:
American National Corp.
First Capital Corp. of Chicago
First Chicago Financial Corp.
First National Bank of Chicago
First Chicago Trading Co.

FIRST INTERSTATE BANCORP
707 Wilshire Boulevard
Los Angeles, CA 90017
(213) 614-3001
Primary Business: Bank holding company
Chairman: Joseph J. Pinola
CEO: Joseph J. Pinola
Vice-Chairman: Norman Barker, Jr.
President: Edward M. Carson
Executive Vice-President and General Counsel: William J. Boggaard
Executive Vice-President (Personnel): Gerald L. Shott
Gross Operating Income: $2.56 billion
Net Worth: $2.51 billion
# of Employees: 35,000

Subsidiaries:
Commercial Alliance Corp.
Credit Alliance Corp.
Leasing Service Corp.
First Interstate Bank, Ltd.
First Interstate Discount Brokerage

IRVING BANK CORP.
One Wall Street
New York, NY 10005
(212) 635-1111
Primary Business: Bank holding company
Chairman of the Board: Joseph A. Rice
CEO: Joseph A. Rice
President: Samuel F. Chevalier
Executive Vice-President: John J. Houseman

Senior Vice-President (Personnel):
  Bruno E. Ziolkowski
Net Worth: $955 million
# of Employees: 9,700

Subsidiaries:
Bank of Babylon
Dutchess Bank and Trust Co.
Endicott Trust Co.
Hayes National Bank
Irving Business Centers, Inc.

MANUFACTURERS HANOVER CORP.
270 Park Avenue
New York, NY 10017
(212) 286-6000
Primary Business: Bank holding
  company
Chairman: John F. McGillicuddy
CEO: John F. McGillicuddy
President: John R. Torell III
Vice-Chairman: John J. Evans
Vice-Chairman: Edward A. Farley
Personnel Director: Martin H.
  Zuckerman
Revenue: $8.3 billion
Net Worth: $3.6 billion
# of Employees: 31,570

Subsidiaries:
CIT Group Holdings, Inc.
Manufacturers Hanover Trust Co.
Manufacturers Hanover Financial
  Services
Manufacturers Hanover Venture Capital

J. P. MORGAN & CO., INC.
23 Wall Street
New York, NY 10015
(212) 483-2323
Primary Business: Holding company
Chairman: Lewis T. Preston
President: Robert V. Lindsay
Vice-Chairman: Boris S. Berkovitch
Senior Vice-President and Auditor:
  Penelope A. Flugger

Gross Operating Earnings: $6.56 billion
Net Worth: $4.4 billion
# of Employees: 12,939

Subsidiaries:
Morgan Community Development Corp.
Morgan Data Services, Inc.
Morgan Futures Corp.
Morgan Guaranty International Bank
Morgan Holdings Corp.
J. P. Morgan Lease Funding Corp.
Morgan Portfolio Corp.

Miscellaneous Facts: Every day,
  employees who work at corporate
  headquarters receive a free lunch.
  Company clients include 96 of the 100
  largest corporations in the world.

SECURITY PACIFIC CORP.
333 S Hope Street
Los Angeles, CA 90071
(213) 613-6211
Primary Business: Bank holding
  company
Chairman: Richard J. Flamson III
CEO: Richard J. Flamson III
President: George F. Moody
Vice-Chairman: Robert H. Smith
Executive Vice-President and General
  Counsel: Russell A. Freeman
Executive Vice-President (Personnel):
  Irving Margol
Gross Operating Earnings: $5.25 billion
Net Worth: $2.5 billion
# of Employees: 29,930

Subsidiaries:
SP Insurance Services, Inc.
Security Pacific Financial Corp.
Security First Co.
Security Pacific Capital Corp.
Security Pacific Leasing Corp.
Security Pacific National Bank
Pacific Southwest Realty Co.
Security Pacific Brokers, Inc.
Security Pacific Midwest

BEVERAGES AND TOBACCO

Alcoholic Beverages

ANHEUSER-BUSCH COMPANIES, INC.
One Busch Plaza
St. Louis, MO 63118
(314) 577-2000
Primary Business: Brewer of beer, food products
Chairman of the Board: August A. Busch III
President: Dennis P. Long
Executive Vice-President: Michael J. Roarty
Vice-President (Beer Planning): Charles W. Wirtel
Vice-President (Sales): Joseph E. Martino
Sales: $7.2 billion
Net Worth: $1.9 billion
# of Employees: 38,461

Subsidiaries:
Anheuser-Busch, Inc.
Betts Baking Co.
Busch Entertainment Co.
Colonial Baking Co.
El Charrito, Inc.
Herby's Foods
Kilpatrick's Bakeries, Inc.
Eagle Snacks, Inc.
Campbell Taggart, Inc.
St. Louis National Baseball Club, Inc.

Attractions:
Adventure Island
The Dark Continent
The Old Country
Sesame Place

Miscellaneous Facts: Brews more beer than any other brewery in the world. Everyone who works here is entitled to two free cases of beer a month. The company owns the St. Louis Cardinals baseball team. Founded in 1875. Brews Budweiser, Michelob, Busch, Bud Light, Michelob Light, Natural Light, LA, King Cobra. Sold 68 million barrels of beer in 1985.

BACARDI CORP.
General Post Office Box 3549
San Juan, PR 00936
(809) 795-1560
Primary Business: Bottles and sells rum
Chairman of the Board: Alfred P. O'Hara
CEO: Manuel Luis del Valle
President: Manuel Luis del Valle
Vice-President: Mario S. Belaval
Vice-President: Adolfo T. Comas Bacardi
Sales: $270 million
Net Worth: $220 million
# of Employees: 741

Subsidiaries:
Castleton Beverage Corp.
Castleton Development Corp.
Lloyd's Electronics, Inc.
Sunray de Puerto Rico, Inc.
Willmark Electronics, Inc.

BROWN-FORMAN, INC.
850 Dixie Highway
Louisville, KY 40210
(502) 585-1100
Primary Business: Holding company, spirits
Chairman of the Board: W. L. Lyons Brown, Jr.
CEO: W. L. Lyons Brown, Jr.
Vice-Chairman: Owsley Brown Frazier
Vice-President: Owsley Brown II
Sales: $1 billion
Net Worth: $465 million
# of Employees: 6,700

Subsidiaries:
Brown-Forman Brands, Ltd.
Carolina Soap & Candle Makers
Hartmann Luggage Co., Inc.
Keepsake, Inc.
Lenox Candles, Inc.
Rosenthal Jewelry, Inc.
Early Times Distillers
Jack Daniel Distillery
Southern Comfort Corp.

CALIFORNIA COOLER CO.
2601 Tee Pee Drive
Stockton, CA 95205
(209) 466-7000
Primary Business: Manufactures wine
   coolers
Chairman of the Board: Michael M.
   Crete
Sales: $100 million
# of Employees: 500

Miscellaneous Facts: Division of Brown-
   Forman, Inc.

ADOLPH COORS CO.
Golden, CO 80401
(301) 279-6565
Primary Business: Beer
Chairman: William K. Coors
CEO: William K. Coors
President: Joseph Coors
Vice-President (Public Relations):
   Marvin D. Johnson
Vice-President (Sales): Frank L. Spinosa
Vice-President (Brewing): Norman E.
   Kuhl
Sales: $1.13 billion
Net Worth: $890 million
# of Employees: 9,650

Subsidiaries:
Coors Porcelain Co.
Advantage Health Systems
Coors Biotech Products Co.
Coors Distributing
Roberts Rice Mill
Suncoa Foods, Inc.
Alumina Ceramics
Rocky Mountain Water Co.

G. HEILEMAN BREWING CO., INC.
100 Harborview Plaza
LaCrosse, WI 54601
(608) 785-1000
Primary Business: Brewing, baking
Chairman of the Board: Russell G.
   Cleary
CEO: Russell G. Cleary
President: Russell G. Cleary
Senior Executive: John D. Isherwood
Executive Vice-President (Sales):
   Ronald W. Rizzo
Corporate Director (Brewing): Hans
   Reuther
Sales: $1.3 billion

Net Worth: $298 million
# of Employees: 7,200

Plants:
Barrel O' Fun Snack Foods
Dick Bros. Bakery Co.
Emrich Baking Co.
Johnson Nut Co.
Our Own Bakeries, Inc.
Willmar Cookie Co.
Blitz-Weinhard Brewing
Carling National Brewing
G. Heileman Brewing Co., Inc.
Jacob Schmidt Brewing
Lone Star Brewing Co.
Ranier Brewing Co.
Sterling National Brewing
Val Blatz Brewing Co., Inc.

**JACK DANIEL DISTILLERY LEM
   MOTLOW PROP., INC.**
Main Street
Lynchburg, TN 37352
(615) 759-4221
Primary Business: Maker of Tennessee
   whiskey
Chairman: Martin S. Brown
CEO: Martin S. Brown
President: David J. Mahanes
Vice-President (Sales): James M.
   Gustave
Sales: $90 million
# of Employees: 550

Miscellaneous Facts: Subsidiary of
   Brown-Forman, Inc.

MILLER BREWING CO.
3939 W Highland Boulevard
Milwaukee, WI 53201
(414) 931-2000
Primary Business: Beer
Chairman: John A. Murphy
CEO: William K. Howell
President: William K. Howell
Vice-President (Brewing and Research):
   Vincent S. Bavisotto
Vice-President (Sales): Leonard J.
   Goldstein
Vice-President (Corporate Affairs):
   Alan G. Easton
Sales: $2.92 billion
# of Employees: 11,000

Miscellaneous Facts: Subsidiary of Philip

Morris, Inc. Is the second-largest brewer in the world. Founded in 1855 by Frederic Miller. Brands include Miller High Life, Miller Light, Lowenbrau, Miller Genuine Draft, Magnum, Meister Brau and Milwaukee's Best. Famous for its Miller Light commercials on television.

PABST BREWING CO.
Post Office Box 766
Milwaukee, WI 53201
(414) 223-3500
Primary Business: Beer, ale, malt
Chairman: Lutz E. Isseib
Vice-President (Sales): R. Craig Werle
Vice-President (Advertising): Richard J. Ratcheson
Revenue: $752.36 million
# of Employees: 3,500

Subsidiary:
Pabst Brewing Co./Tumwater Div.

Miscellaneous Facts: Subsidiary of S & P Holding Co.

SEAGRAM CO., LTD. (THE)
375 Park Avenue
New York, NY 10152
(212) 572-7000
Primary Business: Distilled beverages, wine
Chairman: Edgar M. Bronfman
CEO: Edgar M. Bronfman
President: Philip E. Beekman
Department Chairman: Charles R. Bronfman
Executive Vice-President (Manufacturing): Melvin W. Griffin
Vice-President (Human Resources): Ronald J. Watkins
Sales: $2.82 billion
# of Employees: 14,000

Divisions:
Seagram International
The House of Seagram
Perennial Sales Co.
375 Spirits Co.
Seagram Distillers Co.
The Seagram Wine Co.
Summit Sales Co.
Seagram Vinters

Miscellaneous Facts: Bruce Willis is national spokesman for Seagram's wine coolers. Incorporated in 1928 in Canada as Distillers Corporation-Seagrams, Ltd. Present name adopted in 1975.

THE STROH BREWERY CO.
100 River Place
Detroit, MI 48207
(313) 446-2000
Primary Business: Beer, ice cream
Chairman: Peter W. Stroh
President: Roger Fridholm
Executive Vice-President (Sales and Marketing): J. Wayne Jones
Vice-President (Corporate Affairs): William V. Weatherston
Sales: $1.50 billion
# of Employees: 6,800

Miscellaneous Facts: Subsidiary of The Stroh Companies, Inc. Manufactures 12 brands of beer.

Juices

OCEAN SPRAY CRANBERRIES, INC.
225 Water Street
Plymouth, MA 02360
(617) 747-1000
Primary Business: Cranberry juice cocktail, other kinds of juices
Chairman: Stuart Pedersen
Vice-Chairman: William Atwood
President: Harold Thorkilsen
Senior Vice-President (Corporate Service): Curtis L. Collison, Jr.
Vice-President (Logistics): Arch MacIsaac
Sales: $565.62 million
Net Worth: $109 million
# of Employees: 1,462

Subsidiary:
Milne Food Products, Inc.

TREESWEET PRODUCTS CO.
9801 Westheimer
Houston, TX 77042
(713) 789-2222
Primary Business: Canned juices, frozen concentrates

Chairman: C. E. Owens
CEO: C. E. Owens
President: John W. Hunt
Vice-President (Sales): Richard R.
  Kantner
Vice-President (Human Resources):
  John J. Gemperle
# of Employees: 400

TREE TOP, INC.
2nd and Railroad Avenue
Selah, WA 98942
(509) 697-7251
Primary Business: Apple juice, dried
  fruit products
Chairman: Cragg Gilbert
President: Dennis J. Colleran
Vice-President (Sales): Ken Davidson
Vice-President (Operations): LeRoy
  Fletcher
Sales: $160 million
# of Employees: 500

TROPICANA PRODUCTS, INC.
1001 13th Avenue, E
Bradenton, FL 33508
(813) 747-4461
Primary Business: Chilled juices and
  citrus drinks
Chairman: Spencer J. Volk
CEO: Spencer J. Volk
President: Spencer J. Volk
Vice-President (Sales): Karl J. Maggard
Vice-President (Distribution): Robert G.
  Powers
Vice-President (Marketing): Robert L.
  Weisman
# of Employees: 3,000

Miscellaneous Facts: Subsidiary of
  Beatrice Companies, Inc.

WELCH FOODS, INC., A
   COOPERATIVE
100 Main Street
Concord, MA 01742
(619) 371-1000
Primary Business: Grape products,
  juice, jams
Chairman: J. Roy Orton
President: Everett N. Baldwin
Senior Vice-President (Marketing): Dan
  P. Dillon

Vice-President (Sales): H. K. Kelley
Vice-President (Personnel): Tom Gettig
Sales: $238.5 million
# of Employees: 1,230

Miscellaneous Facts: Subsidiary of
  National Grape Co-operative Assn.

Soft Drinks

BUBBLE UP CO., INC.
600 S Federal
Chicago, IL 60605
(312) 633-3230
Primary Business: Manufactures soft
  drink concentrates
President: Roy Gurvey
Executive Vice-President: Michael Flynn

Miscellaneous Facts: Subsidiary of IC
  Industries, Inc.

THE COCA-COLA CO.
310 North Avenue, NW
Atlanta, GA 30313
(404) 676-2121
Primary Business: Soft drinks, motion
  pictures
Chairman of the Board: Robert C.
  Goizveta
President: Donald R. Keough
Senior Executive Vice-President: Claus
  M. Halle
Executive Vice-President: A. Garth
  Hamby
Director, Employment: Jim Erbar
Sales: $7.36 billion
Net Worth: $2.7 billion
# of Employees: 39,6000

Subsidiaries:
Belmont Springs Water Co.
Coca-Cola Bottlers Enterprises
CPT Holdings
Gottlieb International Sales
Columbia Pictures Industries
General Bottling Co.
General Beverage Co.
Embassy Communications
Tandem Productions

Joint Ventures:
Tri-Star Pictures
Presto Products, Inc.

Miscellaneous Facts: World's leading soft-drink marketer. Maker of Sprite, Diet Sprite, Minute Maid Orange soda and lemon-lime soda, Fresca, Fanta, Hi-C fruit drinks and Nutri-Foods International Products. Coca-Cola is sold in more than 155 countries. Incorporated in 1919 in Delaware.

DAD'S ROOT BEER CO.
600 S Federal
Chicago, IL 60605
(312) 463-4600
Primary Business: Concentrate for franchise bottlers of root beer
President: Roy Gurvey
Executive Vice-President: Michael Flynn
Marketing Manager: Sheldon Adelman
# of Employees: 49

Miscellaneous Facts: Subsidiary of IC Industries, Inc.

DR PEPPER CO.
Post Office Box 225086
Dallas, TX 75265
(214) 824-0331
Primary Business: Soft drinks manufacturing
Chairman of the Board: W. W. Clements
CEO: W. W. Clements
President: John R. Albers
Vice-President (Franchise): Donald L. Antle
Vice-President (Corporate Relations): Jim Ball
# of Employees: 450

Subsidiary:
Premier Beverages, Inc.

PEPSICO, INC.
Anderson Hill Road
Purchase, NY 10577
(914) 253-2000
Primary Business: Soft drinks and snack foods
Chairman: Donald M. Kendall
CEO: Donald M. Kendall
President: D. Wayne Calloway
Chief Financial Officer: Michael H. Jordon

Vice-President (Personnel): J. Roger King
Executive Vice-President (Beverages): Victor A. Bonomo
Revenue: $8.70 billion
Net Worth: $1.84 billion
# of Employees: 150,000

Subsidiaries:
Frito-Lay, Inc.
Pizza Hut, Inc.
Taco Bell
Seven-Up International
Contract Beverages Co.
MEI Corp.
Brainerd Wadena Beverages Co.
La Petite Boulangerie, Inc.
Kentucky Fried Chicken

Miscellaneous Facts: Incorporated in Delaware September 18, 1919, as Loft, Inc. Present name adopted in 1965, with the merger of Pepsi-Cola and Frito-Lay. There are 16 Pepsi-Cola plants in the Soviet Union. Products include: Pepsi, Mountain Dew, Slice, Ruffles, Doritos, Fritos, Cheetos, Tostitos and O'Grady's.

ROYAL CROWN COMPANIES, INC.
41 Perimeter Center E, NE
Atlanta, GA 30346
(404) 394-6120
Primary Business: Soft drinks, citrus juices
Chairman of the Board: William T. Young
President: Donald A. McMahon
Vice-President (Corporate Communications): Arnold Belasco
President (Citrus Division): Ben Adams
Revenue: $490.07 million
# of Employees: 4,800

Subsidiaries:
Adams Packing Assn.
Arby's, Inc.
Athens Furnitures, Inc.
Frederick Cooper Lamps Co., Inc.
Couroc of Monterey, Inc.
Hoyne Industries, Inc.
National Picture and Frame Co.

Miscellaneous Facts: Subsidiary of Chesapeake Financial Corp.

SCHWEPPES U.S.A.
High Ridge Park
Stamford, CT 06905
(203) 329-0911
Primary Business: Soft drinks
    manufacturer
President: John C. Carson
Vice-President (Sales): Kenneth E.
    Walsh
# of Employees: 150

THE SEVEN-UP CO.
121 S Meramec
St. Louis, MO 63105
(314) 889-7777
Primary Business: Soft drinks and food
    products
CEO: Edward W. Frantel
President: Edward W. Frantel
Executive Vice-President (Soft Drink
    Group): Charles W. Schmid
Executive Vice-President (Food Group):
    Gerard J. Martin
Sales: $658 million
# of Employees: 4,000

Miscellaneous Facts: Subsidiary of Philip
    Morris Companies, Inc. Company
    toll-free consumer information
    number is (800) 325-7272.

SQUIRT & CO.
777 Brooks Avenue
Holland, MI 49423
(619) 396-1281
Primary Business: Soft drink
    manufacturer
Chairman: James F. Brooks
CEO: James F. Brooks
President: James W. F. Brooks
Vice-President (Human Resources):
    Dennis H. Eade
Vice-President (Special Products):
    Gerald O. Keel
Sales: $70 million
# of Employees: 275

Miscellaneous Facts: Subsidiary of Squirt
    Enterprises, Inc.

Tobacco Products

AMERICAN BRANDS, INC.
245 Park Avenue
New York, NY 10167
(212) 880-4200
Primary Business: Tobacco and food
    products
Chairman of the Board: Edward W.
    Whittemore
CEO: Edward W. Whittemore
President: Virginius B. Lougee III
Senior Vice-President and General
    Counsel: Arnold Henson
Vice-President (Public Affairs): Robert
    J. Rukeyser
Manager, Human Resources: Dennis
    Doherty
Sales: $6.9 billion
Net Worth: $2.1 billion
# of Employees: 75,700

Subsidiaries:
The Franklin Life Insurance Co.
James B. Beam Distilling Co.
The Andrew Jergens Co.
Master Lock Co.
Sunshine Biscuits
Bell Brand Foods
American Cigar
The American Tobacco Co.
Golden Belt Mfg. Co.

Miscellaneous Facts: Some of the
    products made by American Brands
    and subsidiaries are Carlton, Silk Cut,
    Pall Mall and Lucky Strike cigarettes;
    Master Locks; Cheez-It, Hi Ho and
    Honey Gram crackers; Titleist and
    Pinnacle golf balls; Jim Beam
    Whiskey; and Jergens products.
    Incorporated in 1986 in Delaware by
    merger with American Brands
    Holding Co.

CULBRO CORP.
387 Park Avenue, S
New York, NY 10016
(212) 561-8700
Primary Business: Manufactures tobacco
    products
Chairman of the Board: Edgar M.
    Cullman
CEO: Edgar M. Cullman
President: Edgar M. Cullman, Jr.

Vice-Chairman: Joseph E. Whitwell
Senior Vice-President: Richard F.
  Bonini
Personnel Director: Robert Grimaldi
Sales: $1.9 billion
Net Worth: $140 million
# of Employees: 6,125

Subsidiaries:
HF, Inc.
Flaks
Eli Witt Co.
Culbro Machine Systems
The Snacktime Co.
General Cigar & Tobacco Co.
Helme Tobacco Co.

PHILIP MORRIS COMPANIES, INC.
120 Park Avenue
New York, NY 10017
(212) 880-5000
Primary Business: Holding company,
  cigarettes, soft drinks, wine
Chairman: Hamish Maxwell
CEO: Hamish Maxwell
President: John A. Murphy
Vice-Chairman: Hugh Cullman
Vice-President (Corporate Affairs):
  Stanley S. Scott
Vice-President (Human Resources):
  William J. O'Connor
Revenue: $15.81 billion
Net Worth: $4.7 billion
# of Employees: 114,000

Subsidiaries:
General Foods Corp.
Miller Brewing Co.
The Seven-Up Co.
Mission Viejo Realty Group, Inc.
Philip Morris Credit Corp.

Miscellaneous Facts: Some of the
  products made by the company are:
  Marlboro, Benson & Hedges, Merit,
  Virginia Slims, Parliament Lights,
  Players, Cambridge, Saratoga and
  English Ovals. See General Foods
  Corp. and Miller Brewing Co. for
  more products. Incorporated in 1985 in
  Virginia to become holding company
  for Philip Morris, Inc. Marlboro is the
  largest-selling cigarette in the world.
  Miller is the second-largest-selling
  beer in the nation.

STANDARD COMMERCIAL
  TOBACCO, INC.
2201 Miller Road
Wilson, NC 27893
(919) 291-5507
Primary Business: Tobacco dealers
Chairman of the Board: Ery W. Kehaya
CEO: Ery W. Kehaya
President: Marvin W. Coughill
Executive Vice-President: J. Alec G.
  Murray
Revenue: $520 million
Net Worth: $92 million
# of Employees: 5,000

Subsidiaries:
Curo-Green Nursery, Inc.
Jas. I. Miller Tobacco Co.

UNITED STATES TOBACCO CO.
100 W Putnam Avenue
Greenwich, CT 06830
(203) 661-1100
Primary Business: Maker of tobacco and
  pipes
Chairman of the Board: Louis F. Bantle
CEO: Louis F. Bantle
President: Nicholas A. Bouniconti
Vice-Chairman: R. L. Rossi
Executive Vice-President: Thomas
  O'Grady
Sales: $480 million
Net Worth: $323 million
# of Employees: 3,741

Subsidiaries:
Honduran Cigar Imports, Ltd.
House of Windsor, Inc.
Mastercraft Pipes, Inc.
National Pen & Pencil Co.
Sparta Industries

UNIVERSAL LEAF TOBACCO CO.,
  INC.
Hamilton Street
Richmond, VA 23230
(804) 359-9311
Primary Business: Tobacco processing
Chairman of the Board: G. L. Crenshaw
CEO: G. L. Crenshaw
President: H. H. Harrell
Vice-Chairman: T. R. Towers
Vice-Chairman: W. L. Chandler
Personnel Director: W. L. Grubbs, Jr.
Revenue: $1.07 billion

Net Worth: $261 million
# of Employees: 14,000

Subsidiaries:
Blakely Peanut Co.

Dunnington-Beach Tobacco Co.
Latco, Inc.
Lawyers Title Insurance Co.
J. P. Taylor Co., Inc.

CHEMICALS

AIR PRODUCTS & CHEMICALS, INC.
Box 538
Allentown, PA 18105
(215) 481-4911
Primary Business: Industrial gases
Chairman of the Board: Edward Donley
CEO: Edward Donley
President: Dexter F. Baker
Vice-Chairman: Leon C. Holt, Jr.
Vice-President (Public Affairs): William J. Kendrick
Vice-President (Human Resources): Donald T. Shire
Revenue: $1.74 billion
Net Worth: $1.1 billion
# of Employees: 19,000

Subsidiaries: APCI, Inc.
Air Products, Inc.
Air Products Finance Co.
Arcair Co.
Butler Industrial Gas Co.
Catad, Inc.
Houdry Process Corp.
Prodair Corp.
Project Construction Corp.
Stearns Catalytic Corp.
Stearns-Roger, Inc.

Miscellaneous Facts: Incorporated in 1961 in Delaware by merger with subsidiary, Air Products, Inc.

BROWNING-FERRIS INDUSTRIES, INC.
14701 St. Mary's Lane
Houston, TX 77079
(713) 870-8100
Primary Business: Solid and chemical waste collection and disposal
Chairman of the Board: Harry J. Phillips, Sr.
President: John E. Drury
Vice-President (General Sales): Edward J. Crane
Vice-President (Employee Relations): C. P. J. Mooney III
Personnel Director: Stephen C. Shomette
Revenue: $1 billion
Net Worth: $465 million
# of Employees: 15,000

Subsidiaries:
Active Disposal Co.
Beach Disposal, Inc.
BFI Aviation Services, Inc.
Browning-Ferris Industries of Alabama
Captiva Disposal, Inc.
CECOS Environmental, Inc.
Disposal Specialists, Inc.
Empire Sweeping Co.
Indoco, Inc.
Karas Trucking Co., Inc.
Niagra Landfill, Inc.
Wasteco, Inc.

Miscellaneous Facts: There is a Browning-Ferris Industries subsidiary in every state in the country (not listed above).

CELANESE CORP.
1211 Avenue of the Americas
New York, NY 10036
(212) 719-8000
Primary Business: Petrochemicals, fibers, plastics
Chairman of the Board: John D. Macomber
CEO: John D. Macomber
President: John D. Macomber
Vice-President (Personnel): Kenneth G. Anderson
Vice-President: James J. Bigham
Vice-President: Richard M. Clarke
Revenue: $3.33 billion
Net Worth: $1.2 billion
# of Employees: 33,000

Subsidiaries:
Celanese Canada, Inc.
Celanese Plastics & Specialties Co.
VCSC, Inc.
VirChem Export, Inc.
Virginia International
Winterlawn Chemical Corp.

Divisions:
Celanese Chemical Co., Inc.
Celanese Fibers Operations
Celanese International Co.

Miscellaneous Facts: Incorporated in 1918 in Delaware as The American Cellulose & Chemical Manufacturing

Co. Name changed to Celanese Corp. of America in 1927. Present name adopted in 1966.

DOW CHEMICAL CO.
2030 Willard H. Dow Center
Midland, MI 48674
(517) 636-1000
Primary Business: Plastics, industrial and agricultural chemicals
Chairman of the Board: Robert W. Lundeen
CEO: Paul F. Oreffice
President: Paul F. Oreffice
Vice-President and General Counsel: Wayne M. Hancock
Executive Vice-President: Hunter W. Henry
Vice-President (Human Resources): Robert Tate
Revenue: $11.42 billion
# of Employees: 49,800

Subsidiaries:
Admiral Equipment Co.
Merrell Dow Pharmaceuticals, Inc.

Divisions:
Eastern Div.
Louisiana Div.
Michigan Div.
Oyster Creek Div.
Dow Corning Corp.

Miscellaneous Facts: Founded in 1897 by Herbert H. Dow. Products include Saran Wrap, Ziploc storage bags, Styrofoam, Spray 'N' Wash, Glass Plus, and Fantastik. Operates over 400 plants around the world.

HERCULES, INC.
Hercules Plaza
Wilmington, DE 19894
(302) 594-5000
Primary Business: Chemical products
Chairman of the Board: Alexander F. Giacco
CEO: Alexander F. Giacco
President: Alexander F. Giacco
Vice-Chairman: Robert J. Leahy
Vice-President and General Counsel: S. Maynard Turk
Vice-President: Edward J. Sheehy
Revenue: $2.57 billion

Net Worth: $1.5 billion
# of Employees: 26,000

Subsidiaries:
Champlain Cable Corp.
Hercules Overseas Corp.
Hercules Trading Corp.
Lexteco, Inc.
Mica Corp.
Simmonds Precision Products, Inc.

Miscellaneous Facts: Incorporated in 1912 in Delaware.

INTERNATIONAL FLAVORS & FRAGRANCES, INC.
521 W 57th Street
New York, NY 10019
(212) 765-5500
Primary Business: Aroma chemicals manufacturer
Chairman of the Board: Eugene P. Grisanti
CEO: Eugene P. Grisanti
Senior Vice-President: Bernard Chant
Senior Vice-President: Harry Fields
Sales: $467 million
# of Employees: 3,590

MINNESOTA MINING & MFG. CO.
3M Center
St. Paul, MN 55101
(612) 733-1110
Primary Business: Abrasives, chemicals, health care products
Chairman: Lewis W. Lehr
CEO: Lewis W. Lehr
President (U.S. Operations): Allen F. Jacobson
Executive Vice-President (Life Sciences): J. E. Robertson
Vice-President (Human Resources): Christopher J. Wheeler
Revenue: $7.70 billion
Net Worth: $4 billion
# of Employees: 86,700

Divisions:
Electronic Products Div.
TelComm Products Div.
Engineering Systems Div.
PhotoColor Div.
Audio Visual Div.
Automotive Trades Div.
Automotive Specialties Div.

Industrial Tape Div.
Orthopedic Products Div.
Household Products Div.
Consumer Specialties Div.

Miscellaneous Facts: Trade name: "3M."
Company makes 45,000 different
products, from Scotch-Brand tape and
videocassettes to orthopedic casts to
reflective coatings for street signs.

MONSANTO CO.
800 North Lindbergh Boulevard
St. Louis, MO 63166
(314) 694-1000
Primary Business: Plastics, resins, man-
made fibers
Chairman: Louis Fernandez
CEO: Richard J. Mahoney
President: E. H. Harbison, Jr.
Vice-President (Public Affairs): J. F.
Hussey
Personnel Director: B. Blitstein
Revenue: $6.69 billion
Net Worth: $3.4 billion
# of Employees: 56,754

Subsidiaries:
AstroTurf Industries
Monsanto Electronics Material Co.
Fisher Controls International Co.
The NutraSweet Co.
G. D. Searle and Co.
Monsanto Agricultural Co.
Monsanto Chemical Co.

Miscellaneous Facts: Incorporated in
1933 in Delaware as Monsanto
Chemical Co. Present name adopted
in 1964.

MORTON THIOKOL, INC.
110 N Wacker Drive
Chicago, IL 60606
(312) 621-5200
Primary Business: Manufacturer and
marketer of specialty chemicals, high-
technology propulsion systems and
salt
Chairman: Charles S. Locke
CEO: Charles S. Locke
President: Robert C. Hyndman
Group Vice-President (Aerospace): V.
Edwin Garrison

Vice-President (Human Resources):
Hugh C. Marx
Vice-President (Legal) and General
Counsel: Robert B. Gerrie
Sales: $2 billion
Net Worth: $636 million
# of Employees: 17,5000

Divisions: Armstrong Products Co.
Morton Chemical Co.
Polymer Industries Div.
Chemical Group
Coated Film Products
Aerospace Group
Space Div.
Strategic Div.
Morton Salt Div.
Ponse Salt Industries Corp.

Miscellaneous Facts: Formed in
September of 1982 from the merger of
Morton-Norwick Products, Inc., and
Thiocol Corp. Manufactures Morton
table salt, Trident I fleet ballistic
missiles, and many other defense
products.

NALCO CHEMICAL CO.
2901 Butterfield Road
Oak Brook, IL 60521
(312) 887-7500
Primary Business: Specialized chemicals
manufacturer
Chairman of the Board: W. H. Clark, Jr.
CEO: W. H. Clark, Jr.
Executive Vice-President: L. J. Palmer
Executive Vice-President (Staff
Operations): K. V. Davis
Vice-President (Human Resources): J.
F. Lambe
Revenue: $664 million
# of Employees: 4,751

NATIONAL DISTILLERS &
CHEMICAL CORP.
99 Park Avenue
New York, NY 10016
(212) 949-5000
Primary Business: Chemicals
manufacturer
Chairman of the Board: Drummond C.
Bell
CEO: Drummond C. Bell
President: John H. Stookey
Vice-President: F. Donald Brigham

Vice-President (Corporate Relations):
Richard A. Tilghman
Revenue: $2.24 billion
# of Employees: 10,343

NATIONAL SERVICE INDUSTRIES, INC.
1180 Peachtree Street, NE
Atlanta, GA 30309
(404) 892-2400
Primary Business: Linen service,
cleaning chemicals
Chairman of the Board: Erwin Zaban
CEO: Erwin Zaban
President: Signey Kirschner
Senior Vice-President: Robert H.
Creviston
Senior Vice-President: David Levy
Sales: $1.07 billion
Net Worth: $417 million
# of Employees: 18,861

Divisions:
Atlantic Envelope Co.
Blocke Industries
Certified Leasing Co.
Lithonia Lighting Co.
Marketing Service Div.
National Linen & Uniform Service
North Brothers Co.
Selig Chemical Industries
Zep Manufacturing Co.

OLIN CORP.
120 Long Ridge Road
Stamford, CT 06904
(203) 356-2000
Primary Business: Industrial chemicals
Chairman of the Board: John M.
Henske
CEO: John M. Henske
President: John W. Johnstone
Executive Vice-President: Richard R.
Berry
Vice-President (Public Affairs): George
H. Nusloch
Vice-President (Human Resources):
Richard N. Williams
Sales: $1.7 billion
Net Worth: $686 million
# of Employees: 17,800

Subsidiaries:
Olin Hunt Specialty Products, Inc.
Rockor, Inc.

Larse Corp.
Pacific Electro-Dynamics, Inc.
Physics International Co.

Miscellaneous Facts: Incorporated in
1892 in Virginia as Mathieson Alkali
Works. Name adopted in 1969.

PENNWALT CORP.
Three Parkway
Philadelphia, PA 19102
(215) 587-7000
Primary Business: Chemicals, health
products
Chairman: Edwin E. Tuttle
CEO: Edwin E. Tuttle
President: Seymour S. Preston III
Vice-President (Personnel): Anthony P.
Fortino
Director of Advertising and Public
Relations: Peter J. McCarthy
Vice-President (Health): Isaac R.
McGraw
Revenue: $1.05 billion
Net Worth: $334 million
# of Employees: 13,900

Subsidiaries:
Automatic Power, Inc.
Cook's Lubrication Products Div.
May Products Co.
Ozark-Mahoning Co.
Wyandotte Southern R.R.

Divisions:
Decco Tilt Belt Div.
Flourochemicals Div.
Pennwalth Corp., Keystone Div.
Stokes Div.
Wallace & Tiernan Div.

Miscellaneous Facts: Incorporated in
1850 in Pennsylvania as Pennsylvania
Salt Manufacturing Co. Present name
adopted in 1969.

ROHN & HAAS CO.
Independence Mall W
Philadelphia, PA 19105
(215) 592-3000
Primary Business: Industrial and
agricultural chemicals
Chairman: Vincent L. Gregory, Jr.
CEO: Vincent L. Gregory, Jr.
President: Donald L. Felley

Group Vice-President (Corporate
   Business): John P. Mulroney
Vice-Chairman: John C. Haas
Group Vice-President and General
   Counsel: John T. Subak
Sales; $2.04 billion
Net Worth: $965 million
# of Employees: 11,379

Subsidiaries:
Electro-Materials Corp. of America
Furane Products Co.
Rohm & Haas Bayport, Inc.
Rohm & Haas Credit Corp.

Miscellaneous Facts: Incorporated in
   1917 in Delaware.

SCM CORP.
299 Park Avenue
New York, NY 10171
(212) 752-2700
Primary Business: Chemicals, coatings
   and resins
Chairman: Paul H. Elicker
President: D. George Harris
Vice-President (Corporate
   Communications): Gerard F.
   Stoddard
Vice-President and General Counsel:
   Richard Sexton
Director, Consumer Affairs: Charles A.
   Molloy
Sales: $1.96 billion
# of Employees: 24,500

TENNECO CORP.
Post Office Box 2482
Houston, TX 77001
(713) 757-2131
Primary Business: Holding company,
   chemicals
Chairman of the Board: J. L. Ketelsen
President: J. L. Ketelsen
Vice-President: E. L. Capps
Vice-President: Kenneth W. Reese
# of Employees: 66,000

Miscellaneous Facts: Subsidiary of
   Tenneco, Inc. Company owns its own
   country club and $11 million fitness
   center for employee use. It is the
   youngest company among the top 25
   Fortune 500 firms.

UNION CARBIDE CORP.
Old Ridgebury Road
Danbury, CT 06817
(203) 794-2000
Primary Business: Chemicals and carbon
   products
Chairman: Warren M. Anderson
CEO: Warren M. Anderson
President: Alec Flamm
Vice-President: John A. Stichnoth
Director of Communications: J. Walter
   Goetz
Sales: $9.50 billion
Net Worth: $4.9 billion
# of Employees: 98,366

Subsidiaries:
Amko Service Co.
Bakers Welding Supply Co.
Bently Sales Co., Inc.
Harvey Co.
Linox Co.
R.S. McCracken, Inc.
Presto Welding Supplies, Inc.
STP Corp.
Soilserve, Inc.
Unigas, Inc.

Miscellaneous Facts: Incorporated in
   1917 in New York as Union Carbide &
   Carbon Corp. Present name adopted
   in 1957.

UNITED STATES BORAX &
CHEMICAL CORP.
Post Office Box 75128
Los Angeles, CA 90010
(213) 381-5311
Primary Business: Chemicals
   manufacturer
President: Dr. C. L. Randolph
Executive Vice-President: R. E. Kendall
Senior Vice-President: T. M. Cromwell
Vice-President (Employee Relations): J.
   H. Hallahan
# of Employees: 2,000

UNIVAR CORP.
1600 Norton Building
Seattle, WA 98104
(206) 447-5911
Primary Business: Distributes industrial
   chemicals
Chairman of the Board: James H.
   Wiborg

CEO: R. E. Engebrecht
President: R. E. Engebrecht
Vice-Chairman: M. M. Harris
Chairman of the Executive Committee:
  Robert D. O'Brien
Sales: $951 million
# of Employees: 3,050

WITCO CHEMICAL CORP.
520 Madison Avenue
New York, NY 10022
(212) 605-3800
Primary Business: Special-purpose
  chemical products
Chairman: William Wishnick
CEO: William Wishnick

President: William J. Ashe
Executive Vice-President: Dennis
  Andrevzzi
Executive Vice-President: J. L. Kennedy
Revenue: $1.38 billion
Net Worth: $374 million
# of Employees: 8,000

Subsidiaries:
Aero Oil Co., Inc.
Witco Corp., Allied Kelite Div.
Argus Chemical
Chemprene
Richardson Battery Parts
Southwest Petro Chem, Inc.
Witco International Sales Corp.

COMMUNICATIONS

Broadcasting

CAPITAL CITIES/ABC, INC.
24 E 51st Street
New York, NY 10022
(212) 421-9595
Primary Business: Owns and operates
  broadcasting stations
Chairman of the Board: Thomas S.
  Murphy
CEO: Daniel B. Burke
President: Thomas B. Burke
Executive Vice-President: Joseph P.
  Dougherty
Executive Vice-President: John B.
  Fairchild
Vice-President (Human Resources):
  John Frisoli
Revenue: $939.70 million
Net Worth: $734 million
# of Employees: 8,600

Subsidiaries:
Capital Cities Cable, Inc.
American Traveler
Cablecom-General of Altus, Inc.
Trenton Cable TV, Inc.
Capital Cities Media, Inc.

Divisions:
Fort Worth Star-Telegram
KFSN-TV
KZLA AM-FM

Miscellaneous Facts: Captial Cities
  Communications, Inc., acquired ABC
  for $3.52 billion in 1986 and changed
  the name to Capital Cities/ABC, Inc.
  Owns 80 percent of ESPN, Arts &
  Entertainment and parts of Lifetime,
  CNN, MTV and USA networks.

CBS, INC.
51 W 52nd Street
New York, NY 10019
(212) 975-4321
Primary Business: Broadcasting,
  publishing, music, films
Chairman of the Board: William S.
  Paley

President: Lawrence Tisch
Senior Vice-President (Corporate
  Affairs): William Lilley III
Senior Vice-President (Administration):
  H. P. MacCowatt
Vice-President (Personnel): Joan
  Showalter
Revenue: $4.92 billion
Net Worth: $1.5 billion
# of Employees: 30,000

Subsidiaries:
CBS-Fox Video, Inc.
Columbia Television
Tri-Star Pictures
April Music
Columbia Recording

Divisions:
CBS Records
Columbia House
CBS Toys
CBS Magazines

Magazines:
American Photographer
Car and Driver
Cycle
Field & Stream
Modern Bride
Popular Photography
Road & Track
The Runner
Skiing
Stereo Review
Woman's Day

Miscellaneous Facts: Incorporated in
  1927 in New York as United
  Independent Broadcasters, Inc.
  Present name adopted in 1974.

METROMEDIA, INC.
1 Harmon Plaza
Secaucus, NJ 07094
(201) 348-3244
Primary Business: TV and radio
  broadcasting
Chairman of the Board: John W. Kluge
CEO: John W. Kluge
President: John W. Kluge

Executive Vice-President: Stuart
Subotnick
Senior Vice-President (Broadcasting):
Robert M. Bennett
Director, Labor Relations: Allan Frost,
Esq.
Revenue: $763 million
# of Employees: 5,500

Subsidiaries:
Harlem Globetrotters, Inc.
Ice Capades, Inc.
Metromedia Producers Corp.
Metromedia Broadcasting Corp.

Radio Stations:
WIP (PA)
KRLD (TX)
KHOW-AM (CO)
WCBM (MD)
WNEW-AM (NY)
WNEW-FM (NY)
KMET-FM (CA)

TV Stations:
KRLD-TV (TX)
KRIV-TV (TX)
KTTV (CA)
WCVB-TV (MA)
WFLD-TV (IL)
WNEW-TV (NY)
WTTG (DC)

NATIONAL BROADCASTING CO., INC.
30 Rockefeller Placa
New York, NY 10020
(212) 664-4444
Primary Business: Network radio and
television broadcasting
Chairman: Robert C. Wright
CEO: Robert C. Wright
Vice-Chairman: Irwin Segelstein
Executive Vice-President (Corporate
Communications): M. S. Rukeyser
Director, Personnel (NBC Sports):
Ronald Mason
Director, Personnel (NBC News): Peter
Spinner

Miscellaneous Facts: Subsidiary of RCA
Corp.

RCA CORP.
30 Rockefeller Plaza
New York, NY 10020
(212) 621-6000

Primary Business: TV receivers,
videocassettes, TV and radio
broadcasting
Chairman: Thornton F. Bradshaw
CEO: Robert R. Frederick
President: Robert R. Frederick
Executive Vice-President (Corporate
Affairs): Kenneth W. Bilby
Executive Vice-President (Corporate
Service): George A. Fadler
Revenue: $8.97 billion
Net Worth: $2.5 billion
# of Employees: 87,000

Divisions:
Aerospace & Defense Div.
Broadcast Systems Div.
Consumer Electronics
Distributor & Special Products Div.
RCA Laboratories
RCA Service Co.
RCA Records
Solid State Div.
Coronet Industries, Inc.
National Broadcasting Co.
RCA Communications, Inc.
RCA Music Service
RCA Network Services, Inc.
RCA Sales Corp.

Miscellaneous Facts: Subsidiary of
General Electric Co.

TAFT BROADCASTING CO.
1718 Young Street
Cincinnati, OH 45210
(513) 721-1414
Primary Business: Operates radio and
TV stations
Chairman of the Board: Charles S.
Mechem, Jr.
CEO: Charles S. Mechem, Jr.
President: Dudley S. Taft
Executive Vice-President: George E.
Castrucci
Executive Vice-President (Television):
Jack Sander
Executive Vice-President (Radio and
Cable): Carl J. Wagner
Revenue: $472 million
Net Worth: $1.2 billion
# of Employees: 2,700

Operating Companies:
The Taft Entertainment Co.
Taft Merchandising Group

The Sy Fischer Co.
Taft Entertainment Television
Worldvision Enterprises
Ruby-Spears Enterprises
Hanna-Barbera Productions
Titus Productions
Cine Guarantors
Southern Star Productions
Taft Entertainment Motion Pictures

TELE-COMMUNICATIONS, INC.
5455 S Valentia Way
Englewood, CO 80111
(303) 771-8200
Primary Business: Broadcasting
Chairman of the Board: Bob Magness
CEO: John C. Malone
President: John C. Malone
Senior Vice-President: Stewart D. Blair
Senior Vice-President: Donne F. Fisher
Revenue: $577 million
Net Worth: $373 million
# of Employees: 4,716

Subsidiary:
Community Tele-Communications, Inc.

TURNER BROADCASTING SYSTEM, INC.
100 International Boulevard
Atlanta, GA 30348
(404) 827-1700
Primary Business: Cable production, broadcasting
Chairman of the Board: R. E. Turner
President: R. E. Turner
Executive Vice-President: Robert J. Wussler
Vice-President (Personnel): William M. Shaw
Vice-President (Corporate Communications): Arthur Sando
Sales: $351 million
Net Worth: $29 million
# of Employees: 2,062

Subsidiaries:
Atlanta Hawks, Inc.
Atlanta Braves, Inc.
Atlanta Chiefs, Inc.
Braves Productions, Inc.
CNN
MGAM Entertainment Co.
RET Corp.
SuperStation, Inc.

TBS Productions, Inc.
Turner Music Publishing, Inc.
Turner Network Television, Inc.
Turner Omni Ventures, Inc.

VIACOM INTERNATIONAL, INC.
1211 Avenue of the Americas
(212) 575-5175
Primary Business: Worldwide syndication of TV programs
Chairman of the Board: Ralph M. Baruch
CEO: Terrence A. Elkes
President: Terrence A. Elkes
Executive Vice-President: Kenneth F. Gorman
Vice-President (Human Resources): Kenneth Meyer
Sales: $444 million
Net Worth: $603 million
# of Employees: 4,400

Subsidiaries:
Film Intex Corp.
Viacom Broadcasting, Inc.
Cable Health Network, Inc.
Telecasters, Inc.
Telerama, Inc.

Affiliates:
Showtime/The Movie Channel, Inc.
All Media, Inc.
MTV Networks, Inc.

Publishing

DE LUXE CHECK PRINTERS, INC.
1080 W Country Road, F.
St. Paul, MN 55112
(612) 483-7111
Primary Business: Bank checks, deposit ticket printing
Chairman: Eugene R. Olson
CEO: Eugene R. Olson
President: Harold V. Haverty
Senior Vice-President (Sales): W. N. Hansen
Vice-President (Personnel): T. J. Quigley
Revenue: $682.82 million
Net Worth: $299 million
# of Employees: 10,237

Subsidiary:
Chex Systems, Inc.

DOUBLEDAY & CO., INC.

245 Park Avenue
New York, NY 10017
(212) 984-7561
Primary Business: Book publishing
President and Publisher: Nancy Evans t
President (Book Shop Division): Gary
  Del Vecchio
Manager, Public Relations: Nancy
  Tuckerman
Sales: $500 million
# of Employees: 6,000

Subsidiaries:
Dell Publishing Co., Inc.
Doubleday Broadcasting Co., Inc.
Doubleday Sports, Inc.
Feffer & Simons, Inc.
J. G. Ferguson Publishing Co.

Book Clubs:
Collectibles Limited
Doubleday Book Club
Ecstasy Romance Club
Fireside Theatre
The Literary Guild
Military Book Club
Mystery Club
Readers Select Books
Science Fiction Book Club
Miscellaneous Facts: A Division of the
  Bantam/Doubleday/Dell Publishing
  Group

DOW JONES & CO., INC.

22 Cortlandt Street
New York, NY 10007
(212) 285-5000
Primary Business: News publishing
Chairman of the Board: Warren H.
  Phillips
CEO: Warren H. Phillips
President: Ray Shaw
Senior Vice-President: Frederick G.
  Harris
Vice-President: Frank C. Breese III
Sales: $965 million
Net Worth: $505 million
# of Employees: 6,300
Subsidiaries:
American Demographics, Inc.
Richard D. Irwin, Inc.
Ottaway Newspapers, Inc.

THE DUN & BRADSTREET CORP.

299 Park Avenue
New York, NY 10171
(212) 593-6800
Primary Business: Publisher, business
  service
Chairman of the Board: Charles W.
  Moritz
CEO: Charles W. Moritz
President: Robert E. Weissman
Executive Vice-President: John C. Holt
Executive Vice-President (Human
  Resources): Charles J. Wielgus
Revenue: $2.9 billion
Net Worth: $1.2 billion
# of Employees: 54,000

Subsidiaries:
Compumark, Inc.
DataQuest, Inc.
A. C. Nielsen Co.
Official Airline Guides
SalesNet
Technical Data Resources
Technical Publishing
Zytron

Miscellaneous Facts: Incorporated in
  1973 in Delaware as part of company
  reorganization. Present name adopted
  in 1979. Former name The Dun &
  Bradstreet Companies, Inc.

ENCYCLOPAEDIA BRITANNICA, INC.

310 S Michigan Avenue
Chicago, IL 60604
(312) 347-7000
Primary Business: Book publishing
Chairman of the Board: Robert P.
  Gwinn
President: Peter B. Norton
Editor-in-Chief: Philip W. Goetz
Personnel Director: Jeanne Holle
Sales: $345 million
# of Employees: 1,100

Subsidiaries:
Britannica Home Library Services
EB (USA)
Encyclopaedia Britannica Educational
  Corp.
Library Resources, Inc.
Merriam-Webster, Inc.

GANNETT CO., INC.
P. O. Box 7858
Washington, DC 20044
(202) 284-6000
Primary Business: Newspaper
publishing, broadcasting, outdoor
advertising
President and CEO: John J. Curley
Vice Chairman: Douglas H.
McCorkindale
Vice-President (Labor Relations): John
B. Jaske
Executive Vice-President/Marketing:
Cathleen P. Black
Revenue: $2.8 billion
Net Worth: $1.4 billion
# of Employees: 36,000

Subsidiaries:
90 Daily Newspapers including *USA
Today*
USA Weekend
Lou Harris and Associates
Literature Control Services
Gannett News Media
Gannett International
Gannett National News
GTG Entertainment
Gannett News Service
Gannett Outdoor

Miscellaneous Facts: Owns sixteen radio
and eight television stations plus many
other newspapers. Incorporated in
1972 in Delaware as successor to
company with the same name.

HARPER & ROW PUBLISHERS, INC.
10 E 53rd Street
New York, NY 10022
(212) 207-7000
Primary Business: Book publishing
President: George Craig
Vice-President and General Counsel:
Edward A. Miller
Vice-President (Personnel): Chester S.
Logan
Revenue: $181.24 million
Net Worth: $64 million
# of Employees: 1,800

Subsidiaries:
Ballinger Publishing Co.
Basic Books, Inc.
J. B. Lippincott Co.

Divisions:
Adult Trade Div.
Barnes & Noble Div.
College Div.
General Books Group
Harper & Row San Francisco
International Div.
Junior Books Div.

THE HEARST CORP.
959 Eighth Avenue
New York, NY 10019
(212) 262-5700
Primary Business: Publisher of
newspapers, books and magazines
Chairman of the Board: Randolph A.
Hearst
CEO: Frank A. Bennack, Jr.
President: Frank A. Bennack, Jr.
Executive Vice-President: Gilbert C.
Maurer
Vice-President and General Counsel:
Harvey L. Lipton
Director, Corporate Communications:
James F. O'Donnell
# of Employees: 13,000

Publications:
American Druggist
Diversion
Motor Magazine
Colonial Homes
Connoisseur
Cosmopolitan
Country Living
Good Housekeeping
Harper's Bazaar
House Beautiful
Motor Boating & Sailing
Popular Mechanics
Redbook
Sports Afield
Town & Country

Operations:
Avon Books Div.
William Morrow & Co., Inc.
Hearst Radio, Inc.
Arts & Entertainment Network
Lifetime Cable Network

HOUGHTON MIFFLIN CO.
One Beacon Street
Boston, MA 02107
(617) 725-5000

Primary Business: Book publishing
Chairman: Harold T. Miller
President: Richard W. Young
Vice-President (Personnel): Joan P.
  Bowman
Vice-Chairman: Richard B. Gladstone
Sales: $277.21 million
Net Worth: $138 million
# of Employees: 1,897

Subsidiaries:
The Riverside Publishing Co.
Ticknor & Fields
Clarion Books

Divisions:
College Div.
Educational Software Div.
Financial & Corporate Services
International Div.
School Div.
Trade & Reference Div.

KNIGHT-RIDDER NEWSPAPERS, INC.
One Herald Plaza
Miami, FL 33101
(305) 376-3800
Primary Business: Newspaper publishing
Chairman: Alvah H. Chapman, Jr.
CEO: Alvah H. Chapman, Jr.
President: James K. Batten
Senior Vice-President (News): Larry
  Jinks
Vice-President (Personnel): Douglas
  Harris
Vice-President (Circulations): Donald
  A. Nizen
Revenue: $1.66 billion
Net Worth: $696 million
# of Employees: 22,000

Divisions:
KOLD-TV
KTVY-TV
WALA-TV
WJRT-TV
WKRN-TV
WPRI-TV
WTEN

Newspapers:
Akron Beacon Journal
Fort Wayne News-Sentinel
Long Beach Press-Telegram
Miami Herald
Detroit Free Press

San Jose Mercury News
Seattle Times

Miscellaneous Facts: Incorporated in
1976 in Florida as successor to
company with the same name, which
was formed as a result of the
consolidation of a number of
newspapers in 1941. Company delivers
more newspapers to homes in
America than any other newspaper
publisher.

MCGRAW-HILL, INC.
1221 Avenue of the Americas
New York, NY 10020
(212) 512-2000
Primary Business: Publisher of books
  and services
Chairman of the Board: Harold W.
  McGraw, Jr.
CEO: Joseph L. Dionne
President: Joseph L. Dionne
Senior Vice-President (Human
  Resources): William W. Mauritz
Vice-President (Public Affairs): Donald
  S. Rubin
Revenue: $1.04 billion
Net Worth: $776 million
# of Employees: 14,792

Subsidiaries:
McGraw-Hill Broadcasting Co.
Electronic Markets & Information
  Systems
Standard & Poor's Corp.
Data Resources, Inc.
Systemetrics, Inc.

Divisions:
McGraw-Hill Book Co.
McGraw-Hill Information Systems Co.
McGraw-Hill Publications Co.
Chemical Engineering
Chemical Week
Coal Age
Engineering & Mining Journal
Modern Plastics
Textile World

MARVEL COMIC GROUP
387 Park Avenue S
New York, NY 10016
(212) 576-9200
Primary Business: Comic book publisher
CEO: James E. Galton

Miscellaneous Facts: Subsidiary of Cadence Industries Corp.

MEREDITH CORP.
1716 Locust Street
Des Moines, IA 50336
(515) 284-3000
Primary Business: Publishing, broadcasting
Chairman of the Board: E. T. Meredith III
CEO: Robert A. Burnett
President: Robert A. Burnett
Senior Vice-President: James E. Conley
Vice-President (Corporate Relations): Donald L. Arnold
Sales: $450 million
Net Worth: $228 million
# of Employees: 2,859

Publications:
Better Homes and Gardens Books
Better Homes and Gardens Cook Book Club
Country Home Magazine
List Marketing
Metropolitan Home Magazine
Meredith Newspapers
Meredith Publishing Services
Successful Farming Magazine
Syndication Services

NEWS AMERICA PUBLISHING, INC.
210 South Street
New York, NY 10002
(212) 815-8800
Primary Business: Newspaper and magazine publisher
Chairman of the Board: K. Rupert Murdoch
CEO: Martin Singerman
President: Martin Singerman
Vice-President and General Counsel: Lawrence B. Kessler
Personnel Director: Lucy Lambert
Sales: $1.8 billion
# of Employees: 11,000

Subsidiaries:
Automobile Magazine
Elle Magazine
European Travel & Life
New York Post
New York Magazine Company
San Antonio Express-News

Star Magazine
New Women Magazine
The Boston Herald
Twentieth Century-Fox Film Corp.
Fox Television Stations, Inc.

Joint Venture:
CBS/Fox Company

NEWSWEEK, INC.
444 Madison Avenue
New York, NY 10022
(212) 350-4000
Primary Business: Publishing
President: Mark M. Edmiston
Executive Vice-President: S. H. Price
Editor-in-Chief: Richard Smith
Vice-President and General Counsel: Alan R. Finberg
Sales: $302 million
# of Employees: 1,500

Miscellaneous Facts: Subsidiary of The Washington Post Co.

THE NEW YORK TIMES CO.
229 W 43rd Street
New York, NY 10036
(212) 556-1234
Primary Business: Newspaper, magazine and book publishing
Chairman: Arthur Ochs Sulzberger
Vice-Chairman: Sydney Gruson
President: Walter Mattson
Vice-President (Corporate Personnel): Guy T. Garrett, Jr.
Vice-President (Books): William T. Kerr, Jr.
Public Affairs Director: Marjorie W. Longley
Revenue: $1.32 billion
Net Worth: $588 million
# of Employees: 10,750

Affiliates:
Avon Park Sun, Inc.
Banner-Independent
Claiborne Progress
Cruising World
Daily News
The Family Circle, Inc.
Florence Times Daily
Golf Digest
Houma Daily Courier
Lakeland Ledger
Lexington Dispatch

The Messenger
The Press Democrat
Sebring News
State Gazette
Tennis Magazine

A. C. NIELSEN CO.
Nielsen Plaza
Northbrook, IL 60062
(312) 498-6300
Primary Business: Market research
Chairman of the Board: Henry Burk
CEO: Henry Burk
President: Norman E. Harden
Executive Vice-President: D. R.
  McCurry
Vice-President (Communications):
  Robert Bregenzer
Director, Personnel: V. H. Field
# of Employees: 23,000

Miscellaneous Facts: Subsidiary of The
  Dun & Bradstreet Corp.

PENTHOUSE INTERNATIONAL, LTD.
1965 Broadway
New York, NY 10023
(212) 496-6100
Primary Business: Magazine publisher
Chairman of the Board: Bob Guccione
CEO: Bob Guccione
President: Bob Guccione
Vice-Chairman: Kathy Keeton
Senior Vice-President (Graphics): Frank
  De Vino
Personnel Director: Robyn Wisneski
Sales: $185 million
# of Employees: 359

Divisions:
The McCord Corp.
Omni Publications International, Ltd.

PLAYBOY ENTERPRISES, INC.
919 N Michigan Avenue
Chicago, IL 60611
(312) 751-8000
Primary Business: Magazine publishing
Chairman: Hugh M. Hefner
CEO: Hugh M. Hefner
President: Christie Hefner
Executive Vice-President: Richard S.
  Rosenzweig

Senior Vice-President (Law and
  Administration): Howard Shapiro
Director of Personnel: Russell Ringl
Revenue: $187.14 million
Net Worth: $82.7 million
# of Employees: 1,025

Subsidiaries:
Boarts International, Inc.
Playboy Clubs International, Inc.
Playboy Programs, Inc.
Playboy Programming Distribution Co.,
  Inc.
Playboy Sales, Inc.

RAND MCNALLY & CO.
8255 W Central Park Avenue
Skokie, IL 60076
(312) 673-9100
Primary Business: Book printing,
  publishing, map making
Chairman: Andrew McNally III
President: Andrew McNally IV
Executive Vice-President: William J.
  Bold
Vice-President (Map Division): Arthur
  DuBois
Vice-President (Purchasing): Irwin List
Sales: $150 million
# of Employees: 3,000

Subsidiaries:
Book Manufacturing Group
Rand McNally TDM, Inc.
Rand McNally-INFOMAP

RANDOM HOUSE, INC.
201 E 50th Street
New York, NY 10022
(212) 751-2600
Primary Business: Book publishing
Chairman: Robert L. Bernstein
CEO: Robert L. Bernstein
President: Robert L. Bernstein
Vice-President and General Counsel:
  Gerald E. Hollingsworth
Vice-President (Marketing): Richard H.
  Liebermann
# of Employees: 1,500

Miscellaneous Facts: Subsidiary of
  Advance Publications, Inc. Employees
  can select ten free books a year and
  buy others at half price.

READER'S DIGEST ASSN., INC.
Pleasantville, NY 10570
(914) 769-7000
Primary Business: Publishing periodicals
Chairman: George V. Grune
CEO: George V. Grune
President: William J. Cross
Vice-Chairman: Richard F. McLoughlin
Vice-President and Editor-in-Chief:
  Kenneth O. Gilmore
Vice-President (Personnel): J. Edward
  Hall
# of Employees: 3,100

Subsidiaries:
QSP, Inc.
RD Mfg. Corp.
Reader's Digest Sales & Services, Inc.
Reader's Digest Services, Inc.
Source Telecomputing Corp.

Miscellaneous Facts: Publishes one of
  the most popular magazines in the
  world. Has a bus service that brings
  employees to work. A community
  garden is located on corporate
  headquarters grounds so employees
  can grow vegetables.

SCHOLASTIC, INC.
730 Broadway
New York, NY 10003
(212) 505-3000
Primary Business: Publishes magazines
  and books for school and home
Chairman of the Board: Richard
  Robinson
CEO: Richard Robinson
President: Richard Robinson
Executive Vice-President: Richard M.
  Spaulding
Vice-President (Family Computing):
  Claudia Gohl
Vice-President (Human Resources):
  Katherine Ryden
Revenue: $167 million
Net Worth: $29 million
# of Employees: 1,590

Subsidiaries:
California School Book Fairs, Inc.
Scholastic Book Fairs, Inc.
Scholastic Productions, Inc.

SIMON & SCHUSTER, INC.
1230 Avenue of the Americas
New York, NY 10020
(212) 245-6400
Primary Business: Publishing and
  distributing books
Chairman: Richard E. Snyder
President: Richard E. Snyder
Executive Vice-President: Enzo Vialardi
Vice-President (Purchasing): Richard A.
  Koplitz
Sales Range: $300–$400 million
# of Employees: 2,000

Miscellaneous Facts: Division of Gulf &
  Western Industries, Inc.

TECHNICAL PUBLISHING
1301 S Grove Avenue
Barrington, IL 60010
(312) 381-1840
Primary Business: Publishes business
  magazines
President: John K. Abely
Executive Vice-President: Robert L.
  Dickson
Vice-President (Circulation): Joseph
  Zaccaria
# of Employees: 771

Miscellaneous Facts: Subsidiary of Dun
  & Bradstreet Corp.

TIME, INC.
Time Life Building
New York, NY 10020
(212) 586-1212
Primary Business: Magazine, newspaper
  and book publishing
Chairman: Ralph P. Davidson
CEO: J. Richard Munro
President: J. Richard Munro
Corporate Vice-President (Public
  Affairs): Donald M. Wilson
Editor-in-Chief: Henry A. Grunwald
Executive Vice-President: Gerald M.
  Levin
Revenue: $3.07 billion
Net Worth: $1.2 billion
# of Employees: 19,000

Subsidiaries:
American Family Publishers
American Television & Communications
  Corp.

Book of the Month Club
541 Fairbanks Corp.
Home Box Office
HBO Pictures
Burke Marketing Services
Media Services
Progressive Farmer, Inc.
Time-Life Books, Inc.
Time-Life Video

Miscellaneous Facts: Incorporated in
1983 in Delaware as successor to
company with the same name
incorporated in 1922. It is the largest
magazine publisher in the United
States and one of the largest firms in
the cable TV industry.

THE TIMES MIRROR CO.
Times Mirror Square
Los Angeles, CA 90053
(213) 972-3700
Primary Business: Newspaper, magazine
and book publishing
Chairman: Otis Chandler
CEO: Robert F. Erburu
President: Robert F. Erburu
Senior Vice-President and General
Counsel: John E. Flick
Vice-President (Public Affairs): Donald
S. Kellermann
Revenue: $2.97 billion
Net Worth: $974 million
# of Employees: 28,000

Subsidiaries:
Los Angeles Times
Call-ChrOnical Newspapers, Inc.
The Denver Post Corp.
The H. M. Gousha Co.
Graphic Controls Corp.
KDFW-TV
KTBC-TV
National Journal
Newsday, Inc.
Sporting News Publishing Co.
Times Mirror Cable TV
Times Mirror Magazines

Miscellaneous Facts: Incorporated in
1884 in California.

TIMES MIRROR MAGAZINES
380 Madison Avenue
New York, NY 10017
(212) 687-3000

Primary Business: Magazine and book
publishing
Chairman of the Board: Herbert K.
Schnall
President: John A. Scott
Executive Vice-President: John Condon
Sales: $120 million
# of Employees: 400

Miscellaneous Facts: Subsidiary of The
Times Mirror Co.

TRIBUNE CO.
435 N Michigan Avenue
Chicago, IL 60611
(312) 222-9100
Primary Business: Publishes daily papers
CEO: S. R. Cook
President: S. R. Cook
Vice-President (Legal): L. Gunnels
Vice-President (Corporate Relations): J.
E. Hayes
Vice-President (Employee Relations): P.
E. Heraty
Revenue: $1.79 billion
Net Worth: $908 million
# of Employees: 18,700

Subsidiaries:
Chicago National League Ball Club
Chicago Tribune Co.
New Building, Inc.
New York News, Inc.
Tribune Broadcasting Co.
KTLA, Inc.
WPIX, Inc.
WGNO, Inc.
Tribune Media Services, Inc.

WASHINGTON POST CO.
1150 15th Street, NW
Washington, DC 20017
(202) 223-6000
Primary Business: Newspaper and
magazine publishing
Chairman: Katharine Graham
CEO: Katharine Graham
President: Richard D. Simmons
Vice-President and General Counsel:
Alan R. Finberg
Vice-President (Corporate Affairs):
Guyon Knight
Revenue: $984.30 million
Net Worth: $349 million
# of Employees: 5,200

Subsidiaries:
Daily Herald Co.
Newsweek, Inc.
Post-Newsweek Stations, Inc.

Robinson Terminal Warehouse Corp.

Miscellaneous Facts: Incorporated in 1947 in Delaware.

COMPUTERS

AMDAHL CORP.
1250 E Arques Avenue
Sunnyvale, CA 94086
(408) 746-6000
Primary Business: Mainframe computers
Chairman: Eugene R. White
CEO: John C. Lewis
President: John C. Lewis
Senior Vice-President (Corporate
    Strategy): William F. O'Connell, Jr.
Vice-President (Communications): Paul
    Hachigian
Sales: $779.41 million
Net Worth: $428 million
# of Employees: 7,000

Divisions:
Amdahl Communications Systems Div.
Education & Professional Services Div.
Peripheral Products Div.

APPLE COMPUTER, INC.
20525 Mariana Avenue
Cupertino, CA 95014
(408) 996-1010
Primary Business: Personal Computer
    Systems
CEO: John Sculley
President: John Sculley
Executive Vice-President (Sales and
    Marketing): William Campbell
Executive Vice-President (Product
    Operation): Delbert W. Yolam
Vice-President and General Counsel:
    Albert A. Eisenstat
Revenue: $1.51 billion
Net Worth: $464 million
# of Employees: 4,500

Groups:
Accessory Products Group
Apple II
Apple 32
Mackintosh

Miscellaneous Facts: Everyone who
    works for Apple gets a computer, and
    is allowed to keep it after a year. The
    first company in history to make the
    Fortune 500 in less than five years. An
    estimated 300 employees have become
    millionaires at Apple. Company toll-
    free information number is (800)
    538-9696.

**COMMODORE INTERNATIONAL,
    LTD.**
1200 Wilson Drive
West Chester, PA 15380
(215) 431-9100
Primary Business: Computer systems,
    business and personal
Chairman: I. Gould
CEO: Marshall I. Smith
President: Marshall I. Smith
Vice-President and General Counsel:
    Joseph C. Benedetti
Sales: $1.27 billion
Net Worth: $324 million
# of Employees: 3,000

Subsidiaries:
Commodore Business Machines, Inc.
Commodore Realty, Inc.

COMPAQ COMPUTER CORP.
20555 FM 149
Houston, TX 77070
(713) 370-0670
Primary Business: Manufacturer of
    computers
CEO: Joseph R. Canion
President: Joseph R. Canion
Senior Vice-President: James M.
    Eckhart
Vice-President (Communications):
    James D. D'Arezzo
Vice-President (Human Resources):
    Cecil C. Parker
Sales: $329 million
Net Worth: $109 million
# of Employees: 1,500

CONTROL DATA CORPORATION
8100 34th Avenue, S
Minneapolis, MN 55440
(612) 853-8100
Primary Business: Computer systems
Chairman: William C. Norris
CEO: William C. Norris
President: Robert M. Price

Department Chairman: Norbert R. Berg
Vice-President and General Counsel:
  Daniel R. Pennie
Manager, Human Resources: Carole
  Wojiak
Revenue; $5.03 billion
Net Worth: $1.7 billion
# of Employees: 50,352

Subsidiaries:
Arbat Systems Limited
CCEC, Inc.
The City Loan Service
Commercial Credit Business Services,
  Inc.
Commercial Credit Mortgage Company
Commercial Credit Plan, Inc.
Myers Park Properties, Inc.
Brokerage Service Corp.
AmeriTour Auto Club, Inc.
Amity Savings & Loan Corp.
Control Data Services Corp.
Union Investment, Inc.
Gulf Insurance Co.
ERA General Agency Corp.

DATA GENERAL CORP.
4400 Computer Drive
Westboro, MA 01580
(617) 366-8911
Primary Business: Digital Computers
President: Edson D. deCastro
Executive Vice-President: Herbert J.
  Richman
Senior Vice-President: David L.
  Chapman
Vice-President (Human Resources):
  Donald Bateman
Revenue: $1.16 billion
Net Worth: $594 million
# of Employees: 14,370

Divisions:
Desktop Div.
Federal Systems Div.
Field Engineering Div.
Information Systems Div.
Systems Development Div.
Technical Products Div.

Miscellaneous Facts: Incorporated in
  1968 in Delaware.

DIGITAL EQUIPMENT CORP.
146 Main Street
Maynard, MA 01754
(617) 897-5111
Primary Business: Digital Computers,
  designs
President: Kenneth H. Olsen
Vice-President (Corporate Relations):
  Albert E. Mullin, Jr.
Vice-President (Computer Software
  Service): Don K. Busiek
Vice-President (Personnel): John Sims
Revenue: $6.68 billion
# of Employees: 89,000

Subsidiaries:
Digital Equipment Corp. de Puerto Rico
Digital Equipment Corp. International
Digital, Inc.
Digital International Sales Corp.

Miscellaneous Facts: The largest
  manufacturer of minicomputers in the
  nation. The first company to make
  computers to be used on desktops.
  Incorporated in 1957 in
  Massachusetts.

HARRIS CORP.
1025 W Nasa Boulevard
Melbourne, FL 32919
(305) 727-9100
Primary Business: Advanced
  communication products
Chairman: Joseph A. Boyd
CEO: Joseph A. Boyd
President: John T. Hartley
Senior Vice-President: Wesley C.
  Cantrell
Senior Vice-President (Finance): Bryan
  R. Roub
Vice-President: Raymond J. Oglethorpe
Sales: $1.99 billion
Net Worth: $1.66 billion
# of Employees: 30,000

Divisions:
Dracon Div.
Farinon Div.
Network Services Div.
Computer Systems Div.
Government Information Systems Div.
Harris/3M Document Products, Inc.

Miscellaneous Facts: Incorporated in
  1926 in Delaware as Harris-Seybold-
  Potier Co. Present name adopted in
  1974.

HEWLETT-PACKARD CO.

3000 Hanover Street
Palo Alto, CA 94304
(415) 857-1501
Primary Business: Manufactures
electronic, medical instrumentation
Chairman: David Packard
President: John A. Young
Vice-Chairman: William R. Hewlett
Director of Public Relations: David B.
Kirby
Director of Personnel: Arthur Dauer
Sales: $65 billion
Net Worth: $3.9 billion
# of Employees: 84,000

Divisions:
Andover Div.
Colorado Networks Div.
Computer Systems Div.
Greeley Div.
Loveland Instruments
Northwest IC Div.
Personal Software Div.
Printed Circuit Div.
Signal Analysis Div.

Miscellaneous Facts: Founded in 1939 by
William Hewlett and David Packard.
Introduced first computer in 1966, and
in 1983, developed the world's first
desktop mainframe. In 1985,
contributed more than $30 million of
its equipment to high schools, colleges
and universities. Has ten different
recreation areas ranging from a beach
villa in Malaysia to a ski chalet in the
German Alps where employees can go
for a modest price.

INTERNATIONAL BUSINESS
MACHINES

Old Orchard Road
Armonk, NY 10504
(914) 765-1900
Primary Business: Information handling
systems
Chairman: John F. Akers
Senior Vice-President: Jack D. Kuehler
Vice-Chairman: Paul J. Rizzo
Vice-President (Communications):
David E. McKinney
Vice-President (Personnel): Walter E.
Burdick
Sales: $50.09 billion
Net Worth: $31.9 billion
# of Employees: 405,545

Subsidiaries:
Rolm Corp.
IBM Credit Corp.
IBM World Trade Corp.

Divisions:
Customer Service Div.
Federal Systems Div.
IBM Instruments, Inc.
Data Systems Div.
Communication Products Div.
Information Products Div.
General Products Div.

Miscellaneous Facts: Incorporated in
1911 in New York as Computing-
Tabulating-Recording Co. In 1924,
merged with International Business
Machines Corp., and assumed its
present name. The world's largest
computer and office equipment
company. Makes more profit after
taxes than any other company in the
world.

NCR CORP.

1700 S Patterson Boulevard
Dayton, OH 45479
(513) 415-5000
Primary Business: Business information
systems, computer systems
Chairman: Charles E. Exley, Jr.
CEO: Charles E. Exley, Jr.
President: Charles E. Exley, Jr.
Vice-President (Customer Service): V.
F. Bean
Vice-President (Communications):
Stephen N. Bowen
Vice-President (Personnel Resources):
James E. McElwain
Revenue: $4.07 billion
Net Worth: $2 billion
# of Employees: 62,000

Divisions:
Financial Systems Development &
Production Div.
Microelectronics Div.
Retail Systems Development &
Production Div.
Micrographic Systems Div.
Office Systems Div.
Personal Computer Div.

PRIME COMPUTER, INC.
Prime Mark, M515-60
Natick, MA 01760
(617) 655-8000
Primary Business: Designs and sells
  minicomputers
Chairman of the Board: David L. Dunn
CEO: Joe M. Henson
President: Joe M. Henson
Vice-President (Sales): W. L. Brubaker
Vice-President (Human Resources):
  Lawrence M. Bronstein
Revenue: $769 million
Net Worth: $479 million
# of Employees: 8,115

THE TELEX CORP.
6422 E 41st Street
Tulsa, OK 74135
(918) 627-2333
Primary Business: Manufactures
  computers
Chairman of the Board: S. J. Jatras
CEO: S. J. Jatras
President: G. L. Bragg
Group Vice-President: Ansel Kleiman
Sales: $709 million
Net Worth: $270 million
# of Employees: 7,500

Subsidiaries:
Telex Communications, Inc.
Telex Computer Products, Inc.

UNISYS CORP.
Burroughs Place
Detroit, MI 48232
(313) 972-7000
Primary Business: Computer systems
CEO: W. Michael Blumenthal
President: Paul G. Stern
Executive Vice-President: Donald E.
  Young
Senior Vice-President (Human
  Resources): Richard H. Bierly
Vice-President: Hollis L. Caswell
Sales: $4.81 billion
Net Worth: $2.3 billion
# of Employees: 65,000

Subsidiaries:
BMX, Inc.
Burroughs Export, Inc.
Burroughs Finance Corp.
Burroughs Information Systems

Burroughs International Co.
Burroughs Overseas Sales Co., Ltd.
Burroughs Transport Corp.
Graftek
Joseph & Cogan Assoc., Inc.
Memorex Corp.
Systems Development Corp.
Systems Research

Miscellaneous Facts: Incorporated in
  1984 in Delaware as successor to
  Burroughs Corp., which was
  incorporated in 1905 as Burroughs
  Adding Machine Co. Present name
  adopted in 1986.

WANG LABORATORIES, INC.
One Industrial Avenue
Lowell, MA 01851
(617) 459-5000
Primary Business: Computing
  equipment, word processing systems
Chairman: An Wang
CEO: An Wang
President: An Wang
Senior Vice-President (Sales &
  Marketing): J. Carl Masi
Senior Vice-President (Human
  Resources): Edwin Devin
Vice-President (Corporate
  Communications): Harold Ano
Revenue: $2.32 billion
Net Worth: $1.24 billion
# of Employees: 30,000

Subsidiaries:
InteCom, Inc.
Walsh Greenwood Information Systems,
  Inc.

XEROX CORP.
Stamford, CT 06904
(203) 329-8700
Primary Business: Maker of copiers and
  duplicators, computer equipment
Chairman: David T. Kearns
CEO: David T. Kearns
Vice-Chairman: William F. Galvin
Executive Vice-President: Melvin
  Howard
Senior Vice-President: Paul A. Allaire
Vice-President (Personnel): Douglas M.
  Reid
Revenue: $9 billion
Net Worth: $7.6 billion
# of Employees: 103,457

Groups:
Business Equipment Group
Reprographic Business Group
Systems Group
Diversified Business Group

Products and Service

ACTIVISION, INC.
2350 Bayshore Frontage Road
Mountain View, CA 94043
(415) 960-0410
Primary Business: Designs, makes and
sells computer entertainment software
Chairman: J. H. Levy
CEO: J. H. Levy
President: J. H. Levy
Senior Vice-President: Gregory
Fischback
Vice-President (Product Development):
Kenneth Coleman
Vice-President and General Counsel: R.
L. Smith McKeithen
Sales: $27.19 million
Net Worth: $37 million
# of Employees: 96

Subsidiary:
Activision International, Inc.

ADVANCED MICRO DEVICES, INC.
901 Thompson Place
Sunnyvale, CA 94068
(408) 732-2400
Primary Business: Monolithic integrated
circuits for computers
Chairman: W. J. Sanders III
CEO: W. J. Sanders III
President: W. J. Sanders III
Executive Vice-President: Anthony
Holbrook
Senior Vice-President (Sales and
Marketing): Steve Zelenick
Vice-President (Human Resources):
Stan W. Winvick
Revenue: $931.08 million
Net Worth: $445 million
# of Employees: 15,000

Miscellaneous Facts: Incorporated in
1969 in Delaware.

ASHTON-TATE CO.
10150 W Jefferson Boulevard
Culver City, CA 90230
(213) 204-5570
Primary Business: Computer products
Chairman of the Board: Carmelo J.
Santoro
President: Edward M. Esber
Executive Vice-President: Ronald S.
Posner
Vice-President: C. W. Ratliff
Vice-President: Harvey Jeane
Revenue: $82.28 million
Net Worth: $29.95 million
# of Employees: 475

COMPUTER SCIENCES CORP.
2100 E Grand Avenue
El Segundo, CA 90245
(213) 615-0311
Primary Business: Computer services
Chairman of the Board: William R.
Hoover
CEO: William R. Hoover
President: William R. Hoover
Vice-President: George Barratt
Vice-President (Personnel): L. Scott
Sharpe
Revenue: $723 million
Net Worth: $186 million
# of Employees: 14,100

Groups:
Systems Group
Industry Services Group
Information Network Services Group

COMPUTERVISION CORP.
15 Crosby Drive
Bedford, MA 01730
(617) 274-1800
Primary Business: Automation products
Chairman of the Board: Martin Allen
CEO: James R. Berrett
President: James R. Berrett
Senior Vice-President: Philip L. Read
Vice-President (Communications):
James A. Baar
Vice-President (Human Resources): Lon
F. Bonczek, Jr.
Revenue: $556 million
Net Worth: $263 million
# of Employees: 6,530

Subsidiaries:
CIS, Inc.
Computervision International Corp.

Miscellaneous Facts: Incorporated in 1975 in Delaware as successor to company incorporated in 1969.

DE VRY, INC.
2201 W Howard Street
Evanston, IL 60202
(312) 328-8100
Primary Business: Training in electronics and computers
CEO: P. A. Clement
Revenue: $146 million

Miscellaneous Facts: Subsidiary of Bell & Howell Co.

INTEL CORP.
3065 Bowers Avenue
Santa Clara, CA 95051
(408) 987-8080
Primary Business: Computer memory circuits
Chairman: Gordon E. Moore
CEO: Andrew S. Grove
President: Andrew S. Grove
Vice-Chairman: Robert N. Noyce
Senior Vice-President: Jack C. Carsten
Director, Human Resources: Richard Sermone
Revenue: $1.63 billion
Net Worth: $1.8 billion
# of Employees: 21,500

Groups:
Components Technology & Manufacturing Group
Microcomputer Group
Systems Group

MEMOREX CORP.
San Tomas at Central Expressway
Santa Clara, CA 95052
(408) 987-1000
Primary Business: Develops, manufactures, markets computer equipment
Chairman: Clarence W. Spangle
CEO: Clarence W. Spangle
Executive Vice-President: James C. Castle
Vice-President (Technology): Frank J. Sordello
Vice-President (President, Communication Group): John J. Mitcham
Revenue: $719.22 million
# of Employees: 11,100

Miscellaneous Facts: Subsidiary of Burroughs Corp.

STORAGE TECHNOLOGY CORP.
2270 S 88th Street
Louisville, CO 80027
(303) 673-5151
Primary Business: Computer peripheral equipment
Chairman: R. R. Poppa
CEO: R. R. Poppa
President: Thomas F. Wands
Vice-President (Human Resources): Norman B. Barth
General Counsel: Alan A. Kenney
Revenue: $808.58 million
# of Employees: 15,197

CONSTRUCTION

GUY F. ATKINSON CO. OF CALIFORNIA
10 W Orange Avenue
San Francisco, CA 94080
(415) 876-1000
Primary Business: Heavy construction
Chairman of the Board: G. T. McCoy
CEO: T. W. Halligan
President: T. W. Halligan
Vice-Chairman: Ray N. Atkinson
Senior Vice-President: Jonathan Goodier
Personnel Director: Bob Schwab
Sales: $1 billion
Net Worth: $180 million
# of Employees: 15,00

Subsidiaries:
G. F. Atkinson Construction Co.
Atkinson Dynamics Co.
Bingham-Williamette Co.
Lake Center Industries
Monterey Construction Co.
Tyger Construction Co.

BECHTEL GROUP, INC.
Post Office Box 3965
San Francisco, CA 94119
(415) 768-1234
Primary Business: Engineering, construction
Chairman of the Board: S. D. Bechtel, Jr.
President: A. P. Yates
Executive Vice-President: R. P. Godwin
Vice-President: D. M. Slavich
Personnel Director: Bill Gilham
Sales: $8.06 billion
Net Worth: $760 million
# of Employees: 29,000

Subsidiaries:
Bechtel Power Corp.
Bechtel, Inc.
Bechtel Civil & Minerals, Inc.
Becon Construction Co., Inc.

Divisions:
Hydro & Community Facilities Div.
Advanced Technology Div.
Bechtel Petroleum, Inc.
Houston Div.

Ann Arbor Power
San Francisco Power

BECOR WESTERN, INC.
1100 Milwaukee Avenue, S
Milwaukee, WI 53172
(414) 768-4000
Primary Business: Construction
Chairman of the Board: Norris K. Ekstrom
CEO: Norris K. Ekstrom
President: William B. Winter
Vice-President: Thomas G. Folliard
Vice-President (Human Resources): Charles R. Revie
Revenue: $407 million
Net Worth: $191 million
# of Employees: 5,300

Subsidiaries:
Brad Foote Gear Works, Inc.
Bucyrus Disc., Inc.
Bucyrus International, Inc.
Western Gear Corp.

BLOUNT, INC.
4520 Executive Park Drive
Montgomery, AL 30116
(205) 272-8020
Primary Business: Construction
Chairman of the Board: Winton Blount
CEO: Winton Blount
President: Oscar J. Reak
Executive Vice-President: Frank H. McFadden
Vice-President (Human Resources): D. Joseph McInnes
Revenue: $847 million
Net Worth: $127 million
# of Employees: 10,000

Subsidiaries:
Blount Agri/Industrial Corp.
Blount Energy Resource Corp.
Blount International, Ltd.
Blount Development Corp.
Blount Specialty Steel Corp.
Omark Industries, Inc.

Miscellaneous Facts: Incorporated in 1971 in Delaware.

BUTLER MFG. CO.

BMA Tower
Kansas City, MO 64141
(816) 968-3000
Primary Business: Manufactures pre-engineered buildings
Chairman of the Board: George C. Dillon
CEO: George C. Dillon
President: Robert H. West
Executive Vice-President: Donald H. Pratt
Vice-President: John R. Moran
Revenue: $428 million
Net Worth: $140 million
# of Employees: 3,000

Subsidiaries:
Cucon, Inc.
Butler International Co.
Butler Pan-American Co.

CBI INDUSTRIES, INC.

800 Jorie Boulevard
Oak Brook, IL 60521
(312) 654-7000
Primary Business: Holding company, fabrication and construction
Chairman: W. A. Pogue
CEO: W. A. Pogue
President: W. A. Pogue
Vice-Chairman: John E. Jones
Vice-President (Research): Jon Hagstrom
Senior Vice-President and General Counsel: C. O. Ziemer
Sales: $899.97 million
Net Worth: $567 million
# of Employees: 10,000

Subsidiaries:
CBI Offshore, Inc.
Chicago Bridge & Iron Co.
CBI Co., Ltd.
Liquid Carbonic Corp.
Na-Con Services, Inc.
Sea-Con Services, Inc.
Walker Process Corp.

CENTEX CORP.

4600 Republic Bank Tower
Dallas, TX 75201
(214) 748-7901
Primary Business: Builder of homes
Chairman of the Board: Frank Crossen
CEO: Frank Crossen
President: Laurence E. Hirsch
Vice-Chairman: Paul Seegers
Executive Vice-President: Harry J. Leonhardt
Revenue: $1.2 billion
Net Worth: $301 million
# of Employees: 4,500

Subsidiaries:
J. W. Bateson Co.
Centex Cement Enterprises, Inc.
Centex Development Co.
Centex Homes Enterprises
M. H. Golden Co.
Rooney Enterprises, Inc.

DOVER CORP.

277 Park Avenue
New York, NY 10172
(212) 826-7160
Primary Business: Manufactures elevators
Chairman of the Board: Thomas C. Sutton
CEO: Gary L. Roubos
President: Gary L. Roubos
Vice-President; John F. McNiff
Vice-President: John B. Apple
Sales: $1.3 billion
Net Worth: $559 million
# of Employees: 16,193

Subsidiaries:
Dieterich Standard Corp.
Pathway Bellows, Inc.
Sargent Industries
Central Research Labs
Kahr Bearing
Pico Operations
Stillman Seal

FLUOR CORP.

3333 Michelson Drive
Irvine, CA 92730
(714) 975-2000
Primary Business: Worldwide engineering construction
Chairman of the Board: D. S. Tappan, Jr.
CEO: D. S. Tappan, Jr.
President: B. Mickel
Vice-President (Human Resources): C. J. Bardley
Vice-President (Corporate communications): J. O. Rollans

Sales: $4.40 billion
Net Worth: $1.03 billion
# of Employees: 26,958

Subsidiaries:
Daniel International Corp.
Fluor Engineers, Inc.
Fluor Drilling Services, Inc.
St. Joe Minerals Corp.
A. T. Massey Coal Co.

PULTE HOME CORP.
6400 Farmington Road
West Bloomfield, MI 48033
(313) 661-1500
Primary Business: Construction
Chairman of the Board: James Grosfeld
CEO: James Grosfeld
President: Robert Burgess
Senior Vice-President: Richard Staky
Sales: $773 million
Net Worth: $169 million
# of Employees: 1,500

Subsidiaries:
ICM Mortgage
Puerto Rican Operations
Southern Californian Div.

THE RYLAND GROUP, INC.
Post Office Box 4000
10221 Wincopin Circle
Columbia, MD 21044
(301) 730-7222
Primary Business: Construction
Chairman of the Board: C. E. Peck
CEO: C. E. Peck
President: C. E. Peck
Director, Public Affairs: Nancy L. Smith
Senior Vice-President: Thurman W.
  Bretz
Sales: $496 million
Net Worth: $80 million
# of Employees: 1,400

Subsidiary:
Ryland Mortgage Co.

THE TURNER CORP.
633 Third Avenue
New York, NY 10017
(212) 878-0400
Primary Business: Commercial
  contractors
Chairman of the Board: H. D. Conant

CEO: H. D. Conant
President: H. D. Conant
President (Diversified): R. D. Kupfer
President (Construction): A. T. McNeill
Senior Vice-President: K. H. Wanderer
Sales: $2.5 billion
Net Worth: $66 million
# of Employees: 2,900

Subsidiaries:
B-F-W Construction Co., Inc.
Universal Construction Co.
F. N. Thompson, Inc.
Trans-Con Construction Co., Inc.
Turner Construction Co.

Materials

AMERICAN STANDARD
40 W 40th Street
New York, NY 10018
(212) 703-5100
Primary Business: Building products
Chairman of the Board: William A.
  Marquard
CEO: William B. Boyd
President: William G. Roth
Vice-President (Human Resources):
  James C. Workman
Vice-President (Communications):
  Jeanne M. Golly
Revenue: $3.21 billion
Net Worth: $926 million
# of Employees: 49,500

Divisions:
American Standard Heat Transfer Div.
Light Commercial Unitary Div.
Process Transport Div.
The Trane Company Div.
WABCO Fluid Power Div.
Cardwell Westinghouse Div.

Miscellaneous Facts: Incorporated in
  1926 in Delaware as American
  Radiator & Standard Sanitary Corp.
  Present name adopted in 1967.

CARLISLE CORP.
1600 Columbia Plaza
250 E Fifth Street
Cincinnati, OH 45202
(513) 241-2500
Primary Business: Construction products

Chairman of the Board: George F. Dixon, Jr.
CEO: Malcolm C. Myers
President: Robert J. Deffeyes
Executive Vice-President: Jerome H. Eichert
Vice-President: Gerald L. Doerger
Sales: $481 million
# of Employees: 5,100

Subsidiaries:
Braemer Corp.
Continental Carlisle Corp.
Digital Controls Corp.
Zetaco, Inc.

CECO INDUSTRIES, INC.
1400 Kensington Road
Oak Brook, IL 60522
(312) 789-1400
Primary Business: Holding company, construction products
Chairman of the Board: Ned Ochiltree, Jr.
CEO: Erwin E. Schulze
President: Erwin E. Schulze
Senior Vice-President: Merce E. Kersten
Senior Vice-President: Howard E. Jessen
Vice-President (Human Resources): R. S. Hintz
Sales: $582 million
Net Worth: $145 million
# of Employees: 8,100

Subsidiaries:
The Ceco Corp.
Formwork Services, Inc.
Linden Post-Tensioning Corp.
Research Systems Group, Inc.

CERTAINTEED CORP.
Post Office Box 860
Valley Forge, PA 19482
(215) 341-7000
Primary Business: Manufactures building material
Chairman of the Board: John T. Gurash
CEO: Michel L. Besson
President: Michel L. Besson
Senior Vice-President: Myron P. Simmons
Vice-President (Employee Relations): Thomas A. Dougherty

Sales: $1.9 billion
Net Worth: $420 million
# of Employees: 7,832

Subsidiaries:
Certainteed Foreign Sales Corp.
Certainteed/Daymond, Inc.
CertainTeed Weaving Corp.
Fluid Systems Hawaii, Inc.
HBR Utilities Leasing Corp.

Miscellaneous Facts: Incorporated in 1917 in Maryland as Certain-Teed Products Corp. Present name adopted in 1983.

KOPPERS CO., INC.
Koppers Building
Pittsburgh, PA 15219
(412) 227-2000
Primary Business: Construction products
Chairman: C. R. Pullin
CEO: C. R. Pullin
Vice-President (Communication Group): J. R. Beidler
Vice-President (Human Resources): Richard C. Hawkins
Sales: $1.82 billion
Net Worth: $239 million
# of Employees: 15,000

Subsidiaries:
Broderick & Gibbons, Inc.
Davidson Mineral Properties
Eastern Rock Prod., Inc.
Fairfield Bridge Company, Inc.
The General Crushed Stowe Co.
Sim J. Harris Co.
Ivy Steel & Wire Co., Inc.
Kaiser Sand & Gravel Co.
The McMichael Co.
Parr, Inc.
Nello L. Teer Co.
Thiem Co.

Miscellaneous Facts: Incorporated in 1944 in Delaware.

LONE STAR INDUSTRIES
One Greenwich Plaza, Box 5050
Greenwich, CT 06836
(203) 661-3100
Primary Business: Cement, concrete products
Chairman: James E. Stewart
CEO: James E. Stewart

President: Robert F. Kizer
Vice-President (Sales): Wallace G.
  Irmscher
Vice-President (Personnel): Gerald I.
  Hyde
Senior Vice-President and General
  Counsel: John J. Martin
Revenue: $939 million
Net Worth: $296 million
# of Employees: 7,000

Subsidiaries:
Cement Financial Corp.
Lone Star Cement, Inc.
Lone Star Properties, Inc.

MANVILLE CORP.
Post Office Box 5108
Denver, CO 80217
(303) 978-2000
Primary Business: Building materials
Chairman of the Board: John A.
  McKinney
CEO: John A. McKinney
President: Josh T. Hulce
Vice-President (Corporate Relations):
  Curtis G. Linke
Senior Vice-President (Human
  Resources): Charles L. Hite
Revenue: $1.87 billion
Net Worth: $1.2 billion
# of Employees: 20,500

Subsidiaries:
Manville Building Materials Corp.
Manville Forest Products Corp.
Manville Products Corp.
Manville International Corp.
Johns-Manville Corp.

Miscellaneous Facts: Incorporated in
  1981 in Delaware as successor to
  Johns-Manville Corp., incorporated in
  1926.

**OWENS-CORNING FIBERGLAS
  CORP.**
Fiberglass Tower
Toledo, OH 43604
(419) 248-8000
Primary Business: Manufactures glass
  fiber products
Chairman: William Boeschenstein
CEO: William W. Boeschenstein
President: William W. Boeschenstein

Executive Vice-President: Fowler
  Blauvelt
Vice-President (Marketing
  Communications): Joseph J. Doherty
Sales: $3.32 billion
Net Worth: $944 million
# of Employees: 25,800

Divisions:
Ladish Co.
Oregon Metallurgical Corp.
Trumbull Asphalt-General Office

Miscellaneous Facts: Pink Panther
  commercials are company trademark.
  Operates 40 manufacturing plants in
  the U.S. Incorporated in 1938 in
  Delaware.

TEXAS INDUSTRIES
8100 Carpenter Freeway
Dallas, TX 75247
(214) 637-3100
Primary Business: Building materials
Chairman of the Board: Ralph B.
  Rogers
CEO: Robert D. Rogers
President: Robert D. Rogers
Executive Vice-President: Fergus J.
  Walker, Jr.
Vice-President (Human Resources):
  Brooke E. Brewer
Sales: $282 million
Net Worth: $160 million
# of Employees: 3,000

Subsidiaries:
Athens Brick Co.
Brookhollow Corp.
Dolphin Construction Co.
United Cement Co.

USG CORP.
101 S Wacker Drive
Chicago, IL 60606
(312) 321-4000
Primary Business: Building materials
Chairman of the Board: Robert J. Day
CEO: Robert J. Day
President: Robert J. Day
Vice-Chairman: H. M. Stover
Executive Vice-President: Eugene Miller
Vice-President (Human Resources):
  Harold E. Pendexter
Sales: $2.5 billion

Net Worth: $984 million
\# of Employees: 22,100

Subsidiaries:
A. P. Green Refractories Co.
L & W Supply Co.
Masonite Corp.

VULCAN MATERIALS CO.
One Metroplex Drive
Birmingham, AL 35209
(205) 877-3000

Primary Business: Construction,
  chemicals
Chairman of the Board: W. Houston
  Blount
CEO: Herbert A. Sklenar
President: Herbert A. Sklenar
Executive Vice-President: Lee K. Baily
Senior Vice-President (Human
  Resources): R. Morrieson Lord
Sales: $971 million
Net Worth: $564 million
\# of Employees: 5,900

CONSUMER PRODUCTS

Appliances

ALLEGHENY INTERNATIONAL, INC.
Post Office Box 456
Pittsburgh, PA 15230
(412) 562-4000
Primary Business: Small household
  appliances
Chairman of the Board: Robert J.
  Buckley
CEO: Robert J. Buckley
President: Graemer K. Hilton
Senior Vice-President (Human
  Resources): F. George Scott
Vice-President (Public Affairs): George
  C. Oehmler
Revenue: $2.11 billion
Net Worth: $537 million
# of Employees: 52,000

Operating Units:
The Arnold Engineering Co.
Bra-Con/Rob-Con
HTL Industries, Inc.
Allegheny International Exercise Co.
Almet/Lawnlite, Inc.
Sunbeam Appliance Co.
Sunbeam Leisure Products Co.
Wilkinson Sword, Inc.

Miscellaneous Facts: Incorporated in
  1929 in Pennsylvania as Allegheny
  Steel Co. Present name adopted in
  1981.

AMANA REFRIGERATION, INC.
Amana IA 52204
(319) 622-5511
Primary Business: Kitchen appliances
Chairman of the Board: Alex A. Meyer
President: Henry J. Meyer
Vice-President (Customer Service):
  David W. Moore
Senior Vice-President (Marketing): John
  A. Kammerer II
Sales: $400 million
# of Employees: 2,900

Miscellaneous Facts: Subsidiary of
  Raytheon Co.

BLACK & DECKER CORP.
701 E Joppa Road
Towson, MD 21204
(301) 583-3900
Primary Business: Power tools,
  household products
Chairman of the Board: Nolen D.
  Archebald
CEO: Nolen D. Archebald
President: Nolen D. Archebald
Executive Vice-President: William
  Stevens
Executive Vice-President: Alan W.
  Larson
Director, Personnel: William Christian
Revenue: $1.53 billion
Net Worth: $683 million
# of Employees: 23,000

Subsidiary:
Wisconsin Knife Works, Inc.

Miscellaneous Facts: Incorporated in
  1910 in Maryland as the Black and
  Decker Manufacturing Co. Present
  name adopted in 1985.

EMERSON ELECTRONIC CO.
8000 W Florissant Avenue
St. Louis, MO 63136
(314) 553-2000
Primary Business: Electrical-electronic
  products and systems
Chairman: Charles F. Knight
CEO: Charles F. Knight
President: E. L. Keyes, Jr.
Vice-President (Corporate Sales):
  Charles O. Planting
Vice-President (Corporate Service): E.
  L. Clary
Vice-President (Manpower
  Development): A. A. Gilbert
Sales: $4.68 billion
Net Worth: $2.2 billion
# of Employees: 61,000

Subsidiaries:
A & M Ludwig Corp.
Beckman Industrial Technology
Branson Corp.
Cedar Grove Operations

Eni Power Systems
Sweco, Inc.
SKIL Corp.

Divisions:
Alco Controls Div.
Emerson Motors Div.
Rittenhouse Div.
Electronics & Space Div.
Commercial Cam Div.
Hurst Manufacturing
Weed-Eater Div.

Miscellaneous Facts: Incorporated in
1890 in Missouri as Emerson Electric
Manufacturing Co. Present name
adopted in 1964.

GENERAL ELECTRIC CO.
3135 Easton Turnpike
Fairfield, CT 06431
(203) 373-2211
Primary Business: Diversified
manufacturing
Chairman: John F. Welch, Jr.
CEO: John F. Welch, Jr.
Vice-Chairman: Edward E. Hood, Jr.
Vice-President (Corporate Public
Relations): Joyce Hergenham
Vice-President (Corporate Customer
Relations): Cecil S. Semple
Vice-President (Corporate Employee
Relations): Arthur V. Puccini
Revenue: $27.95 billion
Net Worth: $13.9 billion
# of Employees: 330,000

Affiliates:
General Electric CAE INternational,
Inc.
General Electric Railcar Services Corp.
Kidder, Peabody & Co., Inc.
Ladd Petroleum Corp.
Lighting Group
Major Appliance Group
RCA Corp.
Semiconductor Div.
Decimus Corp.
Kerr Leasing, Inc.

Miscellaneous Facts: Founded in 1878 to
support the inventor Thomas Edison.
Spent $2.6 billion on research and
development in 1985. The world's
leading supplier of electric motors.
One of the world's leaders in medical
diagnostic imaging equipment. During
any given year, approximately 50
percent of GE's employees are
enrolled in some kind of company-
paid education program.

HAMILTON BEACH CO.
99 Scoville
Waterbury, CT 06706
(203) 573-1199
Primary Business: Kitchen appliances
President: John J. Flaherty
Personnel Director: Mark Eaks
Sales: $180 million

Miscellaneous Facts: Division of First
City Industries, Inc.

HOUSEHOLD INTERNATIONAL, INC.
2700 Sanders Road
Prospect Heights, IL 60070
(312) 564-5000
Primary Business: Maker of household
improvement appliances
Chairman: Donald C. Clark
CEO: Donald C. Clark
President: Donald C. Clark
Senior Vice-President and General
Counsel: J. Richard Hull
Senior Vice-President (Government and
Public Affairs): James L. McCormick
Vice-President (Human Resources):
Robert C. Eimers
Sales: $3.32 billion
Net Worth: $2.7 billion
# of Employees: 43,000

Subsidiaries:
Household Financial Services
EFI Fund Management
HFC Income Tax Service
National Car Rental System, Inc.
King-Seely Thermos Co.
Alexander Hamilton Insurance Co.
GC Electronics, Inc.
P.I. Liquidating Corp.
Shannon Mining Co.
Thorsen Tool Co.

MAGIC CHEF, INC.
740 King Edward Avenue
Cleveland, TN 37311
(615) 472-3371
Primary Business: Gas and electric
ranges, microwave ovens

Chairman: S. B. Rymer, Jr.
CEO: S. B. Rymer, Jr.
President: S. B. Rymer, Jr.
Vice-President (Finance): A. H.
  Rohrbaugh
Advertising Manager: Joseph Bagwell
Human Resources Director: William R.
  Foust
Sales: $1.05 billion
# of Employees: 7,341

MAYTAG CORP.
403 W Fourth Street, N
Newton, IA 50108
(515) 792-8000
Primary Business: Automatic washers
  and dishwashers
CEO: D. J. Krumm
President: D. J. Krumm
Vice-President (Personnel): Jay R.
  Storey
Sales Manager: G. E. Ankeny
Public Relations Director: R. J. Hoover
Sales: $1.7 billion
# of Employees: 14,703

Subsidiaries:
Dixie Narco
Toastmaster

Divisions:
Admiral Home Appliances
Magic Chef, Inc.
Maytag Co.

PREMARK INTERNATIONAL, INC.
2211 Sanders Road
Norbrook, IL 60062
(312) 498-8000
Primary Business: Household goods
Chairman of the Board: Warren L. Batts
CEO: Warren L. Batts
Senior Vice-President: John M. Costigan
Vice-President (Communications):
  Becky W. Osterberg
Sales: $1.8 billion
# of Employees: 20,000

Operations:
Food Equipment Group
Tupperware
Ralph Wilson Plastics Co.
The West Bend Co.

ROPER CORP.
1905 W Court Street
Kankakee, IL 60901
(815) 937-6000
Primary Business: Home appliances
Chairman of the Board: C. M. Hoover
CEO: R. E. Cook
President: R. E. Cook
Vice-President (Sales): Jerry Cope
Personnel Director: Raymond G.
  Warmoth
Revenue: $566 million
Net Worth: $83 million
# of Employees: 5,000

Subsidiaries:
Appliance Group
Outdoor Power Equipment Group

THE SINGER CO.
8 Stamford Forum
Post Office Box 10151
Stamford, CT 06904
(203) 356-4200
Primary Business: Consumer sewing
  machines and motors
Chairman: Joseph B. Flavin
President: WIlliam F. Schmied
Vice-President (Corporate Relations):
  Thomas L. Elliott, Jr.
Senior Vice-President and General
  Counsel: Paul D. O'Connor, Jr.
Sales: $2.52 billion
Net Worth: $563 million
# of Employees: 50,000

Divisions:
Dalmo Victor Div.
HRB-Singer Div.
Kearfott Div.
Link Flight Simulation Div.
Librascope Div.
American Meter Div.
Motor Products Div.
Sewing and Furniture Div.

Miscellaneous Facts: Incorporated in
  1873 in New Jersey as The Singer
  Manufacturing Co. Present name
  adopted in 1963.

SKIL CORP.
4801 W Peterson Avenue
Chicago, IL 60646
(312) 286-7330

Primary Business: Portable power tools, electric hammers, drills, saws
President: George M. Sherman
Vice-President (Marketing): Jack Watson
Vice-President (Sales and Service): L. Storm Bailey
Vice-President (Employee and Public Relations): Ronald J.Staub
Revenue: $163.80 million
# of Employees: 4,000

Miscellaneous Facts: Subsidiary of Emerson Electric Co.

THE STANLEY WORKS
1000 Stanley Drive
New Britain, CT 06053
(203) 225-5111
Primary Business: Hardware, tools
Chairman: Donald W. Davis
CEO: Donald W. Davis
President: Richard H. Ayers
Group Vice-President (Tools Div.): Robert G. Windham
Vice-President (Public Affairs): Ronald F. Gilrain
Sales: $1.16 billion
Net Worth: $502 million
# of Employees: 14,400

Subsidiaries:
Mac Tools, Inc.
Stanley Bostich, Inc.
Stanley Structures, Inc.
Stanley Vidmar, Inc.
Taylor Rental Corp.

Divisions:
Stanley Air Tools Div.
Stanley Magic Door Div.
Stanley Hardware Div.
Stanley Steel Div.
Stanley Tools Div.
Multi Elmac Co.

SUNBEAM CORP.
2001 S York Road
Oak Brook, IL 60521
(312) 654-1900
Primary Business: Manufactures small electrical appliances
President: T. J. Albani
Vice-President (Human Resources): D. W. Hike

Vice-President (Taxes): R. J. Weiland
# of Employees: 13,000

Miscellaneous Facts: Subsidiary of Allegheny International, Inc.

TORO CO.
8111 Lyndale Avenue, S
Minneapolis, MN 55420
(612) 888-8801
Primary Business: Lawn, garden and snow removal equipment
Chairman: Stephen F. Keating
CEO: Kendrick B. Melrose
President: Kendrick B. Melrose
Vice-President (Sales and Marketing): Ralph D. Murray
Vice-President (Customer Relations): James R.Watson
Revenue: $280.25 million
Net Worth: $80 million
# of Employees: 4,095

Subsidiary:
Lumalite, Inc.

THE WEST BEND CO.
400 W Washington
West Bend, WI 53095
(414) 334-2311
Primary Business: Small appliance manufacturer
President: A. J. English

Miscellaneous Facts: Subsidiary of Premark International, Inc.

WHIRLPOOL CORP.
Administrative Center
Benton Harbor, MI 49022
(616) 926-5000
Primary Business: Household laundry washing machines and dryers
Chairman: Jack D. Sparks
CEO: Jack D. Sparks
President: Jack D. Sparks
Executive Vice-President: Samuel M. Bateman
Executive Vice-President: Robert L. Brintnall
Vice-President (Human Resources): Ed Dunn
Revenue: $3.44 billion
Net Worth: $1.2 billion
# of Employees: 23,573

Subsidiaries:
Heil-Quaker Corp.
Whirlpool Acceptance Corp.

Miscellaneous Facts: Began as the Upton Co. in 1911. In 1929, it merged with Nineteen Hundred Washer Co. to become Nineteen Hundred Corp. Renamed Whirlpool Corp. in 1950. Merged with Seeger Refrigerator Co. in 1955 and name changed to Whirlpool-Seeger Corp. Name changed back to Whirlpool Corp. in 1957.

Home Furnishings

ARMSTRONG WORLD INDUSTRIES, INC.
Lancaster, PA 17604
(717) 397-0611
Primary Business: Interior furnishings
Chairman of the Board: Joseph L. Jones
CEO: Joseph L. Jones
President: Joseph L. Jones
Executive Vice-President: William W. Adams
Executive Vice-President: Lawrence E. Bish
Vice-President (Human Resources): Jack Jordan
Revenue: $1.57 billion
Net Worth: $647 million
# of Employees: 19,992

Divisions:
E B Carpet Mills
Applied Color Systems, Inc.
Armstrong Export Sales Co.
Armstrong Finance Corp.
Thomasville Furniture Industries, INC.

Miscellaneous Facts: Company toll-free number is (800) 233-3823.

CORNING GLASS WORKS
Houghton Park
Corning, NY 14830
(607) 974-9000
Primary Business: Glass manufacturer
Chairman of the Board: James R. Houghton
CEO: James R. Houghton
Chairman, Executive Committee: Amory Houghton, Jr.

Vice-President (Personnel): Richard C. Marks
Vice-President (Communications): Susan B. King
Sales: $1.7 billion
Net Worth: $1 billion
# of Employees: 26,900

Subsidiaries:
Corning Engineering
Corning Enterprises, Inc.
Corning International Services, S.A.
Corning Investments
Steuben Glass

Associated Companies:
Dow Corning Corp.
Pittsburgh Corning Corp.
Siecor Corp.
Owens Corning Fiberglas Corp.

Miscellaneous Facts: Incorporated in 1936 in New York as a consolidation of companies.

H. B. FULLER CO.
2400 Kasota Avenue
St. Paul, MN 55108
(612) 645-3401
Primary Business: Industrial adhesives, coatings, floor equipment
Chairman: E. L. Anderson
CEO: A. L. Anderson
President: A. L. Anderson
Vice-Chairman: D. G. Croonquist
Senior Vice-President (Operations): Robert Odom
Vice-President (Human Resources): James A. Metts
Sales: $447.98 million
Net Worth: $113 million

Divisions:
Building Products Div.
Caribbean Export Div.
Foster Products Div.
Industrial Coatings Div.
Linear Products Div.
Monarch Div.

GRANTREE CORP.
2501 SW First Avenue
Box 3210
Portland, OR 97201
(503) 223-1161
Primary Business: Furniture rental and sales

Chairman: Walker M. Treece
CEO: Walker M. Treece
President: Walker M. Treece
Executive Vice-President: Gary A.
  Kisling
Vice-President (Rental): Charles P.
  Murphy
Vice-President (Retail): LaVern J.
  Bender
Revenue: $82.16 million
# of Employees: 1,200

LA-Z-BOY CHAIR CO.
1284 N Telegraph Road
Monroe, MI 48161
(313) 242-1444
Primary Business: Upholstered furniture
Chairman: E. M. Knabusch
President: C. T. Knabusch
Vice-President (Sales): P. W. Wright
Vice-President (Fabric): R. C.
  Waterfield
Vice-President (Personnel): L. E.
  Roussey
Sales: $310.74 million
Net Worth: $129 million
# of Employees: 4,504

Miscellanous Facts: Operates ten plants
  across the United States.

LEGGETT & PLATT, INC.
1 Leggett Road
Carthage, MO 64836
(417) 358-8131
Primary Business: Household furniture
  products
Chairman of the Board: Harry M.
  Cornell, Jr.
CEO: Harry M. Cornell, Jr.
President: Felix E. Wright
Senior Vice-President (Marketing):
  Ralph V. Johnson
Vice-President (Personnel): Max H.
  McCann
Sales: $424 million
Net Worth: $107 million
# of Employees: 6,700

Subsidiaries:
Bedline Manufacturing Co.
Fleet Service Corp.
L&L Plant Food, Inc.
Leggett Wire Co.
Merit Steel Co., Inc.

LEVITZ FURNITURE CORP.
1317 NW 167th Street
Miami, FL 33169
(305) 625-6421
Primary Business: Furniture and home
  furnishings
Chairman: Robert M. Elliot
CEO: Robert M. Elliot
President: George H. Bradley
Vice-President (Personnel): Frank W.
  Bonhein
Vice-President (Consumer Relations):
  Eleanor R. Eckardt
Revenue: $800.44 million
Net Worth: $57.7 million
# of Employees: 5,600

HERMAN MILLER, INC.
8500 Byron Road
Zeeland, MI 49464
(616) 772-3300
Primary Business: Office and health
  furniture
Chairman: Max O. DePree
CEO: Max O. DePree
Vice-President (Sales and Marketing):
  Joseph N. Schwartz
Vice-President (Corporate Service):
  Richard H. Ruch
Vice-President (Marketing): David
  Armstrong
Sales: $402.50 million
Net Worth: $170 million
# of Employees: 3,600

RUBBERMAID, INC.
1147 Akron Road
Wooster, OH 44691
(216) 264-6464
Primary Business: Rubber and plastic
  products
Chairman: Stanley C. Gault
CEO: Stanley C. Gault
President: Robert E. Fowler, Jr.
Senior Vice-President (Human
  Resources): Thomas W. Ward
Senior Vice-President and General
  Counsel: James A. Morgan
Revenue: $566.42 million
Net Worth: $239 million
# of Employees: 4,400

Subsidiaries:
Canford Mfg. Corp.

Gott Corp.
Little Tikes, Inc.
Rubbermaid Specialty Products
Rubbermaid Commercial Products, Inc.

SCOVILLE, INC.
500 Chase Parkway
Waterbury, CT 06708
(203) 757-6061
Primary Business: Housing products
Chairman: William F. Andrews
CEO: William F. Andrews
President: William F. Andrews
Executive Vice-President: James A. Rankin
Vice-President and General Counsel: Stewart S. Hudnut
Vice-President (Corporate Relations): P. F. Beetz, Jr.
Revenue: $824.99 million
# of Employees: 14,875

SHAW INDUSTRIES, INC.
616 E Walnut Avenue
Dalton, GA 30722
(404) 278-3812
Primary Business: Carpet manufacturer
Chairman of the Board: Julius C. Shaw
CEO: Robert E. Shaw
Senior Vice-President: W. N. Little
Senior Vice-President: William C. Lusk, Jr.
Sales: $519 million
Net Worth: $122 million
# of Employees: 4,700

THOMASVILLE FURNITURE INDUSTRIES
401 E Main Street
Thomasville, NC 27360
(919) 475-1361
Primary Business: Wooden furniture
CEO: Frederick B. Starr
President: Frederick B. Starr
Executive Vice-President: Frank W. Burr
Vice-President (Personnel): Carlyle A. Nance, Jr.
Sales: $229.60 million
# of Employees: 5,550

Miscellaneous Facts: Subsidiary of Armstrong World Industries, Inc.

WICKES COMPANIES, INC.
2240 Ocean Park Boulevard
Santa Monica, CA 90405
(213) 452-0161
Primary Business: Lumber supplies, furniture, department, apparel stores
Chairman: Sanford C. Sigoloff
CEO: Sanford C. Sigoloff
President: Sanford C. Sigoloff
Senior Vice-President (Human Resources): Lawrence P. Friedman
Senior Vice-President (Strategic Planning): Seymour Strasberg
Revenue: $3.03 billion
Net Worth: $976 million
# of Employees: 28,000

Subsidiaries:
Kayser-Roth Corp.
Her Majesty Industries, Inc.
Kayser-Roth International
Builders Emporium
Leath Home Furnishings
Mode O'Day
Sequoia Supply, Inc.
Wickes Furniture
Wickes Lumber

Household

AMERICAN HOME PRODUCTS CORP.
685 Third Avenue
New York, NY 10017
(212) 968-1000
Primary Business: Household products, drugs
Chairman: John W. Culligan
CEO: John W. Culligan
President: John R. Stafford
Senior Vice-President; Robert G. Blount
Vice-President (Industrial Relations): Joseph R. Bock
Director of Personnel: Edward Berhrendt
Sales: $4.59 billion
Net Worth: $2 billion
# of Employees: 47,298

Subsidiaries:
Adams Plastics Co., Inc.
American Home Foods
Ayerst Laboratories
Boyle-Midway, Inc.
Home Products, Inc.

Luck's, Inc.
John F. Murray Advertising Agency
E. J. Branch & Sons
Whitehall Laboratories

Miscellaneous Facts: Some of the products made by company and subsidiaries: Advil, Anacin, Anacin 3, Dristan, Preparation H, Primatene, Denorex, Chef Boy-Ar-Dee, Smurf Cereal, Mama Leone's, Dennison's, Franklin Crunch 'N' Munch, Ranch Style Beans, Gulden's, Woolite, Pam, Easy Off, Black Flag, Roach Ender, Dry Breezes. Incorporated in 1926 in Delaware.

AMWAY CORP.
7575 East Fulton Road, SE
Ada, MI 49301
(616) 676-6000
Primary Business: Household products
Chairman of the Board: Jay Van Andel
President: Richard M. DeVos
Vice-President (Communications): Nan Van Andel
Executive Vice-President (Sales and Marketing): Gordon A. Teska
Director of Public Relations: Casey Wondergem
Revenue: $1 billion
# of Employees: 6,000

Subsidiaries:
Amway Communications Corp.
Amway Grand Plaza Hotel
Mutual Broadcasting System
Nutralite Products, Inc.

CLOROX CO.
1221 Broadway
Oakland, CA 94612
(415) 271-7000
Primary Business: Household bleach, cleaning products
Chairman of the Board: Calvin S. Hatch
CEO: Charles R. Weaver
Executive Vice-President: John W. Collins
Executive Vice-President: Sheldon N. Lewis
Personnel Director: J. M. Burke
Sales: $974.57 million
Net Worth: $432 million
# of Employees: 5,600

Subsidiaries:
Food Service Products Co.
The EVB Co.
Grocery Store Products Co.
The Kingsford Co.

Divisions:
Household Products Div.
Olympic Stain Div.

Miscellaneous Facts: Brand names include Clorox bleach, Formula 409, Fresh Step, Hidden Valley Ranch, Kingsford, Kitchen Bouquet, Liquid Plumber, Litter Green, Lucite, Match Light, Olympic, Salad Crispins, Soft Scrub, Twice as Fresh. Incorporated in 1973 in California as successor to company incorporated in 1957 with the same name.

DIXIE PRODUCTS BUSINESS
Post Office Box 6000, River Park
Norwalk, CT 06856
(203) 854-2000
Primary Business: Food and beverage products
Group Executive: Charles M. Foster
# of Employees: 9,393

Miscellaneous Facts: Subsidiary of James River Corp.

HOOVER CO.
101 E Maple Street
North Canton, OH 44720
(216) 499-9200
Primary Business: Vacuum cleaning equipment manufacturer
Chairman: Merle R. Rawson
CEO: Merle R. Rawson
President: Merle R. Rawson
Executive Vice-President: Joseph R. Cutinella
Vice-President (Marketing): Eugene O. Hatfield
Director, Public Relations: H. E. Buker
Revenue: $666.85 million
Net Worth: $190 million
# of Employees: 15,500

Subsidiaries:
Chemko Commercial Products Div.
Hoover Export Corp.
Hoover Worldwide Corp.

ONEIDA, LTD.
Kenwood Station
Oneida, NY 13421
(315) 361-3000
Primary Business: Sterling, silverplate and stainless tableware
Chairman: John L. Marcellus, Jr.
CEO: John L. Marcellus, Jr.
President: John L. Marcellus, Jr.
Honorary Chairman: Pierrepont T. Noyes
Vice-Chairman: Robert E. Sanderson
Revenue: $275.25 million
Net Worth: $86 million
# of Employees: 3,500

Subsidiaries:
Buffalo China, Inc.
Camden Wire Co., Inc.

Divisions:
Oneida Silversmiths Div.
Consumer Products Div.
Hotel & Restaurant Div.
International Operations
Special Sales Div.

PRESTO PRODUCTS, INC.
670 N Perkins Street
Appleton, WI 54911
(414) 739-9471
Primary Business: Manufactures plastic food wrap
President: Lawrence W. Wirth

Miscellaneous Facts: Subsidiary of The Coca-Cola Co.

PROCTER & GAMBLE CO.
301 E Sixth Street
Cincinnati, OH 45202
(513) 983-1100
Primary Business: Soaps, detergents, cleaners
Chairman: Owen B. Butler
CEO: John G. Smale
President: John G. Smale
Vice-President (Sales): Louis A. Pritchett
Vice-President (Personnel): Samuel H. Pruett
Vice-President (Advertising): Robert V. Goldstein
Sales: $12.95 billion
Net Worth: $5 billion
# of Employees: 62,500

Subsidiaries:
Ben Hill Griffin Citrus Co.
Crush International, Inc.
The Folger Coffee Co.
Hines-Park Foods, Inc.
Norwich Eaton Pharmaceuticals, Inc.
Procter & Gamble Commercial Co.
Procter & Gamble Distr. Co.
Procter & Gamble Mfg. Co.
Procter & Gamble Paper Prods. Co.
Procter & Gamble Productions, Inc.

Miscellaneous Facts: Company is usually the largest advertiser in the United States.

Personal

ARM & HAMMER
469 N Harrison Street
Princeton, NJ 08540
(609) 683-5900
Primary Business: Manufactures consumer products
Vice-President: James L. Rogula
Vice-President (Human Resources): Dennis Moore
Sales: $137 million

Miscellaneous Facts: Division of Church & Dwight Co., Inc.

ARMOUR-DIAL, INC.
Greyhound Towers
Phoenix, AZ 85013
(602) 248-2800
Primary Business: Soaps, shampoos, deodorants
CEO: Edward J. Walsh
President: Edward J. Walsh
Executive Vice-President: William T. Bennett
Senior Vice-President (Sales): William H. Windham
Vice-President (Employee Relations): Russell C. Bayne
Sales: $473 million
# of Employees: 5,000

Miscellaneous Facts: Subsidiary of Armour and Co.

AVON PRODUCTS, INC.
9 W 57th Street
New York, NY 10019
(212) 546-6015
Primary Business: Cosmetics, toiletries, health care products
CEO: Hicks B. Waldron
President: John S. Chamberlin
Executive Vice-President: Raymond F. Bentele
Executive Vice-President: Stephen F. Nagy
Director, Personnel: Bill Baer
Sales: $3.414 billion
Net Worth: $1.1 million
# of Employees: 38,700

Subsidiaries:
Avon Fashions, Inc.
Brights Creek, Inc.
Foster Medical Corp.
Great American Magazines, Inc.
James River Traders, Inc.
Mallinckrodt, Inc.

Miscellaneous Facts: The world's leading beauty company. Founded in New York City by David H. McConnell. First called The California Perfume Co. Avon Products, Inc., adopted as corporate name in 1950. Avon sells the broadest range of quality beauty products available from any single source. Markets more than 650 products in the U.S.

BAUSCH & LOMB, INC.
One Lincoln First Square
Rochester, NY 14604
(716) 338-6000
Primary Business: Contact lenses and accessories
Chairman of the Board: Daniel E. Gill
CEO: Daniel E. Gill
President: Daniel E. Gill
Senior Vice-President: Jay T. Holmes
Senior Vice-President: Stephen P. Belbely
Director, Employee Relations: Don Errigo
Revenue: $533.56 million
Net Worth: $327 million
# of Employees: 7,700

Divisions:
Bausch & Lomb Insurance Co.
Bausch & Lomb Opthalmic Instruments
Bausch & Lomb Opticare, Inc.
Charles River Laboratories, Inc.
Optical Systems Div.
Personal Products Div.
Sports Optics Div.
Sunglass Div.

Miscellaneous Facts: Incorporated in 1908 in New York as Bausch & Lomb Optical Co. Present name adopted in 1960.

BRISTOL-MYERS CO.
345 Park Avenue
New York, NY 10154
(212) 546-4000
Primary Business: Toiletries, medicines
Chairman of the Board: Richard L. Gelb
Vice-Chairman: Bruce S. Gelb
Vice-Chairman: William R. Miller
Senior Vice-President: Wayne A. Davidson
Senior Vice-President: Garth F. Dimon
Revenue: $4.91 billion
Net Worth: $2.1 billion
# of Employees: 36,200

Subsidiaries:
Boclaro, Inc.
Clairol, Inc.
Mead, Johnson & Co., Inc.
Monarch Crown Corp.
Pelton & Crane Co., Inc.
The Drackett Co.
Westwood Pharmaceuticals, Inc.

Miscellaneous Facts: Incorporated in 1933 in Delaware.

CHESEBROUGH-POND'S, INC.
33 Benedict Place
Greenwich, CT 06830
(203) 661-2000
Primary Business: Petroleum jelly products, creams, beauty aids
Chairman: Ralph E. Ward
CEO: Ralph E. Ward
President: George F. Goebeler
Vice-President (Personnel): Ted C. Mullins
Vice-President (Public Affairs): Kenneth R. Lightcap
Revenue: $1.86 billion

Net Worth: $625 million
# of Employees: 21,327

Subsidiaries:
Adolph's, Ltd.
Erno Laszio, Ltd.
Prince Manufacturing Co.
Ragu Foods, Inc.
Stauffer Chemical Co.

Divisions:
Bass Div.
Prince Div.
Prince Matchabelli Div.
Grit Publishing Co.

Miscellaneous Facts: Incorporated in 1880 in New York as Chesebrough Manufacturing Co. Present name adopted in 1955.

CLAIROL, INC.
345 Park Avenue
New York, NY 10154
(212) 546-5000
Primary Business: Markets personal care products
President: C. Benjamin Brooks, Jr.
# of Employees: 2,750

Miscellaneous Facts: Company toll-free consumer number is (800) 223-5800. Subsidiary of Bristol-Myers Co.

COLGATE-PALMOLIVE CO. (DELAWARE)
300 Park Avenue
New York, NY 10022
(212) 310-2000
Primary Business: Soaps, detergents, toilet articles
Chairman: Keith Crane
CEO: Reuben Mark
President: Reuben Mark
Executive Vice-President: Silas M. Ford
Vice-President (Human Resources): Benjamin C. Davis. Jr.
Revenue: $4.91 billion
Net Worth: $1.2 billion
# of Employees: 42,800

Subsidiaries:
Bike Athletic Co.
Etonic, Inc.
The Kendall Co.
Anatros Corp.

MedaSonics, Inc.
NDM Corp.
Riviana Foods, Inc.
Hill's Pet Products, Inc.

Divisions:
Associated Products Div.
Household Products Div.
Hoyt Laboratories
Sterno Div.
Louie Glass Co.

Miscellaneous Facts: Incorporated in 1923 in Delaware as Eastern Operating Co. Name changed to Palmolive shortly thereafter. Present name adopted in 1953.

CONAIR CORP.
11 Executive Avenue
Edison, NJ 08817
(201) 287-4800
Primary Business: Personal and hair care appliances
Chairman: Leandro P. Rizzuto
President: Leandro P. Rizzuto
Executive Vice-President: Maurice Lucas
Vice-President (Consumer Appliances): R. Diamond
Senior Vice-President: Salvatore T. DiMascio
Sales: $259.62 million
Net Worth: $55 million
# of Employees: 973

Subsidiaries:
Zotos International, Inc.
Belfaire Products, Inc.

THE DIAL CORP.
Greyhound Towers
Phoenix, AZ 85013
(602) 248-2800
Primary Business: Personal care products
CEO: Edward J. Walsh
Sales: $1 billion
# of Employees: 5,000

Miscellaneous Facts: Subsidiary of The Greyhound Corp.

FABERGE, INC.

1345 Avenue of the Americas
New York, NY 10105
(212) 735-9300
Primary Business: Perfumery, cosmetics
and hair care products
Chairman: Daniel J. Manella
CEO: Daniel J. Manella
President: Daniel J. Manella
Executive Vice-President (Sales): Henry
O. Dow
Vice-President (Fragrances): Morton
Begun
Director, Personnel: Mercedes Colon
Revenue: $254.91 billion
# of Employees: 3,000

Miscellaneous Facts: Subsidiary of
McGregor Corp.

FULLER BRUSH CO.

Westport Addition, Box 729
Great Bend, KS 67530
(316) 792-1711
Primary Business: Chemicals, cosmetics,
brushes, brooms
President: Leonard Dunlap
Executive Vice-President: Richard E.
Benner
Director of Personnel: Robert Hekrick
Sales Range: $70–$100 million
# of Employees: 1,842

Miscellaneous Facts: Subsidiary of Sara
Lee Corp.

GILLETTE CO.

Prudential Tower Building
Boston, MA 02199
(617) 421-7000
Primary Business: Razors and blades,
toiletries and grooming aids
Chairman: Colman M. Mockler, Jr.
CEO: Colman M. Mockler, Jr.
President: Joseph F. Turley
Vice-President (Public Relations): David
A. Fausch
Senior Vice-President (Legal): Joseph
E. Mullaney
Vice-President (Corporate Planning):
Paul N. Fruitt
Revenue: $2.29 billion
Net Worth: $898 million
# of Employees: 29,400

Divisions:
Misco, Inc.
Paper Mate Div.
Personal Care Div.
Oral-B Laboratories
Braun, Inc.
Safety Razor Div.
Corporate Internal Development
Gillette Research Institute

Miscellaneous Facts: Founded in 1901 by
King C. Gillette. Began as Safety
Razor Co. Products include Oral-B,
Jafra, White Rain, Dry Idea, Apri,
Liquid Paper, Paper Mate pens,
Braun shavers.

HELENE CURTIS INDUSTRIES, INC.

325 N Wells Street
Chicago, IL 60604
(312) 661-0222
Primary Business: Shampoos,
conditioners, hair care products
Chairman: Gerald Gidwitz
President: Ronald J. Gidwitz
Sales Manager (Professional Div.):
James Marino
Sales Manager (Consumer Products
Div.): Robert Kelly
Director, Personnel: Jack L. Calabro
Revenue: $370.35 million
Net Worth: $67 million
# of Employees: 2,300

Subsidiaries:
Helene Curtis, Inc.
Helene Curtis, Ltd.

Divisions:
Consumer Products Div.
International Div.
Professional Div.

THE ANDREW JERGENS CO.

2535 Spring Grove Avenue
Cincinnati, OH 45214
(513) 421-1400
Primary Business: Personal care
products manufacturer
CEO: James L. Pahes
President: James L. Pahes
Sales: $133 million

Miscellaneous Facts: Subsidiary of
American Brands.

JOVAN, INC.
980 N Michigan Avenue
Chicago, IL 60611
(312) 951-7000
Primary Business: Fragrances,
  cosmetics, toiletries
President: Richar E. Meyer
Vice-President (Sales): Neil Rocklin
Director of Personnel: Sheryl Fisher
Sales: $100 million
# of Employees: 1,000

THE KENDALL CO.
One Federal Street
Boston, MA 02110
(617) 423-2000
Primary Business: Manufactures
  consumer products
CEO: J. Dale Sherrat
# of Employees: 12,000

Miscellaneous Facts: Subsidiary of
  Colgate-Palmolive Co.

LEVER BROTHERS CO.
390 Park Avenue
New York, NY 10022
(212) 688-6000
Primary Business: Soaps, detergents,
  household products
Chairman: Gordon K. G. Stevens
CEO: Gordon K. G. Stevens
Division Vice-President (Sales, Food
  Div.): Leonard C. Giambronc
Vice-President (Personal Products Div.):
  Arthur C. Unger
Vice-President (Personnel): P. Edward
  Bohlender
Director of Public Affairs: Humphrey
  Sullivan
Sales: $2.04 billion
# of Employees: 5,720

Divisions:
Foods Div.
Household Products Div.
Industrial Div.
Personal Products Div.
Special Markets Div.

Miscellaneous Facts: Subsidiary of
  Unilever United States, Inc.

MARY KAY COSMETICS, INC.
8787 Stemmons Freeway
Dallas, TX 75247
(214) 630-8787
Primary Business: Cosmetics, toiletries
Chairman: Mary Kay Ash
President: Richard R. Rogers
Vice-President (Marketing): Richard C.
  Bartlett
Vice-President (Manufacturing): Patrick
  E. Howard
Vice-President (Human Resources):
  Betty Bessler
Sales: $277.50 million
Net Worth: $163.7 million
# of Employees: 1,500

Miscellaneous Facts: Subsidiary of Mary
  Kay Holding Co. All employees
  receive $200 worth of cosmetics a
  year. Each employee receives a
  birthday card and a free lunch for two
  on birthday.

MAX FACTOR & CO.
700 Fairfield Avenue
Stamford, CT 06904
(203) 326-6600
Primary Business: Cosmetics, makeup
President (U.S. Div.): Paul Masturgo
Executive Vice-President (U.S. Sales):
  Lin Stinson
Vice-President (Fragrance): Cheryl Scott
  Daniels
Vice-President (Public Relations): Carol
  Walters
Sales: $520 million
# of Employees: 9,000

Miscellaneous Facts: Subsidiary of
  Norton Simon, Inc.

MENNEN CO.
Hanover Avenue
Morristown, NJ 07960
(201) 631-9000
Primary Business: Baby care products,
  men's toiletries
Chairman: L. Donald Horne
CEO: L. Donald Horne
President: Harold Danenberg
Vice-Chairman: G. Jeff Mennen
Vice-President (Human Resources): M.
  Marcus
Vice-President (Sales): Bill Boswell

Sales: $200 million
# of Employees: 2,200

MERLE NORMAN COSMETICS, INC.
9130 Bellanca Avenue
Los Angeles, CA 90045
(213) 641-3000
Primary Business: Cosmetics
Chairman: J. B. Nethercutt
CEO: J. B. Nethercutt
President: Gary Hollister
Executive Vice-President: Richard
Nolind
Vice-President (Perfumery): Ralph
Garcia
Vice-President (Training): Alice Nichols
Sales: $90 million
# of Employees: 1,000

Miscellaneous Facts: Employees are
driven to company picnic in a
procession of Rolls-Royces,
Duesenbergs, Pierce-Arrows,
Packards and other classic
automobiles owned by company
chairman. Employees can get prime
rib, trout and spare rib lunches for 25
cents, and they receive free snacks
during morning and afternoon breaks.

MINNETONKA, INC.
Jonathan Inous Center
Chaska, MN 55318
(612) 448-4181
Primary Business: Manufacturing of
fragrances and toiletries
President: Robert Taylor
Vice-President (Group III): Robin R.
Burns
Vice-President: Ronald L. Whipperman
Sales: $124 million
Net Worth: $33 million
# of Employees: 400

Subsidiaries:
Andromeda Toiletries, Inc.
Calvin Klein Cosmetics Co.
Claire Burke, Inc.
Village Bath Products, Inc.
Village International, Inc.

NEUTROGENA CORP.
5755 W 96th Street
Los Angeles, CA 90045
(213) 642-1150

Primary Business: Soaps and sensitive
skin care products
CEO: Lloyd E. Cotsen
President: Lloyd E. Cotsen
Senior Vice-President: Allan H.
Kurtzman
Vice-President (Dermatologics Div.):
Mel Ader
Sales: $59.22 million
# of Employees: 230

REVLON, INC.
767 Fifth Avenue
New York, NY 10022
(212) 572-5000
Primary Business: Nail enamel, lipsticks,
makeup
Chairman: Michel C. Bergerac
CEO: Michel C. Bergerac
President: Michel C. Bergerac
Senior Executive Vice-President: Paul P.
Woolard
Executive Vice-President: Duane K.
Miller
Senior Vice-President (Personnel): Jay
I. Bennett
Revenue: $2.04 billion
# of Employees: 35,200

Subsidiaries:
Balmain Parfums, Inc.
Barnes-Hind, Inc.
Bill Blass, Inc.
Charles Revson, Inc.
Etherea, Inc.
Meloy Laboratories, Inc.
General Wig Manufacturing, Inc.
The Princess Marcella Borghese, Inc.

Miscellaneous

AMERICAN GREETINGS CORP.
10500 American Road
Cleveland, OH 44144
(216) 252-7300
Primary Business: Greeting cards, gift
wrappings
Chairman of the Board: Irving I. Stone
CEO: Irving I. Stone
President: Morry Weiss
Executive Vice-President: Morton
Wyman
Executive Vice-President: Richard H.
Connor

Personnel Director: William Cowden
Sales: $945.66 million
Net Worth: $425 million
# of Employees: 19,000

Subsidiaries:
A. G. Industries, Inc.
AmToy, Inc.
Drawing Board Greeting Cards
Plus Mark, Inc.
The Summit Corp.

Divisions:
American Greetings Div.
Designers Collection
Ripley Graphics

Miscellaneous Facts: The world's largest publicly owned manufacturer and distributor of greeting cards. Markets characters such as Holly Hobbie, Ziggy, Strawberry Shortcake, Care Bears and Popples. Founded in 1906 by Jacob Sapirstein. According to company, nine out of ten consumers who purchase greeting cards are women.

AMERICAN LOCKER CO., INC.
15 W Second Street
Jamestown, NY 14701
(716) 664-9600
Primary Business: Maker of coin and key controlled lockers and locks
President: Alex Ditonto
# of Employees: 48

Miscellaneous Facts: Subsidiary of The American Locker Group, Inc.

AMERICAN TOURISTER, INC.
91 Main Street
Warren, RI 02885
(401) 245-2100
Primary Business: Manufactures luggage
CEO: Harvey Bomes
President: Harvey J. Bomes
Senior Vice-President: John Pulichino
Vice-President (Finance): Michael Robinson
Revenue: $100 million
# of Employees: 1,800

Miscellaneous Facts: Subsidiary of Hillenbrand Industries, Inc.

BIC CORP.
Wiley Street
Milford, CT 06460
(201) 783-2000
Primary Business: Maker of writing instruments
Chairman of the Board: Marcel L. Bich
CEO: Bruno Bich
President: Bruno Bich
Advertising Manager: Dave Furman
Corporate Counsel: Allen S. Lipson
Employee Relations: Philip Lydon
Sales: $246 million
Net Worth: $103 million
# of Employees: 2,100

Miscellaneous Facts: Subsidiary of Bic Societe.

CABOT CORP.
125 High Street
Boston, MA 02110
(617) 423-6000
Primary Business: High conductive inks
Chairman of the Board: Louis W. Cabot
President: Robert A. Charpie
Executive Vice-President: John G. L. Cabot
Executive Vice-President: Samuel B. Coco, Jr.
Revenue: $1.75 billion
Net Worth: $720 million
# of Employees: 7,900

Subsidiaries:
Cabot International Capitol Corp.
Distrigas Corp.
Distrigas of Massachusetts Corp.
Industrial Gas Corp.
Tuco, Inc.

Miscellaneous Facts: Incorporated in 1960 in Delaware as successor to Godfrey L. Cabot, which was established in 1882.

CRAYOLA PRODUCTS DIV.
1100 Church Lane
Easton, PA 18042
(215) 253-6271
Primary Business: Manufactures crayons, water colors
Vice-President: Stephen Yanklowitz
# of Employees: 62

Miscellaneous Facts: Division of Hallmark Cards, Inc.

DURACELL, INC.
Berkshire Industrial Park
Bethel, CT 06801
(201) 796-4000
Primary Business: Batteries
President: William L. Jackson
Senior Vice-President: Bill L. Phillips

Miscellaneous Facts: Subsidiary of Dart & Kraft, Inc.

HALLMARK CARDS, INC.
2501 McGee Trafficway, Box 580
Kansas City, MO 64141
(816) 274-5111
Primary Business: Manufacturing and sale of greeting cards
Chairman of the Board: Donald J. Hall
CEO: Donald J. Hall
President: David H. Hughes
Vice-President (Public Affairs): Charles W. Hucker
Vice-President (Sales): Lanny Julian
Vice-President (Personnel): Lowell Mayone
Sales: $1.5 billion
# of Employees: 20,100 full-time, 5,800 part-time

Subsidiaries:
Binney & Smith, Inc.
Burnes of Boston
Crown Center Redevelopment Corp.
Graphics International, Inc.
Hall's Manufacturing, Inc.

Miscellaneous Facts: The largest greeting card company in the world.

JACUZZI, INC.
11511 New Benton Highway
Little Rock, AR 72209
(501) 455-1234
Primary Business: Pumps and water systems, whirlpool bathtubs
President: Raymond E. Horan
Vice-President: Hugh H. Shull, Jr.
Treasurer: William B. McBride
Sales: $117 million
# of Employees: 1,400

Miscellaneous Facts: Subsidiary of Kidde, Inc.

THE KINGSFORD CO.
1221 Broadway
Oakland, CA 94612
(415) 271-7000
Primary Business: Manufactures charcoal briquets
Vice-President: W. E. Lynn

Miscellaneous Facts: Subsidiary of The Clorox Co.

MCCULLOCH CORP.
Post Office Box 92180
Los Angeles, CA 90009
(213) 827-7111
Primary Business: Chainsaws, portable generators
CEO: Donald V. Marchese
President: Donald V. Marchese
Vice-President (Sales and Marketing): William J. Gamble
Director of Public Relations: Doreen McIntire
# of Employees: 1,000

MASTER LOCK CO.
2600 N 32nd Street
Milwaukee, WI 53210
(414) 444-2800
Primary Business: Padlocks, locker locks
CEO: George F. Villwock
President: George F. Villwock
Vice-President (Marketing and Sales): Peter U. Jung
Vice-President (Manufacturing): Earl G. Stintzi
Service Manager: Roger L. Owen
Sales: $85.38 million
# of Employees: 1,250

PAPER MATE DIV.
Prudential Tower Building
Boston, MA 02199
(617) 421-7000
Primary Business: Ball and porous point pens, refills
President: Joel P. Davis
Vice-President (Marketing): Carmen A. Comite
Vice-President (Sales): Robert P. Hanafee

Miscellaneous Facts: Subsidiary of Gillette Co.

PARKER PEN USA, LTD.
One Parker Place
Janesville, WI 53545
(608) 755-7000
Primary Business: Fountain and ball
  point pens
Chairman: George Parker
CEO: Mitchell S. Fromstein
President: Mitchell S. Fromstein
Vice-President (Human Resources):
  Peter J. Bentley
Vice-President (Public Affairs): Roger
  E. Axtell
Sales: $843.71 million
Net Worth: $118 million
# of Employees: 5,485

Subsidiary:
Panoramic Corp.

Miscellaneous Facts: Subsidiary of the
  Parker Pen Co., Ltd.

RAYOVAC CORP.
101 E Washington Avenue
Madison, WI 53703
(608) 252-7400
Primary Business: Maker of dry cell
  batteries
Chairman: Lionel N. Sterling
President: Thomas F. Pyle
Executive Vice-President: Robert B.
  Goergen
Vice-President (Sales): Gary E. Wilson
Sales: $215 million
# of Employees: 2,100

SAMSONITE CORP.
11200 E 45th Avenue
Denver, CO 80239
(303) 373-2000

Primary Business: Luggage
  manufacturer
President: Malcolm Conplish
Vice-President (Marketing): Thomas
  Leonard
Vice-President (Operations): Norman
  Newton
# of Employees: 2,600

Miscellaneous Facts: Subsidiary of
  Beatrice Companies, Inc.

SCHLAGE LOCK CO.
2401 Bayshore Boulevard
San Francisco, CA 94134
(415) 466-1100
Primary Business: Builders of hardware,
  locks
President: David W. Lasier
Vice-President (President, Schlage
  Div.): Jerold H. Tuft
Sales Manager: John Gamble
Sales: $270 million
# of Employees: 3,300

Miscellaneous Facts: Subsidiary of
  Ingersol-Rand Co.

WD-40 CO.
Post Office Box 80607
San Diego, CA 92138
(619) 275-1400
Primary Business: Lubricant and rust
  arresting compound
President: John S. Barry
Vice-President (Marketing): Gerlad C.
  Schleif
Secretary: Harlem F. Harmsen
Revenue: $57.31 million
Net Worth: $25 million
# of Employees: 49

ELECTRIC UTILITIES

AMERICAN ELECTRIC POWER CO., INC.
One Riverside Plaza
Columbus, OH 43215
(614) 223-1000
Primary Business: Electric light and power
Chairman: W. S. White, Jr.
CEO: W. S. White, Jr.
President: Richard E. Disbrow
Vice-President: G. P. Maloney
Treasurer: Peter J. DeMaria
Revenue: $4.95 billion
Net Worth: $3,867,016,000
# of Employees: 23,333

CENTRAL AND SOUTH WEST CORP.
Post Office Box 600164
Dallas, TX 75226
(214) 754-1000
Primary Business: Holding company, utilities
Chairman of the Board: Durwood Chalker
CEO: Durwood Chalker
President: B. J. Harris
Executive Vice-President: John E. Taulbee
Senior Vice-President: Stanley P. Wilson
Sales: $2.7 billion
Net Worth: $2 billion
# of Employees: 9,301

Subsidiaries:
Central Power & Light Co.
Central & South West Fuels, Inc.
Central and South West Services, Inc.
Public Service Co. of Oklahoma
Transok, Inc.
West Texas Utilities Co.

THE COLUMBIA GAS SYSTEM, INC.
20 Montchanin Road
Wilmington, DE 19807
(302) 429-5000
Primary Business: Natural gas utility
Chairman of the Board: J. H. Croom
CEO: J. H. Croom
President: J. H. Croom
Executive Vice-President: J. D. Little

Executive Vice-President: J. P. Cornell
Revenue: $4.6 billion
Net Worth: $1.7 billion
# of Employees: 11,000

Subsidiaries:
Big Marsh Oil Co.
Commonwealth Propane, Inc.
Columbia Distribution Companies
Columbia Gulf Transmission Co.
Columbia Hydrocrabon Corp.

COMMONWEALTH EDISON CO.
Post Office Box 767
Chicago, IL 60690
(312) 294-4321
Primary Business: Electricity
Chairman: James J. O'Connor
CEO: James J. O'Connor
President: James J. O'Connor
Vice-Chairman: Wallace B. Behnke, Jr.
Manager, Nuclear Safety: Frank A. Palmer
Manager, Customer Service: David W. Nocchi
Revenue: $4.93 billion
Net Worth: $6.6 billion
# of Employees: 18,900

Subsidiaries:
Chicago & Illinois Midland Railroad Co.
Commonwealth Edison of Indiana
Commonwealth Research Corp.
Cotter Corp.
Edison Development Co., Inc.

KANSAS CITY POWER & LIGHT CO.
1330 Baltimore Avenue
Kansas City, MO 64141
(816) 556-2200
Primary Business: Electric utility
Chairman of the Board: Arthur J.Doyle
CEO: Arthur J. Doyle
President: Arthur J. Doyle
Executive Vice-President: Louis C. Rasmussen
Senior Vice-President: Samuel P. Cowley
Vice-President (Human Resources): W. H. Miller

Sales: $596 million
Net Worth; $1 billion
# of Employees: 2,863

Subsidiaries:
Red Hill Coal Co.
Utility Fuel Co.
Wymo Fuels, Inc.

PACIFIC GAS & ELECTRIC CO.
77 Beale Street
San Francisco, CA 94106
(415) 781-4211
Primary Business: Electricity, gas, water
Chairman: Frederick W. Mielke, Jr.
CEO: Frederick W. Mielke, Jr.
President: Barton W. Shakelford
Vice-President (Customer Operations):
   George F. Clifton, Jr.
Vice-President (Community Relations):
   J. Y. DeYoung
Vice-President (Rates): Stephen P.
   Reynolds
Revenue: $7.83 billion
Net Worth: $5.07 billion
# of Employees: 28,400

Subsidiaries:
Alaska California LNG Co.
Eureka Energy Co.
Gas Lines, Inc.
PG&E Gas Supply Co.
Pacific Conservation Services Co.

SAN DIEGO GAS & ELECTRIC CO.
Post Office Box 1831, 101 Ash Street
San Diego, CA 92112
(619) 696-2000
Primary Business: Electric utility
Chairman of the Board: Thomas A.
   Page
CEO: Thomas A. Page
President: Thomas A. Page
Executive Vice-President: Jack E.
   Thomas
Senior Vice-President: Gary D. Cotton
Vice-President (Human Resources):
   George A. F. Weida
Sales: $1.7 billion
Net Worth: $1.3 billion
# of Employees: 4,830

Subsidiaries:
Califia Co.
New Albion Resources Co.
Pacific Diversified Co.

SOUTHERN CALIFORNIA EDISON CO.
2244 Walnut Grove Avenue
Rosemead, CA 91770
(818) 302-1212
Primary Business: Electric service
Chairman: Howard P. Allen
CEO: Howard P. Allen
President: H. Frederick Christie
Vice-President (Fuel Supply): R. H.
   Bridenbecker
Vice-President (Human Resources): C.
   E. Hathaway
Vice-President and General Counsel:
   John R. Bury
Sales: $4.90 billion
# of Employees: 16,866

SOUTHERN CO.
64 Perimeter Center E
Atlanta, GA 30346
(404) 393-0650
Primary Business: Electricity
President: Edward L. Addison
Vice-President: Alan R. Barton
Vice-President: A. W. Dahlberg
Vice-President: Joseph M. Farley
Sales: $6.12 billion
Net Worth: $6 billion
# of Employees: 31,121

Subsidiaries:
Alabama Power Co.
Georgia Power Co.
Gulf Power Co.
Mississippi Power Co.
Southern Company Services, Inc.
Southern Electric International, Inc.
Southern Electric Investments, Inc.

TEXAS UTILITIES CO.
2001 Bryan Tower
Dallas, TX 75201
(214) 653-4600
Primary Business: Electricity (holding
   company)
Chairman: Perry G. Brittain
CEO: Perry G. Brittain
President: Jerry Farrington
Executive Vice-President: Erle Nye
Treasurer: H. A. Horn
Revenue: $3.93 billion
Net Worth: $4.3 billion
# of Employees: 16,208

Subsidiaries:
Basic Resources, Inc.
Chaco Energy Co.
Texas Utilities Electric Co.
Texas Utilities Fuel Co.

UNITED ILLUMUNATING CO.
80 Temple Street
New Haven, CT 06506
(203) 787-7200

Primary Business: Electric utility
Chairman of the Board: J. D. Fassett
CEO: George W. Edwards
President: George W. Edwards
Executive Vice-President: R. L. Fiscus
Vice-President (Human Resources):
    Harold J. Moore, Jr.
Sales: $515 million
Net Worth: $675 million
# of Employees: 1,501

ELECTRONICS

ANALOG DEVICES, INC.
Route One, Industrial Park
Norwood, MA 02062
(617) 329-4700
Primary Business: Analog-digital
  converters
Chairman: Ray Stata
President: Ray Stata
Group Vice-President (Components):
  Jerald G. Fishman
Group Vice-President (Sales): Melvin J.
  Sallen
Vice-President (Human Resources):
  Henrich F. Krabbe
Sales: $313.40 million
Net Worth: $195 million
# of Employees: 4,800

Divisions:
Analog Devices Semiconductor
Component Test Systems Div.
Computer Labs Div.
Industrial Automation Div.
Interface Products Div.

Miscellaneous Facts: Incorporated in
  1964 in Massachusetts.

ARROW ELECTRONICS, INC.
767 Fifth Avenue
New York, NY 10153
(212) 935-6100
Primary Business: Electronic parts
Chairman of the Board: John C.
  Waddell
CEO: John C. Waddell
President: Stephen P. Kaufman
Executive Vice-President: Thomas M.
  Davidson
Vice-President: T. Wayne Anthony
Revenue: $740 million
Net Worth: $80 million
# of Employees: 2,500

Subsidiary:
Schuylkill Metals Corp.

AVNET, INC.
767 Fifth Avenue
New York, NY 10153
(212) 644-1050

Primary Business: Electric component
  parts
Chairman of the Board: Anthony R.
  Hamilton
CEO: Anthony R. Hamilton
President: Leon Machiz
Senior Vice-President: Sylvester Herlihy
Senior Vice-President: Joseph Brown
Vice-President (Resource Management):
  Morton Vogel
Revenue: $1.5 billion
Net Worth: $603 million
# of Employees: 9,700

Miscellaneous Facts: Owns and operates
  155 divisions and subsidiaries in the
  U.S. Incorporated in 1955 in New
  York.

BAIRNCO CORP.
200 Park Avenue
New York, NY 10166
(212) 490-8722
Primary Business: Electronic products
Chairman of the Board: Glenn W. Baily
President: Glenn W. Baily
Vice-President: Robert J. Prata
Director, Public Relations: Ray
  Schumack
Sales: $537 million
Net Worth: $167 million
# of Employees: 5,000

Subsidiaries:
Craftlite
Diamond F/Timely Lighting
Genlyte Group, Inc.
Keene Corp.
Howe Corp.

EATON CORP.
1111 Superior Avenue, NE
Cleveland, OH 44114
(216) 523-5000
Primary Business: Electronic and
  electrical products
Chairman: E. M. de Winot
CEO: E. M. de Winot
President: James R. Stover
Vice-President (Human Resources):
  John D. Evans

Vice-President (Corporated Affairs):
  Marshall Wright
Revenue: $3.51 billion
Net Worth: $1.3 billion
# of Employees: 43,000

Subsidiaries:
Analytical Assessments Corp.
Eaton Credit Corp.
Eaton International Corp.
Eaton-Kenway, Inc.
Eaton Leasing Corp.
Pacific-Sierra Research Corp.

Divisions:
AIL Div.
Air Controls Div.
Airflex Div.
Automation Products Div.
Axle and Brake Div.
Microwave Products Div.
Golf Grip Div.

Miscellaneous Facts: Incorporated in
  1916 in Ohio as the Trobensen Axle
  Co. Name changed in 1923 to the
  Eaton Axle & Spring Co. as a result
  of several acquisitions. Name changed
  again in 1932 and in 1965. Present
  name adopted in 1971.

EG & G, INC.
45 William Street
Wellesley, MA 02181
(617) 237-5100
Primary Business: Develops electronic
  systems
Chairman of the Board: Dean W. Freed
CEO: Dean W. Freed
President: John M. Kucharski
Senior Vice-President: David J.
  Beaubien
Senior Vice-President: Charles C. Dunn
Director, Human Resources: Richard F.
  Murphy
Revenue: $1.7 billion
Net Worth: $203 million
# of Employees: 23,000

Divisions:
EG & G Electronic Components
EG & G Special Projects
Aerial Measurement Opers.
EG & G Las Vegas Opers.
EG & G San Ramon Opers.
EG & G Automotive Research
EG & G ORTEC

EG & G Reticon
EG & G Rotron

**ELECTRO SCIENTIFIC INDUSTRIES,
INC.**
13900 NW Science Park Drive
Portland, OR 97229
(503) 641-4141
Chairman: William D. Walker
CEO: William D. Walker
President: William D. Walker
Vice-Chairman: Douglas C. Strain
Vice-President (Manufacturing): Wally
  Masters
Sales: $84.08 million
Net Worth: $55 million
# of Employees: 1,100

Subsidiary:
Palomar Systems and Machines

GENERAL SIGNAL CORP.
High Ridge Park
Stamford, CT 06904
(203) 357-8800
Primary Business: Electronic controls
  and systems
Chairman of the Board: David T.
  Kimball
President: David T. Kimball
Vice-Chairman: Glenn E. Ronk
Personnel Director: Eileen Joyce
Director of Communications: Nino J.
  Fernandez
Sales: $1.88 billion
Net Worth: $903 million
# of Employees: 85,000

Subsidiaries:
SGE Voorlas
Hevi-Duty Electric
Nelson Electric
Henschel Corp.
Kayex Corp.
Micro Automation, Inc.

GOULD, INC.
10 Gould Center
Rolling Meadows, IL 60008
(312) 640-4000
Primary Business: Biophysical
  instrumentation
Chairman: William T. Ylvisaker
CEO: William T. Ylvisaker

President: James F. McDonald
Executive Vice-President (Defense
  Systems): Henry J. Peppers
Director of Public Relations: Gerard F.
  Corbett
Revenue: $1.40 billion
Net Worth: $674 million
# of Employees: 19,600

Divisions:
Advanced Systems Development Div.
Circuit Div.
Computer Systems Div.
Ocean Systems Div.
Design & Test Systems Div.
Microware Products
Foil Div.
Semiconductor Div.

Miscellaneous Facts: Incorporated in
  1928 in Delaware as National Battery
  Co. Present name adopted in 1969.

KOLLMORGEN CORP.
60 Washington Street
Hartford, CT 06106
(203) 547-0600
Primary Business: Electric motors,
  tachometers
Chairman: Robert L. Swiggett
CEO: James E. Swiggett
President: James E. Swiggett
Vice-Chairman: George P. Stephan
Senior Scientific Officer: Herbert E.
  Torberg
General Counsel: Donald L. Borod
Revenue: $326.20 million
Net Worth: $99 million
# of Employees: 5,400

Subsidiaries:
Crystal Specialties, Inc.
ISG, Inc.
PCK Elastometrics, Inc.
Photocircuits Atlanta, Inc.
Questel Enterprises, Inc.
West Lane Properties

Divisions:
Additive Products Div.
Multiwire-EED Div.
Inland Motor Div.
MacBeth Div.

MOTOROLA, INC.
1303 E Algonquin Road
Schaumburg, IL 60194
(312) 397-5000
Primary Business: Automotive and
  industrial electronic equipment
Chairman: Robert W. Gavlin
CEO: Robert W. Gavlin
President: John F. Mitchell
Vice-Chairman: William J. Weisz
Executive Vice-President (Personnel):
  Robert N. Swift
Corporate Vice-President (Public
  Relations): Toni Dewey
Sales: $5.53 billion
Net Worth: $2.3 billion
# of Employees: 90,900

Subsidiaries:
CTX International
Codex Corp.
Computer X, Inc.
Emtek Health Care Systems, Inc.
Modar Electronics, Inc.
Motorola Cellular Service, Inc.
Motorola International
Tegal Corp.

Miscellaneous Facts: Founded in 1928 by
  Paul V. Galvin as the Galvin
  Manufacturing Corp. Name changed
  to Motorola, Inc., in 1947.

NORTH AMERICAN PHILIPS CORP.
100 E 42nd Street
New York, NY 10017
(212) 697-3600
Primary Business: Electrical-electronic
  components
Chairman of the Board: Cees Bruynes
CEO: Cees Bruynes
President: Cees Bruynes
Executive Vice-President: Frank
  Hopkins
Executive Vice-President: Richard A.
  Daunoras
Personnel Manager: William Conrad
Sales: $4.3 billion
Net Worth: $986 million
# of Employees: 57,400

Subsidiaries:
Advance Transformer Co.
Airpax Corp.
Philips Home Products
Anchor Brush Co., Inc.

Mepco/Centralab, Inc.
Dialight Corp.
Magnavox CATV Systems, Inc.
The Selmer Co.
Ohmite Mfg. Co.
Philips Business Systems, Inc.
Philips Medical Systems, Inc.

Miscellaneous Facts: Subsidiary of
Philips International B.V.

PERKIN-ELMER CORP.
Main Avenue
Norwalk, CT 06856
(203) 762-1000
Primary Business: Analytical
instruments
Chairman: Horace G. McDonnell
CEO: Horace G. McDonnell
President: Gaynor N. Kelley
Executive Vice-President: William W.
Chorske
Senior Vice-President: Mercade A.
Cramer, Jr.
Vice-President (Human Resources):
Thomas W. Barnard
Sales: $1.38 billion
Net Worth: $562 million
# of Employees: 15,500

Subsidiaries:
Metco Div.
Materials & Surface Tech. Group
Prekin-Elmer Cetus Instruments

Divisions:
Applied Science Div.
Electro-Optical Div.
Oak Brook Instrument Dept.
Military Systems Div.

Miscellaneous Facts: Incorporated in
1939 in New York.

PITNEY BOWES, INC.
Walter H. Wheeler Jr. Drive
Stamford, CT 06926
(203) 356-5000
Primary Business: Postage meters and
mailing equipment
Chairman: George G. Harvey
CEO: George B. Harvey
President: George B. Harvey
Vice-President (Corporate
Communications): Thomas F.
McGarry

Vice-President (Employee Relations):
Robert C. Rugen
Vice-President (Customer Service):
Archil Martin
Revenue: $1.73 billion
Net Worth: $694 million
# of Employees: 26,500

Subsidiaries:
Data Documents, Inc.
Dictaphone Corp.
Monarch Marking Systems, Inc.
Pitney Bowes Business Supplies
Pitney Bowes Business Systems, U.S.
Pitney Bowes Credit Corp.
Wheeler Group, Inc.

Miscellaneous Facts: Founded in 1920,
Pitney Bowes makes nine of every ten
postage meters made in the U.S.

RAYCHEM CORP.
300 Constitution Drive
Menlo Park, CA 94025
(415) 361-3333
Primary Business: Electronic hook-up
wire and cable
Chairman: Paul M. Cook
CEO: Paul M. Cook
President: Robert M. Halperin
Senior Vice-President: Robert J. Saldich
Vice-President (Administration):
William A. Berry
Revenue: $629.86 million
Net Worth: $322 million
# of Employees: 8,000

Subsidiary:
Bentley-Harris Mfg. Co.

Miscellaneous Facts: Incorporated in
1957 in California as Raytherm Corp.
Present name adopted in 1960.

SONY CORP. OF AMERICA
9 W 57th Street
New York, NY 10019
(212) 371-5800
Primary Business: Electronic equipment
Chairman of the Board: Norio Ohga
CEO: Kenji Tamiya
President: Neil Vander Dussen
Senior Vice-President (Human
Resources): John Stern
Corporate Communications: Fred
Wahlstrom

Sales: $6.7 billion
Net Worth: $2.2 billion
# of Employees: 43,000

Divisions:
Consumer Video Div.
Consumer Audio Products Div.
Information Products Div.
Component Products Div.
Sony Magnetic Products Co.
Sony Service Co.

Miscellaneous Facts: Subsidiary of Sony
   Corp., Tokyo

SQUARE D. CO.
1415 S Roselle
Palatine, IL 60067
(312) 397-2600
Primary Business: Safety switches,
   circuit breakers, switchboards
Chairman: Dalton L. Knauss
CEO: Dalton L. Knauss
President: Robert E. King
Vice-President (Marketing): Richard A.
   Hegeman
Vice-President (Sales): R. M. O'Neal
Vice-President (Personnel Relations): J.
   M. Veha
Revenue: $1.36 billion
Net Worth: $496 million
# of Employees: 21,200

Subsidiaries:
Engineered Systems, Inc.
General Semiconductor, Inc.
Ircon, Inc.
KB-Denver, Inc.
Ramsey Controls, Inc.
Topaz, Inc.
United States Robots
Yates Industries, Inc.
Yin, Inc.

TEKTRONIX, INC.
4900 W.W. Griffith Drive
Beaverton, OR 97005
(503) 627-7111
Primary Business: Cathode ray
   oscilloscopes—electronic laboratory
Chairman: John D. Gray
CEO: Earl Wantland
President: Earl Wantland
Vice-Chairman: Howard Vollum
Vice-President and General Council:
   Allan Leedy, Jr.

Sales: $1.33 billion
Net Worth: $839 million
# of Employees: 20,800

Subsidiaries:
CAE Systems
The Grass Valley Group, Inc.
Tektronix Export Corp.
V-R Information Systems, Inc.

Miscellaneous Facts: Tektronix is the
   largest private employer in Oregon.

TELEX CORP.
6422 E 41st Street
Tulsa, OK 74101
(913) 627-2333
Primary Business: Maker of aircraft
   high-fidelity stereo devices
Chairman of the Board: S. J. Jatras
CEO: S. J. Jatras
President: S. J. Jatras
Group Vice-President: Ansel Kleiman
Group Vice-President: G. L. Bragg
Revenue: $709.43 million
Net Worth: $270 million
# of Employees: 7,526

Subsidiaries:
Telex Communications, Inc.
Telex Computer Products, Inc.
Tulsa Computer Products, Ltd.

TEXAS INSTRUMENTS, INC.
Post Office Box 225474
Dallas, TX 75265
(214) 995-2011
Primary Business: Semiconductor
   devices, calculators, computers
Chairman: Mark Shepherd, Jr.
CEO: Jerry R. Junkins
President: Jerry R. Junkins
Vice-President (Corporate
   Communications): Liston M. Rice, Jr.
Vice-President (Personnel): William E.
   Wetsel
Sales: $4.94 billion
Net Worth: $1.9 billion
# of Employees: 77,000

Operations:
Consumer Products
Control Products
Data Systems Group
Defense Systems & Electronics Group
Geophysical Service, Inc.

Government Products
Materials and Control Groups
Semiconductor Products

WESTINGHOUSE ELECTRIC CORP.
Gateway Center, Westinghouse Building
Pittsburgh, PA 15222
(412) 642-3800
Primary Business: Electrical equipment
Chairman: D. D. Danforth
CEO: D. D. Danforth
President: N. M. Nelson
President (Learning Corp.): N. M.
  Nelson
Executive Vice-President (Nuclear
  Energy Systems): T. Stern
Executive Vice-President (Defense): H.
  B. Smith
Revenue: $10.26 billion
Net Worth: $3.7 billion
# of Employees: 145,000

Subsidiaries:
Coal Ridge Properties, Inc.
Westinghouse Elevator Co.
Group W Radio
KFWB Radio
KJQY Radio
KODA Radio
Group W Systems
Group W Television
Group W Productions

Home Entertainment Products

AMPEX CORP.
401 Broadway
Redwood City, CA 94063
(415) 367-2011
Primary Business: Cassettes, stereo
  equipment
Chairman of the Board: Arthur H.
  Hausman
CEO: Roy H. Ekrom
President: Roy H. Ekrom
Executive Vice-President: Charles A.
  Steinberg
Vice-President: David J. Chapman
Personnel Director: Bill Hilton
Revenue: $502 million
# of Employees: 6,649

Miscellaneous Facts: Subsidiary of The
  Signal Companies, Inc.

KRACO ENTERPRISES, INC.
505 E Euclid
Compton, CA 90224
(213) 774-2550
Primary Business: Rubber and vinyl
  floor mats, stereo tape decks, speakers
Chairman: Maurice H. Kraines
President: Lawrence M. Kraines
Senior Vice-President (Sales): Steve
  Kraines
Vice-President (Auto Division): Mark
  Boone
Sales: $150 million
# of Employees: 700

MARANTZ CO., INC.
20525 Nordhoff Street
Chatsworth, CA 91311
(818) 998-9333
Primary Business: Home entertainment
  products
Chairman: Joseph S. Tushinsky
CEO: Joseph S. Tushinsky
President: Fred C. Tushinsky
Senior Vice-President (Sales and
  Marketing): Harvey Schneider
Sales: $44.05 million
Net Worth: $14.9 million
# of Employees: 173

Subsidiaries:
Marantz Piano Co., Inc.
Rentabeta International
Superscope, Inc.
Superscope Tape Duplicating Products,
  Inc.

MATSUSHITA ELECTRIC CORP. OF
  AMERICA
One Panasonic Way
Secaucus, NJ 07094
(201) 348-7400
Primary Business: Manufactures
  electronic goods
Chairman of the Board: M. Matsushita
CEO: K. Seki
President: K. Seki
Vice-President: T. Doi
Vice-President: I. Perlman
Sales: $25 billion

Subsidiaries:
Panafac Corp.
Panasonic Finance, Inc.
Panasonic Hawaii, Inc.

Miscellaneous Facts: Subsidiary of
Matsushita Electric Industrial Co.,
Ltd., Osaka, Japan. Specializes in the
brands of Panasonic, Technics and
Quasar.

PANASONIC CO.
One Panasonic Way
Secaucus, NJ 07094
(201) 348-7000
Primary Business: Radios, TVs,
phonographs, tape recorders
CEO: Akiya Imura
President: Akiya Imura
Vice-President (Merchandising): Steve
Asada
General Manager (TV Div.): Paul
Adams
# of Employees: 1,030

SANYO ELECTRIC, INC.
1200 W Artesia Boulevard
Compton, CA 90220
(213) 537-5830
Primary Business: Portable radios and
tape recorders
Chairman of the Board: Yoshimi
Takemoto
President: Nobuhiro Arimoto
General Counsel: Brian Mulherin
Communications Manager: John Rinek
# of Employees: 600

Divisions:
Home Appliance Div.
O.E.M. Div.

TOSHIBA AMERICA, INC.
375 Park Avenue
New York, NY 10152
(212) 308-2040
Primary Business: TVs, VCRs, tape
recorders
Chairman: Nobuo Ishizaka
CEO: Nobuo Ishizaka
President: Ryoui Suzuki
Executive Vice-President: Toshioki
Masuda
Executive Vice-President: J. Paul Michie
Sales: $1 billion
# of Employees: 2,000

Miscellaneous Facts: Subsidiary of
Toshiba Corp.

ZENITH ELECTRONICS CORP.
1000 N Milwaukee Avenue
Glenview, IL 60025
(312) 391-7000
Primary Business: TVs, video recorders,
parts and accessories
Chairman: Jerry K. Pearlman
CEO: Jerry K. Pearlman
President: Jerry K. Pearlman
Executive Vice-President: Robert B.
Hansen
Executive Vice-President: Karl H. Horn
Vice-President (Human Resources):
David W. Denton
Sales: $1.71 billion
Net Worth: $437 million
# of Employees: 30,000

Subsidiaries:
Heath Co.
Inteq, Inc.
Zenith Data Systems Corp.

ENTERTAINMENT

AMC ENTERTAINMENT, INC.
10 W 14th Street
Kansas City, MO 64105
(816) 474-6150
Primary Business: Exhibits motion
  pictures
CEO: S. H. Durwood
Executive Vice-President: J. H. Resnick
Executive Vice-President: R. D. Leslie
Personnel Director: Mary Jean Brown
Revenue: $200.31 million
Net Worth: $75 million
# of Employees: 800 full-time, 2,800
  part-time

Subsidiaries:
AMC International, Inc.
AMC Film Marketing, Inc.
AMC Operations
AMERICAN Multi-Cinema, Inc.

**COLUMBIA PICTURES INDUSTRIES,
  INC.**
711 Fifth Avenue
New York, NY 10022
(212) 751-4400
Primary Business: Production and
  distribution of motion pictures
Chairman: Francis T. Vincent, Jr.
CEO: Francis T. Vincent, Jr.
President: Richard C. Gallop
Vice-President (Corporate
  Communications): Raymond A.
  Boyce
Vice-President (Human Resources):
  Susan B. Garelli
# of Employees: 3,200

Miscellaneous Facts: Subsidiary of The
  Coca-Cola Co.

WALT DISNEY PRODUCTIONS
500 S Buena Vista Street
Burbank, CA 91521
(818) 840-1000
Primary Business: Motion picture and
  TV production, amusement park
Chairman of the Board: Michael D.
  Eisner
CEO: Michael D. Eisner

President: Frank G. Wells
Vice-President (Corporate
  Communications): Erwin D. Okun
Chairman, Executive Committee:
  Raymond L. Watson
Revenue; $1.65 billion
# of Employees: 24,000

Miscellaneous Facts: When traveling on
  company business, employees always
  fly first class.

GENERAL CINEMA CORP.
27 Boylston Street
Chestnut Hill, MA 02167
(617) 232-8200
Primary Business: Movie exhibition
Chairman of the Board: Richard A.
  Smith
CEO: Richard A. Smith
President: Robert J. Tarr, Jr.
Vice-Chairman: J. Atwood Ives
Vice-President (Human Resources):
  Thomas C. Colbert
Sales: $966 million
Net Worth: $386 million
# of Employees: 12,000

Divisions:
General Cinema Beverages, Inc.
General Cinema Theatres, Inc.
WGRZ-TV

Miscellaneous Facts: Incorporated in
  1950 in Delaware as MidWest Drive-
  In Theatres, Inc. Name changed in
  1960 to General Drive-In Corp.
  Present name adopted in 1964.

LORIMAR-TELEPICTURES CORP.
3970 Overland Avenue
Culver City, CA 90230
(213) 202-2312
Primary Business: Motion pictures,
  television series
Chairman of the Board: Merv Adelson
CEO: Merv Adelson
Executive Vice-President: J. Anthony
  Young
Senior Vice-President: Barbara S.
  Brogliatti

Senior Vice-President: Robert
  Giovannettone
Revenue: $441 million
Net Worth: $240 million
# of Employees: 1,126

Subsidiaries:
Bozell, Jacobs Kenyon & Eckhardt
The Brillstein Co.
California Video Center
Karl Lorimar Home Video, Inc.
Muppet Magazine
US Magazine
Lorimar-Telepictures Music Group

MCA, INC.
100 Universal City Plaza
Universal City, CA 91608
(818) 985-4321
Primary Business: TV and motion
  picture production, record
  manufacturing
Chairman: Lew R. Wasserman
CEO: Lew R. Wasserman
President: Sidney Jay Sheinberg
Executive Vice-President: Thomas
  Wertheimer
Vice-President: Frank Price
Personnel Manager: Rick Larsen
Revenue: $1.65 billion
Net Worth: $1.3 billion
# of Employees: 16,200

Subsidiaries:
MCA Videodisc, Inc.
MCA New Ventures, Inc.
MCA Records, Inc.
MA Recreation Services
MCA Television, Ltd.
The Putnam Publishing Group, Inc.
Spencer Gifts, Inc.
Universal Amphitheatre
Universal City Studios, Inc.
Universal Film Exchanges, Inc.
Womhopper's Wagon Works Restaurant
Yosemite Park & Curry Co.

MGM/UA ENTERTAINMENT CO.
10202 W Washington Boulevard
Culver City, CA 90230
(213) 558-5000
Primary Business: Produces feature-
  length motion pictures
Vice-Chairman: Frank E. Rosenfelt
President: Alan Ladd, Jr.

Vice-President (Corporate Relations):
  Arthur E. Rockwell
Vice-President (Facilities): Arnold
  Shupack
Sales: $706.90 million
# of Employees: 2,700

Subsidiary:
MGM/UA Home Entertainment Group

MTV NETWORKS, INC.
1775 Broadway
New York, NY 10019
(212) 484-8680
Primary Business: Owns and operates
  TV rock music video service
Chairman: A. L. Lewis, Jr.
CEO: D. H. Horowitz
President: D. H. Horowitz
Executive Vice-President: R. W.
  Pittman
Senior Vice-President: M. S. Mitzner
Sales: $109.54 million
# of Employees: 450

ORION PICTURES CORP.
711 Fifth Avenue
New York, NY 10022
(212) 758-5100
Primary Business: Produces and
  distributes motion pictures
Chairman: Arthur B. Krim
CEO: Eric Pleskow
President: Eric Pleskow
Executive Vice-President: William
  Bernstein
Senior Vice-President (Business
  Affairs): Robert A. Geary
Revenue: $223 million
Net Worth: $112 million
# of Employees: 625

Subsidiaries:
Orion Home Entertainment Corp.
Orion Pictures Distribution Corp.
Orion Television, Inc.
Orion TV Productions, Inc.

Divisions:
Orion Classics
Orion Pictures International

PARAMOUNT PICTURES CORP.
One Gulf and Western Plaza
New York, NY 10023
(212) 333-4128
Primary Business: Produces and
  distributes motion pictures
Chairman: Frank Mancuso
CEO: Frank Mancuso
Executive Vice-President: Richard
  Zimbert
Vice-President (Corporate
  Communications): Jon J. Gould
Vice-President (Human Resources):
  Sherry Harris
Sales Range: $100–$200 million
# of Employees: 3,600

Miscellaneous Facts: Subsidiary of Gulf
& Western Industries, Inc.

**TWENTIETH CENTURY-FOX FILM
CORP.**
10201 W Pico Boulevard
Los Angeles, CA 90035
(213) 277-2211
Primary Business: Motion pictures, TV
  programs
Chairman: Barry Diller
CEO: Barry Diller
Executive Vice-President: Gerald K.
  Bergman
Executive Vice-President: Burton I
  Monasch
Director of Public Relations: Jerry
  Greenberg
Revenue: $847.26 million
# of Employees: 3,280

UNITED ARTISTS CORP.
10202 W Washington Boulevard
Culver City, CA 90230
(213) 558-5000

Primary Business: Distribution of
  motion pictures
President: Richard Berger
Executive Vice-President: Sidney H.
  Sapsowitz
Senior Vice-President (Entertainment):
  Karla Davidson
Vice-President (Labor Relations):
  Ronald M. Bruno
# of Employees: 1,913

Miscellaneous Facts: Subsidiary of
MGM/UA Entertainment Co.

WARNER COMMUNICATIONS, INC.
75 Rockefeller Plaza
New York, NY 10019
(212) 484-8000
Primary Business: Entertainment/
  communication
Chairman: Steven J. Ross
CEO: Steven J. Ross
Office of the President: Bert W.
  Wasserman
Vice-Chairman: Ted Ashley
Executive Vice-President and General
  Counsel: Martin D. Payson
Senior Vice-President: Alberto Cribiore
Revenue: $2.02 billion
Net Worth: $563 million
# of Employees: 10,000

Subsidiaries:
Atlantic Recording Corp.
Licensing Corp. of America
Warner Cable Communications, Inc.
Warner Brothers, Inc.
Warner Brothers Records, Inc.
Warner Home Video
Warner Publishing, Inc.
Warner Special Products
WEA Corp.
WEA International
WEA Manufacturing

FINANCIAL SERVICES

AMERICAN EXPRESS CO.
American Express Plaza
New York, NY 10004
(212) 640-2000
Primary Business: Credit cards, travelers
checks
Chairman of the Board: James D.
Robinson III
President: Louis V. Gerstner, Jr.
Executive Vice-President: Howard L.
Clark, Jr.
Executive Vice-President: Harry L.
Freeman
Vice-President (Human Resources):
Richard J. Murphy
Revenue: $12.89 billion
Net Worth: $4.04 billion
# of Employees: 70,456

Subsidiaries:
American Express Credit Corp.
American Express Publishing Corp.
Fireman's Fund Insurance Companies
American Express International
Banking Corp.
Shearson Lehman Brothers, Inc.
Warner Amex Cable Communications,
Inc.
IDS Financial Services, Inc.
The Boston Co.
American Express Travel Related
Services Co.
IDS Life Insurance Co.

Miscellaneous Facts: Card holders
charged over $55 billion in goods in
1985. Publishes *Travel & Leisure* and
Food & Wine magazines.

AMERICAN GENERAL CORP.
2727 Allen Parkway
Houston, TX 77019
(713) 522-1111
Primary Business: Holding company,
financial services
Chairman of the Board: Harold S. Hook
CEO: Harold S. Hook
President: Michael J. Poulos
Vice-Chairman: H. J. Bremermann, Jr.
Vice-Chairman: Andrew Delaney
Personnel Director: Deidra Johnson

Revenue: $5.30 billion
Net Worth: $3.3 billion
# of Employees: 16,367

Subsidiaries:
AGC Life Insurance Co.
American General Life & Accident
Insurance
GUC Corp.
American General Investment Corp.
American General Services Co.
Guardsman Life Insurance Co.
Hawaiian Life Insurance Co.
Intereal Co.
Interstate Fire Insurance Co.
Knickerbocker Corp.
Lincoln American Corp.
Marcaso Co., Inc.

**AMERICAN STOCK EXCHANGE,
INC.**
89 Trinity Place
New York, NY 10006
(212) 302-1000
Primary Business: Securities exchange
Chairman: Arthur Levitt, Jr.
Vice-Chairman: Daniel P. Tully
Senior Vice-President (Sales and
Support): Robert A. Smith
Senior Vice-President (Securities):
Benjamin D. Krouse
Vice-President (Press Relations):
Gordon Stewart
# of Employees: 692

BENEFICIAL CORP.
1100 Carr Road
Wilmington, DE 19809
(302) 798-0800
Primary Business: Consumer loans, sales
finance
Chairman of the Board: Finn M. W.
Caspersen
CEO: Finn M. W. Caspersen
Vice-President (Public Affairs): Ann
Stephenson
Senior Vice-President (Legal): James H.
Gilliam, Jr.
Revenue: $1.80 billion
Net Worth: $992 million
# of Employees: 13,700

Subsidiaries:
Beneficial Finance Co. of New Jersey
American Centennial Insurance Co.
BFC Agency, Inc.
Eva Gabor International, Ltd.
Midland International Corp.
Wasco Insurance Agency, Inc.
Southwest American Life Insurance Co.

H & R BLOCK, INC.
4410 Main Street
Kansas City, MO 64111
(816) 753-6900
Primary Business: Prepares income tax
  returns
Honorary Chairman: Richard Bloch
President: Henry Bloch
Vice-President (Corporate
  Development): James J. Moran
Legal: Robert Coleman
Revenue: $415.63 million
Net Worth: $245 million
# of Employees: 2,000

Subsidiaries:
Block Management Co.
Path Management Industries
Personnel Pool of America, Inc.
Compuserve, Inc.

Divisions:
Medical Personnel Pool
Personnel Pool

Miscellaneous Facts: Incorporated in
  1955 in Missouri.

DEAN WITTER FINANCIAL
  SERVICES, INC.
101 California Street
San Francisco, CA 94111
(415) 955-6000
Primary Business: Holding company,
  investment banker, securities dealer
Chairman of the Board: Robert M.
  Gardiner
President: Philip J. Purcell
Executive Vice-President: John J.
  Detterick
Revenue: $2.5 billion
# of Employees: 16,000

Subsidiary:
Dean Witter Reynolds, Inc.

Miscellaneous Facts: Subsidiary of Sears
  Roebuck and Co.

DINERS CLUB INTERNATIONAL
575 Lexington Avenue
New York, NY 10043
(212) 906-2481
Primary Business: Credit card system
Chief Operating Officer: Philip Heasley
Executive Vice-President (Marketing):
  Richard Vampe
Senior Vice-President (Sales): Robert
  Schwarze
Sales: $2.50 billion
# of Employees: 1,350

Miscellaneous Facts: Subsidiary of
  Citibank N.A. Consumer toll-free
  number is (800) 525-9135.

FEDERAL NATIONAL MORTGAGE
  ASSN.
3900 Wisconsin Avenue, NW
Washington, DC 20016
(202) 537-7000
Primary Business: Serves as mortgage
  market facility
Chairman: David O. Maxwell
CEO: David O. Maxwell
President: Mark J. Fiedy
Senior Vice-President Corporate
  Affairs): Douglas M. Bibby
Executive Vice-President and General
  Counsel: Caryl S. Bernstein
Revenue: $8.86 billion
Net Worth: $1.34 billion
# of Employees: 1,700

GREAT WESTERN FINANCIAL
  CORP.
8484 Wilshire Boulevard
Beverly Hills, CA 90211
(213) 852-3411
Primary Business: Holding company
Chairman: James F. Montgomery
CEO: James F. Montgomery
President: Robert B. Holmes
Senior Vice-President (Corporate
  Communications): Ian D. Campbell
Senior Vice-President (Investor
  Relations): Monroe Morgan
Vice-President (Personnel): Tobi
  Lombardi
Total Income: $2.87 billion
Net Worth: $1.19 billion
# of Employees: 7,003

Subsidiaries:
Aristar, Inc.
Blazer Financial Services
Bryant Financial Corp.
California Reconveyance Co.
GWF Securities Corp.
Great Western Leasing

GULF AND WESTERN, INC.
One Gulf & Western Plaza
New York, NY 10023
(212) 333-7000
Primary Business: Consumer and
   commercial financing
Chairman: Martin S. Davis
President: Martin S. Davis
Executive Vice-President (Government
   Relations): Lawrence Levinson
Vice-President (Corporate
   Communications): Jerry Sherman
Assistant Vice-President (Human
   Resources): Diane Kenny
Revenue: $3.09 billion
Net Worth: $174 billion
# of Employees: 65,377

Units:
Famous Music
Madison Square Garden Corp.
Miss Universe
Paramount Pictures Corp.
Associates Corp. of America
Prentice-Hall, Inc.
Simon & Schuster, Inc.

Miscellaneous Facts: Incorporated in
   1967 in Delaware. Name changed to
   Michigan Plating & Stamping Co. in
   1955, in 1958 changed to Gulf &
   Western Corp., and then in 1960 to
   Gulf & Western Industries. Present
   name adopted in 1986.

THE E. F. HUTTON GROUP, INC.
One Battery Park Plaza
New York, NY 10004
(212) 742-5000
Primary Business: Investment banking
   and brokerage
Chairman: Robert Fomon
President: Thomas P. Lynch
Vice-Chairman: W. Robert Wigley, Jr.
Revenue: $3.17 billion
Net Worth: $810 million
# of Employees: 17,500

Subsidiaries:
E. F. Hutton Insurance Group, Inc.
E. F. Hutton & Company, Inc.

INTEGRATED RESOURCES, INC.
666 Third Avenue
New York, NY 10017
(212) 551-6000
Primary Business: Financial services
Chairman of the Board: Selig A. Zises
CEO: Selig A. Zises
President: Arthur H. Goldberg
Senior Executive Vice-President:
   William L. Adair
Senior Executive Vice-President: Jay D.
   Chazanoff
Revenue: $440 million
Net Worth: $449 million
# of Employees: 2,453

Subsidiaries:
Bartmil, Inc.
Dascit/White & Winston, Inc.

MERRILL LYNCH & CO., INC.
165 Broadway
New York, NY 10006
(212) 637-7455
Primary Business: Holding company,
   security brokers
Chairman: William A. Schreyer
CEO: William A. Schreyer
President: Daniel P. Tully
Vice-Chairman: Dakin B. Ferris
Executive Vice-President: Jerome P.
   Kenney
Revenue: $6.04 billion
Net Worth: $2.3 billion
# of Employees: 41,500

Subsidiaries:
Merrill Lynch Hubbard, Inc.
Merrill Lynch, Pierce, Fenner & Smith,
   Inc.
Family Life Insurance Co.
Merrill Lynch Government Securities,
   Inc.
Merrill Lynch Leasing, Inc.

NEW YORK STOCK EXCHANGE,
   INC.
11 Wall Street
New York, NY 10005
(212) 623-3000

Primary Business: Stock exchange
Chairman: John J. Phelan, Jr.
Executive Vice-Chairman: William M. Ellinghaus
President: Robert J. Birnbaum
Executive Vice-President (Public Affairs): Donald L. Calvin
Senior Vice-President (Human Resources): Leonard W. Brustman, Jr.
# of Employees: 1,746

PAINE WEBBER, INC.
1285 Avenue of the Americas
New York, NY 10019
(212) 713-2000
Primary Business: Stock brokerage service
Chairman: Donald B. Marron
CEO: Donald B. Marron
President (Paine Webber Capital, Inc.): Jack L. Rivkin
President (Capital Markets Group): Michael J. Johnston
President (Consumer Markets Group): Donald E. Nickelson
Revenue: $1.9 billion
Net Worth: $431 million
# of Employees: 12,000

Subsidiaries:
Paine Webber Capital, Inc.
Paine Webber, Inc.
Paine Webber, Inc. Consumer Markets
Paine Webber International, Inc.

SALOMON, INC.
1221 Avenue of the Americas
New York, NY 10020
(212) 764-3700
Primary Business: Financial services
Chairman of the Board: John H. Gutfreund
CEO: John H. Gutfreund
President: John H. Gutfreund
Senior Vice-President: Walter E. Baker
Executive Vice-President: Raymond L. Golden
Revenue: $27 billion
Net Worth: $2.9 billion
# of Employees: 6,300

Subsidiaries:
Phibro Energy, Inc.
Philipp Brothers, Inc.
Salomon Brothers, Inc.

SHEARSON LEHMAN BROTHERS, INC.
600 Montgomery Street
San Francisco, CA 94111
(415) 321-6000
Primary Business: Financial services
Chairman: Sanford I. Weill
CEO: Peter A. Cohen
President: Peter A. Cohen
Executive Vice-President (Commodities): Jack H. Lehman III
Executive Vice-President (Sales): Joel Margolies
Revenue: $1.32 billion
# of Employees: 14,500

Subsidiary:
Shearson Lehman Mortgage Corp.

Miscellaneous Facts: Subsidiary of American Express Co.

SOUTHMARK CORP.
1601 LBJ Freeway, Suite 800
Dallas, TX 75234
(214) 241-8787
Primary Business: Financial services
Chairman of the Board: Gene E. Phillips
CEO: Gene E. Phillips
President: Gene E. Phillips
Vice-Chairman: William S. Friedman
Executive Vice-President: D. Vinson Marley
Personnel Manager: Janice Townsend
Revenue: $573 million
Net Worth: $700 million
# of Employees: 25,000

Subsidiaries:
Carlsberg Financial Corp.
Exchange Network
National American Corp.
Pacific Standard Life
Southmark Capital

STUDENT LOAN MARKETING ASSN.
1050 Thomas Jefferson Street, NW
Washington, DC 20007
(202) 333-8000
Primary Business: Financial services
Chairman of the Board: Edward A. McCabe
CEO: Edward A. Fox
President: Edward A. Fox

Executive Vice-President: Ronald F. Hunt
Senior Vice-President (Personnel): Gerald Cohen
Assets: $1.1 billion
Net Worth: $704 million
# of Employees: 861

TENNESSEE VALLEY AUTHORITY
400 W Summit Hill Drive
Knoxville, TN 37902
(615) 632-2101
Primary Business: Resource development
Chairman of the Board: C. H. Dean, Jr.
General Manager: W. F. Willis
Sales: $4.40 billion
# of Employees: 33,357

VALUE LINE, INC.
711 Third Avenue
New York, NY 10017
(212) 687-3965
Primary Business: Investment advisory service
Chairman of the Board: Arnold Bernhard
CEO: Arnold Bernhard
President: Jean Bernhard Buttner
Executive Vice-President: Mark K. Tavel
Senior Vice-President: Samuel Eisenstadt
Revenue: $56 million
Net Worth: $25 million
# of Employees: 400

FOOD

Convenience Stores

CIRCLE K CORP.
4500 S 40th Street
Phoenix, AZ 85040
(602) 437-0600
Primary Business: Operates grocery
  stores
Chairman: Karl Eller
CEO: Karl Eller
President: Robert E. Hutchinson
Senior Vice-President: Bill J. Farmer
Senior Vice-President: William H.
  Remmers
Senior Vice-President (Human
  Resources): Charles Shoumaker
Sales: $1.7 billion
Net Worth: $122 million
# of Employees: 16,657

Subsidiaries:
Bauman Co., Inc.
Circle K Convenience Stores, Inc.
Circle K General, Inc.
Idaho Outdoor Advertising, Inc.

Miscellaneous Facts: Operates 2,699
  convenience grocery stores in the
  Southwest United States.

**NATIONAL CONVENIENCE STORES,
  INC.**
100 Waugh Drive
Houston, TX 77007
(713) 863-2200
Primary Business: Operates convenience
  stores
Chairman of the Board:R. C. Steadman
CEO: V. H. Van Horn
President: V. H. Van Horn
Senior Vice-President: T. W. Ewens
Vice-President (Marketing): C. R. Jones
Revenue: $927 million
Net Worth: $96 million
# of Employees: 7,630

SOUTHLAND CORP.
2828 N Haskell Avenue
Dallas, TX 75221
(214) 828-7011
Primary Business: Convenience food
  stores, dairy products
Chairman: John P. Thompson
CEO: John P. Thompson
President: Jere W. Thompson
Senior Vice-President (Stores): S. R.
  Dole
Vice-President (Dairies): C. O.
  Beshears
Vice-President (Public Relations): Allen
  C. Liles
Revenue: $12.03 billion
Net Worth: $1.49 billion
# of Employees: 61,000

Divisions:
Gristede Brothers
Charles & Co.
Adohr Farms Div.
Bancroft Dairy Div.
Oak Farms Div.
Specialty Products Div.
Velda Farms Div.
7-Eleven Convenience Food Stores
Chief Auto Parts Group
Western Gasoline Div.
Southland International

Miscellaneous Facts: Incorporated in
  1961 in Texas as Southland Corp. of
  Texas. Present name adopted in 1963.
  Owns and operates 7-Eleven stores
  across the country.

Distributors

ALLEGHENY BEVERAGE CORP.
Macke Circle
Cheverly, MD 20781
(301) 341-6000
Primary Business: Vending and manual
  food service
Chairman of the Board: Morton M.
  Lapides
CEO: Morton M. Lapides
President: Morton M. Lapides

Vice-Chairman: Edward A. Weisman
Senior Vice-President: Harry J. Conn
Director of Personnel: Jim Hart
Sales: $495.60 million
# of Employees: 41,000

CANTEEN CORP.
1430 Merchandise Mark
Chicago, IL 60654
(312) 661-7500
Primary Business: Sells food, beverages
through vending machines
Chairman: L. Edwin Smart
CEO: Robert A. Kozlowski
President: Robert A. Kozlowski
Vice-Chairman: James T. McGuire
Vice-President (Food Service): Kenneth
R. Davidson
Sales: $854 million
# of Employees: 16,900

CFS CONTINENTAL, INC.
100 S Wacker Drive
Chicago, IL 60606
(312) 368-7500
Primary Business: Maker and distributor
to food service industry
Chairman: Robert H. Cohn
Vice-Chairman: Stanley Owens
President: Alvin W. Cohn
Executive Vice-President: Donald W.
Hansen
Vice-President: Louis Leichentritt
Revenue: $1.04 billion
# of Employees: 4,100

RYKOFF-SEXTON, INC.
761 Terminal Street
Los Angeles, CA 90021
(213) 622-4131
Primary Business: Food service
wholesaler
CEO: Roger W. Coleman
President: Roger W. Coleman
Executive Vice-President: Chris Adams
Vice-President: Herbert L. Jaffe
Vice-President: Victor B. Chavez
Sales: $853 million
Net Worth: $86 million
# of Employees: 5,000

Subsidiaries:
John Sexton & Co.
S. E. Rykoff & Co.

SCRIVNER, INC.
1301 SE 59th Street
Oklahoma City, OK 73126
(405) 670-4571
Primary Business: Wholesale and retail
foods
Chairman: Jerry D. Metcalf
CEO: Jerry D. Metcalf
President: D. Clark Ogle
Vice-President (Food Service):
Dominick J. Lombardo
Vice-President and General Counsel:
Bryan J. Keller
Revenue: $2.17 billion
# of Employees: 5,000

Subsidiary:
S. M. Flickinger Co., Inc.

SERVOMATION CORP.
88 Gatehouse Road
Stamford, CT 06904
(203) 964-5000
Primary Business: Operates vending
machines
Chairman of the Board: William A.
Vella
Sales: $563 million

Miscellaneous Facts: Subsidiary of
Allegheny Beverage Corp.

SKY CHEFS
Post Office Box 619777
Dallas-Fort Worth Airport, TX 75261
(817) 792-2123
Primary Business: Airline catering
President: J. J. O'Neill
Sales: $332 million

Miscellaneous Facts: Subsidiary of AMR
Corp.

SYSCO CORP.
1177 W Loop S
Houston, TX 77027
(713) 877-1122
Primary Business: Wholesale distributor
of foods
Chairman of the Board: John F.
Woodhouse
CEO: John F. Woodhouse
President: Bill M. Lindig
Senior Chairman of the Board: John F.
Baugh

124

Executive Vice-President: E. James
Lowrey

Grocery Stores

ALBERTSON'S, INC.
250 Parkcenter Boulevard
Boise, ID 83726
(208) 344-7441
Primary Business: Owns and operates
supermarkets and drug stores
Chairman of the Board: Warren E.
McCain
CEO: Warren E. McCain
President: John B. Carley
Senior Vice-President (Human
Resources): Gerald R. Rudd
Revenue: $5.06 billion
Net Worth: $454 million
# of Employees: 30,000

Subsidiaries:
Albertson's Liquor, Inc.
Albertson's Realty, Inc.
Albertson's Trucking, Inc.
Texas Albertson's, Inc.

Miscellaneous Facts: Founded in 1939 by
Joe Albertson in Boise, Idaho. In the
last ten years, sales have increased 298
percent. Operates 444 stores in 17
states.

ALLIED SUPERMARKETS, INC.
8711 Meadowdale
Detroit, MI 48228
(313) 943-3300
Primary Business: Supermarkets
Chairman of the Board: David K.Page
CEO: David K. Page
President: Lon D. Makanoff
Senior Vice-President: Elmer L. Blatz
Vice-President: Donald R. Gapp
Personnel Director: Jack Masek
Sales: $529.80 million
Net Worth: $52 million
# of Employees: 3,191

Miscellaneous Facts: Incorporated in
1982 in Michigan as successor to
company incorporated in 1926.

ALPHA BETA CO.
777 S Harbor Boulevard
La Habra, CA 90631
(714) 738-2141
Primary Business: Supermarkets
President: Richard P. Gladden
Executive Vice-President: Robert O.
Kuchenbecker
Senior Vice-President: Tom Zaricki
Vice-President (Human Relations): John
Gibson
# of Employees: 18,800

Miscellaneous Facts: Subsidiary of
American Stores Co.

AMERICAN STORES CO.
Post Office Box 27447
Salt Lake City, UT 84127
(801) 539-0112
Primary Business: Operates food and
drug stores
Chairman: L. S. Skaggs
President: Thomas A. King
Executive Vice-President and General
Counsel: Thomas H. Sunday
Senior Vice-President (Public
Relations): Michael T. Miller
Director of Personnel: Gary Schultz
Sales: $13.89 billion
Net Worth: $676 million
# of Employees: 120,000

Subsidiaries:
Acme Markets, Inc.
Alpha Beta Co.
American Stores Buying Co.
Jewel Companies, Inc.

Divisions:
Buttrey Food Stores
Jewel Food Stores
Osco Drugs, Inc.
Sav-On Drugs, Inc.
Star Market Co.
Skaggs Companies, Inc.
Skaggs Alpha Beta Co.

Miscellaneous Facts: Incorporated in
1965 in Delaware as Skaggs Drug
Centers, Inc. Present name adopted in
1979.

BIG BEAR, INC.
770 West Goodale Boulevard
Columbus, OH 43212
(614) 464-6500

Primary Business: Operates chain of
supermarkets
President: M. J. Knilans
Vice-President: R. D. Wickerham
Vice-President: D. W. Godfrey
Personnel Director: D. Hampshire
Sales: $747 million
Net Worth: $52 million
# of Employees: 7,581

Subsidiary:
Big Bear Stores Co.

BORMAN'S, INC.
Post Office Box 446
Detroit, MI 48232
(313) 270-1000
Primary Business: Operates chain of
supermarkets
President: Paul Borman
Vice-President: Daniel Church
Vice-President (Personnel): Jim Smith
Vice-President: Ted Simon
Revenue: $1.02 billion
Net Worth: $22 million
# of Employees: 7,182

Subsidiaries:
Arnolds, Inc.
Carton Co., Inc.
Detroit Pure Milk Co.
Welsey's Quaker Maid, Inc.

Miscellaneous Facts: Incorporated in
1969 in Delaware as successor to
Borman Food Stores, Inc.

BRUNO'S, INC.
2620 13th Street, W
Birmingham, AL 35201
(205) 785-9400
Primary Business: Operates
supermarkets
Chairman of the Board: Joe Bruno
CEO: Angelo J. Bruno
President: Angelo J. Bruno
Senior Vice-President: Lee J. Bruno
Personnel Director: Randolph Page
Sales: $886 million
Net Worth: $153 million
# of Employees: 6,298

FISHER FOODS, INC.
5300 Richmond Road
Bedford Heights, OH 44146
(216) 292-7000
Primary Business: Grocery retailer
Chairman of the Board: Carl H. Linder
CEO: Carl H. Linder
President: Robert L. Hayden
Senior Vice-President: Robert R.
Gerber
Vice-President (Human Resources):
James Crytzer
Sales: $494 million
Net Worth: $63 million
# of Employees: 4,000

Subsidiaries:
Fisher Properties, Inc.
Heritage Wholesalers

Divisions:
Eagle Ice Cream Div.
Fazio's Northern Ohio
Omar Bakeries, Inc.

GIANT FOOD, INC.
Post Office Box 1804
Washington, DC 20013
(301) 341-4100
Primary Business: Retail food and drug
stores
Chairman: Israel Cohen
CEO: Israel Cohen
President: Israel Cohen
Vice-President (Consumer Affairs): O.
Donna Matthews
Vice-President (Personnel): Jeremiah E.
Donovan
Vice-President (Pharmacy Operations):
Emanuel Richman
Revenue: $2.14 billion
Net Worth: $271 million
# of Employees: 19,300

Subsidiaries:
Bursil, Inc.
GFS Realty, Inc.
Giant Construction Co.
Landover Wholesale Tobacco Corp.
Leco Inc.
Warex-Jessup, Inc.
Shaw Community Supermarket
Giant Automatic Money Systems
Cole Engineering
Bayside Traffic Services, Inc.

GRAND UNION CO.
100 Broadway
Elmwood Park, NJ 07407
(201) 794-2000
Primary Business: Retail food chain
Chairman: Floyd Hall
CEO: Floyd Hall
President: Joseph J. McCaig
Vice-President (Service Departments):
  Buck Jones
Vice-President (Labor Relations):
  Charles Barrett
Revenue: $2.6 billion
# of Employees: 31,000

**THE GREAT ATLANTIC & PACIFIC
TEA CO., INC.**
2 Paragon Drive
Montvale, NJ 07654
(201) 573-9700
Primary Business: Chain grocery stores
Chairman: James Wood
CEO: James Wood
President: Louis Sherwood
Vice-President (Human Resources):
  Thomas L. Garrette
Vice-President (Grocery): Peter R.
  Lavoy
Vice-President (Communications):
  Michael J. Rourke
Sales: $5.88 billion
Net Worth: $1.03 billion
# of Employees: 45,000

Subsidiaries:
Compass Foods, Inc.
Kohl's Food Stores
Super Fresh Food Markets
Super Market Service Corp.
Supermarket Services, Inc.

Miscellaneous Facts: Subsidiary of
  Tengelman Group, West Germany.

THE KROGER CO.
1014 Vine Street
Cincinnati, OH 45201
(513) 762-4000
Primary Business: Supermarkets, drug
  stores
Chairman: Lyle Everingham
CEO: Lyle Everingham
President: William G. Kagler
Group Vice-President (Merchandising):
  George Irwin

Vice-President and General Counsel:
  George A. Leonard
Director, Public Relations: Paul Bernish
Revenue: $17.12 billion
Net Worth: $1.15 billion
# of Employees: 150,000

Subsidiaries:
Dillon Companies, Inc.
Hook Drugs, Inc.
SupeRx Drugs

LUCKY STORES, INC.
6300 Clark Avenue
Dublin, CA 94568
(415) 833-6000
Primary Business: Operates retail food
  markets
Chairman: S. Donley Ritchey
CEO: John M. Lillie
President: John M. Lillie
Executive Vice-President: Lawrence A.
  Del Santo
Senior Vice-President: Theodore F.
  Brunner
Vice-President (Personnel): Thomas F.
  Herman
Revenue: $9.38 billion
Net Worth: $609 million
# of Employees: 65,300

Subsidiaries:
Cal-Pharm, Inc.
Checker Auto Parts, Inc.
Emilco, Inc.
Hancock Textile Co., Inc.
Lucky Stores, Inc.
Markets, Inc.
Marydoug, Inc.
Seventeen One, Inc.
Shopper's Markets, Inc.
T-Chem Co.
Walnut Creek Canning Co.
Yellow Front Div.

Miscellaneous Facts: Incorporated in
  1931 in California as Peninsula Stores,
  Ltd. Present name adopted in 1940.

PUBLIX SUPER MARKETS, INC.
2040 George Jenkins Boulevard
Lakeland, FL 33802
(813) 688-1188
Primary Business: Food markets
Chairman: Charles H. Jenkins

Chairman, Executive Committee:
George W. Jenkins
Vice-President (Public Relations): Mark
C. Hollis
Vice-President (Advertising): R.
William Schroter
Vice-President (Personnel): E. H. Ruth
Sales: $3.20 billion
# of Employees: 37,000

Miscellaneous Facts: Company is one of
the largest employee-owned
companies in the world.

SAFEWAY STORES, INC.
201 Fourth Street
Oakland, CA 94660
(415) 891-3000
Primary Business: Chain retail food
stores
Chairman: Peter A. Magowan
CEO: Peter A. Magowan
President: James A. Rowland
Senior Vice-President (Public
Relations): Robert E. Bradford
Senior Vice-President (Personnel): John
L. Repass
Sales: $19.65 billion
Net Worth: $1.6 billion
# of Employees: 148,800

Miscellaneous Facts: Incorporated in
1926 in Maryland.

SUPER FOOD SERVICES, INC.
3185 Elbee Road
Dayton, OH 45439
(513) 294-1731
Primary Business: Wholesale food
distributor
Chairman of the Board: Jack Twymann
CEO: Jack Twymann
President: Jack Twymann
Senior Vice-President: George Gayda
Vice-President (Human Resources):
Richard Metzger
Sales; $1.4 billion
Net Worth: $61 million
# of Employees: 1,860

Subsidiary:
General Merchandise Services, Inc.

SUPERMARKETS GENERAL CORP.
301 Blair Road
Woodbridge, NJ 07095
(201) 499-3000
Primary Business: Retail chain
supermarkets
Chairman of the Board: Alex A.
Aidekman
CEO: Leonard Lieberman
President: Leonard Lieberman
Executive Vice-President: James D.
Dougherty
Vice-President (Human Resources):
Maureen McGurl
Sales: $5.12 billion
Net Worth: $346 million
# of Employees: 52,193

Divisions:
Purity Supreme
Purity Supreme, Inc.
Rickel Home Centers
SCG Drugstore Merchandising Div.

SUPER VALU STORE, INC.
11840 Valleyview Road
Eden Prarie, MN 55344
(612) 828-4000
Primary Business: Wholesale groceries
Chairman of the Board: Michael W.
Wright
CEO: Michael W. Wright
President: Michael W. Wright
Executive Vice-President: Sumner H.
Goldman
Vice-President (Communications):
Michael Mulligan
Vice-President (Human Resources):
Robert C. Tortelli
Sales: $7.9 billion
Net Worth: $534 million
# of Employees: 26,575

Subsidiaries:
Cub Foods
J. M. Jones Co.
The Lewis Grocer Co.
Planmark, Inc.
Preferred Products, Inc.
Risk Planners, Inc.
Shopko Stores, Inc.
Westen Grocers, Inc.

VONS GROCERY CO.
10150 Lower Azusa Road
El Monte, CA 91731
(818) 597-1400
Primary Business: Supermarket chain
Chairman: Roger E. Stangeland
CEO: Roger E. Stangeland
President: William S. Davila
Group Vice-President (Perishables):
  Robert J. Kelly
Vice-President (Meat Div.): Robert W.
  Clark
Vice-President (Pharmacy): Carl Vitalie
# of Employees: 18,000

Miscellaneous Facts: Subsidiary of The
  Vons Companies, Inc. Operates more
  than 190 supermarkets.

WALDBAUM, INC.
Hemlock and Boulevard
Central Islip, NY 11722
(516) 248-5600
Primary Business: Supermarket retailer
President: Ira Waldbaum
Executive Vice-President: Aaron
  Malinsky
Vice-President (Sales): Ernest Brown
Vice-President (Safety and Claims):
  Dominic Piccininni
Sales: $1.71 billion
Net Worth: $128 million
# of Employees: 6,500

WINN-DIXIE STORES, INC.
5050 Edgewood Court
Jacksonville, FL 32203
(904) 783-5000
Primary Business: Chain grocery stores
Chairman: Robert D. Davis
CEO: A. Dan Davis
President: A. Dan Davis
Executive Vice-President: Frank L.
  James
Senior Vice-President: S. W. Evans
Revenue: $7.77 billion
Net Worth: $646 million
# of Employees: 36,600 full-time, 28,700
  part-time

Divisions:
Winn-Dixie Tampa
Winn-Dixie Orlando
Winn-Dixie Miami
Winn-Dixie Jacksonville

Winn-Dixie Atlanta
Winn-Dixie Charlotte
Winn-Dixie Greenville
Winn-Dixie New Orleans
Winn-Dixie Louisville
Winn-Dixie Montgomery
Winn-Dixie Raleigh
Winn-Dixie Fort Worth

Ice Cream

BASKIN-ROBBINS ICE CREAM CO.
31 Baskin-Robbins Place
Glendale, CA 91201
(818) 965-0031
Primary Business: Ice cream shops

Miscellaneous Facts: Subsidiary of
  Allied-Lyons North American Corp.

BON BON CO. OF AMERICA
1620 N Spring Street
Los Angeles, CA 90012
(213) 221-2395
Primary Business: Ice cream
  manufacturer
General Manager: Ed Gassmann

Miscellaneous Facts: Subsidiary of
  Carnation Co.

DREYER'S GRAND ICE CREAM, INC.
5929 College Ave.
Oakland, CA 94618
(415) 652-8187
Primary Business: Ice cream products
Chairman of the Board: Gary T. Rogers
President: William F. Cronk III
Vice-President (Sales): Norman Lawson
Sales: $84.22 million
Net Worth: $31 million
# of Employees: 575

Subsidiary:
Edy's, Inc.

ESKIMO PIE CORP.
530 E. Main Street
Richmond, VA 23219
(804) 782-1800
Primary Business: Licenses ice cream
  manufacturers

Chairman of the Board: David P.
Reynolds
President: Fenton N. Hord
Vice-President and Treasurer: W. M.
Fariss, Jr.
Sales: $39.74 million
# of Employees: 920

FRIENDLY ICE CREAM CORP.
1855 Boston Road
Willbraham, MA 01095
(413) 543-2400
Primary Business: Operates restaurants
President: John F. Cauley

Miscellaneous Facts: Subsidiary of
Hershey Foods Corp. Operates 752
restaurants in 17 states.

POPSICLE INDUSTRIES, INC.
110 Route 4
Englewood, NJ 07631
(201) 567-8500
Primary Business: Ice cream supplies
CEO: Rupert A. Walters
President: Rupert A. Walters
Vice-President (Sales): Eugene Welka
Vice-President (Marketing): Paul Kadin
Sales: $50 million
# of Employees: 200

Miscellaneous Facts: Subsidiary of Sara
Lee Corp.

Restaurants and Fast Food

A & W RESTAURANTS
One Parklane Boulevard
Dearborn, MI 48126
(313) 271-9300
Primary Business: Fast food restaurants,
root beer
Chairman of the Board: A. Alfred
Taubman
CEO: A. Alfred Taubman
President: Howard W. Berkowitz
Vice-President (Franchising): Lamont
Burningham
Vice-President and Chief Financial
Officer: Phillip S. Schaefer
Sales: $170 million
# of Employees: 500

Miscellaneous Facts: Subsidiary of
Taubman Investment Co.

BURGER KING CORP.
7360 N Kendall Drive
Miami, FL 33156
(305) 596-7011
Primary Business: Fast food restaurants
Chairman of the Board: J. Jeffrey
Cambell
President: Jerome B. Ruenheck
Executive Vice-President: Jay Darling
Executive Vice-President: Bill deLaet
Personnel Director: Joan Lefkowitz
Sales: $2.80 billion
# of Employees: 160,000

Miscellaneous Facts: Subsidiary of The
Pillsbury Co.

CHURCH'S FRIED CHICKEN, INC.
Post Office Box BH001
San Antonio, TX 78284
(512) 735-9392
Primary Business: Operates fast food
restaurants
Chairman: J. David Bamberger
CEO: J. David Bamberger
President: Richard F. Sherman
Executive Vice-President: James S.
Parker
Vice-President (Franchising): George N.
Samaras
Vice-President (Personnel): Norman D.
Mecham
Revenue: $545.33 million
Net Worth: $264 million
# of Employees: 13,500

Subsidiary:
Ron's Krispy Fried Chicken, Inc.

COLLINS FOOD INTERNATIONAL,
INC.
5400 Alla Road
Los Angeles, CA 90066
(213) 827-2300
Primary Business: Operates restaurant
chains
Chairman of the Board: James A.
Collins
CEO: James A. Collins
President: Richard P. Bermingham
Vice-Chairman: Rushton O. Backer
Vice-President (Human Resources): Lee
Clancy
Revenue: $468 million
Net Worth: $113 million
# of Employees: 9,900

Subsidiaries:
CFI Insurers, Ltd.
CFI Pty., Ltd.
Collins Foodservice, Inc.
Collins Foods International, Ltd.
Kentucky Fried Chicken of California
Sizzler Restaurants International, Inc.

Miscellaneous Facts: Operates 250
  Kentucky Fried Chicken outlets and
  465 Sizzler Restaurants.

DENNY'S, INC.
16700 Valley View Avenue
La Mirada, CA 90638
(714) 739-8100
Primary Business: Restaurants,
  doughnut shops
Chairman of the Board: Verne H.
  Winchell
CEO: Vern O. Curtis
President: Vern O. Curtis
Vice-President (Human Resources):
  Stephen F. Joyce
Vice-President and General Counsel:
  Terrence J. Wallock
Sales: $1.05 billion
Net Worth: $301 million
# of Employees: 45,000

Subsidiary:
El Pollo Loco

Divisions:
Denny's Restaurants
Winchell's Donut House

DUNKIN' DONUTS, INC.
Post Office Box 317
Randolph, MA 02368
(617) 961-4000
Primary Business: Developing and
  franchising doughnut shops
Chairman of the Board: Robert M.
  Rosenberg
President: Thomas R. Schwarz
Senior Vice-President (Marketing):
  Sidney J. Feltenstein, Jr.
Vice-President (Personnel): Richard
  Power
Revenue: $90.30 million
Net Worth: $53 million
# of Employees: 2,100

Division:
Dunkin' Donuts of America, Inc.

HOWARD JOHNSON CO.
One Howard Johnson Plaza
Boston, MA 02125
(617) 848-2350
Primary Business: Operates and supplies
  restaurant chain
Chairman: G. Michael Hostage
Vice-Chairman: E. J. Durgin
Vice-President (Employee Relations):
  Michael A. Jones
Revenue: $587.78 million
# of Employees: 27,600

CARL KARCHER ENTERPRISES, INC.
1200 N Harbor Boulevard
Anaheim, CA 92801
(714) 774-5796
Primary Business: Fast food restaurants
Chairman: C. N. Karcher
CEO: C. N. Karcher
President: Donald F. Karcher
Group Vice-President: L. C. Pannier
Vice-President (Human Resources):
  John Kubas
Sales: $321.13 million
# of Employees: 14,500, including part-
  time

Miscellaneous Facts: Known as Carl's
  Junior.

KENTUCKY FRIED CHICKEN CORP.
Post Office Box 32070
Louisville, KY 40232
(502) 456-8300
Primary Business: Fast food restaurants
Chairman of the Board: Richard P.
  Mayer
CEO: Richard P. Mayer

Subsidiaries:
KFC Corp.
KFC International Corp.

Miscellaneous Facts: Subsidiary of RJR
  Nabisco, Inc.

MCDONALDS CORP.
One McDonald Plaza
Oak Brook, IL 60521
(312) 575-3000
Primary Business: Fast food restaurants
Chairman: Fred L. Turner
CEO: Fred L. Turner

President: Michael P. Quinlan
Executive Vice-President: G. Brent
  Cameron
Vice-President (Personnel): Stan Stein
Revenue: $3.41 billion
Net Worth: $2.2 billion
# of Employees: 37,000

THE MARCUS CORP.
212 W Wisconsin Avenue
Milwaukee, WI 53203
(414) 272-6020
Primary Business: Restaurant, hotel
  operations
Chairman of the Board: Ben Marcus
CEO: Ben Marcus
President: Stephen Marcus
Vice-President: Richard Heintz
Sales: $131 million
Net Worth: $69 million
# of Employees: 8,400

Subsidiaries:
Mar's Big Boy Corp.
Marcus Hotel Corp.
Marcus Theatres Corp.

PIZZA HUT, INC.
9111 E Douglas
Wichita, KS 67207
(316) 681-9000
Primary Business: Franchises and
  operates pizza restaurants
CEO: Arthur G. Gunther
President: Arthur G. Gunther
Vice-President (Public Relations): Larry
  H. Whitt
Vice-President (Personnel): David
  Zemelman
Vice-President (Franchising): Robert C.
  Hunter
Revenue: $725 million
# of Employees: 36,000

Miscellaneous Facts: Subsidiary of
  Pepsico.

SAGA CORP.
One Saga Lane
Menlo Park, CA 94025
(415) 854-5150
Primary Business: Operates restaurants
Chairman of the Board: Charles A.
  Lynch

CEO: Charles A. Lynch
President: Jeffrey O. Henley
Executive Vice-President: Francis W.
  Cash
Revenue: $1.2 billion

Miscellaneous Facts: Subsidiary of
  Mariott Corp.

SHONEY'S, INC.
1727 Elm Hill Pike
Nashville, TN 37210
(615) 361-5201
Primary Business: Operates chain of
  restaurants
Chairman of the Board: R. L. Danner
CEO: R. L. Danner
President: Gary Spoleta
Vice-Chairman: J. Mitchell Boyd
Vice-President (Personnel): Mickey
  Skelton
Revenue: $630 million
Net Worth: $217 million
# of Employees: 22,000

Divisions:
Captain D's Restaurant Div.
Lee's Famous Recipe Restaurant Div.
Shoney's Restaurant Div.
Specialty Restaurant Div.

STRAW HAT PIZZA
6400 Village Parkway
Dublin, CA 94568
(415) 829-1500
Primary Business: Pizza restaurants
President: Everett Jefferson
Vice-President (Franchising): John A.
  Kubas
Vice-President (Human Resources):
  Dennis E. Swanson
Sales: $90 million
# of Employees: 2,225

Miscellaneous Facts: Subsidiary of
  Marriott Corp.

WENDY'S INTERNATIONAL, INC.
4288 W Dublin Granville Road
Dublin, OH 43017
(614) 764-3100
Senior Chairman and Founder: R.
  David Thomas
CEO: Robert L. Barney

President: Ronald P. Fay
Executive Vice-President (Franchise
  Operations): Thomas C. Copeland III
Vice-President (Corporate
  Communications): Dennis L. Lynch
Revenue: $2.7 billion
Net Worth: $364 million
# of Employees: 145,000

Subsidiary:
Sisters International, Inc.

Miscellaneous Facts: Founded by R.
  David Thomas.

WINCHELL'S DONUT HOUSE
16424 Valley View
La Mirada, CA 90638
(714) 670-5300
Primary Business: Doughnut shops
Senior Vice-President: John D. Hatch
Sales: $185 million

Miscellaneous Facts: Division of
  Denny's, Inc.

FOOD PROCESSING FIRMS

ALPO PET FOODS, INC.
Rte 309 and Pope Road
Allentown, PA 18104
(215) 395-3301
Primary Business: Pet food
  manufacturer
CEO: Joseph Sestak
Sales: $350 million
# of Employees: 1,384

Miscellaneous Facts: Subsidiary of
  Grandmet USA, Inc.

AMERICAN MAIZE-PRODUCTS CO.
250 Harbor Drive
Stamford, CT 06904
(203) 356-9000
Primary Business: Corn products
Chairman of the Board: William Siegler
  III
CEO: William Siegler III
President: Leslie C. Liabo
Vice-President: Alan J. Edly
Vice-President: Edgar G. Gates
Revenue: $414 million
Net Worth: $20 million
# of Employees: 2,500

Subsidiaries:
American Fructose Corp.
Lloyd Home & Building Centers, Inc.
Jno. H. Swisher & Son, Inc.

AMFAC, INC.
44 Montgomery Street
San Francisco, CA 94104
(415) 772-3300
Primary Business: Food processing
Chairman of the Board: H. A. Walker,
  Jr.
CEO: Myron Du Bain
President: Myron Du Bain
Executive Vice-President: Ronald H.
  Dykehouse
Vice-President (Communications): Keith
  V. Mabee
Vice-President (Employee Relations):
  Richard D. Baum
Revenue: $2.40 billion
Net Worth: $406 million
# of Employees: 21,000

Subsidiaries:
Amfac Cameo Stores, Inc.
Amfac Communities, Inc.
Amfac Distribution Corp.
Amfac Financial Inc.
Amfac Foods
Amfac Garden Perry's, Inc.
Amfac Hawaii, Inc.
Amfac Energy, Inc.
Amfac Hotels & Resorts, Inc.
Amfac Nurseries Cole, Inc.

Miscellaneous Facts: Incorporated in
  1918 in Hawaii as Americans Factors,
  Inc. Present name adopted in 1966.

ANDERSON, CLAYTON & CO.
1100 Louisiana, Box 2538
Houston, TX 77252
(713) 651-0641
Primary Business: Diversified foods,
  insurance
Chairman of the Board: T. J. Barlow
CEO: W. F. Guinee, Jr.
President: W. F. Guinee, Jr.
Vice-President (Consumer Products): R.
  R. Bachman
Vice-President (Law): Don C.
  McDonald
Vice-President (Personnel): B. B.
  McMenamy
Sales: $1.83 billion
Net Worth: $570 million
# of Employees: 17,800

Subsidiaries:
American Founders Life Insurance Co.
Gaines Foods, Inc.
Great South Warehouses, Inc.
Igloo Corp.
Impact Extrusions, Inc.
Ranger Insurance Co.
Ranger Lloyds

Divisions:
ACCO Feeds Div.
Anderson Clayton Foods Div.
Purity Cheese Co.

ARCHER-DANIELS-MIDLAND CO.
4666 Faries Parkway
Decatur, IL 62526
(217) 424-5200
Primary Business: Bakery and durum flours
Chairman of the Board: Dwayne O. Andreas
CEO: Dwayne O. Andreas
President: James R. Randall
Group Vice-President: Michael A. Andreas
Vice-President: Martin L. Andreas
Revenue: $4.90 billion
Net Worth: $1.6 billion
# of Employees: 8,875

Subsidiaries:
ADM Feed Corp.
American River Transportation Co.
Ardanco, Inc.
Coeval, Inc.
Columbia Peanut Co.
Fleischmann Malting Co.
Gooch Foods, Inc.
Miller Hauling Co.
Supreme Sugar Co., Inc.

BEATRICE COMPANIES, INC.
2 N LaSalle Street
Chicago, IL 60602
(312) 782-3820
Primary Business: Holding Co., Foods
Chairman of the Board: William W. Granger, Jr.
Executive Vice-President: Frank E. Grzelecki
Executive Vice-President: David E. Lipson
Manager, Human Resources: Pam Tehringer
Revenue: $12.60 billion
Net Worth: $3.2 billion
# of Employees: 100,000

Subsidiaries:
Lark Luggage Co.
Samsonite Corp.
Waterloo Industries, Inc.
International Playtex, Inc.
Danskin, Inc.
Max Factor & Co.
Arrowhead Drinking Water Co.
Tropicana Products, Inc.
Aunt Nellie's Foods, Inc.
Fisher Nut Co.

La Choy Food Products, Inc.
Lowrey's, Inc.
Rosarita Mexican Foods Co.
Avis, Inc.
STP Corp.

BORDEN
277 Park Avenue
New York, NY 10172
Primary Business: Manufacturer of foods and chemicals
Chairman of the Board: Eugene J. Sullivan
CEO: Eugene J. Sullivan
President: Eugene J. Sullivan
Executive Vice-President: R. J. Ventres
Executive Vice-President: H. G. Lambroussis
Vice-President (Personnel): Alan L. Miller
Sales: $4.57 billion
Net Worth: $1.67 billion
# of Employees: 32,200

Subsidiaries:
Bayamon Can Corp.
Chevy Chase, Inc.
Wyler Foods Div.
Borden Consumer Products, Inc.
Buckeye Potato Chip Co.
Caribbean Snacks, Inc.
Cheese-Tek Corp.
El Molino Foods, Inc.
Guy's Foods, Inc.
Morton Foods, Inc.

Miscellaneous Facts: Maker of Eagle Brand products, ReaLemon, Creamette Brand, Wylers, Elmers Glue, Krylon Paints and Cottage Fried Potato Chips. Founded by Gail Borden, Jr.

BUMBLE BEE SEAFOOD PRODUCTS
Post Office Box 1017
San Diego, CA 92112
(619) 560-0404
Primary Business: Manufacturer of seafood products
President: Pat Rose

Miscellaneous Facts: Division of Castle & Cooke, Inc.

CAMPBELL SOUP CO.
Campbell Place
Camden, NJ 08103
(609) 342-4800
Primary Business: Food products
Chairman of the Board: William S. Cashel, Jr.
CEO: R. Gordon McGovern
President: R. Gordon McGovern
President, International: John Argabrite
Director, Personnel: John Dieleuterio
Vice-President (Sales): Carl Stinnet
Revenue: $3.66 billion
Net Worth: $1.2 billion
# of Employees: 44,647

Subsidiaries:
CSC Advertising, Inc.
Campbell Finance Corp.
Camsco Mushroom Co., Inc.
Champion Valley Farms, Inc.
H.T. Restaurants, Inc.
Juice Bowl Products, Inc.
Martino's Bakery
Mrs. Paul's Kitchen
Snow King Frozen foods, Inc.
Pepperidge Farm, Inc.
Peitros Corp.
Valley Tomato Products, Inc.
Vlasic Foods, Inc.

Miscellaneous Facts: Founded in 1869 in New Jersey by Abraham and Joseph Campbell. Women are 44 percent of the work force. Has more than 1,000 products on the market. Brand names include Campbell soups, Prego, Swanson, Hungry-Man, Le Menu, Plump & Juicy, Franco-American, V-8 Juice, Snowking, Winschuler's, Mrs. Paul's, Vlasic, Domsea, Triange Brand, Pepperidge Farm, Godiva Chocolates, Pietro's Pizza.

CAMPBELL TAGGART, INC.
6211 Lemmon Avenue
Dallas, TX 75209
(214) 358-9211
Primary Business: Baked goods
CEO: C. B. Lane, Jr.
President: C. B. Lane, Jr.
Executive Vice-President: Jose M. Rubi
Vice-President (Education): Howard Chambers
Vice-President (Human Resources): Harold D. Scaneard

Revenue: $1.26 billion
# of Employees: 22,911

Miscellaneous Facts: Subsidiary of Anheuser-Busch.

CARNATION CO.
5045 Wilshire Boulevard
Los Angeles, CA 90036
(213) 932-6000
Primary Business: Processing and sale of food and grocery products
Chairman of the Board: H. E. Olsen
CEO: Timm F. Crull
Vice-Chairman: Carl L. Angst
Vice-President (Communications): R. N. Matthews
Vice-President (Human Resources): Tony Burnham
# of Employees: 22,400

Subsidiaries:
Bon Bon Co. of America, Inc.
Carnation Export Corp.
Eagle Realty Corp.
Favorite Foods, Inc.
Hawaiian Grain Corp.
Tomorrow Products, Inc.

Miscellaneous Facts: Subsidiary of Nestle Holdings Co.

CASTLE & COOKE, INC.
Post Office Box 7330
San Francisco, CA 94120
(415) 986-3000
Primary Business: Food processing, merchandising
Chairman of the Board: Henry B. Clarke, Jr.
CEO: Robert D. Cook
President: Robert D. Cook
Executive Vice-President: I. Homer Eaton
Vice-President and General Counsel: Robert R. Nielsen
Vice-President (Human Resources): Mary Stanyne
Revenue: $1.5 billion
Net Worth: $343 million
# of Employees: 37,000

Subsidiaries:
A&W Beverages, Inc.
Blue Goose Growers, Inc.
Kohala Corp.

Lanai Co., Ltd.
Flexi-Van Corp.
Intelect, Inc.

Divisions:
Hawaiian Equipment Co.
Bumble Bee Seafood Products
Dole Processed Products

CONAGRA, INC.
One Central Park E
Omaha, NB 68102
(402) 978-4000
Primary Business: Manufactures
  prepared frozen foods
Chairman of the Board: Charles M.
  Harper
CEO: Charles M. Harper
Executive Vice-President: George K.
  Gosko
Senior Vice-President (Human
  Resources): Harold F. Schuler
Vice-President (Public Affairs): Martin
  G. Colladay
Sales: $5.5 billion
Net Worth: $481 million
# of Employees: 30,000

Operating Companies:
Armour Food Co.
Berger & Co.
Country Skillet Catfish Co.
Pfaelzer Brothers
Home Brands Co.
Sea-Alaska Products Co.
Caribbean Basic Foods Co.
Peavey Co.

CPC INTERNATIONAL, INC.
P.O. Box 8000
Englewood Cliffs, NJ 07632
(201) 894-4000
Primary Business: Salad dressing, corn
  oil, snack meals
Chairman of the Board: James W.
  McKee, Jr.
CEO: James R. Eiszner
President: James R. Eiszner
Executive Vice-President: Ivan A. Burns
Executive Vice-President: Paul Craven
Sales; $4.37 billion
Net Worth: $1.3 billion
# of Employees: 38,000

Divisions:
Best Foods U.S.
CPC Foodservice
Knorr, Special Products Unit
S.B. Thomas, Inc.
Acme Resin Corp.
Amerchol Corp.
Peterson/Puritan, Inc.

DEAN FOODS CO.
3600 River Road
Franklin Park, IL 60131
(312) 625-6200
Primary Business: Process dairy
  products
Chairman of the Board: Kenneth J.
  Douglas
CEO: Kenneth J. Douglas
President: Howard M. Dean, Jr.
Senior Vice-President: William J.
  Corbett
Senior Vice-President: John V. Guckien
Sales: $923 million
Net Worth: $29 million
# of Employees: 4,630

Subsidiaries:
Atkins Pickle Co., Inc.
Bell Dairy Products, Inc.
Creamland Dairies, Inc.
Dean Milk Co., Inc.
Green Bay Foods Co.
Harts Dairy, Inc.
Juice Service, Inc.

Miscellaneous Facts: Incorporated in
1969 in Delaware.

DEL MONTE CORP.
Post Office Box 3575
San Francisco, CA 94119
(415) 442-4000
Primary Business: Canned and dried
  fruits and vegetables
Chairman of the Board: R. A. Fox
CEO: R. A. Fox
Vice-President (Corporate Relations):
  Henry Sandbach
Vice-President (Employee Relations): J.
  W. Farlow
Vice-President (Personnel): Don Sipes
Revenue: $2.06 billion
# of Employees: 37,000

Miscellaneous Facts: Subsidiary of R. J.
  Reynolds Industries, Inc.

DI GIORGIO CORP.
One Maritime Plaza
San Francisco, CA 94111
(415) 765-0100
Primary Business: Distributes forest
  products
Chairman of the Board: R. Di Giorgio
CEO: Peter F. Scott
President: Peter F. Scott
Vice-President: Robert E. Mellor
Sales: $1.2 billion
Net Worth: $110 million
# of Employees: 3,800

Subsidiaries:
Carando, Inc.
DG Shelter Products Co.
Serv-A-Portion, Inc.
White Rose Food Corp.

DOLE CITRUS
2151 E D Street
118 B Suite
Ontario, CA 91764
(714) 983-0203
Primary Business: Packs, grows and sells
  citrus fruits
President: William Swinford
Vice-President: David Palmer
Sales: $60 million
# of Employees: 400

DOLLY MADISON BAKERIES
12 E Armour Boulevard
Kansas City, MO 64111
(816) 561-6600
Primary Business: Operates bakeries

Miscellaneous Facts: Division of
  Interstate Bakeries Corp.

FARMER BROTHERS CO.
20333 S Normandie Avenue
Torrance, CA 90502
(213) 775-2451
Primary Business: Manufactures coffee
  and spices
Chairman of the Board: Roy F. Farmer
CEO: Roy F. Farmer
President: Roy F. Farmer
Director of Personnel: Beverly Stillson
Director of Purchasing: Carol Halfaker
Sales: $194 million
Net Worth: $81 million
# of Employees: 1,180

Subsidiary:
FBC Finance Co.

Divisions:
Brewmatic Co. Div.
Custom Coffee Plan Div.
Route Sales Div.
Spice Products Div.

THE FEDERAL CO.
1755 D Lynnfield, Suite 149
Memphis, TN 38119
(901) 761-3610
Primary Business: Manufactures
  consumer food products
Chairman of the Board: Lewis K.
  McKee
CEO: R. Lee Taylor II
President: R. Lee Taylor II
Vice-President: John T. Stout
Vice-President: W. F. Baily
Revenue: $1.28 billion
Net Worth: $243 million
# of Employees: 11,000

Subsidiaries:
Diana Fruit Preserving Co.
Dixie Portland Flour Mills
Globe Products Co., Inc.
Holly Farms Poultry Industries
National By-Products, Inc.
Rustico Products Co.
The White Lily Foods Co.

FISHER NUT CO.
2327 Wycliff
St. Paul, MN 55114
(612) 645-0635
Primary Business: Dry roasted nut
  manufacturer
Vice-President: Roger Schrankler

Miscellaneous Facts: Subsidiary of
  Beatrice Companies, Inc.

THE FOLGER CO.
One Procter & Gamble Plaza
Cincinnati, OH 45202
(513) 983-1100
Primary Business: Maker of coffee
  products
President: J. E. Pepper
# of Employees: 958

Miscellaneous Facts: Subsidiary of the
  Procter & Gamble Co.

FOREMOST DAIRIES, INC.
100 Spear Street
San Francisco, CA 94105
(415) 546-1600
Primary Business: Dairy products
Chairman: Nicholas Wallner
President: Allen A. Meyer
Vice-President (Finance): R. Timothy
  Leister
Vice-President (Personnel): Carl
  Connell
Sales: $600 million
# of Employees: 2,700

Miscellaneous Facts: Subsidiary of
  Knudsen Foods, Inc.

R. T. FRENCH CO.
One Mustard Street
Rochester, NY 14609
(716) 482-8000
Primary Business: Makes mustard,
  potato products
CEO: R. Silkett
President: R. Silkett
Vice-President (Personnel): J. J. Cahill
Vice-President: R. R. Hartel
Vice-President: K. D. Simonson
Sales: $50 million
# of Employees: 1,800

Miscellaneous Facts: Subsidiary of
  Reckitt & Colman, North America,
  Inc.

GENERAL FOODS
250 North Street
White Plains, NY 10625
(914) 335-2500
Primary Business: Makes coffee, cereals,
  frozen food products
Chairman: James L. Ferguson
CEO: James L. Ferguson
President: Phillip L. Smith
Vice-President (Sales): Lloyd A. Nelson
Vice-President (Consumer Affairs):
  Gabrielle J. Hermann
Vice-President (Corporate Personnel):
  C. R. Blundell
Sales: $9.09 billion
Net Worth: $5.63 billion
# of Employees: 56,000

Subsidiaries:
Entenmann's, Inc.

Oscar Mayer Food Corp.
Ronzoni Food Corp.

Divisions:
Claussen Pickle Co.
Louis Rich Co.
Maxwell House Div.
Beverage Div.

Miscellaneous Facts: Subsidiary of Philip
  Morris Companies, Inc.

GENERAL MILLS
9200 Wayzata Boulevard
Minneapolis, MN 55426
(612) 540-2311
Primary Business: Manufactures
  breakfast cereals, food products
Chairman: H. Brewster Atwater, Jr.
CEO: H. Brewster Atwater, Jr.
Vice-Chairman: F. Caleb Blodgett
Vice-President (Corporate
  Communications): Dean Belbas
Vice-President (Nutrition): Ivy M.
  Celender, M.D.
Senior Vice-President (Personnel): John
  L. Frost
Revenue: $4.28 billion
Net Worth: $1.02 billion
# of Employees: 64,000

Subsidiaries:
The Furniture Group America, Inc.
Eddie Bauer, Inc.
The Olive Garden
Red Lobster Inns of America
Leeann Chin's, Inc.
The Talbots, Inc.
Vroman Foods, Inc.

Divisions:
The Gorton Group Div.
Minnetonka Div.
Yoplait USA
Betty Crocker Div.
Sperry Div.

Miscellaneous Facts: Products include
  Cheerios, Honey Nut Cheerios, Total,
  Lucky Charms, Fiber One, Rocky
  Road, Circus Fun, S'mores Crunch,
  Wheaties, Betty Crocker Products,
  Hamburger and Tuna Helper,
  Oriental Classics, Bisquick, Gold
  Medal, Pop Secret, Yoplait, Gorton's
  Seafood. Incorporated in 1928 in
  Delaware. Company has more than 60
  subsidiaries.

GENERAL NUTRITION
921 Penn Avenue
Pittsburgh, PA 15222
(412) 288-4600
Primary Business: Makes vitamins,
 minerals and nutritional food
CEO: Jerry D. Horn
President: G. A. Daum
Vice-Chairman: B. J. Shakarian
Vice-President: G. R. Banjamin
Vice-President: G. E. McTuek
Sales: $390.35 million
Net Worth: $95 million
# of Employees: 6,500–7,000

Divisions:
General Nutrition Centers
General Nutrition Corp.
General Nutrition Mills

GERBER PRODUCTS CO.
445 State Street
Fremont, MI 49412
(616) 928-2000
Primary Business: Baby food, baby
 clothing and toys
Chairman: Carl G. Smith
CEO: Carl G. Smith
President: Leo D. Goulet
Vice-President (Sales): Samuel J.
 Bourgeois
Vice-President (Nutrition Sciences):
 George A. Purvis
Director, Human Resources: Jay B.
 Hartfield
Revenue: $929.44 million
Net Worth: $374 million
# of Employees: 14,470

Subsidiaries:
Atlanta Novelty
Cornucopia Farms, Inc.
Buster Brown Apparel, Inc.
Century Products, Inc.
Gerber Finance
Kent, Inc.
Gerber Life Insurance Co.
Walter M. Moyer Co., Inc.
Bates Nitewear Co.
Reliance Products Co.

Miscellaneous Facts: Founded in 1927 as
 Fremont Canning Co. Company name
 changed in 1941. According to the
 company, the Gerber baby is the
 second most recognized corporate
image in the world. Gerber sells 168
types of baby food today. Singer Kate
Smith is a former spokesperson.

GREEN GIANT CO.
Pillsbury Center
200 S Sixth Street
Minneapolis, MN 55402
(612) 330-4966
Primary Business: Canned and frozen
 vegetables
Chairman: William H. Spoor, Pillsbury
 Co.
CEO: John M. Stafford
President: John M. Stafford
General Manager, Frozen Vegetables:
 G. Klingl
General Manager, Canned Vegetables:
 K. Reis
Senior Vice-President (Human
 Resources): Timmothy Sullivan
Revenue: $485.67 million
# of Employees: 6,600

Miscellaneous Facts: Subsidiary of
 Pillsbury Co.

H. J. HEINZ CO.
600 Grant Street
Pittsburgh, PA 15219
(412) 237-5757
Primary Business: Canned and
 processed foods, food preparations
Chairman: Henry J. Heinz II
CEO: Anthony J. F. O'Reilly
President: Anthony J. F. O'Reilly
Chairman (Weight Watchers Int'l):
 Albert Lippert
Senior Vice-President: Richard B.
 Patton
Director, Public Relations: T. H.
 McIntosh
Revenue: $3.95 billion
Net Worth: $1.4 billion
# of Employees: 45,000

Miscellaneous Facts: Some of the brand
 names made by the company are
 Weight Watchers, Worcestershire
 Sauce, Star Kist, 9-Lives, Jerry
 Treats, Oreida Foods, La Pizzeria,
 Goodcookie, and Steak-umm
 products. Incorporated in 1900 in
 Pennsylvania. Makes more catsup
 than any other company in the world.

For Christmas, every employee receives a gift.

HERSHEY FOOD CORP.
Post Office Box 814
Hershey, PA 17033
(717) 534-4000
Primary Business: Food manufacturing and services
Chairman: Richard A. Zimmerman
CEO: Richard A. Zimmerman
President: Kenneth L. Wolfe
Vice-President (Corporate Communications): Kenneth L. Bowers
Vice-President (Human Resources): William P. Noyes
Sales: $1.98 billion
Net Worth: $727 million
# of Employees: 15,200

Divisions:
Cory Food Services, Inc.
Friendly Ice Cream Corp.
Hershey Chocolate Co.
Hershey Pasta Group

Miscellaneous Facts: Founded in 1903 by Milton Hershey. Company owns its own town. Along Chocolate Avenue, street lights are shaped like Hershey Kisses. Some of the products made by the company are Reese's, Kit-Kat, Rolo, New Trail, Twizzlers, Brown Cow and Skor. Other brand names are American Beauty, San Giorgio, Scinner, Delmonico, P&R and Light & Fluffy.

HILLS BROS. COFFEE, INC.
2 Harrison Street
San Francisco, CA 94105
(415) 546-4600
Primary Business: Maker of ground and instant coffee
Chairman: P. J. Miller
President: N. E. Dean
Vice-President (Sales): Robert J. Otto
Vice-President (Food Services): Charles E. Pugh
Sales: $350 million
# of Employees: 750

Miscellaneous Facts: Subsidiary of Nestle Holdings, Inc.

HOOLY SUGAR CORP.
100 Chase Stone Center
Colorado Springs, CO 80903
(303) 471-0123
Primary Business: Manufacturer of sugar and sugar products
Chairman of the Board: Michael S. Buchsbaum
CEO: Charles Azarow
President: Charles Azarow
Vice-Chairman: J. E. A. Rich
Director, Human Resources: A. L. Sharp
Director, Public Relations: Nola F. Winters
Revenue: $259 million
Net Worth: $61 million
# of Employees: 940

Subsidiary:
HSC Export Corp.

G.E.O.A. HORMEL & CO.
501 16th Avenue NE
Austin, MN 55912
(507) 437-5611
Primary Business: Meat packing and food processing
Chairman of the Board: Richard L. Knowlton
CEO: Richard L. Knowlton
President: Richard L. Knowlton
Executive Vice-President: Raymond J. Asp
Director, Public Relations: Allan Krejci
Vice-President (Human Resources): David A. Larson
Sales: $1.5 billion
Net Worth: $311 million
# of Employees: 7,000

Subsidiaries:
Algona Food Equipment Co.
Farm Fresh Catfish Co.
Hormel International Corp.

Divisions:
Dole Foods
Deli Div.
Food Services Div.
Grocery Products Div.

Miscellaneous Facts: Incorporated in 1928 in Delaware.

HUNT-WESSON FOOD, INC.
1645 W Valencia Drive
Fullerton, CA 92634
(714) 680-1000
Primary Business: Maker of canned
tomato products
CEO: Frederick B. Rentschler
President: Frederick B. Rentschler
Executive Vice-President: Albert J.
Crosson
Vice-President (Marketing): James F.
Frawley
Sales: $940 million

Miscellaneous Facts: Subsidiary of
Norton Simon, Inc.

IC INDUSTRIES
111 E Wacker Drive
Chicago, IL 60601
(312) 565-3000
Primary Business: Holding company,
consumer and commercial products
Chairman: William B. Johnson
CEO: William B. Johnson
President: C. L. Pecchenio
Senior Vice-President (Consumer
Service): Bruce S. Chelberts
Senior Vice-President (Corporate
Affairs): Wendell W. Larsen
Vice-President (Personnel): Ronald
Wright
Revenue: $4.73 billion
Net Worth: $1.6 billion
# of Employees: 45,384

Divisions:
Abex Corp. Amsco
Jetway Div.
National Water Lift Div.
Railroad Products Group
Remco Hydraulics
Pet, Inc.
Bubble-Up Co., Inc.
Dad's Root Beer Co.
Hussmann Corp.
Illinois Center Corp.
LaSalle Properties, Inc.

Miscellaneous Facts: Incorporated in
1962 in Delaware as Illinois Central
Industries, Inc. Present name adopted
in 1975.

INTERSTATE BAKERIES CORP.
12 E Armour Boulevard
Kansas City, MO 64177
(816) 561-6600
Primary Business: Holding company,
bakery goods
Chairman of the Board: Howard P.
Berkowitz
CEO: Robert W. Hatch
President: Robert W. Hatch
Executive Vice-President: R. A.
Bevalqua
Vice-President (Human Resources):
Wade L. Glassburn
Sales: $703 million
Net Worth: $70 million
# of Employees: 11,200

Subsidiary:
Interstate Brands Corp.

JENOS, INC.
200 Live Oak Gardens
Casselberry, FL 32707
(305) 830-2400
Primary Business: Manufactures frozen
foods
Chairman: Michael J. Paulucci
CEO: Michael J. Paulucci
President: Robert J. Leighton
Executive Vice-President (Sales): Jeffrey
L. Carpenter
Sales: $200 million
# of Employees: 1,200

KAL KAN FOODS, INC.
3386 E 44th Street
Vernon, CA 90058
(213) 587-2727
Primary Business: Maker of foods for
dogs and cats
President: John Barrow
Vice-President (Administration and
Personnel): John Bridgeman
Vice-President (Marketing): A. Poe
Sales: $250 million
# of Employees: 1,000

KELLOGG CO.
Post Office Box 3599
One Kellogg Square
Battle Creek, MI 49016
(616) 961-2000

Primary Business: Cereals, toaster
pastries, food products
Chairman: William E. LaMothe
CEO: William E. LaMothe
President: Gerald D. Robinson
Vice-President (Public Affairs): Joseph
M. Stewart
Vice-President (Employee Relations):
Robert L. Kreviston
Vice-President (Quality and Nutrition):
R. Franta
Sales: $2.60 billion
Net Worth: $683 million
# of Employees: 17,290

Subsidiaries:
Fearn International, Inc.
Kellogg Sales Co.
Mrs. Smith's Frozen Foods Co.
Salada Foods, Inc.
Whitney's Foods, Inc.

*Miscellaneous Facts:*Incorporated in
1922 in Delaware as a reorganization
of Kellogg Toasted Corn Flakes Co.

KNUDSEN FOODS, INC.
Box 2335 Terminal Annex
Los Angeles, CA 90051
(213) 744-7000
Primary Business: Dairy food products
Chairman of the Board: Dee R.
Bangerter
CEO: Dee R. Bangerter
President: David F. Greenawalt
Vice-Chairman: Fallen A. Meyer
Senior Vice-President (Sales and
Marketing): John C. Thompson
Sales: $484 million
# of Employees: 2,200

Miscellaneous Facts: Subsidiary of Winn
Enterprises.

KRAFT, INC.
Kraft Court
Glenview, IL 60025
(312) 998-2726
Primary Business: Dairy products,
processed food products
Chairman: John M. Richman
CEO: John M. Richman
Senior Vice-President (Human
Resources): J. A. Mitchell
Vice-President (Public Relations): N. E.
Toft

Revenue: $8.1 billion
# of Employees: 50,000

Subsidiaries:
Duracell, Inc.
Kraft, Inc., Dairy Group
Frusen Gladje, Ltd.
Celestial Seasonings, Inc.
Churny Cheese, Inc.
Lender's Bagel Bakery

LAND O'LAKES, INC.
4001 Lexington Avenue, N
Arden Hills, MN 55126
(612) 481-2222
Primary Business: Food processing
Chairman of the Board: Claire Sandness
CEO: Ralph Hofstad
President: Ralph Hofstad
Vice-President (Research): David
Hettinga
Personnel Director: Don Renquist
Sales: $2.3 billion
Net Worth: $385 million
# of Employees: 7,300

Subsidiaries:
Lea Foods
Petroleum Resources Co.

Divisions:
Land O'Lakes, Inc., Agricultural
Service
Lake to Lake Dairy

LEA & PERRINS, INC.
15-01 Pollitt Drive
Fair Lawn, NJ 07410
(201) 791-1600
Primary Business: Sauces
President: Dennis Newnham
Treasurer: Joe Hermann
Sales: $35 million
# of Employees: 95

Miscellaneous Facts: Subsidiary of
Imperial Food's America, Inc.

THOMAS J. LIPTON, INC.
800 Sylvan Avenue
Englewood Cliffs, NJ 07632
(201) 567-8000
Primary Business: Tea, dried soups,
salad dressings
CEO: H. M. Tibbetts

President: H. M. Tibbetts
Vice-President (Beverages): G. B.
  Boycks
Vice-President (Corporate Relations):
  D. J. Carroll
Vice-President (Personnel): W. K.
  Godfrey
Sales: $1 billion
# of Employees: 5,500

Subsidiary:
Lawry's Foods, Inc.

Divisions:
Good Humor Corp.
Knox Gelatin, Inc.
Lipton Professional Soccer, Inc.
Pennsylvania Dutch-Megs, Inc.
Sahadi Products Co.

Miscellaneous Facts: Subsidiary of
  Unilever United States, Inc.

MCCORMICK & CO., INC.
11350 McCormick Road
Hunt Valley, MD 21031
(301) 667-7301
Primary Business: Spices, herbs,
  vegetable products
Chairman: Harry K. Wells
CEO: Harry K. Wells
President: Hillsman V. Wilson
Vice-President (Corporate
  Communications): John W. Felton
Vice-President (General Counsel):
  James J. Harrison, Jr.
Sales: $788.36 million
Net Worth: $261 million
# of Employees: 6,800

Divisions:
Food Service
Special Div.
Schilling Plant
TB Time Foods
International Group
Gilroy Foods
McCormick Properties, Inc.

Miscellaneous Facts: Incorporated in
  1915 in Maryland. Company is one of
  the largest spice makers in the United
  States.

MCILHENNY CO.
Avery Island, LA 70513
(318) 365-8173

Primary Business: Hot pepper sauce,
  Bloody Mary mix
President: Edward M. Simmons
Vice-President: Paul C. P. McIlhenny
Vice-President: E. P. Terrell III
# of Employees: 155

Miscellaneous Facts: Subsidiary of E.
  McIlhenny's Son Corp. Maker of
  Tabasco brand products.

MALT-O-MEAL CO.
2601 IDS Tower
Minneapolis, MN 55402
(612) 338-8551
Primary Business: Breakfast cereals
President: Glenn S. Brooks
Vice-President: Donovan Pautzke
Vice-President: John Lettman
Sales: $35 million
# of Employees: 250

MONFORT OF COLORADO, INC.
1930 AA Street Box G
Greeley, CO 80631
(303) 353-2311
Primary Business: Cattle products
Chairman: Roland L. Madelli
CEO: Kenneth Monfort
President: Kenneth Monfort
Group Vice-President (Beef Sales):
  Joseph H. Meilinger
Vice-President (Portion Food Sales):
  Robert B. Parris
Sales: $1.44 billion
Net Worth: $911 million
# of Employees: 3,561

Subsidiaries:
Monfort Energy Resources, Inc.
Monfort Food Distributing Co.
Monfort Foreign Sales Corp.
Monfort Transportation Co.
Summit Trading Co., Inc.
Weld Agricultural Credit, Inc.
Weld Insurance Co., Inc.

MORTON SALT DIV.
110 N Wacker Drive
Chicago, IL 60606
(312) 621-5200
Primary Business: Produces and sells salt
  for table use
President: W. E. Johnston, Jr.

Vice-President (Sales): J. F. Poe
Vice-President (Manufacturing): R. L.
  Pierdbon
Sales: $336 million
# of Employees: 3,400

Miscellaneous Facts: Division of Morton
  Thiokol, Inc.

MRS. FIELDS
333 Main Street
Park City, UT 84640
(801) 649-1304
Primary Business: Maker of cookies
Chairman: Randy Fields
President: Deborah Fields

MRS. PAUL'S KITCHENS, INC.
5830 Henry Avenue
Philadelphia, PA 19128
(215) 483-4000
Primary Business: Maker of prepared
  frozen foods
President: Richard J. Baker
Sales: $108 million

Miscellaneous Facts: Subsidiary of
  Campbell Soup Co.

MRS. SMITH'S FROZEN FOODS CO.
South and Charlotte streets
Pottstown, PA 19464
(215) 326-2600
Primary Business: Frozen pies and
  waffles
CEO: A. G. Langbow
President: A. G. Langbow
Senior Vice-President (Manufacturing):
  Littleton Johnson
Vice-President (Sales and Marketing):
  R. D. Bademan
# of Employees: 2,165

RJR NABISCO, INC.
Post Office Box 2959
Winston-Salem, NC 27102
(919) 773-2000
Primary Business: Tobacco & food
  products
Chairman of the Board: J. Tylee Wilson
CEO: J. Tylee Wilson
President: F. Ross Johnson
Vice-Chairman: Edward A. Horrigan,
  Jr.

Senior Vice-President (Human
  Resources): Rodney E. Austin
Senior Vice-President (Public Affairs):
  Marshall B. Bass
Sales: $16.6 billion
Net Worth: $6.4 billion
# of Employees: 147,513

Subsidiaries:
Beaulieu Vineyard
Nabisco Brands, Inc.
Planters & Life Savers
Del Monte Corp.
R.J. Reynolds Tobacco Co.
Madera Glass Co.
Zantigo Corp.
Bear Creek Corp.
Jackson & Perkins Co.
RJR Archer, Inc.
All Brand Importers, Inc.
Banana Processors, Inc.
HI Continental Corp.

Miscellaneous Facts: Incorporated in
  1970 in Delaware as R. J. Reynolds
  Industries, Inc. Present name adopted
  in 1986.

NABISCO BRANDS, INC.
Nabisco Brands Plaza
Parsippany, NJ 07054
(201) 898-7100
Primary Business: Nut products,
  margarine, other food products
Chairman: Robert M. Schaeberle
CEO: F. Ross Johnson
President: James O. Welch, Jr.
Senior Vice-President (Personnel):
  Andrew S. Barrett
Senior Vice-President (Corporate
  Affairs): Michael M. Masterpool
Revenue: $6.25 billion
# of Employees: 68,200

Subsidiary:
Nabisco Brands, Ltd.
Planters

Miscellaneous Facts: Subsidiary of RJR
  Nabisco, Inc.

NESTLE FOODS CORP.
100 Manhattenville Road
Purchase, NY 10577
(914) 251-3000
Primary Business: Chocolate bar

products, freeze-dried coffee
Chairman: James M. Biggar
CEO: C. A. MacDonald
President: C. A. MacDonald
Senior Vice-President: P. Kamber
Senior Vice-President: B. E. Gensamer
Vice-President (Human Resources):
  Robert Buritt
Sales: $1 billion
# of Employees: 6,000

Miscellaneous Facts: Subsidiary of Nestle
  Holdings, Inc.

THE NUTRASWEET CO.
Post Office Box 1111
Skokie, IL 60076
(312) 982-7000
Primary Business: Sugar substitute
  manufacturer
CEO: Robert B. Shapiro
President: Robert B. Shapiro
# of Employees: 1,026

Miscellaneous Facts: Subsidiary of
  Monsanto.

ORE-IDA FOODS CO., INC.
Post Office Box 10
Boise, ID 83707
(208) 383-6100
Primary Business: Frozen foods
President: Paul Cordory
Vice-President (Sales and Marketing):
  Dietmar Kluth
Vice-President (Human Resources):
  Donald E. Masterson, Jr.
Vice-President (Logistics): Lee
  Bonovrant
Sales: Over $500 million
# of Employees: 4,200

OSCAR MAYER & CO.
Post Office Box 7188
Madison, WI 53707
(608) 241-3311
Primary Business: Meat products
Chairman: Jerry M. Hiegel
CEO: Jerry M. Hiegel
President: James W. McVey
Vice-President (Consumer Affairs):
  Phyllis A. Lovrien
Group Vice-President (Marketing):
  Thomas F. Duesler

Vice-President (Personnel): Pat Richter
Revenue: $1.77 billion
# of Employees: 14,547

Miscellaneous Facts: Subsidiary of
  General Foods Corp.

PEPPERIDGE FARM, INC.
Post Office Box 5500
Norwalk, CT 06856
(203) 846-7000
Primary Business: Makes bakery
  products
President: W. A. Schmidt
Sales: $42.5 million

Miscellaneous Facts: Subsidiary of
  Campbell Soup Co.

PILLSBURY CO.
200 S Sixth Street
Minneapolis, MN 55402
(612) 330-4966
Primary Business: Prepared baking
  mixes, refrigerated dough products
Chairman: John M. Stafford
CEO: John M. Stafford
President: John M. Stafford
Executive Vice-President: J. Jeffrey
  Campbell
Senior Vice-President (Human
  Resources): Timothy Sullivan
Senior Vice-President: Richard T.
  Crowder
Revenue: $5.67 billion
Net Worth: $1.3 billion
# of Employees: 92,900

Subsidiaries:
Azteca Corn Products Corp.
Burger King Corp.
Fox Deluxe Pizza Co.
Green Giant Co.
Haagen-Dazs Co., Inc.
Jeno's Inc.
Pioneer Food Industries, Inc.
Pillsbury Grain Export, Inc.
Quik Wok
Sedvito Ice Cream Corp.
Steak & Ale Corp.
Totino's
Van de Kamp's Frozen Foods

Miscellaneous Facts: Some of the
  company brand names are Pillsbury,
  Green Giant, Hungry Jack, Totinos,

Haagen-Dazs, Van De Kamps, Jeno's Pizza, Chef Saluto, Figurines, Godfather's Pizza, and Quik Wok.

PROGRESSO FOODS CORP.
365 W Passaic Street
Rochelle Park, NJ 07662
(201) 368-9450
Markets Italian-style food products
CEO: Gaspar Taormina
# of Employees: 500

Miscellaneous Facts: Subsidiary of Ogden Corp.

QUAKER OATS CO.
Post Office Box 9001
Chicago, IL 60609
(312) 222-7111
Primary Business: Foods, pet foods
Chairman: William D. Smithburg
CEO: William D. Smithburg
President: Frank J. Morgan
Executive Vice-President (U.S. Foods): Hedric E. Rhodes
Vice-President (Human Resources): Lawrence Baytos
Vice-President (Corporate Affairs): Deborah E. Kelley
Sales: $334 billion
Net Worth: $786 million
# of Employees: 30,000

Subsidiaries:
Arden, Inc.
Golden Grain Macaroni, Inc.
Ardmore Farms
Liqui-Dey
Wolf Brand Products

Divisions:
SVC Div.
Ghirardelli Chocolate Co.
Mission Macaroni Div.
Vernell's Candy Co.
Grocery Specialties
Fisher-Price Div.
Specialty Retailing

Miscellaneous Facts: Some of the cereals made are Cap'n Crunch, Oh's, Life, Quaker Natural Cereals, Crunchy Nut and Honey Graham. Brand names include Aunt Jemima, Gatorade, Celeste, Kibbles 'n Bits, Ken-l Ration, Burger, Snausages and Fisher-Price. Incorporated in 1901 in New Jersey.

RAGU FOODS, INC.
33 Benedict Place
Greenwich, CT 06830
(203) 661-2000
Primary Business: Manufactures food products
President: Charles R. Perrin
# of Employees: 514

Miscellaneous Facts: Subsidiary of Cheesebrough-Pond's, Inc.

RALSTON PURINA CO.
Checkerboard Square
St. Louis, MO 63164
(314) 982-1000
Primary Business: Poultry and livestock feeds, dry dog and cat foods, cereals
Chairman: William P. Stiritz
CEO: William P. Stiritz
President: William P. Stiritz
Group Vice-President: P. H. Hatfield
Group Vice-President: W. H. Jones
Director, Human Resources: Robert Bell
Sales: $598 billion
Net Worth: $997 million
# of Employees: 70,000

Subsidiaries:
Van Camp Sea Food Co.
Bremner Biscuit Co.
Continental Baking Co., Inc.

Miscellaneous Facts: Founded in 1894. One of the largest producers of dry dog and dry, soft and moist cat food. One of the largest wholesalers of fresh bakery products in the U.S. Products include Almond Delight, Beancorn-Wheat Chex, Sun Flakes, Sun-Maid Hot Cereal, Rainbow Bright, Hostess Snacks, Grain Land, Happy Dog, Happy Kitten, Puppy Chow, Dog Chow, Cat Chow and G.I. Joe Action Figures.

SARA LEE CORP.
3 First National Plaza
Chicago, IL 60602
(312) 726-2600
Primary Business: Frozen desserts, processed meats, seafood
Chairman: John H. Beyan, Jr.
CEO: John H. Beyan, Jr.

President: Robert E. Elberson
Senior Vice-President (Human
  Resources): Joseph F. Neely
Vice-President (Corporate Affairs):
  Robert L. Laver
Sales: $8.1 billion
Net Worth: $999 million
# of Employees: 90,900

Subsidiaries:
Aris Isotoner, Inc.
Bali Co.
Chef Pierre, Inc.
The Fuller Brush Co.
Hollywood Brands, Inc.
The Jimmy Dean Meat Co., Inc.
Lyons Restaurants, Inc.
PYA/Monarch, Inc.
Popsille Industries, Inc.
Hanes DSD

Divisions:
Coach Leatherware
Kahn's & Co.
Gallo Salame
Hi-Brand Foods
Hillshire Farm Co.
Hanes Hosiery, Inc.
L'Eggs Products, Inc.

Miscellaneous Facts: Some of the
  company brand names are Gourmet
  Entree, Smoky Hollow, King Cotton,
  Martenn, Chef Pierre, Gallo Salame,
  Cook's Pantry, Hillshire Farm, Butter
  Nut, Pay Day, Jimmy Dean, Big
  Stick, Fruit-sicle, Fudgesicle, Popsicle,
  Rudy's Farm, Kayo, Aris, Isotoner,
  Hanes, Slenderalls, Today's Girl,
  Underalls, L'Eggs and Sheer
  Elegance. Incorporated in 1941 in
  Maryland as South Street Co. Present
  name adopted in 1985.

SENECA FOODS CORP.
74 Seneca Street
Dundee, NY 14837
(607) 243-7171
Primary Business: Canned fruits and
  vegetables
Chairman: A. S. Wolcott
CEO: A. S. Wolcott
President: J. G. Kayser
Executive Vice-President: F. W. Leick
Executive Vice-President: D. P. Naeye
Sales: $215 million
# of Employees: 1,500

Miscellaneous Facts: Subsidiary of S.S.
  Pierce Co., Inc.

J.M. SMUCKER CO.
Strawberry Lane
Orrville, OH 44667
(216) 682-0015
Primary Business: Preserves, jams,
  jellies, syrups
Chairman: Paul H. Smucker
CEO: Paul H. Smucker
President: Timothy P. Smucker
Executive Vice-President: Richard K.
  Smucker
Vice-President (Sales): Edwin Dountz
Vice-President (Personnel): Bruce E.
  Fike
Revenue: $230.93 million
Net Worth: $88 million
# of Employees: 1,400

Subsidiaries:
H.B. DeViney Co.
Mary Ellen, Inc.

STAR-KIST FOODS, INC.
582 Tuna Street
Terminal Island, CA 90731
(213) 548-4411
Primary Business: Tuna, sardines,
  anchovies
Chairman: Joseph J. Bogdanovich
CEO: Richard L. Beattie
President: Richard L. Beattie
Vice-President (Sales): Allyn A. Ayotte
Vice-President (Marketing—Pet Foods
  Div.): Will H. Gassett

Miscellaneous Facts: Subsidiary of H.J.
  Heinz Co.

STOUFFER FOODS
57550 Harper Road
Solon, OH 44139
(216) 248-3600
Primary Business: Frozen food
  manufacturer
President: Robert McGuigan

Miscellaneous Facts: Subsidiary of Nestle
  Holdings, Inc.

SUNKIST GROWERS, INC.
Post Office Box 7888
Van Nuys, CA 91409
(213) 986-4800
Primary Business: Fresh and processed
  oranges
Chairman: J. V. Newman
President: R. L. Hanlin
Vice-Chairman: D. E. Armstrong
Vice-Chairman: R. E. Bodine
Vice-Chairman: H. S. Chase
Sales Range: $700–$750 million
Net Worth: $58 million
# of Employees: 1,500

SWIFT INDEPENDENT PACKING CO.
115 W Jackson Boulevard
Chicago, IL 60604
(312) 431-3500
Primary Business: Holding company,
  beef, lamb and pork processing
Chairman: John A. Copeland
CEO: John A. Copeland
President: J. Douglas Gray
Senior Vice-President (Sales): William J.
  Zautcke
Senior Vice-President (Beef and Lamb):
  Richard C. Knight
Vice-President (Employee Relations):
  Harry A. Niese
Sales: $2.97 billion
Net Worth: $29 million
# of Employees: 6,500

THORN APPLE VALLEY, INC.
18700 W Ten Mile
Southfield, MI 48075
(313) 552-0700
Primary Business: Fresh pork products
Chairman of the Board: Henry S.
  Dorfman
CEO: Henry S. Dorfman
President: Joel Dorfman
Vice-Chairman: Allen Charivpski
Sales: $664.80 million
Net Worth: $33 million
# of Employees: 3,100

Subsidiaries:
Coast Refrigerated Trucking Co., Inc.
National Food Express, Inc.
Packer Security Patrol, Inc.
Thorn Apple Valley Foreign Sales Corp.
Wayne By-Products Co.

TILLAMOOK COUNTY CREAMERY
Post Office Box 313
Tillamook, OR 97141
(503) 842-4481
Primary Business: Cheese and fluid milk
Chairman of the Board: Edward Myers
President: Edward Myers
Vice-President: Rudolph Fenk
Treasurer: Robert L. Berkey
Sales: $66 million
# of Employees: 240

TYSON FOODS, INC.
2210 W Oaklawn Drive
Springdale, AR 72764
(501) 756-4000
Primary Business: Processed poultry
Chairman of the Board: Don Tyson
CEO: Don Tyson
President: Leland Tollett
Executive Vice-President: Gerald
  Johnston
Senior Vice-President (Sales): Donald
  E. Wray
Sales: $1.5 billion
Net Worth: $176 million
# of Employees: 24,000

Subsidiaries:
Coatal Rental & Rigging Corp.
Dixie Distributors, Inc.
Dixie Home Farms, Inc.
Howard County Foods, Inc.
Poultry Growers, Inc.
Tyson-Carolina, Inc.
Tyson Export Sales, Inc.
Tyson Express
Valmac Industries, Inc.

UNITED BRANDS CO.
1271 Avenue of the Americas
New York, NY 10020
(212) 307-2000
Primary Business: Diversified food, food
  processing
Chairman of the Board: Carl H. Linder
CEO: Carl H. Linder
President: Ronald F. Walker
Vice-President (Public Affairs): G.
  Burke Wright
Vice-President (Personnel): John R.
  Treadwell
Sales: $3.36 billion
Net Worth: $224 million
# of Employees: 42,000

Subsidiaries:
Chiquita Brands, Inc.
Vernors, Inc.
John Morrell & Co.
Bob Ostrow Co.
Partridge Meats, Inc.
Roberts & Oake, Inc.

VAN DE KAMP'S FROZEN FOODS
6621 E Pacific Coast Highway
Long Beach, CA 90803
(213) 544-4481
Primary Business: Frozen foods
President: Steven Pokress
Vice-President (Operations): Richard
  Koob
Vice-President (Sales): Peter Nolan
Vice-President (Purchasing): Bill
  Diederich
# of Employees: 400–500

VLASIC FOODS, INC.
33200 W 14 Mile Road
West Bloomfield, MI 48033
(313) 851-9400
Primary Business: Pickles, sauerkraut
Chairman: Robert J. Vlasic
CEO: J. R. Scales
President: J. R. Scales
Senior Vice-President: G. L. Hettich, Jr.
Senior Vice-President: William B.
  Nance

Miscellaneous Facts: Subsidiary of
  Campbell Soup Co.

**WEIGHT WATCHERS
  INTERNATIONAL, INC.**
800 Community Drive
Manhasset, NY 11030
(516) 627-9200
Primary Business: Conducts classes to
  reduce weight
Chairman: Albert Lippert
CEO: Charles M. Berger
President: Charles M. Berger
Vice-President (Franchise and
  Licensing): D. T. Fisher
Vice-President (Marketing and
  Operations): Lelio G. Parducci
Revenue: $78.30 million
# of Employees: 7,700

Miscellaneous Facts: Subsidiary of H.J.
  Heinz Co.

Candy and Snack Food Processing Firms

E.J. BRACH & SONS
4656 W Kinzie
Chicago, IL 60644
(312) 626-1200
Primary Business: Candy manufacturer
President: Ned E. Mitchell

Miscellaneous Facts: Subsidiary of
  American Home Products Corp.

CORNNUTS, INC.
10229 Pearmain Street
Oakland, CA 94603
(415) 632-0977
Primary Business: Toasted corn snacks
President: M. E. Holloway
Vice-President: R. K. Holloway
Sales Manager: Joe Heaney

EAGLE SNACKS, INC.
One Busch Place
St. Louis, MO 63118
(314) 587-3941
Primary Business: Makes snack foods
Chairman of the Board: John H. Purnell

Miscellaneous Facts: Subsidiary of
  Anheuser-Busch Companies, Inc.

FRITO-LAY, INC.
Frito-Lay Tower
Dallas, TX 75235
(214) 351-7000
Primary Business: Corn chips, potato
  chips, corn snacks
Chairman: Willard C. Korn
CEO: Willard C. Korn
President: Willard C. Korn
Senior Vice-President (Sales and
  Marketing): W. Leo Kiely III
Vice-President (Public Affairs): T. A.
  Fassburg
Vice-President (Personnel): John
  Varnson
Sales: $1 billion
# of Employees: 28,000

Miscellaneous Facts: Subsidiary of
  Pepsico., Inc.

GHIRARDELLI CHOCOLATE CO.
1111 139th Avenue
San Leandro, CA 94578
(415) 357-8400
Primary Business: Chocolate products
CEO: Dennis DeDomenico

Miscellaneous Facts: Division of The
Quaker Oats Co.

GODIVA CHOCOLATIER, INC.
450 Park Avenue
New York, NY 10022
(212) 486-8750
Primary Business: Candy manufacturer
President: Thomas A. Fey

Miscellaneous Facts: Subsidiary of
Campbell Soup Co.

GRANNY GOOSE FOODS, INC.
930 98th Avenue
Oakland, CA 94603
(415) 635-5400
Primary Business: Manufacturing of
potato chips and snacks
President: Wesley Felton
Vice-President (Marketing): Jim Clizbe
Sales: Over $50 million
# of Employees: 700

Miscellaneous Facts: Subsidiary of G.G.
Industries, Inc.

KEEBLER CO.
One Hollow Tree Lane
Elmhurst, IL 60125
(312) 833-2900
Primary Business: Cookies, crackers,
snacks
CEO: Thomas M. Garvin
President: Thomas M. Garvin
Senior Vice-President (Sales and
Distribution): William L. Daniels
Vice-President (Human Resources and
Services): John J. Kelly
Sales: $876.75 million
Net Worth: $154 million
# of Employees: 9,000

Bakeries:
Atlanta Bakery
Bluffton Bakery
Cincinnati Bakery
Denver Bakery

Grand Rapids Bakery
Macon Bakery
Van Nuys Bakery
Raleigh Bakery

LAURA SCUDDER'S, INC.
1525 N Raymond Avenue
Anaheim, CA 92801
(714) 772-5151
Primary Business: Snack foods, potato
chips
President: Joseph W. Halligan
Senior Vice-President (Marketing):
Frank Martin
Personnel Director: Norman Landsberg
Sales: Over $100 million
# of Employees: 1,200

LIFE SAVERS DIV.
6 Campus Drive
Parsippany, NJ 07054
(201) 898-7100
Primary Business: Candy manufacturer

Miscellaneous Facts: Division of RJR
Nabisco, Inc.

M&M/MARS
High Street
Hackettstown, NJ 07840
(201) 852-1000
President: Howard Walker
Senior Vice-President (Brands): J.
Langdon
Vice-President (Sales): P. B. Joyce

Miscellaneous Facts: Division of Mars,
Inc.

MOTHER'S CAKE & COOKIE CO.
810 81st Avenue
Oakland, CA 94621
(415) 569-2323
Primary Business: Cookies
Chairman: Pierre Jean Everaert
President: Michel Laverne
Vice-President (Sales): Robert A.
Curran
Vice-President (Manufacturing): Mark
Bernel
Sales: $80 million
# of Employees: 800

NALLEY'S FINE FOODS
3303 S 35th Street
Tacoma, WA 98411
(206) 383-1621
Primary Business: Potato chips and
other snack foods
CEO: J. William Petty
President: J. William Petty
Vice-President (Distribution): Larry
Hile
Vice-President (Marketing): Thomas C.
Tussing
Sales: $132 million
# of Employees: 800

PETER PAUL CADBURY, INC.
New Haven Road
Naugatack, CT 06770
(203) 729-0221
Primary Business: Confectionery
Chairman: Robert E. Ix
President: J. A. Hanlon
Vice-President (Marketing): D. Dawson
Vice-President (Sales): C. D. Trallo
# of Employees: 1,250

Miscellaneous Facts: Subsidiary of
Cadbury Schweppes Holdings, Inc.

PLANTERS
East Hanover, NJ 07936
(201) 884-0500
Primary Business: Nuts, nut products,
snacks
President: Fred Corrado
Vice-President (Sales): T. M. Finnigan
Vice-President (Marketing): R. B.
Trurenbrod
Director of Personnel: W. M. Jones
# of Employees: 1,200

Miscellaneous Facts: Subsidiary of
Nabisco Brands, Inc.

SEE'S CANDY SHOPS, INC.
210 El Camino Real
San Francisco, CA 94080
(415) 583-7307
Primary Business: Candy
Chairman: Warren E. Buffett
President: Charles N. Huggins
Vice-President and General Manager:
Richard Van Doren
Sales Range: $100–$110 million
# of Employees: 1,200

Miscellaneous Facts: Subsidiary of
Berkshire Hathaway, Inc.

SUNSHINE BISCUITS, INC.
245 Park Avenue
New York, NY 10167
(212) 880-4200
Primary Business: Biscuits, crackers,
cookies
CEO: Howard E. Fraga
President: Howard E. Fraga
Vice-President (Sales): John F. Klarich
Vice-President (Operations): Arthur G.
Murray
Vice-President (Marketing): Joseph P.
Simrany
Sales: $473 million
# of Employees: 4,850

Miscellaneous Facts: Subsidiary of
American Brands, Inc.

TOOTSIE ROLL INDUSTRIES, INC.
7401 S Cicero Avenue
Chicago, IL 60629
(312) 838-3400
Primary Business: Candy and other
confectionery products
Chairman: Melvin J. Gordon
CEO: Melvin J. Gordon
President: Ellen R. Gordon (Mrs.)
Vice-President (Manufacturing): John
Newlin, Jr.
Vice-President (Marketing and Sales):
Thomas E. Core
Revenue: $93.12 million
Net Worth: $53 million
# of Employees: 1,100

Subsidiaries:
Henry Eisen Advertising Agency, Inc.
The Sweets Co., Inc.
The Sweets Mix Co., Inc.
Tri International Co.
Tootsie Roll Express
Tootsie Roll–Latin America

TOPPS CHEWING GUM, INC.
254 36th Street
Brooklyn, NY 11232
(718) 768-8900
Primary Business: Chewing gum
Chairman of the Board: Arthur T.
Shorin

CEO: Arthur T. Shorin
Vice-President: Louis Walker
Vice-President (Sales): James
  McBrearty
Director, Human Resources: Bert Falk
Sales: $71 million
Net Worth: $22 million
# of Employees: 1,000

WM. WRIGLEY, JR., CO.
410 N Michigan Avenue
Chicago, IL 60611
(312) 644-2121
Primary Business: Chewing gum
CEO: William Wrigley

President: William Wrigley
Executive Vice-President: Bozdar
  Bulovic
Vice-President (Personnel): E. W.
  Swanson, Jr.
Vice-President (Marketing): Ronald O.
  Cox
Revenue: $590.53 million
Net Worth: $229 million
# of Employees: 5,600

Subsidiaries:
Amurol Products Co.
L.A. Dreyfus Co.
Four-Ten Corp.
The Northwestern Chemical Co.
Zeno Manufacturing Co.

HEALTH

Products

ABBOTT LABORATORIES
Abbott Park
North Chicago, IL 60064
(312) 937-6100
Primary Business: Health care products
Chairman: Robert A. Schoellhorn
CEO: Robert A. Schoellhorn
Executive Vice-President: Charles J. Aschauer, Jr.
Vice-President (Personnel): O. Ralph Edwards
Vice-President (Public Affairs): David C. Jones
Sales: $3.10 billion
Net Worth: $1.6 billion
# of Employees: 33,500

Divisions:
Abbott Diagnostic Div.
Abbott International Div.
Chemical & Agricultural Div.
Hospital Products Div.
Pharmaceutical Products Div.
Ross Laboratories Div.

Miscellaneous Facts: Incorporated March 6, 1900, in Illinois as Abbott Alkaloidal Co. Present name adopted in 1914.

AMERICAN CYANAMID CO.
One Cyanamid Plaza
Wayne, NJ 07470
(201) 831-2000
Primary Business: Medical, agricultural, consumer products
Chairman: George J. Sella, Jr.
CEO: George J. Sella, Jr.
President: George J. Sella, Jr.
Vice-Chairman: William A. Liffers
ExecutiveVice-President: Frank V. Atlee
Vice-President (Personnel): W. P. Brown
Sales: $3.86 billion
Net Worth: $1.6 billion
# of Employees: 39,000

Subsidiary:
Formica Corp.

Miscellaneous Facts: Incorporated in 1907 in Maine.

AMERICAN HOSPITAL SUPPLY CORP.
One American Plaza
Evanston, IL 60201
(312) 866-4000
Primary Business: Manufacturing medical supplies
Chairman: Karl D. Bays
President: Frank A. Ehrmann
Executive Vice-President: Robert J. Simmons
Vice-President (Personnel): Ralph V. Seaman, Jr.
Sales: $3.45 billion
Net Worth: $1.4 billion
# of Employees: 31,300

Divisions:
American Abbey Medical
American ACMI
American Convertors
American Critical Care
American General Health Care
American Micro Scan
American Physicians Service & Supply

BAXTER TRAVENOL LABORATORIES, INC.
One Baxter Parkway
Deerfield, IL 60015
(312) 948-2000
Primary Business: Diversified medical care products
Chairman: William B. Graham
CEO: Vernon R. Loucks, Jr.
President: Vernon R. Loucks, Jr.
Senior Vice-President and General Counsel: G. Marshall Abbey
Senior Vice-President (Scientific Affairs): Robert A. Patterson
Sales: $1.8 billion
Net Worth: $894 million
# of Employees: 32,000

Subsidiaries:
Omnis Surgical, Inc.
Travenol International, Inc.
Travenol Labs, Inc.
Travenol International Services

Divisions:
Compucare, Inc.
Dayton Flexible Products Div.
Americas and Pacific Div.
Hospital Products Div.

Miscellaneous Facts: Incorporated in
1931 in Delaware as Baxter
Laboratories, Inc. Present name
adopted in 1976.

BECTON, DICKENSIN & CO.
Mack Centre Drive
Paramus, NJ 07652
(201) 967-3700
Primary Business: Health care products
Chairman: Wesley J. Howe
CEO: Wesley J. Howe
President: Wesley J. Howe
Vice-Chairman: Henry P. Becton
Senior Vice-President: Raymond V.
Gilmartin
Executive Vice-President: Photios T.
Paulson
Sales: $1.2 billion
Net Worth: $606 million
# of Employees: 17,600

Miscellaneous Facts: Incorporated in
1906 in New Jersey.

BERGEN BRUNSWIG CORP.
1900 Avenue of the Stars
Los Angeles, CA 90067
(213) 879-4991
Primary Business: Wholesale distributor
of health care products
Chairman: Emil P. Martini, Jr.
CEO: Emil P. Martini, Jr.
President: Robert E. Martini
Executive Vice-President: Dwight A.
Steffenson
Senior Vice-President: John Calasibetta
Vice-President (Human Resources):
Jerold O. Gutman
Sales: $1.7 billion
Net Worth: $139 million
# of Employees: 3,365

Subsidiaries:
Bergen Brunswig Drug Co.
Syntex Corp.
Syntex Dental Products, Inc.

Miscellaneous Facts: Incorporated in
1956 as Essex Drug Co. Present name
adopted in 1969.

BINDLEY WESTERN INDUSTRIES
4212 W 71st Street
Indianapolis, IN 46268
(317) 298-9900
Primary Business: Wholesale drug
distributor
Chairman: W. E. Bindley
President: W. E. Bindley
Vice-President: D. W. Swaim
Vice-President: S. L. Asher
Sales: $566.68 million
Net Worth: $35 million
# of Employees: 48

Subsidiary:
Bindley Western Drug Co., Inc.

JOHNSON & JOHNSON
Johnson & Johnson Plaza
New Brunswick, NJ 08933
(201) 524-0400
Primary Business: Pharmaceuticals,
medical devices
Chairman: James E. Burke
CEO: James E. Burke
President: David R. Clare
Vice-President (Public Relations):
Lawrence G. Foster
General Counsel: George S. Frazza
Vice-President (Finance): J. C. Walcott
Sales: $6.12 billion
Net Worth: $3.92 billion
# of Employees: 77,400

Subsidiaries:
Johnson & Johnson Cardiovascular
Chicopee
Codman & Shurtleff, Inc.
Critikon, Inc.
Devro, Inc.
Ethicon, Inc.
Iolab Corp.
Janssen Pharmaceutica, Inc.
Johnson & Johnson Baby Products Co.
McNeil Consumer Products Co.
Noramco, Inc.

Ortho Diagnostic Systems, Inc.
Personal Products Co.
Pitman-Moore, Inc.
Vistakon, Inc.

Miscellaneous Facts: Founded in 1885 by
Robert Wood Johnson, James Wood
Johnson, Edward Mead Johnson.
Incorporated in 1887. Some of the
products made by company are Band-
Aid Brand products, Tylenol,
Johnson's Baby Shampoo, Stayfree
Maxi-pads, Reach Toothbrushes,
Micatin, Act Floride Rinse, Sine-Aid,
Sure and Nature and Assure.
Company toll-free consumer number
is (800) 526-2433. Company is one of
the largest health care companies in
the U.S.

ELI LILLY & CO.
Lilly Corporate Center
Indianapolis, IN 46285
(317) 261-2000
Primary Business: Manufactures and
sells health products
Chairman: Richard D. Wood
CEO: Richard D. Wood
President: Richard D. Wood
Vice-Chairman: Thomas H. Lake
Executive Vice-President: Cornelius W.
Peitinga, PhD.
Executive Vice-President: Thomas A.
Klingaman
Sales: $3.3 billion
Net Worth: $2.3 billion
# of Employees: 28,700

Subsidiaries:
Advanced Cardiovascular Systems, Inc.
Cardiac Pacemakers, Inc.
Eli Lilly International Corp.
Eli Lilly & Co., Inc.
Elizabeth Arden, Inc.
ELCO Management

MC KESSON CORP.
One Post Street
San Francisco, CA 94104
(415) 983-8300
Primary Business: Drug and health care
Chairman: Neil E. Harlan
CEO: Neil E. Harlan
President: Thomas W. Field, Jr.

Vice-President (Finance): Alan
Seelenfreund
Vice-President (Personnel): James I.
Johnston
Vice-President (Corporate Relations):
Marvin L. Krasnansk
Sales: $6.3 billion
Net Worth: $696 million
# of Employees: 17,200

Subsidiaries:
ZI Brands, Inc.
Mohawk Liqueur Corp.
Alhambra National Water Co.
Sparkletts Drinking Water Corp.
Armor All Products Corp.
Tawn.Co.
McKesson International
McKesson Beverage Group
McKesson Drug Co.
Spectro Industries, Inc.

Miscellaneous Facts: Incorporated in
1928 in Maryland as McKesson &
Robbins, Inc. Present name adopted
in 1984.

MERCK & CO., INC.
126 E Lincoln Avenue
Rahway, NJ 07065
(201) 574-4000
Primary Business: Produces products for
restoration of health
Chairman: P. Roy Vagelos, M.D.
CEO: P. Roy Vagelos, M.D.
President: P. Roy Vagelos, M.D.
Executive Vice-President: John E.
Lyons
Senior Vice-President (Human Health):
Jerry T. Jackson
Vice-President (Human Resources):
Walter R. Trosin
Sales: $3.5 billion
Net Worth: $2.8 billion
# of Employees: 30,900

Subsidiaries:
Calgon Corp.
Hubbard Farms, Inc.
Merck Sharp & Dohme, Inc.

Divisions:
Kello
MSD Agvet Div.

Miscellaneous Facts: One of the largest
prescription drug makers in the U.S.

Merck scientists discovered vitamin B_{12}.

MILES LABORATORIES, INC.
1127 Myrtle Street
Elkhart, IN 46515
(219) 264-8111
Primary Business: Antacid tablets, vitamins
Chairman: Klaus H. Risse
CEO: Klaus H. Risse
President: Richard B. Kocher
Honorary Chairman: Walter A. Compton
Executive Vice-President: George E. Davy
Executive Vice-President: Gero D. Mueller
Sales: $1.2 billion
Net Worth: $500 million
# of Employees: 12,000

Divisions:
Consumer Healthcare Div.
Household Products Div.
Miles Laboratories, Inc.
Miles Scientific
Bayvet Div.
Dental Products

Miscellaneous Facts: Subsidiary of Bayer USA.

PFIZER, INC.
235 E 42nd Street
New York, NY 10017
(212) 573-2323
Primary Business: Manufactures health care products
Chairman: E. T. Pratt, Jr.
CEO: E. T. Pratt, Jr.
President: G. D. Laubach
Vice-President (Personnel): Bruce R. Ellig
Vice-President (Public Affairs): Robert L. Shafer
Sales: $4.03 billion
Net Worth: $2.9 billion
# of Employees: 39,200

Subsidiaries:
Composite Metal Products, Inc.
Pfizer International, Inc.
Pfizer Hospital Products Group
Quigley Co., Inc.

Shiley, Inc.
Valley Lab, Inc.

Miscellaneous Facts: Incorporated in 1942 in Delaware as Charles Pfizer & Co., Inc. Present name adopted in 1970.

SCHERING-PLOUGH CORP.
One Geralda Farms
Madison, NJ 07940
(201) 822-7000
Primary Business: Ethical pharmaceutical products
Chairman: Robert P. Luciano
CEO: Robert P. Luciano
President: Robert P. Luciano
Executive Vice-President (Consumer Operations): R. Lee Jenkins
Senior Vice-President (Public Affairs): Allan S. Kushen
Senior Vice-President (Human Resources): Stephen F. Byrd
Sales: $1.87 billion
Net Worth: $1.5 billion
# of Employees: 23,800

Subsidiaries:
American Scientific Labs
Maybelline Co.

Operating Units:
Schering International
Schering Research
Schering Animal Health
Consumer Operations
Wesley-Jessen

G. D. SEARLE & CO.
Post Office Box 1045
Skokie, IL 60076
(312) 982-7000
Primary Business: Prescription and consumer pharmaceuticals
Chairman: Donald H. Rumsfeld
CEO: Donald H. Rumsfeld
President: John E. Robson
Vice-President (President Nutra Sweet Group): Robert B. Shapiro
Vice-President (Corporate Relations): William I. Greener, Jr.
Sales: $1.24 billion
# of Employees: 15,200

SMITHKLINE BECKMAN CORP.
One Franklin Plaza
Philadelphia, PA 19101
(215) 751-4000
Primary Business: Ethical and
  proprietary pharmaceutical products
Chairman: Robert F. Dee
CEO: Henry Wendt
President: Henry Wendt
Vice-President (Corporate Affairs):
  Thomas M. Collins
Vice-President (Personnel): Peter
  Hickman
Sales: $2.95 billion
Net Worth: $2.3 billion
# of Employees: 30,500

Miscellaneous Facts: Incorporated in
  1929 in Pennsylvania.

SQUIBB CORP.
Post Office Box 4000
Princeton, NJ 08540
(609) 921-4000
Primary Business: Prescription and
  nonprescription pharmaceuticals
Chairman: Richard M. Furland
CEO: Richard M. Furland
President: Dennis C. Fill
Executive Vice-President: Charles A.
  Sanders
Senior Vice-President (General
  Counsel): Daniel A. Cuoco
Senior Vice-President (Human
  Resources): Robert E. Humes
Sales: $1.88 billion
Net Worth: $1.4 billion
# of Employees: 24,100

Subsidiaries:
Medical Products Group
Advanced Technology Laboratories
Spacelabs, Inc.
Edward Weck & Co., Inc.
Charles of the Ritz Group, Ltd.
E.R. Squibb & Sons, Inc.

STERLING DRUG, INC.
90 Park Avenue
New York, NY 10016
(212) 907-2000
Primary Business: Pharmaceutical
  products
Chairman: John M. Pietruski
CEO: John M. Pietruski

President: James G. Andrews
Vice-President (Medical Affairs):
  George S. Goldstein
Vice-President (Corporate Planning):
  Robert J. Hennessey
Vice-President (Licensing): Bradley G.
  Lorimier
Sales: $1.83 billion
Net Worth: $936 million
# of Employees: 27,336

Groups:
Sterling Chemical Group
Lehn & Fink Products Group
Sterling International
Sterling Pharmaceutical Group

THORATEC LABORATORIES CORP.
2023 Eighth Street
Berkeley, CA 94710
(415) 841-1213
Primary Business: Medical devices for
  blood conservation
Chairman: Robert J. Harvey
CEO: Robert J. Harvey
President: John E. Chester
Executive Vice-President: Louis A.
  McKellar
Sales: $2.4 billion
# of Employees: 50

THE UPJOHN CO.
7000 Portage Road
Kalamazoo, MI 49001
(616) 323-4000
Primary Business: Pharmaceuticals
Chairman: R. T. Parfet, Jr.
CEO: R. T. Parfet, Jr.
President: Lawrence C. Hoff
Vice-Chairman: Dr. Theodore Cooper
Vice-President: W. L. Parfet
Vice-President (Personnel): Cass S.
  Hough
Sales: $2 billion
Net Worth: $1.8 billion
# of Employees: 20,600

Subsidiary:
Asgrow Seed Co.

WARNER-LAMBERT CO.
201 Tabor Road
Morris Plains, NJ 07950
(201) 540-2000

Primary Business: Health care products
Chairman: Joseph D. Williams
CEO: Joseph D. Williams
President: Melvin R. Goodes
Senior Vice-President: Robert J. Dircks
Vice-President (Public Affairs): Ronald E. Zier
Vice-President (Human Resources): Raymond E. Fino
Sales: $3.2 billion
Net Worth: $891 million
# of Employees: 33,000

Divisions:
American Chicle Group
Consumer Health Products
Parke-Davis

Miscellaneous Facts: Incorporated in 1920 in Delaware as William R. Warner & Co. Present name adopted in 1970. Company toll-free consumer number is (800) 223-0423.

Services

AMERICAN MEDICAL INTERNATIONAL, INC.
414 N Camden Drive
Beverly Hills, CA 90210
(213) 278-6200
Primary Business: Operates hospitals and related services
Chairman: Royce Diener
CEO: Walter L. Weisman
President: Walter L. Weisman
Executive Vice-President: R. Bruce Andrews
Executive Vice-President: Charles P. Reilly
Personnel Director: Linda Carver
Sales: $2.42 billion
Net Worth: $795 million
# of Employees: 40,000

Subsidiaries:
AMI Ambulatory Centers, Inc.
AMI Food & Nutrition Management, Inc.
AMI Psychiatric Services
Eastern Professional Properties
Professional Hospital Services
Stat Records, Inc.

Hospitals:
Anaheim General Hospital

Bellaire General Hospital
Medical Arts Hospital of Dallas
Park Plaza Hospital
Riverside Hospital
St. Mary's Hospital

Miscellaneous Facts: Incorporated in 1976 in Delaware as successor to company incorporated in California in 1956. Name changed to American Medical Enterprises, Inc., in 1965. Present name adopted in 1972.

BEVERLY ENTERPRISES
873 S Fair Oaks Avenue
Pasadena, CA 91105
(818) 577-6111
Primary Business: Operates health care facilities
Chairman: Robert Van Tuyle
CEO: Robert Van Tuyle
President: David R. Banks
Executive Vice-President: Charles Jordan
Executive Vice-President: William M. Wright
Personnel Director: Tom O'Malley
Sales: $1.4 billion
Net Worth: $434 million
# of Employees: 85,500

CHARTER MEDICAL CORP.
577 Mulberry Street
Macon, GA 31201
(912) 742-1161
Primary Business: Hospital management company
Chairman: W. A. Fickling, Jr.
CEO: W. A. Fickling, Jr.
President: Ray Stevenson
Executive Vice-President: James T. McAfee
Vice-President (Human Resources): Robert C. Miller
Sales: $493 million
Net Worth: $380 million
# of Employees: 7,300

COMPREHENSIVE CARE CORP.
18551 Von Karmen Avenue
Irvine, CA 92715
(714) 851-2273
Primary Business: Health care management

Chairman: B. Lee Karns
CEO: B. Lee Karns
President: Richard A. Santoni, Ph.D.
Vice-Chairman: William James Nilol
Personnel Director: Steve Toth
Sales: $190 million
Net Worth: $133 million
# of Employees: 3,800

Subsidiaries:
Quanta Systems Corp.
Robintech, Inc.

GOODWILL INDUSTRIES OF AMERICA, INC.
9200 Wisconsin Avenue
Bethesda, MD 20814
(301) 530-6500
Primary Business: National
   representation, rehabilitation service
   programs
Chairman: F. Lloyd Smith
CEO: David M. Cooney
President: David M. Cooney
Vice-Chairman: Henry J. Ullmann
Vice-President: Joseph E. Pouliot
Sales: $3.99 million
# of Employees: 55

HOSPITAL CORP. OF AMERICA
One Park Plaza
Nashville, TN 37203
(615) 327-9551
Primary Business: Hospital management
   company
Chairman: Thomas F. Frist, Jr.
CEO: Thomas F. Frist, Jr.
President: R. Clayton McWhorter
Vice-Chairman: David G. Williamson,
   Jr.
Senior Vice-President (Public Affairs):
   Samuel H. Howard
Senior Vice-President (Health Plans):
   Joseph C. Hutts, Jr.
Sales: $4.18 billion
Net Worth: $1.7 billion
# of Employees: 100,000

Subsidiaries:
Allied Clinical Laboratories
Ambulatory Services, Inc.
The Center for Health Studies, Inc.
HCA Management Co.
HCA International Co.
HCA Psychiatric

Medic One
Parthenon Insurance Co.
Shepard Ambulance, Inc.
Spokane Ambulance Corp.

Miscellaneous Facts: Manages 240
   hospitals across the country.
   Incorporated in 1960 in Tennessee as
   Park View Hospital, Inc. Present
   name adopted in 1968. Pays its
   employees to keep fit by giving them
   cash for every mile they jog, every lap
   they swim and more. It is one of the
   largest profit-making hospital
   companies in the United States. 80
   percent of employees are women.

HUMANA, INC.
500 W Main Street
Louisville, KY 40202
(502) 580-1000
Primary Business: Hospital services
Chairman: David A. Jones
CEO: David A. Jones
President: Wendell Cherry
Senior Executive Vice-President: Carl F.
   Pollard
Vice-President (Human Resources):
   Michael R. Smith
Vice-President (Public Affairs): George
   L. Atkins
Sales: $2.87 billion
Net Worth: $903 million
# of Employees: 43,800

Subsidiaries:
A.C. Medical, Inc.
ARE, Inc.
Allenmore Community Hospital, Inc.
Allied Health Group, Inc.
House Calls of America, Inc.
American Medicorp. Development Co.

MANOR CARE, INC.
10750 Columbia Pike
Silver Spring, MD 20901
(301) 681-9400
Primary Business: Health care services
Chairman: Stewart Bainum
CEO: Stewart Bainum
President: C. Arnold Renschler
Vice-Chairman: Steward Bainum, Jr.
Senior Vice-President: James H. Rempe
Vice-President (Human Resources):
   John Robertson

Sales: $482 million
Net Worth: $173 million
# of Employees: 17,600

Subsidiaries:
Manor Healthcare Corp.
Quality Inns, Inc.
Quality Inns International, Inc.

NATIONAL MEDICAL ENTERPRISES, INC.
11620 Wilshire Boulevard
Los Angeles, CA 90025
(213) 479-5526
Primary Business: Operates hospitals
Chairman: Richard K. Eamer

CEO: Richard K. Eamer
President: Leonard Cohen
Senior Executive Vice-President: John C. Bedrosian
Vice-President (Communications): Paul J. Russell
Senior Vice-President (Human Resources): Alan R. Ewalt
Sales: $3.6 billion
Net Worth: $1.01 billion
# of Employees: 68,000

Miscellaneous Facts: Owns or operates more than 275 hospitals and psychiatric and nursing facilities across the country.

HEAVY EQUIPMENT

ALLIS-CHALMERS CORP.
Post Office Box 512
Milwaukee, WI 53201
(414) 475-2000
Primary Business: Designs process
control equipment
Chairman: David C. Scott
CEO: W. F. Bcuchc
President: W. F. Bueche
Vice-President: Richard Bueche
Vice-President: C. W. Parker, Jr.
Personnel Director: John Eckl
Sales: $ 1.32 billion
Net Worth: $71 million
# of Employees: 12,700

Subsidiaries:
A-C ESD, Inc.
A-C Hydro, Inc.
A-C Pumps, Inc.
Hartman Material Handling Systems,
Inc.

Miscellaneous Facts: Incorporated in
1913 in Delaware as Allis-Chalmers
Manufacturing Co. Present name
adopted in 1971.

AUTOMATIC TOLL SYSTEMS
144 Kingsbridge Road
Mount Vernon, NY 10550
(914) 699-7000
Primary Business: Makes toll-collecting
equipment
President: Herman Lopata
Sales: $37 million
# of Employees: 240

Miscellaneous Facts: Subsidiary of Basix
Corp.

BEARINGS, INC.
3600 Euclid Avenue
Post Office Box 6925
Cleveland, OH 44101
(216) 881-2828
Primary Business: Makes ball and roller
bearings
Chairman: J. R. Cunin
CEO: J. R. Cunin
President: George L. LaMore

Vice-President (Sales): Fred L. Mohr
Vice-President: Thomas L. Bradley
Sales: $496 million
Net Worth: $127 million
# of Employees: 3,294

Subsidiaries:
Bruening Bearings, Inc.
Dixie Bearings, Inc.

Miscellaneous Facts: Incorporated in
1928 in Delaware as Brown Fence &
Wire Co.

CATERPILLAR TRACTOR CO.
100 NE Adams Street
Peoria, IL 61629
(309) 675-1000
CEO: G. A. Schaefer
President: P. P. Donis
Executive Vice-President: D. U. Fites
Executive Vice-President: D. S. Gould
Vice-President (Personnel): James K.
Ward
Sales: $6.57 billion
Net Worth: $2.8 billion
# of Employees: 58,000

Subsidiaries:
Caterpillar Americas Co.
Caterpillar Capital Co., Inc.
Caterpillar Finance Corp.
Catex Three, Inc.
Solar Turbines International Co.
Towmotor Corp.

Miscellaneous Facts: Incorporated in
1925 in California.

CHICAGO PNEUMATIC TOOL CO.
6 E 44th Street
New York, NY 10017
(212) 850-6800
Primary Business: Maker of air and gas
compressors
CEO: T. P. Latimer
President: T. P. Latimer
Vice-President: R. T. Brandifino
Vice-President (Personnel): J. J. Carey
Sales: $411 million
Net Worth: $133 million
# of Employees: 4,569

Subsidiaries:
Hennessy Industries
Solar Industries, Inc.
Allen Manufacturing Co.
Dynapar Corp.
The Partlow Corp.

CINCINNATI MILACRON, INC.
4701 Marburg Avenue
Cincinnati, OH 45209
(513) 841-8100
Primary Business: Process equipment
  manufacturer
Chairman: James A. D. Geier
CEO: James A. D. Geier
President: C. R. Meyer
Vice-President: Daniel J. Meyer
Vice-President (Human Resources):
  Theodore Mauser
Sales: $660 million
Net Worth: $312 million
# of Employees: 9,707

Subsidiaries:
Cincinnati Milacron-Heald Corp.
L.K. Tool U.S.A., Inc.

CLARK EQUIPMENT CO.
Post Office Box 7008
100 N Michigan Street
South Bend, IN 46634
(219) 239-0100
Primary Business: Heavy equipment
Chairman: James R. Rinehart
CEO: James R. Rinehart
President: James R. Rinehart
Executive Vice-President: L. J.
  McKeenan
Executive Vice-President: F. M. Sims
Senior Vice-President: T. C. Clarke
Sales: $1 billion
Net Worth: $510 million
# of Employees: 12,974

Subsidiary:
Clark Equipment Credit Corp.

Business Groups:
Clark Automative Products Corp.
Clark Components International
Clark Distributions Services Co.
Clark Michigan Co.
Clark Telecommunications
Melroe Co.

COOPER INDUSTRIES, INC.
Post Office Box 4446
Houston, TX 77210
(713) 739-5400
Primary Business: Engines, turbines,
  pumps
Chairman: Robert Cizik
CEO: Robert Cizik
President: Robert Cizik
Vice-President (Personnel): Laurence
  H. Polsky
Vice-President (Public Affairs): Thomas
  W. Campbell
Vice-President and General Counsel:
  Edgar A. Bircher
Sales: $2.03 billion
Net Worth: $1.2 billion
# of Employees: 30,370

Divisions:
Arrow Hart
Bussmann Div.
Midwest Electric Div.
New England Die Casting, Inc.
Metalux Lighting
Cooper Air Tools
McGraw-Edison Service Div.

DEERE & CO.
John Deere Road
Moline, IL 61265
(309) 752-8000
Primary Business: Farm and industrial
  tractors
Chairman: Robert A. Hanson
CEO: Robert A. Hanson
President: Boyd C. Bartlett
Vice-President (Corporate
  Communications): Chester K. Lasell
Vice-President (General Counsel):
  Robert W. Weeks
Sales: $4.40 billion
Net Worth: $2.2 billion
# of Employees: 43,011

Subsidiaries:
John Deere Credit Co.
John Deere Insurance Co.
Capen, Frank, Proctor & Bowles, Inc.
Farm Plan Corp.
John Deere Co.
Ruck River Insurance Co.
Tahoe Insurance Co.

Divisions:
John Deere Co., Minneapolis

John Deere Engine Works
John Deere Foundry
John Deere Harvester Works
John Deere Plow & Planter Works
John Deere Tractor Works

Miscellaneous Facts: Incorporated in
1958 in Delaware, as John
Deere–Delaware Co. Present name
adopted in 1959.

DRESSER INDUSTRIES, INC.
1505 Elm Street
Dallas, TX 75201
(214) 740-6000
Primary Business: Supplies equipment to
energy industry
Chairman: J. J. Murphy
CEO: J. J. Murphy
President: J. J. Murphy
Executive Vice-President: Bill D. St.
John
Vice-President (Human Resources): G.
Leeson
Senior Vice-President: W. E. Bradford
Sales: $3.7 billion
Net Worth: $1.8 billion
# of Employees: 29,600

Subsidiaries:
Dresser Leasing Corp.
Reliance Standard Life Insurance Co.
Dresser Transportation Services Co.

EMHART CORP.
Post Office Box 2730
Hartford, CT 06101
(203) 678-3000
Primary Business: Maker of hardware
and machinery products
Chairman: Peter L. Scott
CEO: Peter L. Scott
President: WIlliam C. Lichtenfels
Vice-President (Human Resources):
Royal E. Cowles
Senior Vice-President
(Communications): John F. Budd, Jr.
Sales: $1.7 billion
Net Worth: $609 million
# of Employees: 30,422

Subsidiaries:
Emhart Industries, Inc.
D.O.M. Security Locks, Inc.
Kwikset Corp.

Notifier Co.
Mite Co.
U.S.M. Credit Corp.

Divisions:
Mallory Timers Div.
Amatron Div.
Textron, Inc.
True Temper Hardware Div.
True Temper Sports Div.
Bostik Industrial Div.

Miscellaneous Facts: Incorporated in
1976 in Virginia.

FMC CORP.
200 E Randolph Drive
Chicago, IL 60601
(312) 861-6000
Primary Business: Agricultural
chemicals, equipment
Chairman: Robert H. Malott
CEO: Robert H. Malott
President: Raymond C. Tower
Vice-President and General Counsel:
Patrick J. Head
Public Relations Director: Patricia D.
Brozowski
Director, Human Resources: Lawrence
E. Holleran
Sales: $3.34 billion
Net Worth: $1.68 billion
# of Employees: 27,000

Divisions:
FMC Finance Corp.
Alkali Chemicals Div.
Fluid Control Div.
Wellhead Equipment Div.
Beverage Equipment Div.
Airline Equipment Div.
Fire Apparatus Div.
Sweeper Div.
Turbo Pump Operations

THE FOXBORO CO.
38 Neponset Avenue
Foxboro, MA 02035
(617) 543-8750
Primary Business: Heavy equipment
Chairman: Earle W. Pitt
CEO: Earle W. Pitt
Executive Vice-President: Charles A.
McKay
Vice-President: Gerald H. Gleason

Sales: $572 million
Net Worth: $259 million
# of Employees: 10,000

INGERSOLL-RAND CO.
200 Chestnut Ridge Road
Woodcliff Lake, NJ 07675
(201) 573-0123
Primary Business: Maker of machinery
  and related products
Chairman: T. A. Holmes
CEO: T. A. Holmes
Executive Vice-President: J. E. Perrella
Executive Vice-President: R. D.
  Wendeborn
Vice-President (Human Resources): R.
  G. Repston
Sales: $2.6 billion
Net Worth: $1.03 billion
# of Employees: 34,740

Subsidiaries:
California Pellet Mill Co.
Air Power Equipment Corp.
I-R Enhanced Recovery
I-R Oilfield Products Co.
I-R Research, Inc.
Ingersoll-Rand Air Sales
Mining Machinery Group
Northern Research Engineering Group
Roconeco
Schlage Lock Co.
Sier Bath Gear Co.
Terry Corp.

Miscellaneous Facts: Incorporated in
  1905 in New Jersey as a combination
  of Ingersoll-Sergeant Drill Co. and the
  Rand Drill Co.

JOY MANUFACTURING CO.
One Oxford Center
301 Grant Street
Pittsburgh, PA 15219
(412) 562-4500
Primary Business: Heavy equipment
  manufacturer
Chairman: A. William Calder
CEO: A. William Calder
President: A. William Calder
Vice-President: Joseph J. Bellas
Vice-President (Human Resources): J.
  R. Glansdrop
Sales: $800 million
Net Worth: $443 million
# of Employees: 7,900

PARKER HANNIFIN CORP.
17325 Euclid Avenue
Cleveland, OH 44112
(216) 531-3000
Primary Business: Components for
  hydraulic power systems
Chairman: Patrick S. Parker
CEO: Paul G. Schoemer
President: Paul G. Schoemer
Vice-Chairman: D. S. Manning
Vice-President (Human Resources):
  John L. Hanson
Director, Communications Services: K.
  Strauss
Sales: $1.46 billion
Net Worth: $577 million
# of Employees: 22,167

Divisions:
Aerospace Hydraulic Div.
Control Systems Div.
Automative Connectors Div.
Clamp Div.
Cliff Impact Div.
Parker Fluidpower Group
Racor Div.
Rotary Actuator Div.
Parker Intercontinental Group

THE TIMKEN CO.
1835 Oveber Avenue, SW
Canton, OH 44706
(216) 438-3000
Primary Business: Tapered Roller
  Bearings
Chairman: W. R. Timken, Jr.
President: J. F. Toot, Jr.
Vice-President (Steel Operations): A. B.
  Glossbrenner
Vice-President (Bearing Operations): P.
  J. Ashton
Vice-President (Communications): D. L.
  Hart
Sales: $1.2 billion
Net Worth: $789 million
# of Employees: 17,764

Subsidiary:
Latrobe Steel Co.

Miscellaneous Facts: Incorporated in
  1904 in Ohio as Timken Roller
  Bearing Axle Co. Present name
  adopted in 1970.

HOME AND OFFICE PRODUCTS AND SERVICES

Products

AVERY INTERNATIONAL
150 N Orange Grove Boulevard
Post Office Box 7090
Pasadena, CA 91103
(818) 304-2000
Primary Business: Self-adhesive labels, office products
Chairman: Charles D. Miller
President: Richard J. Dearson
Senior Vice-President: C. W. Clemen
Vice-President (Human Resources): Karl J. Klein
Sales: $913.02 million
Net Worth: $270 million
# of Employees: 8,774

Subsidiaries:
Avery Label Co.
Soabar

Divisions:
Aigner Co.
Fasson Reflective Products
Fasson Roll Materials

Miscellaneous Facts: Incorporated in 1977 in Delaware as successor to Avery Adhesive Label Corp., incorporated in 1946 in California. Name changed in 1964 to Avery Products Corp. Present name adopted in 1976.

BORG-WARNER CORP.
200 S Michigan Avenue
Chicago, IL 60604
(312) 322-8500
Primary Business: Maker of industrial equipment, air-conditioners
Chairman: James F. Bere
President: C. E. Johnson
Executive Vice-President: Leonard A. Harvey
Executive Vice-President: Robert E. LaRoche

Vice-President (Communication): Robert A. Morris
Sales: $3.91 billion
Net Worth: $1.6 billion
# of Employees: 75,000

Subsidiaries:
Creon Life Insurance Co.
Borg-Warner Industrial Prod. Co.
B-W Automotive
Automotive Components Headquarters
Borg & Beck Transmission Components
Baker Industries, Inc.
Wells Fargo Armored Service Corp.
Pony Express Courier Corp.
Pyrotronics

Miscellaneous Facts: Incorporated in 1978 as successor to company with the same name incorporated in 1967.

KELLY-MOORE PAINT CO., INC.
987 Commercial Street
San Carlos, CA 94070
(415) 592-8337
Primary Business: Paints
Chairman: William E. Moore
President: Joseph P. Cristiano
Vice-President (Sales): Frank L. Skaggs
Vice-President (Paint Store Operations): John M. DeLong
Sales: $136 million
# of Employees: 1,275

MOORE BUSINESS FORMS, INC.
1205 Milwaukee Avenue
Glenview, IL 60025
(312) 480-3000
Primary Business: Business forms and systems
Chairman: D. W. Barr
President: Judson W. Sinclair
Vice-President (Sales and Marketing): J. R. Anderluh
Vice-President (Human Resources): J. A. Heist
Vice-President (Research): J. L. Wilson

Sales: $1.4 billion
# of Employees: 14,558

Divisions:
Moore Business Products Catalog
Moore Business Systems
Moore Data Management Systems
Rediform Office Products
Response Graphics

Miscellaneous Facts: Subsidiary of
Moore Corp., Ltd.

NORTON CO.
120 Front Street
Worcester, MA 01608
(617) 795-5000
Primary Business: Abrasives
Chairman: Donald R. Melville
CEO: Donald R. Melville
President: Donald R. Melville
Vice-Chairman: Richard J. Flynn
Vice-President and General Counsel:
Ronald H. Marcks
Vice-President (Human Resources):
Thomas J. Hourihan
Sales: $1.2 billion
Net Worth: $499 million
# of Employees: 18,100

Subsidiaries:
Norton Christensen, Inc.
Boyles Bros. Drilling Co.

THE O'BRIEN CORP.
450 Grand Avenue
South San Francisco, CA 94080
(415) 761-2300
Primary Business: Paints, enamels,
varnishes
Chairman: Jerome J. Crowley
President: Jerome J. Crowley, Jr.
Vice-President (Trade Sales): Orley H.
Anderson
Vice-President (Research): James J.
Kelly
Sales: $150 million
# of Employees: 1,100

Miscellaneous Facts: Trade name "Fuller
O'Brien Paints."

OLYMPIC STAIN DIV.
2233 112th Avenue, NE
Bellevue, WA 98004
(206) 453-1700

Primary Business: Manufactures interior
and exterior paints
Vice-President: R. C. Richter

Miscellaneous Facts: Division of the
Clorox Co.

RUST-OLEUM CORP.
11 Hawthorn Parkway
Vernon Hills, IL 60061
(312) 367-7700
Primary Business: Rust preventive
coatings
President: Rex Reade
Senior Vice-President (Sales and
Marketing): Daniel C. Ferguson
Executive Vice-President: Wilbert B.
Bartelt
# of Employees: 500

SHAEFFER EATON DIV.
75 S Church Street
Pittsfield, MA 01201
(413) 499-2210
Primary Business: Social stationary,
typewriter papers, fountain pens
Chairman: M. R. Eisner
President: Joseph E. Biafore
Vice-President (Domestic Sales): J. R.
Connor
Vice-President (Domestic Operations):
R. J. Boss
Sales: More than $100 million
# of Employees: 2,500

SHERWIN-WILLIAMS CO.
101 Prospect Avenue, NW
Cleveland, OH 44115
(216) 566-2000
Primary Business: Paints, enamels,
varnishes
Chairman: John G. Breen
CEO: John G. Breen
President: John G. Breen
Vice-President (Human Resources): A.
D. Maine
Director of Corporate Communications:
S. A. Domm
Sales: $2.07 billion
Net Worth: $465 million
# of Employees: 19,437

Subsidiaries:
Sherwin-Williams Canada, Inc.

Contract Transportation Systems Co.
Dupli-Color Products Co., Spray-On
Gray Drug Fair
Sherwin-Williams Development Corp.

Miscellaneous Facts: Some of the paint
brand names are Dutch Boy, Martin-
Seymour, Kem-Tone, Acme and
Rogers. Incorporated in 1884 in Ohio.

STANDARD BRANDS PAINT CO.
4300 W 190th Street
Torrance, CA 90509
(213) 214-2111
Primary Business: Retail paint, home
decorating centers
Chairman: Stuart D. Buchalter
CEO: Stuart D. Buchalter
President: Marvin Wager
Executive Vice-President: Eric Beck
Vice-President: Paul M. Ozawa
Sales: $337 million
Net Worth: $169 million
# of Employees: 3,647

Subsidiaries:
Major Paint Co.
Enterprise Wallcoverings, Inc.
Howells, Inc.
KWAL Paints, Inc.
Zynolyte Products Co.

THE STANDARD REGISTER CO.
600 Albany Street
Dayton, OH 45408
(513) 443-1000
Primary Business: Business forms
Chairman: P. H. Granzow
CEO: J. K. Darragh
President: J. K. Darragh
Vice-President: W. A. Sandusky
Vice-President: W. J. Byrne
Sales: $438 million
Net Worth: $170 million
# of Employees: 4,452

Subsidiaries:
The Rein Co.
Stanfast, Inc.

TENNANT CO.
701 N Lilac Drive
Minneapolis, MN 55422
(612) 540-1200

Primary Business: Floor maintenance
products
Chairman: Roger L.Hale
CEO: Roger L. Hale
Senior Vice-President: Lyle D. Delwiche
Vice-President (Personnel): Kenneth M.
Hall
Manager, Public Relations: Fritz Von
Yeast
Sales: $135 million
Net Worth: $57 million
# of Employees: 1,600

Subsidiary:
Tennant Trend, Inc.

THOMAS INDUSTRIES, INC.
207 E Broadway
Louisville, KY 40202
(502) 582-3771
Primary Business: Residential lighting
fixtures
Chairman: Lee B. Thomas, Sr.
CEO: Thomas R. Fuller
President: Thomas R. Fuller
Executive Vice-President: Gerald W.
O'Pool
Senior Vice-President: Arnold Mulbach
Sales: $291.73 million
Net Worth: $133 million
# of Employees: 3,750

Divisions:
Benjamin Div.
Jet Line Div.
Power Air Div.

WITE-OUT PRODUCTS, INC.
10114 Bacon Drive
Beltsville, MD 20705
(301) 937-5353
Primary Business: Manufacturing of
correction fluid
President: Archibald Douglas
Vice-President: Leslie H. Rhoades
Plant Manager: George Korper
Sales: $3.2 million
# of Employees: 74

Services

AUTOMATIC DATA PROCESSING, INC.
One ADP Boulevard
Roseland, NJ 07068
(201) 994-5000
Primary Business: Electronic data processing services
Chairman: Henry Taub
CEO: Josh Weston
President: Josh Weston
Group President: Ric Duques
Senior Vice-President: Fred S. Lafer
Personnel Director: Lew Levetown
Sales: $1.03 billion
Net Worth: $475 million
# of Employees: 18,500

Subsidiaries:
ADP Collision Estimating Services, Inc.
ADP Network Services International, Inc.
ADP-WHT Corp.

Miscellaneous Facts: Incorporated in 1961 in Delaware.

DYNALECTRON CORP.
1313 Dolly Madison Boulevard
McLean, VA 22101
(703) 356-0480
Primary Business: Technological services for industry
Chairman: Jorge Carnicero
CEO: Daniel R. Bannister
President: Daniel R. Bannister
Executive Vice-President: G. W. Ewalt
Vice-President (Human Relations): Michael Robilolto
Sales: $640 million
Net Worth: $75 million
# of Employees: 14,000

KELLY SERVICES, INC.
999 W Big Beaver Road
Troy, MI 48099
(313) 362-4444
Primary Business: Temporary office help
Chairman: William R. Kelly
President: Terence E. Adderley
Executive Vice-President: Angelo A. Agnello

Executive Vice-President: Thomas Anton
Senior Vice-President (Human Resources): Gene Knapp
Sales: $741.02 million
Net Worth: $129 million
# of Employees: 430,000 (includes all temporary employees

Divisions:
Kelly Girl
Kelly Health Care
Kelly Industrial
Kelly Marketing
Kelly Technical

KIDDE, INC.
Park 80 W Plaza Two
Post Office Box 5555
Saddle Brook, NJ 07662
(201) 368-9000
Primary Business: Security products and services
Chairman: Fred R. Sullivan
President: Fred R. Sullivan
Vice-Chairman: David R. Ficca
Executive Vice-President: Leonard T. Riccardo
Vice-President (Communications): Harvey S. Ekenstierna
Sales: $2.2 billion
Net Worth: $721 million
# of Employees: 48,000

Subsidiaries:
AMS Industries
Bayless Stationers, Inc.
Bear Archery
W. D. Byron & Sons, Inc.
Computrol
Cook Pump Co.
Devine Lighting, Inc.
EAM, Inc.
Fashion, Inc.
Globe Security Systems
Jacuzzi Whirlpool Bath, Inc.
Tommy Armour Golf
Scott Rice Co.

ROLLINS, INC.
2170 Piedmont Road, NE
Atlanta, GA 30324
(404) 888-2000
Primary Business: Operates exterminating service

Chairman: O. Wayne Rollins
CEO: O. Wayne Rollins
President: Gary W. Rollins
Senior Vice-Chairman: R. Randall
  Rollins
Vice-President: Don Olthoff
Sales: $308 million
Net Worth: $34 million
# of Employees: 7,000

ROTO-ROOTER
1400 DuBois Tower
Cincinnati, OH 45202
(513) 762-6690
Primary Business: Sewer, drain and pipe
  cleaning services
CEO: William R. Griffin
President: William R. Griffin

Miscellaneous Facts: Subsidiary of
  Chemed Corp.

SERVICE MASTER INDUSTRIES, INC.
2300 Warrenville Road
Downers Grove, IL 60515
(312) 964-1300
Primary Business: Provides management
  services
Chairman: Kenneth T. Wessner
CEO: C. William Pollard
President: C. William Pollard
Vice-Chairman: Kenneth N. Hansen
Vice-President (People): W. W.
  Hargreaves
Sales: $100 million
Net Worth: $76 million
# of Employees: 8,410

Subsidiaries:
Alimuth Advertising, Inc.
Service Master Management Services
Service Master Investment Co.
Service Direction, Inc.

INSURANCE

ACACIA MUTUAL LIFE INSURANCE CO.
51 Louisiana Avenue
Washington, DC 20001
(202) 628-4506
Primary Business: Life insurance, annuity
Chairman: Duane B. Adams
CEO: Duane B. Adams
President: Duane B. Adams
Vice-President (Personnel): Christie G. Harris
Vice-President (Corporate Communications): Charles L. Larance
Assets: $814.40 million
# of Employees: 1,200

Subsidiaries:
Acacia Financial Corp.
Acacia Insurance Sales Corp.
Acacia National Life Insurance Co.

AETNA CASUALTY & SURETY CO.
151 Farmington Avenue
Hartford, CT 06156
(203) 273-0123
Primary Business: Casualty and surety insurance
Chairman: James T. Lynn
President: William O. Bailey
Senior Vice-President (Employee Benefit Div.): Burton E. Burton
Senior Vice-President (Commercial Insurance Div.): Robert J. Clark
Personnel Director: Robert McAloon
Sales: $3.5 billion
# of Employees: 15,450

Miscellaneous Facts: Subsidiary of Aetna Life & Casualty Co.

AETNA LIFE & CASUALTY CO.
151 Farmington Avenue
Hartford, CT 06156
(203) 273-0123
Primary Business: Life, group, accident and health, pension insurance
Chairman: James T. Lynn
President: William O. Bailey
Senior Vice-President (Employee Benefit Div.): Burton E. Burton
Senior Vice-President (Commercial Insurance Div.): Robert J. Clark
Sales: $15.41 billion
# of Employees: 40,900

Subsidiaries:
The Aetna Casualty & Surety Co.
Aetna Life Insurance & Annuity Co.
Aetna Life Insurance Co.
Aetna Capital Management, Inc.
Federated Investors, Inc.
Ponderosa Homes

ALEXANDER & ALEXANDER SERVICES, INC.
1211 Avenue of the Americas
New York, NY 10036
(212) 840-8500
Primary Business: Insurance brokers
Chairman: Johna Bogardus, Jr.
CEO: Johna Bogardus, Jr.
President: Tinsley H. Irvin
Senior Vice-President: Peter M. Densen
Senior Vice-President: Richard E. Lynn
Revenue: $550.40 million
# of Employees: 15,000

Subsidiaries:
AAMET, Inc.
Alexsis, Inc.
Barros & Carrion, Inc.
Benefacts, Inc.
Corporate Service, Inc.
Illinois R.B. Jones, Inc.
PBA, Inc.
Property Tax Service Co.
Shand, Morahan & Co., Inc.
TIFCO, Inc.
Turner & Shepard, Inc.

ALLSTATE INSURANCE CO.
Allstate Plaza
Northbrook, IL 60062
(312) 291-5000
Primary Business: Insurance
Chairman: Donald F. Craib, Jr.
President: Richard J. Haayen
Vice-President (Sales): William V. Henderson
Vice-President (Corporate Relations): Lawrence H. Williford

Vice-President (Claims): Donald J. Ford
Net Premiums Written: $6.05 billion
# of Employees: 43,000

Subsidiary:
Allstate Life Insurance Co.

Miscellaneous Facts: Subsidiary of Sears, Roebuck and Co.

AMERICAN FAMILY CORP.
932 Wynnton Road
Columbus, GA 31906
(404) 323-3431
Primary Business: Cancer insurance
Chairman: John B. Amos
CEO: John B. Amos
President: Salvador Diaz-Verson, Jr.
Vice-Chairman: Paul S. Amos
Vice-President (Public Information): Michael H. Rhodes
Personnel Director: Alfred Errington
Revenue: $823 million
Net Worth: $274 million
# of Employees: 2,395

Subsidiaries:
American Black Hawk Broadcasting Co.
American Family Broadcasting Co.
American Family LAWS, Inc.
American Family Life Assurance Co.
American Self Care Corp.

AMERICAN INTERNATIONAL GROUP
70 Pine Street
New York, NY 10270
(212) 770-7000
Primary Business: Multinational insurance
CEO: Maurice R. Greenberg
President: Maurice R. Greenberg
Executive Vice-President: Elmer N. Dickinson
Executive Vice-President: Edward E. Matthews
Director of Staffing: Donna Dorn
Revenue: $4.28 billion
Net Worth: $2.8 billion
# of Employees: 24,000

Subsidiaries:
AI Credit Corp.
AIG Oil Rig, Inc.
AIU Insurance Co.
American Life Insurance Co.

Commerce & Industry Insurance Co.
Lexington Insurance Co.
North American Managers, Inc.
United Guaranty Corp.

AMERICAN NATIONAL INSURANCE CO.
One Moody Plaza
Galveston, TX 77550
(409) 763-4661
Primary Business: Life insurance
Chairman: Robert L. Moody
CEO: O. C. Clay
President: O. C. Clay
Senior Chairman: Mary Moody Northern
Vice-President (Personnel): Glenn C. Langley
Sales: $753 million
Net Worth: $1.1 billion
# of Employees: 8,667

Subsidiaries:
American National Life Insurance Co.
American National Property & Casualty Co.
American Printing Co.

CAPITAL HOLDING CORP.
Commonwealth Building
Louisville, KY 40202
(502) 560-2000
Primary Business: Holding company, insurance
Chairman: Tomas C. Simons
CEO: Tomas C. Simons
President: Robert T. Rakich
Executive Vice-President: Irving W. Baily II
Senior Vice-President: Robert W. Crispin
Revenue: $1.7 billion
Net Worth: $1 billion
# of Employees: 8,500

Subsidiaries:
Capital Enterprise Insurance Group
Capital Ventures Corp.
Commonwealth Life Insurance Co.
Georgia International Life Insurance Co.
Home Security Life Insurance Co.
Peoples Life Insurance Co.

THE CHUBB CORP.
15 Mountain View Road
Warren, NJ 07061
(201) 580-2000
Primary Business: Holding company,
  insurance
Chairman: Henry U. Harder
CEO: Henry U. Harder
President: Henry U. Harder
Executive Vice-President: Percy Chubb
  III
Senior Vice-President: Samuel V.
  Gilman, Jr.
Personnel Director: David S. Fowler
Sales: $2.03 billion
Net Worth: $894 million
# of Employees: 7,800

Subsidiaries:
Associated Aviation, Inc.
Associated Aviation Underwriters
Associated Insurers Corp.
Chubb & Son, Inc.
DHC
Chubb Custom Insurance Co.

CIGNA CORP.
One Logan Square
Philadelphia, PA 19103
(215) 557-5000
Primary Business: Insurance
CEO: Robert D. Kilpatrick
President: Hartzel Z. Lebed
Executive Vice-President: Thomas H.
  Dooley
Executive Vice-President: G. Robert
  O'Brien
Executive Vice-President: Andrew M.
  Rouse
Revenue: $14.77 billion
Net Worth: $4.5 billion
# of Employees: 47,943

Subsidiaries:
Cigna Escrow, Inc.
Aetna Insurance Co.
American Lloyds Insurance Co.
Automatic Business Centers, Inc.
Cigna Health Care Group, Inc.
Connecticut General Corp.
Cigna International Corp.
Cigna Insurance Co.
Alaska Pacific Assurance Co.

CINCINNATI FINANCIAL CORP.
11295 Princeton Road
Cincinnati, OH 45214
(513) 771-2000
Primary Business: Holding company,
  insurance
Chairman: John J. Schiff
CEO: John J. Schiff
President: Robert B. Morgan
Vice-President: Robert J. Driehaus
Personnel Director: Charles Ratliff
Sales: $560 million
Net Worth: $391 million
# of Employees: 1,300

Divisions:
CFC Investment Corp.
Cincinnati Insurance Co.
Inter-Olean Insurance Co.
Queen City Indemnity Co.

COMBINED INTERNATIONAL CORP.
222 N Dearborn Street
Chicago, IL 60601
(312) 269-4000
Primary Business: Holding company,
  insurance
Chairman: W. Clement Stone
CEO: Patrick G. Ryan
President: Patrick G. Ryan
Senior Executive Vice-President: Ronald
  K. Holmberg
Executive Vice-President: Gordon A.
  Dancer
Revenue: $1.3 billion
Net Worth: $882 million
# of Employees: 14,000

Subsidiaries:
Combined Insurance Co. of America
Booth Potter Seal Co., Inc.
Charles Ryan & Rivers
Rolibec, Inc.

**CONNECTICUT GENERAL LIFE
  INSURANCE CO.**
900 Cottage Grove Road
Bloomfield, CT 06002
(203) 726-6000
Primary Business: Life, accident and
  health insurance
President: Hartzel Z. Lebed
Executive Vice-President: Thomas H.
  Dooley

Executive Vice-President: G. Robert O'Brien
Senior Vice-President: David G. Devereaux
Revenue: $4.93 billion
# of Employees: 13,000

THE CONTINENTAL CORP.
180 Maiden Lane
New York, NY 10038
(212) 440-3000
Primary Business: Multiple line insurance
Chairman: John P. Mascotte
CEO: John P. Mascotte
President: John H. Bretherick, Jr.
Senior Vice-President: William F. Gleason, Jr.
Vice-President: Edward Harvey
Revenue: $4.6 billion
Net Worth: $1.9 billion
# of Employees: 17,000

Subsidiaries:
AFCO Credit Corp.
American Title Insurance Co.
CIC Financial
CPI Group
Equitable Fire Insurance Co.

EQUITABLE LIFE ASSURANCE
787 Seventh Avenue
New York, NY 10019
(212) 554-1234
Primary Business: Life insurance, annuities
Chairman: Robert F. Froehlke
CEO: John B. Carter
President: John B. Carter
Vice-Chairman: Harry D. Garber
Executive Vice-President and General Counsel: Herbert P. Shyer
Executive Vice-President: Robert W. Barth
Assets: $47.989 billion
# of Employees: 30,200

Subsidiaries:
Equitable Investment Co.
Calvin Bullock, Ltd.
Donaldson, Lufkin & Jenrette, Inc.
Elafund, Inc.
Equico Lessors
Equitable Life Leasing Co.
Equitable Mortgage Resources, Inc.
Equitable Real Estate Group, Inc.

FIREMAN'S FUND CORP.
Harborside Financial Center, Number 2, 10th Floor
Jersey City, NJ 07302
(201) 434-8244
Primary Business: Commercial insurance
Chairman: John J. Byrne
CEO: John J. Byrne
President: William M. McCormick
Executive Vice-President: Joseph W. Brown
Executive Vice-President and General Counsel: Borell L. Kirschen
Revenue: $3.35 billion
Net Worth: $1.34 billion
# of Employees: 12,100

Subsidiaries:
Fireman's Fund Insurance Co.
The American Insurance Co.
Interstate National Corp.
National Surety Corp.
Southern Guaranty Insurance Co.
San Francisco Reinsurance Co.
The Excess & Special Risk Market, Inc.
FAMEX, Inc.

GEICO CORP.
Geico Plaza
Washington, DC 20076
(301) 986-3000
Primary Business: Insurance services
Chairman: William B. Snyder
CEO: William B. Snyder
President: William B. Snyder
Vice-Chairman: Louis A. Simpson
Senior Vice-President: Alvan Sparks, Jr.
Director, Personnel: Patricia M. Corr
Sales: $1.2 billion
Net Worth: $515 million
# of Employees: 5,391

JOHN HANCOCK MUTUAL LIFE INSURANCE CO.
John Hancock Plaza
Boston, MA 02116
(617) 421-6000
Primary Business: Life insurance
Chairman: John G. McElwee
CEO: John G. McElwee
President: E. James Morton
Senior Vice-President (Sales/Staff): Howard D. Allen
Vice-President (Corporate

Communications): David
D'Allesandro
Assets: $26.256 billion
Net Worth: $957 million
# of Employees: 20,700

Subsidiaries:
First Signature Bank & Trust Co.
John Hancock Health Plans, Inc.
John Hancock Advisors, Inc.
John Hancock Capital Corp.

KEMPER CORP.
Long Grove, IL 60049
(312) 540-2000
Primary Business: Nonoperating holding
  company
Chairman: Joseph E. Luecke
CEO: Joseph E. Luecke
President: Joseph E. Luecke
Senior Vice-President: Thomas R.
  Anderson
Senior Vice-President: Donald R. Clark
Director, Corporate Relations: Chuck
  Johanns
Sales: $2.5 billion
Net Worth: $1.1 billion
# of Employees: 15,800

Subsidiaries:
American Motorist Insurance Co.
Batehill, Inc.
Boettcher Investment Corp.
Economy Fire & Casualty Co.
Kemper Financial Services, Inc.
Kemper Reinsurance Co.
Loewi Financial Companies
National Loss Control Service Corp.
PBT Holding Co., Inc.
Sequoia Insurance Co.

MARSH & MCLENNAN COMPANIES, INC.
1221 Avenue of the Americas
New York, NY 10020
(212) 997-2000
Primary Business: Insurance brokers
Chairman: Frank J. Tasco
CEO: Frank J. Tasco
President: A. J. C. Smith
Senior Vice-President: Frank J. Borelli
Vice-President (Personnel): Edward O.
  Cole
Sales: $1.3 billion
Net Worth: $515 million
# of Employees: 17,700

Subsidiaries:
Guy Carpenter & Co., Inc.
Marsh & McLennan, Inc.
The Putnam Companies
William M. Mercer-Meidinger, Inc.

MCORP
1807 Commerce Street
Dallas, TX 75201
(214) 698-5000
Primary Business: Holding company,
  insurance
Chairman: Gene H. Bishop
CEO: Gene H. Bishop
President: John T. Cater
Vice-Chairman: Karl T. Butz, Jr.
Manager, Human Resources: Mark L.
  Pabst
Net Worth: $1.2 billion
# of Employees: 11,694

Subsidiaries:
MCORP Properties
MCORP Financial

METROPOLITAN LIFE INSURANCE CO.
One Madison Avenue
New York, NY 10010
(212) 578-2211
Primary Business: Life and health
  insurance
Chairman: Robert G. Schwartz
CEO: John J. Creedon
President: John J. Creedon
Senior Vice-President (Pensions): Ted
  Athanassiades
Senior Vice-President (Law): J. Austin
  Lyons, Jr.
Senior Vice-President (Human
  Resources): Mark A. Peterson
Assets: $76.49 billion
# of Employees: 36,000

Subsidiaries:
Centennial Equities Corp.
Century 21 Real Estate Corp.
Corporate Health Strategies, Inc.
Cross & Brown Co.
DTSS, Inc.
Metropolitan Life Capital Corp.
Metropolitan Tower Corp.

NEW YORK LIFE INSURANCE CO.

51 Madison Avenue
New York, NY 10010
(212) 576-7000
Primary Business: Life insurance
Chairman: Donald K. Ross
Vice-Chairman: George A. W.
  Bundschuh
President: Jacob B. Underhill
Senior Vice-President and General
  Counsel: David Albenda
Senior Vice-President and General
  Auditor: Leif Rode
Vice-President (Human Resources):
  Richard A. Hansen
Premiums Written: $5.46 billion
Net Worth; $1.5 billion
# of Employees: 9,500

Subsidiaries:
New York Life Insurance & Annuity
  Corp.
New York Life Securities Corp.

NORTHWESTERN MUTUAL LIFE INSURANCE CO.

720 E Wisconsin Avenue
Milwaukee, WI 53202
(414) 271-1444
Primary Business: Life insurance
CEO: Donald J. Schuenke
President: Donald J. Schuenke
Vice-President (Communications):
  Robert O. Carboni
Vice-President (Policy Owner Service):
  James L. Compere
Vice-President (Personnel): James W.
  Ehrenstrom
Assets: $17.90 billion
Net Worth: $837 million
# of Employees: 2,353

Subsidiary:
MGIC Investment Corp.

NORWEST CORP.

1200 Peavy Building
Minneapolis, MN 55479
(612) 372-8268
Primary Business: Insurance, banking
Chairman: Lloyd P. Johnson
CEO: Lloyd P. Johnson
Vice-Chairman: Richard S. Levitt
Director, Investor Relations: Kerry K.
  Noyes
Director, Human Resources: Nancy
  Scherer
Sales: $2.5 billion
Net Worth: $1.2 billion
# of Employees: 15,974

Subsidiaries:
Norwest Audit Services, Inc.
Norwest Mortgage, Inc.

Miscellaneous Facts: Operates 84 offices
  across the country.

THE PRUDENTIAL INSURANCE CO. OF AMERICA

Prudential Plaza–3 Plaza
Newark, NJ 07101
(201) 877-6000
Primary Business: Life and health
  insurance
Chairman: Robert A. Beck
CEO: Robert A. Beck
Vice-Chairman: Garnett L. Keith, Jr.
Vice-Chairman: Robert C. Winters
Total Assets: $91.14 million
# of Employees: 80,398

Subsidiaries:
PRUCO, Inc.
PRUCO Securities Corp.
PRUCO Services, Inc.
Bache Group
Prudential Funding Corp.
Prudential Property & Casualty
  Insurance Co.
Prudential Realty Partnerships, Inc.
Prudential Trust Co.
Prudential Reinsurance Co.
PRUCO Life Insurance Co.

TEACHERS INSURANCE & ANNUITY ASSN. OF AMERICA

730 Third Avenue
New York, NY 10017
(212) 490-9000
Primary Business: Insurance and
  annuities for nonprofit educational
  institutions
Chairman: James G. MacDonald
CEO: James G. MacDonald
President: Walter G. Ehlers
Executive Vice-President and General
  Counsel: Francis P. Gunning
Executive Vice-President: Russell E.
  Bone

Executive Vice-President: J. Daniel Lee,
   Jr.
Assets: $23 billion
# of Employees: 2,476

TRANSAMERICA CORP.
600 Montgomery Street
San Francisco, CA 94111
(415) 983-4000
Primary Business: Diversified service
   company
Chairman: James R. Harvey
CEO: James R. Harvey
President: James R. Harvey
Vice-President (Public Affairs): James
   B. Lockhart
Executive Vice-President: Frank C.
   Herringer
Revenue: $5.04 billion
Net Worth: $1.86 billion
# of Employees: 30,600

Subsidiaries:
Budget Rent a Car Corp.
Fred S. James & Co., Inc.
Transamerica Airlines, Inc.
Transamerica Delaval, Inc.

THE TRAVELERS CORP.
One Tower Square
Hartford, CT 06183
(203) 277-0111
Primary Business: Life, accident, health
   and auto insurance
Chairman: Edward H. Budd
CEO: Edward H. Budd
President: Edward H. Budd
Executive Vice-President: Robert E.
   Bjorhus
Executive Vice-President: John W.
   Heilshorn
General Counsel: George A. McKeon
Total Income: $13.47 billion
Net Worth: $3.9 billion
# of Employees: 29,000

Subsidiaries:
Constitution Plaza, Inc.
Derby Advertising, Inc.
The Plaza Corp.
The Prospect Co.
The Travelers Indemnity Co.
The Travelers Insurance Co.

Miscellaneous Facts: Company toll-free
   consumer number is (800) 243-0191.

JEWELRY

BULOVA WATCH CO., INC.
Bulova Park
Flushing, NY 11370
(718) 565-4200
Primary Business: Watches
Chairman: Harry B. Henshel
President: Andrew H. Tisch
Vice-President (Advertising): George
  Foreman
Vice-President (Marketing): Jerry
  Josephson
Revenue: $145 million
# of Employees: 1,800

Miscellaneous Facts: Subsidiary of the
  Loews Corp.

CASIO, INC.
15 Gardner Road
Fairfield, NJ 07006
(201) 575-7400
Primary Business: Manufactures
  watches, calculators
President: John J. McDonald
Vice-President (Marketing): Ed McNally
Vice-President (Sales): Paul Kudeck
Sales: $350 million
# of Employees: 250

KAY CORP.
320 King Street
Alexandria, VA 22314
(703) 683-3800
Primary Business: Jewelry operating,
  international trading
CEO: Anthonie C. Van Ekris
President: Anthonie C. Van Ekris
Vice-President: Murray Ackerman
General Counsel: Scott L. Spitzer
Sales: $666 million
Net Worth: $59 million
# of Employees: 3,855

Subsidiaries:
Balfour Maclaine, Inc.
Vanekris & Stoett, Inc.
PVO International, Inc.
Seed Tec International, Inc.

Retail Divisions:
Kay Jewelers, Inc.
Marcus & Co., Inc.

JOSTENS, INC.
5501 Norman Grove Drive
Minneapolis, MN 55437
(612) 830-3300
Primary Business: Class rings,
  graduation announcements
Chairman: H. William Lurton
CEO: H. William Lurton
President: Robert W. Leslie
Senior Vice-President (Education): Gary
  L. Buckmiller
Vice-President (Public Affairs): Ellis F.
  Bullock, Jr.
Sales: $570 million
Net Worth: $192 million
# of Employees: 9,000

Subsidiaries:
Jostens Learning Systems, Inc.
Hazel, Inc.
The Jostens Foundation, Inc.
Prescription Learning Corp.

Divisions:
Artex Div.
Business Products Div.
Education Div.
Printing & Publishing Div.
Recognition Div.
Scholastic Div.

TIFFANY & CO.
727 Fifth Avenue
New York, NY 10022
(212) 755-8000
Primary Business: Jewelers
Chairman: William R. Chaney
Senior Vice-President: Lincoln Foster
Vice-President (Public Relations):
  Arlette Brisson

TIME PRODUCTS DIV.
Laurel Hill Church Road
Laurinburg, NC 28352
(919) 276-3101
Primary Business: Clocks and household
  timers
Vice-President: Ralph J. Ronalter, Sr.
Product Manager: William L. Ronalter
Chief Engineer: Leslie G. Ingram
# of Employees: 500

Miscellaneous Facts: Division of
Toastmaster, Inc.

TIMEX GROUP, LTD.
Waterbury, CT 06720
(203) 573-5000
Primary Business: Watches, clocks,
timing instruments
Chairman: T. F. Olsen
President: James W. Binns
Vice-Chairman: Ronald Marsching
Sales: $600 million
# of Employees: 10,000

ZALE CORP.
901 W Walnut Hill Lane
Irving, TX 75038
(214) 580-4000
Primary Business: Retail jewelry
Chairman: Donald Zale
CEO: Bruce A. Lipshy
President: Bruce A. Lipshy
Vice-Chairman: Marvin Zale
Senior Vice-President (Human
Resources): Wayne Majors
Revenue: $1.1 billion
Net Worth: $414 million
# of Employees: 14,500

LEISURE AND RECREATION

Athletic Equipment

AMF, INC.
777 Westchester Avenue
White Plains, NY 10604
(914) 694-9000
Primary Business: Manufacturing
sporting equipment
CEO: Kenneth J. Severinson
Executive Vice-President: Stanley
Groner
Senior Vice-President: Timothy C.
Sullivan
Vice-President and General Counsel:
John S. Johnson
Revenue: $970.52 million
Net Worth: $455 million
# of Employees: 18,738

Subsidiaries:
AMF Apparel Equipment Div.
AMF Cuno Div.
AMF Head, Inc.
AMF Tuboscope, Inc.
AMF Voit, Inc.
AMF Whitley Div.
AMF Wyott Corp.
Ben Hogan Co.

Miscellaneous Facts: Subsidiary of
Minstar, Inc.

BEN HOGAN CO.
2912 W Pafford Street
Fort Worth, TX 76110
(817) 921-2661
Primary Business: Golf products
Chairman: Robert L. Corbett

Miscellaneous Facts: Subsidiary of AMF,
Inc.

BIKE ATHLETIC CO.
Post Office Box 666
Knoxville, TN 37901
(615) 546-4703
Primary Business: Manufactures athletic
equipment
President: John M. Axford

Miscellaneous Facts: Subsidiary of
Colgate-Palmolive Co.

BRUNSWICK CORP.
One Brunswick Plaza
Skokie, IL 60076
(312) 470-4700
Primary Business: Manufactures leisure
products
CEO: Jack F. Reichert
President: Jack F. Reichert
Senior Vice-President (Administration):
James F. Urbanek
Vice-President: Herbert E. Ennis
Vice-President: Richard J. Jordon
Revenue: $1.47 billion
Net Worth: $460 million
# of Employees: 19,400

Subsidiaries:
Brunswick International, Ltd.
Marine Power International, Ltd.
Vapor Corp.
Brunswick Valve & Control, Inc.

Divisions:
Brunswick Div.
Brunswick Recreation Centers
Defense Div.
GPE Controls
Mercury Marine Div.
Technetics Div.
Vapor Div.

Miscellaneous Facts: Founded in 1845 by
John M. Brunswick. Is the oldest
American leisure firm operating as an
independent business today. Famous
for its bowling products and Mercury
motors.

COLT INDUSTRIES, INC.
430 Park Avenue
New York, NY 10022
(212) 940-0400
Primary Business: Handguns, specialty
metals
Chairman: David I. Margolis
CEO: David I. Margolis
President: David I. Margolis

Vice-President (Personnel): Phil
  Berkowitz
Vice-President (Public Relations): John
  F. Campbell
Revenue: $1.87 billion
Net Worth: $343 million
# of Employees: 22,116

Divisions:
Colt Firearms
Holly Carburetor
Crucible Magnetics Div.
Elox Div.
Manasco, Inc.
Pratt & Whitney Machine Tool Div.

HEAD, INC.
4801 N 63rd Street
Boulder, CO 80301
(303) 530-2000
Primary Business: Manufactures tennis
  equipment
CEO: Robert L. Carpenter

Miscellaneous Facts: Subsidiary of
  Minstar, Inc.

HUFFY CORP.
7701 Byers Road
Miamisburg, OH 45342
(513) 866-6251
Primary Business: Maker of bicycles,
  basketball equipment
Chairman: Stuart J. Northrop
CEO: Harry A. Shaw
President: Harry A. Shaw
Vice-President (Marketing): W.
  Anthony Huffman
Director, Human Resources: William
  Noble
Sales: $272.60 million
Net Worth: $64.7 million
# of Employees: 2,800

Subsidiaries:
Gerico, Inc.
Snugli, Inc.
Raleigh Cycle Co. of America
YLC Enterprises, Inc.

**INTERNATIONAL THOROUGHBRED
  BREEDERS, INC.**
202 Abbington Drive
East Windsor, NJ 08520
(609) 443-6111

Primary Business: Breeds thoroughbreds
Chairman: Robert E. Brennan
CEO: Kerry B. Fitzpatrick
President: Kerry B. Fitzpatrick
Net Worth: $195 million
# of Employees: 1,500

Subsidiaries:
Colonial Racing Club, Inc.
Garden State Race Track, Inc.

MASTERCRAFT BOAT CO.
Route 9
Maryville, TN 37801
(615) 983-2178
Primary Business: Manufactures ski
  boats
President: Jon Baird
# of Employees: 105

Miscellaneous Facts: Subsidiary of the
  Coleman Co., Inc.

OSHMAN'S SPORTING GOODS, INC.
2302 Maxwell Lane
Houston, TX 77023
(713) 928-3171
Primary Business: Operates sporting
  goods stores
Chairman: Jeanette Oshman Effron
  (Mrs.)
CEO: Alvin N. Lubetkin
President: Marvin Aronowitz
Senior Vice-President (Operations): Joe
  D. Nanny
Vice-President (Merchandise): Glen B.
  Boyd
Personnel Director: Marshall Wilkes
Revenue: $304.42 million
Net Worth: $62 million
# of Employees: 4,200

Subsidiary:
Abercrombie & Fitch Co.

OUTBOARD MARINE CORP.
100 Sea Horse Drive
Waukegan, IL 60085
(312) 689-6200
Primary Business: Manufactures
  outboard motors
Chairman: C. D. Strang
CEO: C. D. Strang
President: James C. Chapman

Vice-President and General Counsel:
Thomas J. Beeler
Vice-President: Samuel J. Winett
Sales: $880 million
Net Worth: $366 million
# of Employees: 9,540

Divisions:
OMC Lincoln
OMC Parts & Accessories

RALEIGH CYCLE CO. OF AMERICA
22710 72nd Street
Kent, WA 98032
(206) 395-1100
Primary Business: Distributes bicycles
President: Dennis Brockmann
# of Employees: 116

Miscellaneous Facts: Subsidiary of Huffy
Corp.

RAWLINGS SPORTING GOODS
1859 Intertech Road
Fenton, MO 63026
(314) 349-3500
Primary Business: Manufactures
sporting goods
CEO: Robert P. Burrows III
# of Employees: 2,100

Miscellaneous Facts: Subsidiary of Figgie
International Holdings, Inc.

REMINGTON ARMS CO., INC.
Brandywine Building
1007 Market Street
Wilmington, DE 19801
(302) 333-1112
Primary Business: Manufactures
firearms
Director: E. E. Woodacre

Miscellaneous Facts: Subsidiary of E. I.
Du Pont.

SMITH & WESSON
2100 Roosevelt Avenue
Springfield, MA 01102
(413) 781-8300
Primary Business: Sporting and law
enforcement products
CEO: L. J. Deters
President: L. J. Deters

Senior Vice-President (Marketing):
Robert I. Haas
Vice-President (Finance): John M.
Prosser
Vice-President (Sales, Sporting Goods):
Delbert E. Shorb
Sales: $85 million
# of Employees: 2,500

Miscellaneous Facts: Division of Lear
Siegler, Inc.

TIDE CRAFT, INC.
1616 Shreveport Road
Minden, LA 71055
(318) 377-5703
Primary Business: Maker of Fiberglas
boats
Chairman: Melvin Smith
President: Melvin Smith
Sales Manager: Richard Armstrong
Treasurer: Melba Smith
Sales: $6 million
# of Employees: 100

TIDEWATER, INC.
1440 Canal Street
New Orleans, LA 70112
(504) 568-1010
Primary Business: Supplies marine
equipment to companies
Chairman: John P. Laborde
CEO: John P. Laborde
President: Damon B. Bankston
Executive Vice-President: Robert C.
Milton
Executive Vice-President: Sam S.
Allgood
Revenue: $321.2 million
Net Worth: $272 million
# of Employees: 3,200

Subsidiaries:
Pental Insurance Co., Ltd.
Tidewater Compression, Inc.
Tidewater Marine Service, Inc.
Tidewater Realty, Inc.

VOIT CORP.
45 Gould Street
Rochester, NY 14610
(716) 442-4663
Primary Business: Sports equipment,
billiard equipment

President: David H. Goldman
Executive Vice-President: Leon R. Ellin
Vice-President: Bernard A. Frank
Sales: $21.6 million
# of Employees: 600

Hotels and Gaming

BALLY MANUFACTURING CORP.
8700 W Bryn Mawr
Chicago, IL 60631
(312) 399-1300
Primary Business: Hotel-casino,
  amusement parks
CEO: Robert E. Mullane
President: Robert E. Mullane
Executive Vice-President: Roger N.
  Keesee
Executive Vice-President: Donald B.
  Romans
Personnel Director: Lois Balodias
Revenue: $1.35 billion
Net Worth: $368 million
# of Employees: 35,000

Subsidiaries:
Bally Distributing of Nevada, Inc.
Astroworld/Waterworld
Six Flags Great Adventure
Six Flags Great America, Inc.
Six Flags Magic Mountain, Inc.
Six Flags Movieland Wax Museum, Inc.
Six Flags Over Georgia
Six Flags Over Mid-America, Inc.
Six Flags Over Texas, Inc.

Miscellaneous Facts: Trade name
  "Bally." Incorporated in 1968 in
  Delaware.

BEST WESTERN INTERNATIONAL
Post Office Box 10203
Phoenix, AZ 85064
(602) 957-5700
Primary Business: Hotel/motel chain
CEO: Ronald Evans
Vice-President (Sales): Frank Hansen
Vice-President (Marketing): Lawrence
  L. Pelegrin
Director Human Resources: Judy Nelson
# of Employees: 1,000

Divisions:
B-W Advertising Agency, Inc.

B-W Insurance Agency
Best Western Supply Div.
Reservations Services, Inc.

CAESARS WORLD, INC.
1801 Century Park E
Los Angeles, CA 90067
(213) 552-2711
Primary Business: Resort hotels, casinos
Chairman: Henry Gluck
President: J. Terrence Lanni
Vice-Chairman: M. Peter Schweitzer
Vice-President (Communications):
  Julian C. Leone
Vice-President (Personnel): Janet
  Bussiere
Revenue: $620 million
Net Worth: $193 million
# of Employees: 10,660

Subsidiaries:
Caesars New Jersey, Inc.
Boardwalk Regency Corp.
Caesars Atlantic City
Caesars Pocono Resorts
Cove Haven
Paradise Stream
Pocono Palace
Desert Palace, Inc.

Miscellaneous Facts: Incorporated in
  1958 in Florida as Lum's Bar, Inc.
  Name changed to Lum's, Inc., in
  1961. Present name adopted in 1971.

CARLSON COMPANIES, INC.
12755 State Highway 55
Minneapolis, MN 55441
(612) 540-5000
Primary Business: Hotels, inns, resorts
Chairman: Curtis L. Carlson
President: Edwin Gage
Vice-President (Personnel): Terry
  Butorac
Vice-President (Public Relations):
  Thomas D. Jardine
Vice-President (General Counsel): Lee
  Bearmon
Sales: $2.6 billion
# of Employees: 42,000

Subsidiaries:
Colony Resorts, Inc.
Country Kitchen International, Inc.
Radisson Hotel Corp.

National Hotel Corp.
TGI Friday's, Inc.
Carlson Leasing, Inc.
North American Financial Corp.
First Travel Corp.
Ardan, Inc.
Arrowhead Assn.
CSA, Inc.

HILTON HOTELS CORP.
9880 Wilshire Boulevard
Beverly Hills, CA 90210
(213) 278-4321
Primary Business: Hotel management
Chairman: Barron Hilton
CEO: Barron Hilton
President: Barron Hilton
Senior Vice-President (Human
    Resources): William R. McDonald
Senior Vice-President (Corporate
    Affairs): James R. Galeraith
Director of Public Relations: Patrick J.
    Barry
Revenue: $712 million
Net Worth: $651 million
# of Employees: 34,000

Divisions:
Hilton Hotels Div.
Turtle Bay Hilton & Country Club
Hilton Gaming Div.
Nevada Div.

Miscellaneous Facts: Incorporated in
    1946 in Delaware.

HOLIDAY CORP.
1023 Cherry Road
Memphis, TN 38117
(901) 762-8600
Primary Business: Hotels, gaming/casino
Chairman: Michael D. Rose
CEO: Michael D. Rose
President: Richard J. Goeglein
Senior Vice-President (Human
    Resources): Ben C. Peternell
Vice-President and General Counsel:
    Craig H. Norville
Vice-President (Corporate Relations):
    Robert L. Brannon
Revenue: $1.8 billion
Net Worth: $662 million
# of Employees: 52,800

Subsidiaries:
Duluth Motor Hotels

Minot Motor Hotels
Embassy Suites, Inc.
Gateway Motels, Inc.
Harrah's
Air Corp.
Holiday Inns, Inc.
Nob Nill Casino, Inc.
Industrial Realty, Inc.
Pipers Restaurants, Inc.
Queensgate Investment Co.
Town Park Hotel Corp.

Miscellaneous Facts: Holding company
    for Holiday Inns, Inc. Incorporated in
    1984 in Delaware.

HOST INTERNATIONAL, INC.
34th Street and Pico Boulevard
Santa Monica, CA 90406
(213) 450-7566
Primary Business: Hotels, restaurants
    and gift shops
Chairman: Howard E. Varner
President: Ronald P. Johnson
Senior Vice-President: Arthur T. Spring
Vice-President: Francis W. Cash
Vice-President: Sterling D. Colton
Revenue: $356.73 million
# of Employees: 13,100

HYATT CORP.
200 W Madison
Chicago, IL 60606
(312) 750-1234
Primary Business: Operates hotels
Chairman: Jay A. Pritzker
CEO: Jay A. Pritzker
President: Thomas J. Pritzker
Vice-Chairman: A. N. Pritzker
Vice-President (Human Resources):
    John Hamilton
Revenue: $540 million
# of Employees: 35,000

Subsidiaries:
Hyatt Hotels Corp.
Hyatt International Corp.
Dalfort, Inc.
Braniff, Inc.

LOEWS CORP.
666 Fifth Avenue
New York, NY 10103
(212) 841-1000

Primary Business: Holding company, hotels, motion pictures, tobacco products
Chairman: Laurence A. Tisch
CEO: Laurence A. Tisch
President: Preston R. Tisch
Executive Vice-President: Bernard Myerson
Vice-President: Robert J. Hausman
Vice-President: Kenneth Abrams
Revenue: $6.60 billion
Net Worth: $2.64 billion
# of Employees: 10,200

Subsidiaries:
Bulova Watch Co.
CNA Financial Corp.

Divisions:
Loew's Hotels, Inc.
Regency Hotel
Summit Hotel
Lorillard, Inc.

Miscellaneous Facts: Incorporated in 1969 in Delaware.

MARRIOTT CORP.
Marriott Drive
Washington, DC 20058
(301) 897-9000
Primary Business: Hotels and food service
Chairman: J. W. Marriott, Jr.
President: Frederic V. Malek
Executive Vice-President: John Dasburg
Senior Vice-President (Human Resources): Clifford J. Ehrlich
Sales: $4.2 billion
Net Worth: $848 million
# of Employees: 160,000

Subsidiaries:
Host International
Sage Corp.
Spectrum Foods
Stuart Anderson's Black Angus
The Velvet Turtle
Grandy's, Inc.
Spoons
Straw Hat Pizza
Sunline Cruisers

MOTEL 6, INC.
51 Hitchcock Way
Santa Barbara, CA 93105
(805) 682-6666
Primary Business: Operating motels
Chairman: James A. Lucas
CEO: Roger C. Royce
President: Roger C. Royce
Executive Vice-President: William F. Muster
Senior Vice-President (Quality Control): William J. Matthews
Vice-President (Human Resources): Raymond Lee
Sales: $200 million
# of Employees: 7,200

RAMADA INNS, INC.
3838 E Van Buren Street
Phoenix, AZ 85008
(602) 273-4000
Primary Business: Operates hotels and gaming facilities
Chairman: Richard Snell
CEO: Richard Snell
President: Richard Snell
Vice-President (Corporate Communications): David M. Thompson
Vice-President (Human Resources): Thomas W. Davidson
Revenue: $600.15 million
Net Worth: $249 million
# of Employees: 14,250

Divisions:
Gaming Group
Hotel Group

THE SHERATON CO.
60 State Street
Boston, MA 02109
(617) 367-3600
Primary Business: Owns and operates hotels through subsidiaries
Chairman: John Kapioltas
CEO: John Kapioltas
President: John Kapioltas
Senior Vice-President (Marketing): Sigmund S. Front
Senior Vice-President (Franchise Operations): Joseph A. McInerney
Vice-President (Labor Relations): Carl Madda

Sales: $2.50 billion
# of Employees: 91,200

Miscellaneous Facts: Subsidiary of ITT
Corp.

TRANSWORLD CORP.
605 Third Avenue
New York, NY 10158
(212) 972-4700
Primary Business: Hotel, food service
Chairman: L. Edwin Smart
CEO: L. Edwin Smart
President: C. J. Bradshaw
Vice-Chairman: Frank L. Salizzoni
Vice-President and General Counsel:
John J. O'Keefe, Jr.
Revenue: $2 billion
# of Employees: 87,500

Outdoor Equipment

COACHMEN INDUSTRIES, INC.
601 E Beardsley
Elkhart, IN 46514
(219) 262-0123
Primary Business: Manufactures
recreational vehicles
Chairman: Thomas H. Corson
CEO: Thomas H. Corson
President: Philip G. Lux
Executive Vice-President: G. L. Groom
Personnel Director: James Frahm
Sales: $458 million
Net Worth: $96 million
# of Employees: 3,643

Subsidiaries:
All American Homes, Inc.
Coachmen Housing of Georgia
Fan Coach Co.
The Lux Co., Inc.
Shasta Industries of Pennsylvania, Inc.
Sportscoach Corp. of America
Viking Recreational Vehicles

Miscellaneous Facts: Incorporated in
1964 in Indiana.

COLEMAN CO., INC.
250 N St. Francis Avenue
Wichita, KS 67201
(316) 261-3211

Primary Business: Outing products,
lanterns, camp stoves
Chairman: Sheldon Coleman
Vice-Chairman: Clarence Coleman
Vice-President (Corporate
Communications): Charles B.
McIlwaine
Vice-President (Personnel): Vernon L.
Williams
Sales: $454.49 million
Net Worth: $157 million
# of Employees: 5,200

Subsidiaries:
Coast Catamaran Corp., Hobie Cat.
Golden Eagle
Master Craft Boat Co.
O'Brien International, Inc.
Soniform, Inc.
Western Cutlery Co., Inc.

Divisions:
Camping Trailers Div.
Crosman Airguns Co.
Coleman Flotation Prods.
International Div.
Outing Products Group.

FLEETWOOD ENTERPRISES, INC.
3125 Myers Street
Riverside, CA 92523
(714) 351-3500
Primary Business: Manufactured
housing, travel trailers
Chairman: John C. Crean
CEO: John C. Crean
President: Glenn F. Kummer
Vice-Chairman: William W. Weide
Vice-President (Housing Group): Jon A.
Nord
Vice-President and General Counsel:
William H. Lear
Revenue: $1.42 billion
Net Worth: $288 million
# of Employees: 11,300

Subsidiaries:
Avion Coach Corp.
Continental Lumber
Gold Shield Fiberglass, Inc.
Hauser Lake Lumber Operation, Inc.
Westfield Manufactured Homes, Inc.

Miscellaneous Facts: Nation's largest
producer of manufactured housing
and recreational vehicles. Owns 30
Fleetwood Homes, Inc., across the
country.

IGLOO CORP.
Post Office Box 19322
Houston, TX 77024
(713) 465-2571
Primary Business: Maker of portable
   water coolers, picnic chests
President: J. Futch
President (Impact Extrusions): J. Weis
Vice-President (Sales): John Caldwell
# of Employees: 1,400

Miscellaneous Facts: Subsidiary of
   Anderson, Clayton & Co.

SKYLINE CORP.
2520 Bypass Road
Eklhart, IN 46514
(219) 294-6521
Primary Business: Manufactures
   recreational vehicles
Chairman: A. J. Dello
CEO: A. J. Dello
President: Ronald F. Kloska
Vice-President (Sales): J. Patrick Kerich
Executive Vice-President: William H.
   Lawson
Revenue: $327 million
# of Employees: 3,100

THOUSAND TRAILS, INC.
153255 E 30th Place
Bellevue, WA 98007
(206) 644-1100
Primary Business: Resort campgrounds
Chairman: C. James Jensen
CEO: C. James Jensen
President: C. James Jensen
Executive Vice-President: Melvyn R.
   Kays
Senior Vice-President: Robert M. Mays
Sales: $116.98 million
# of Employees: 1,829

WINNEBAGO INDUSTRIES, INC.
Junction 9 and 69
Forest City, IA 50436
(515) 582-3535
Primary Business: Motor homes, vans
Chairman: John K. Hanson
CEO: Ronald E. Haugen
President: Ronald E. Haugen
Vice-President (Sales and Marketing):
   Fred G. Emmert

Personnel Manager: Jon L. Green
Public Relations Manager: Frank Rotta
Revenue: $410.97 million
Net Worth: $137 million
# of Employees: 2,800

Subsidiaries:
Winnebago Acceptance Corp.
Winnebago International Corp.
Winnebago Realty Corp.

Photographic Products and Services

BELL & HOWELL
5215 Old Orchard Road
Skokie, IL 60077
(312) 470-7100
Primary Business: Photographic
   equipment
Chairman: Donald N. Frey
CEO: Donald N. Frey
President: Gerald Schultz
Vice-President: Gary W. Ampulski
Vice-President: Timothy J. Croasdalle
Vice-President (Human Resources):
   John Kambenis
Sales: $713.55 million
Net Worth: $205,578 million
# of Employees: 10,349

Subsidiaries:
Bell & Howell, Ltd.
Tandy/B & H Home Video
B&H/Columbia Pictures Video Service
DeVry, Inc.

Divisions:
Business Data Products Div.
Phillipburg Div.
Bell & Howell Service Co.
Micro Design Div.
Publications Systems Div.

CANON, INC., U.S.A.
One Canon Plaza
Lake Success, NY 11042
(516) 488-6700
Primary Business: Camera products
Chairman: Takeshi Mitarai
President: Fujio Mitarai
Director of Public Relations: H. Harai
Senior Vice-President (Service): H.
   Kagami

Sales: $96 million
# of Employees: 1,400

Subsidiaries:
Ambassador Office Equipment
Astro Office Products
Canon Business Machines, Inc.
Metropolitan Calculator Systems

Miscellaneous Facts: Subsidiary of
Canon, Inc., Tokyo, Japan.

EASTMAN KODAK CO.
343 State Street
Rochester, NY 14608
(716) 724-4000
Primary Business: Photography
equipment
CEO: Colby H. Chandler
President: Kay R. Whitmore
Senior Vice-President (Corporate
Relations): William L. Sutton
Senior Vice-President and General
Counsel: Kendall M. Cole
Revenue: $10.06 billion
Net Worth: $10 billion
# of Employees: 123,900

Subsidiaries:
Atex, Inc.
Eastman Chemical Products, Inc.
Eastman Gelatine Corp.
Eastman Technology, Inc.
Verbatim Corp.

Miscellaneous Facts: The world's largest
photographic company. Maintains
medical center at company
headquarters, which is staffed by more
than 275 people.

FOTOMAT CORP.
205 Ninth Street, N
St. Petersburg, FL 33701
(813) 823-2027
Primary Business: Photographic supplies
and equipment
Chairman: Ghigeru Suzuki
President: John R. Chase
Vice-President (Human Resources):
Robert E. Nemecek
Vice-President and General Counsel:
Michael H. Alden
Revenue: $180.54 million
Net Worth; $5.9 million
# of Employees: 8,800

Subsidiary:
Portrait World

Miscellaneous Facts: Subsidiary of
Konishiroku Photo Industry Co., Ltd.

FOX PHOTO, INC.
8750 Tesoro Drive
San Antonio, TX 78217
(512) 828-9111
Primary Business: Processes film and
sells photographic equipment
Chairman: Carl D. Newton, Jr.
President: Carl D. Newton III
Senior Vice-President (Dealer Div.):
Don Harman
Senior Vice-President (Retail Div.):
Lloyd E. Swiggum
Personnal Director: Edwin C. Honeck
Revenue: $166 million
# of Employees: 4,300

Subsidiary:
Stanley Redevelopment Corp.

Miscellaneous Facts: Incorporated in
1936 in Texas as Fox Co. Present
name adopted in 1985.

NIKON, INC.
623 Stewart Avenue
Garden City, NY 11530
(516) 222-0200
Primary Business: Photographic and
optical equipment
Chairman: Hiroshi Moromizato
CEO: Yutaka Sasaguchi
President: Yutaka Sasaguchi
Executive Vice-President: Jack Abrams
Executive Vice-President: Walter
Burrmann
Revenue: $180 million
# of Employees: 500

Miscellaneous Facts: Subsidiary of
Nippon Kogaku, KK.

POLAROID CORP.
549 Technology Square
Cambridge, MA 02139
(617) 577-2000
Primary Business: Cameras and film
Chairman: William J. McCune, Jr.
CEO: William J. McCune, Jr.
President: I. M. Booth

Executive Vice-President: Sheldon A. Buckler
Senior Vice-President: Peter O. Kliem
Revenue: $1.27 billion
Net Worth: $916 million
# of Employees: 13,402

Subsidiaries:
Advanced Color Technology, Inc.
Inner City, Inc.
International Polaroid Corp.
Merganser Capital Management Corp.
PMC, Inc.
Polaroid Asia Pacific, Ltd.
Polaroid Caribbean Corp.
Polaroid Foundation
Polint Management Services Corp.
Sage Technology, Inc.

Miscellaneous Facts: Company invented and developed the instant camera, and still controls 75 percent of the market.

Toys

COLECO INDUSTRIES, INC.
999 Quaker Lane, S
Hartford, CT 06110
(203) 725-6000
Primary Business: Recreational and toy products
Chairman: Arnold C. Greenberg
CEO: Arnold C. Greenberg
President: J. Brian Clarke
Executive Vice-President (Sales): Philip Cohen
Executive Vice-President (Marketing): Alfred Kahn
Senior Vice-President (Human Resources): William A. Roskin
Revenue: $774.90 million
Net Worth: $100 million
# of Employees: 6,000

Miscellaneous Facts: Some of the products made by Coleco are The Cabbage Patch Kids (one of the largest selling line of toys in the history of the toy industry), Rambo, Furskins, Wrinkles, Tubtown, J. Livingston Clayton, Hank "Spitball," Thistle, The Force of Freedom, Knight Rider, Transformers and Sesame Street toys. Games include Aggravation, Perfection, Perquackey,

Barrel of Monkeys, My Talking Computer, Little Genius.

FISHER-PRICE TOYS
East Aurora, NY 14052
(716) 687-3000
Primary Business: Toy manufacturer
Executive Vice-President: R. Bruce Sampsell
Sales: $422 million
# of Employees: 6,500

Miscellaneous Facts: Subsidiary of the Quaker Oats Co.

HASBRO, INC.
1027 Newport Avenue
Pawtucket, RI 02861
(401) 727-5000
Primary Business: Toy manufacturer
Chairman: Stephen D. Hassenfeld
CEO: Stephen D. Hassenfeld
President: Alan Hassenfeld
Senior Vice-President (Sales): Lawrence H.Bernstein
Senior Vice-President (Human Resources): Christopher P. Dona
Vice-President (Corporate Affairs): Sylvia Hassenfeld
Revenue: $1.23 billion
Net Worth: $417 million
# of Employees: 7,000

Subsidiaries:
Hasbro Foreign Sales Corp.
Hasbro Industries, Inc.
Hasbro Managerial Services, Inc.
Milton Bradley Co.
Playskool, Inc.
Romper Room Enterprises, Inc.
Tommee Tippee Playskool, Inc.
Pant-Ease Infant Wear Co., Inc.

KENNER PRODUCTS CO.
1014 Vine Street
Cincinnati, OH 45202
(513) 579-4000
Primary Business: Toy manufacturer
CEO: Joe Mendelsohn
President: Joe Mendelsohn
Senior Vice-President (Sales): Pete Kelly
Senior Vice-President (Personnel): John Tamashasky

Sales: $250 million
# of Employees: 2,000

Miscellaneous Facts: Division of General
Mills, Inc.

LIONEL CORP.
441 Lexington Avenue
New York, NY 10017
(212) 818-6300
Primary Business: Maker of precision
electronic components, toys
Chairman: Michael J. Vastola
CEO: Michael J. Vastola
Senior Vice-President and General
Counsel: George A. Padgett
Revenue: $358.26 million
Net Worth: $66.7 million
# of Employees: 5,215

Subsidiary:
Lionel Leisure, Inc.

MATTEL, INC.
5150 Rosecrans Avenue
Hawthorne, CA 90250
(213) 978-5150
Primary Business: Toy products
Chairman: Arthur S. Spear
Vice-Chairman: Glenn A. Hastings
President: Thomas J. Kalinske
Senior Vice-President (Sales and
Merchandising): Loren H. Jildebrand
Vice-President (Corporate Affairs):
Spencer C. Boise
Vice-President (Personnel): Joe McKay
Revenue: $1.05 billion
Net Worth: $435 million
# of Employees: 15,000–20,000

Miscellaneous Facts: One of the largest
toy marketers and manufacturers of
toys in the world. Markets nearly 450
products each year.Began in 1945.
Barbie Doll, one of the world's best
selling toys, was introduced in 1955.
Products include My Child, Masters of
the Universe, He-Man, Heroic
Warriors, Popples, Princess of Power,
The Heart Family, and See 'N Say
toys.

MILTON BRADLEY CO.
443 Shaker Road
East Longmeadow, MA 01028
(413) 525-6411
Primary Business: Toys and games,
puzzles
Chief Operating Officer: George R.
Detomassi, Jr.
Senior Vice-President (Finance): Stanley
Strzempek
Vice-President (Human Resources):
Cristopher Dona
Revenue: $336.96 million
# of Employees: 5,100

Miscellaneous Facts: Division of Hasbro,
Inc.

REVELL, INC.
4223 Glencoe Avenue
Venice, CA 90292
(213) 821-5011
Primary Business: Plastic model hobby
kits and toys
Senior Vice-President: A. R. P. Ghuman
Vice-President (Marketing): Robert
Ziene
Revenue: $47.34 million
# of Employees: 662

Miscellaneous Facts: Subsidiary of
Compagnie Generale de Jouet.

TOMY CORP.
Post Office Box 6252
Carson, CA 90749
(213) 549-2721
Primary Business: Toys
President: David Iida
Vice-President (Sales): Larry Anderson
Vice-President (Marketing): Dan
Oakland
Sales: $180 million
# of Employees: 400

Miscellaneous Facts: Subsidiary of Tomy
Kogyo Co., Inc.

TONKA CORP.
6000 Clearwater Drive
Minnetonka, MN 55345
(612) 936-3300
Primary Business: Metal toys
CEO: Stephen G. Shank

President: Stephen G. Shank
Vice-President (Human Resources):
   David J. Anderson
Vice-President (Marketing): Raymond
   E. McDonald
Vice-President (Sales): Patrick S. Feely
Revenue: $244 million
Net Worth: $61 million
# of Employees: 1,500

Subsidiary:
Tonka Manufacturing, Inc.

Miscellaneous

KIMBALL INTERNATIONAL, INC.
1600 Royal Street
Jasper, IN 47546
(812) 482-1600
Primary Business: Pianos, organs, office
   furniture
Chairman: Thomas L. Habig
CEO: Arnold I. Habig
President: Douglas A. Habig
Executive Vice-President (Keyboard
   Sales): Jim Birk
Vice-President (Human Resources):
   Keith Truelove
Sales: $319.95 million

Net Worth: $160 million
# of Employees: 6,000

Divisions:
Artec
Kimball Office Furniture Co.
Kimball Piano & Organ Co.
Chandler Veneers
Heritage Hills
The Jasper Corp.
Kimball Electronics
Kimball World
Toolpro

UNITED STATES PLAYING CARD CO.
Beech and Park Avenue
Cincinnati, OH 45212
(513) 396-5700
Primary Business: Maker of playing
   cards, games
Chairman: Howard R. Curd
CEO: Leslie J. Racey
President: Leslie J. Racey
Vice-President (Sales): Stewart E.
   Moore
Vice-President (Marketing): Dan F.
   Edelschick
Sales: $54.91 million
# of Employees: 850

METALS

ALUMAX, INC.
400 South El Camino Real
San Mateo, CA 94402
(415) 348-3400
Primary Business: Holding company,
integrated aluminum producers
Chairman: Pierre Gousseland
Vice-Chairman: Mamoru Tabuchi
President: Robert Marcus
Executive Vice-President: George T.
Haymaker, Jr.
Public Relations Director: Robert G.
Miller
Sales: $1.5 billion
# of Employees: 13,059

Subsidiaries:
Alumax Aluminum Corp., Mill Prod.
Alumax Extrusions

Division:
Alumax Home & Specialty Products,
Inc.

Miscellaneous Facts: Incorporated in
1973 in Delaware.

ALUMINUM CO. OF AMERICA
1501 Alcoa Building
Pittsburgh, PA 15219
(412) 553-4545
Primary Business: Primary and
fabricated aluminum manufacturer
Chairman: Charles W. Parry
CEO: Charles W. Parry
President: C. Fred Fetterolf
Senior Vice-President: Richard L.
Fischer
Senior Vice-President: Donald R.
Whitlow
Senior Vice-President: James W. Wirth
Revenue: $5.75 billion
Net Worth: $3.3 billion
# of Employees: 41,000

Subsidiaries:
Alcoa Fuels, Inc.
Alcoa Recycling Co.
Alcoa Steamship Co., Inc.
DEP Industries, Inc.
The Stolle Corp.
Tifton Aluminum Co., Inc.

Miscellaneous Facts: Trade name
"Alcoa." Founded in Pittsburgh in
1888. It is the leading producer of
aluminum products in the world. 45
percent of U.S. power used by Alcoa
is hydroelectric. In 1985, Alcoa
recycled 14.4 billion used aluminum
cans. Collectors of cans were paid
about $200 million in 1985.

AMAX, INC.
Amax Center
Post Office Box 1700
Greenwich, CT 06836
(203) 629-6000
Primary Business: Molybdenum, coal,
iron ore
Chairman: Pierre Gousseland
CEO: Martin V. Alonzo
President: Allen Born
Senior Executive Vice-President
(Metals): John W. Goth
Executive Vice-President and General
Counsel: Malcolm B. Bayliss
Director of Personnel: Patricia Graf
Sales: $2.4 billion
Net Worth: $1.7 billion
# of Employees: 12,400

Subsidiaries:
Amax Engineering & Management
Services Co.
Amax Environmental Services, Inc.
Amax Exploration, Inc.
Amax Materials Research Center

ASARCO, INC.
180 Maiden Lane
New York, NY 10038
(212) 510-1800
Primary Business: Lead, zinc, gold,
silver products
Chairman: Richard D. J. Osborne
CEO: Richard D. J. Osborne
President: Richard D. J. Osborne
Vice-President (Exploration): Richard
L. Brown, Jr.
Vice-President (Sales): E. R. Bergin
Vice-President (Mining): Robert J.
Kupsch

Sales: $1.32 billion
Net Worth: $692 million
# of Employees: 12,500

Subsidiaries:
American Limestone Co.
Asarco Oil & Gas Co.
Bolivian Lead Corp., S.A.
Enthone, Inc.
Neptune Mining Co.
Southern Peru Copper Corp.
Watauga Stone Co.
Lone Star Lead Construction Corp.
Federated Metals Corp.

Miscellaneous Facts: Incorporated in
1899 in New Jersey as American
Smelting and Refining Co. Present
title adopted in 1975.

ATHLONE INDUSTRIES, INC.
200 Webro Road
Parsippany, NJ 07054
(201) 887-9100
Primary Business: Specialty metals
Chairman: Harold J. Miller
President: Harold J. Miller
Executive Vice-President: Daniel J.
    Lyons
Vice-President: Raymond P. Fisher
Manager, Personnel: Evelyn Corcaron
Revenue: $281 million
Net Worth: $51 million
# of Employees: 3,300

Divisions:
Dudley Sports Co.
Henschel Shoe
Reynolds Fasteners, Inc.
Gelfo Manufacturing Co., Inc.
Green River Steel Corp.
Sea Fashions, Inc.

Miscellaneous Facts: Incorporated in
1938 in Delaware as Holland Furnace
Co. Present name adopted in 1966.

BETHLEHEM STEEL CORP.
Bethlehem, PA 18016
(215) 694-2424
Primary Business: Manufacturing and
    sale of steel
Chairman: Donald H. Trautlein
President: Walter F. Williams
Vice-Chairman: Richard M. Smith
Senior Vice-President (Public Affairs):

Curtis H. Barnette
Senior Vice-President (Human
    Resources): John A. Jordon, Jr.
Revenue: $5.39 billion
Net Worth: $1.1 billion
# of Employees: 51,400

Subsidiaries:
Kusan, Inc.
Caradco Corp.
Fiberglass Systems, Inc.
Mastil Corp.
Southeastern-Kusan, Inc.
J. M. Tull Industries, Inc.

Miscellaneous Facts: Incorporated in
1919 in Delaware.

CARPENTER TECHNOLOGY CORP.
101 W Bern Street
Reading, PA 19601
(215) 371-2000
Primary Business: Specialty metals
    manufacturer
CEO: Paul R. Roedel
President: Paul R. Roedel
Senior Vice-President: Carl F. Schweikle
Senior Vice-President: Ralph C.
    Leinbach, Jr.
Sales: $528 million
Net Worth: $319 million
# of Employees: 4,500

Subsidiary:
Eagle Precision Metals Corp.

COMMERCIALS METALS CO.
7800 Stemmons Freeway, N
Dallas, TX 75427
(214) 689-4300
Primary Business: Processes metals
Chairman: Charles W. Merritt
CEO: Stanley A. Rabin
President: Stanley A. Rabin
Vice-President: Lawrence A. Engels
Revenue: $1.1 billion
Net Worth: $125 million
# of Employees: 3,089

COPPERWELD CORP.
2 Oliver Plaza
Pittsburgh, PA 15222
(412) 263-3200
Primary Business: Manufactures metal
    products

Chairman: Anthony J. A. Bryan
CEO: Anthony J. A. Bryan
President: Howell A. Breedlove
Vice-President: Ronald L. Van Meter
Vice-President (Human Resources):
   Wayne A. Nelson
Sales: $442 million
Net Worth: $161 million
# of Employees: 3,000

Subsidiaries:
American Seamless Tubing Co.
Copperwell Steel Co.

Miscellaneous Facts: Incorporated in
   1915 in Pennsylvania as Copperweld
   Steel Co. Present name adopted in
   1973.

CRANE CO.
300 Park Avenue
New York, NY 10022
(212) 415-7300
Primary Business: Steel manufacturer
Chairman: Robert S. Evans
CEO: Robert S. Evans
President: Robert S. Evans
Vice-President: Paul R. Hundt
Vice-President (Human Resources):
   Richard Phillips
Revenue: $792 million
Net Worth: $211 million
# of Employees: 13,000

Subsidiaries:
CF & I Steel Corp.
Deming Pump Co.
Huttig Sash & Door Co.
Medusa Corp.

Miscellaneous Facts: Incorporated in
   1985 in Delaware to succeed company
   with same name incorporated in 1865
   in Illinois.

CYCLOPS CORP.
650 Washington Road
Pittsburgh, PA 15228
(412) 343-4000
Primary Business: Steel concrete forms,
   steel floors and roofs
President: William H. Knoell
Executive Vice-President: James F. Will
Senior Vice-President: William D.
   Dickey

Vice-President (Public Relations):
   Hubert W. Delano
Revenue: $1.27 billion
Net Worth: $193 million
# of Employees: 8,300

Subsidiaries:
Busy Beaver Building Centers, Inc.
E.G. Smith Construction Products

Divisions:
Cosholton Stainless Div.
Cytemp Specialty Steel Div.
Detroit Strip Div.
Sawhill Tubular Div.
Silo Div.
Tex-Tube Div.

CYRUS MINERALS CO.
7200 S Alton Way
Englewood, CO 80112
(303) 740-5000
Primary Business: Owns and operates
   coal mines
Chairman: John C. Duncan
CEO: Kenneth J. Barr
President: Kenneth J. Barr
Vice-President: Donald P. Bellum
Vice-President (Human Resources):
   Roger A. Kaufmann
Revenue: $620 million
Net Worth: $1.1 billion
# of Employees: 4,820

Miscellaneous Facts: Formerly AMOCO
   Minerals Co.

FREEPORT-MCMORAN, INC.
200 Park Avenue
New York, NY 10166
(212) 578-9200
Primary Business: Exploration for
   minerals
Chairman: James R. Moffett
CEO: James R. Moffett
President: Milton H. Ward
Senior Vice-President and General
   Counsel: Edward C. Stebbins
Vice-President (Human Resources):
   Thomas L. Vandegrift
Gross Sales: $847.16 million
Net Worth: $691 million
# of Employees: 5,730

Subsidiaries:
FMI Acquisition, Inc.

FPCO, Inc.
Freeport Coal Co.
Freeport Georgia Co.
Freeport Copper Co.
Freeport Metal Sales Co.

HANDY & HARMAN
850 Third Avenue
New York, NY 10022
(212) 752-3400
Primary Business: Specialty metals
Chairman: M. Wilbur Townsend
President: R. N. Daniel
Group Vice-President: Philip G. McGee
Vice-President (Marketing): George G.
  Cimini
Sales: $556 million
Net Worth: $148 million
# of Employees: 5,680

Subsidiaries:
A-1 Sales, Inc.
American Chemical & Refining Co.
Brunner Engineering & Manufacturing,
  Inc.
Conn-Form Corp.
Daniel Radiator Corp.

HARSCO CORP.
Post Office Box 8888
Camp Hill, PA 17011
(717) 763-7064
Primary Business: Fabricated metal
  products
Chairman: Jeffrey J. Burge
CEO: Jeffrey J. Burge
President: Malcolm W. Gambill
Vice-President (Employee Relations):
  Emile G. deCoen
Vice-President (Public Affairs): Robert
  A. Haynos
Sales: $1.01 billion
Net Worth: $467 million
# of Employees: 11,000

Divisions:
Astro Metallurgical
BMY Co.
Broderick Co.
Can-Tex Industries
Capitol Manufacturing Co.
Fairmont Railway Motors
Sherwood Co.
Hecketi Div.
IKG Industries

Kinnear Div.
Patent Scaffolding Co.
Patterson-Kelley Co.
Plant City Steel Co.
Reed Minerals
Taylor-Wharton Co.

INLAND STEEL INDUSTRIES, INC.
30 W Monroe Street
Chicago, IL 60603
(312) 346-0300
Primary Business: Sheet and strip steel
Chairman: Frank W. Luerssen
CEO: Frank W. Luerssen
President: Robert J. Darnall
Vice-Chairman: O. Robert Nottelmann
Vice-President (Sales): Robert E. Powell
Vice-President (Corporate Planning):
  Joseph D. Corso
Revenue: $2.99 billion
Net Worth: $958 million
# of Employees: 24,900

Subsidiaries:
Inland Steel Co.
Inland Steel Coal Co.
Inland Steel Mining Co.
J.M. Tull Industries, Inc.

Miscellaneous Facts: Incorporated in
  1917 in Delaware as successor to
  company with the same name.

**KAISER ALUMINUM & CHEMICAL
  CORP.**
300 Lakeside Drive
Oakland, CA 94612
(415) 271-3300
Primary Business: Aluminum ingot, foil
  food containers
Chairman: Cornell C. Maier
CEO: Cornell C. Maier
President: A. S. Hutchcraft, Jr.
Senior Vice-President: Jesse D.
  Erickson
Vice-President (Public Relations):
  Robert W. Irelan
Senior Vice-President: H. M. Nelson
Sales: $3.19 billion
Net Worth: $1.1 billion
# of Employees: 16,234

Subsidiary:
Kaiser Development Co.

Miscellaneous Facts: Operates 41
aluminum and chemical plants around
the country.

THE LTV CORP.
2000 Ross Avenue
Dallas, TX 75201
(214) 746-7711
Primary Business: Steel, energy products
Chairman: Raymond A. Hay
CEO: Raymond A. Hay
President: Robert L. Kirk
Executive Vice-President: David H.
Hoag
Senior Vice-President (Personnel):
Walter E. Meyer
Vice-President (Public Relations): John
W. Johnson
Sales: $8.2 billion
Net Worth: $652 million
# of Employees: 56,800

Subsidiaries:
AM General
CKH Corp.
Aliquippa & Southern Railroad Co.
Dearborn Leasing Co.
Olga Coal Co.
Wabush Iron Co., Ltd.
Lykes Equipment Corp.
J.K. Industries, Inc.
Oil States Rubber co.
Ore Finance Co.
Vought Industries, Inc.
Republic Buildings Corp.

THE MARMON GROUP, INC.
39 S LaSalle Street
Chicago, IL 60603
(312) 372-9500
Primary Business: General products,
including steel, automotive, mining
Chairman: J. A. Pritzker
President: Robert A. Pritzker
Executive Vice-President: George A.
Jones
Executive Vice-President: Robert L.
Gluth
Revenue: $2.68 billion
Net Worth: $591 million
# of Employees: 27,600

Subsidiaries:
Accutronics, Inc.
Amarillo Gear Co.

American Box Co.
Cerro Conduit Co.
Penn Aluminum International
Rego Co.
Wells Lamont Corp.
Atlas Bolt & Screw Co.
The Getz Corp.
Leasametric, Inc.
Colson Caster Corp.
Huron Steel Co.
Miles Metal Co.

NATIONAL INTERGROUP, INC.
20 Stanwix Street
Pittsburgh, PA 15222
(412) 394-4100
Primary Business: Holding company,
steel products and mines
Chairman: Howard M. Love
CEO: Howard M. Love
President: James E. Haas
Senior Vice-President (Public Affairs):
Fred E. Tucker
Vice-President and General Counsel: Eli
Krivoshia, Jr.
Sales: $2.29 billion
# of Employees: 16,000

Miscellaneous Facts: Incorporated in
1983 in Delaware.

NATIONAL STEEL CORP.
20 Stanwix Street
Pittsburgh, PA 15222
(412) 394-4100
Primary Business: Manufactures steel
Chairman: Howard M. Love.
CEO: Howard M. Love
President: Kokichi Hagiwara
Senior Vice-President: Stanley C.
Ellspermann
Vice-President and General Counsel: E.
Krivoshia
Sales: $2.08 billion
# of Employees: 12,500

Associated Companies:
Carryore, Ltd.
Mesaba-Cliffs Mining Co.
Pesque Isle Corp.
American Steel Corp.
Mathies Coal Co.
NS Land Co.
National Mines Corp.

NUCOR CORP.
4425 Randolph Road
Charlotte, NC 28211
(704) 366-7000
Primary Business: Manufactures steel,
    steel joints
Chairman: F. Kenneth Iverson
CEO: F. Kenneth Iverson
President: Hugh D. Aycock
Vice-President (Finance): Samuel Siegel
Vice-President and General Manager:
    Hasting M. Crapse
Revenue: $660.26 million
Net Worth: $357 million
# of Employees: 3,600

Divisions:
Nucor Steel Div.
Research Chemicals Div.
Vulcraft Div.

REYNOLDS METALS CO.
6601 Broad Street Road
Richmond, VA 23233
(804) 281-2000
Primary Business: Aluminum products
Chairman: David P. Reynolds
CEO: William O. Bourke
President: William O. Bourke
Executive Vice-President: R. Berncrowl
Vice-President (Personnel): John R.
    McGill
Sales: $3.4 billion
Net Worth: $1.2 billion
# of Employees: 27,400

Subsidiaries:
Alpart Jamaica, Inc.
Alreco Metals, Inc.
Bushnell Plaza Development
El Campo Aluminum Co.

Eskimo Pie Co.
Malakoff Industries, Inc.
New Eastwick Corp.
President Manor Corp.
Reynolds Regency Corp.
Southern Gravure Service, Inc.
Worsley Alumina Property, Ltd.

Miscellaneous Facts: Incorporated in
    1928 in Delaware.

SAGA CORP.
One Saga Lane
Menlo Park, CA 94025
(415) 854-5150
Primary Business: Fabricated structural
    steel
Chairman: Charles A. Lynch
CEO: Charles A. Lynch
Executive Vice-President: Jeffrey O.
    Henley
Vice-President (Human Resources):
    Earl C. Royse
Vice-President (Corporate
    Communications): Gene Elsbree
Revenue: $1.13 billion
# of Employees: 58,000

Subsidiaries:
Spectrum Foods
Stuart Anderson's-Black Angus
The Velvet Turtle
Grandy's, Inc.
Spoons
Straw Hat Pizza

Miscellaneous Facts: Subsidiary of
    Mariott Corp. Company subsidiaries
    feed students at approximately 350
    colleges and universities around the
    country.

OIL AND NATURAL GAS

AMERADA HESS CORP.
1185 Avenue of the Americas
New York, NY 10036
(212) 997-8500
Primary Business: Crude oil and natural
gas
Chairman: Leon Hess
CEO: Philip Kramer
President: Philip Kramer
Group Vice-President: A. T. Jacobson
Senior Vice-President: Bernard T.
Deverin
Vice-President and General Counsel: J.
F. Kelly, Jr.
Revenue: $8.35 billion
Net Worth: $2.5 billion
# of Employees: 8,887

Miscellaneous Facts: Incorporated in
1970 in Delaware as Amerada Corp.
Present name adopted in 1969.

AMERICAN PETROFINA, INC.
Post Office Box 2159
Dallas, TX 75221
(214) 750-2400
Primary Business: Crude oil
Chairman: Paul D. Meek
CEO: Paul D. Meek
Senior Vice-President: K. W. Perry
Vice-President: S. R. West
Vice-President: Guy Patat
Revenue: $2.12 billion
Net Worth: $659 million
# of Employees: 2,750

Subsidiaries:
Fina Oil & Chemical Co.
Cosden Oil & Chemical Co.
Sigma Coatings
Vercon, Inc.

Miscellaneous Facts: Incorporated in
1956 in Delaware.

AMOCO CORP.
200 E Randolph Drive
Chicago, IL 60601
(312) 856-6111
Primary Business: Holding company,
crude oil

Chairman: Richard M. Morrow
CEO: Richard M. Morrow
President: H. Laurance Fuller
Vice-Chairman: James W. Cozad
Vice-President (Public Affairs): Joe P.
Hammond
Vice-President (Human Resources):
Wayne Anderson
Revenue: $29 billion
Net Worth: $12 billion
# of Employees: 53,581

Subsidiaries:
Amoco Chemicals Corp.
Amoco Credit Corp.
Amoco Development Co.
Amoco Leasing Corp.
Amoco Oil Co.
Amoco Pipeline Co.
Amoco Production Co.
Amoco Properties, Inc.
Amoco Realty Co.

Miscellaneous Facts: Incorporated in
1889 in Indiana as Standard Oil Co. In
1931, company was reorganized under
the Indiana General Corporation Act.
Present name adopted in 1985.

ARKLA, INC.
Post Office Box 21734
Shreveport, LA 71120
(318) 266-2700
Primary Business: Natural gas
production
Chairman: Thomas F. McLarty III
CEO: Thomas F. McLarty III
Executive Vice-President: Michael B.
Bracy
Vice-President (Sales): Leo S. Cage
Revenue: $1.2 billion
Net Worth: $465 million
# of Employees: 4,232

Subsidiaries:
Arkansas Cement Corp.
Arkla Chemical Corp.
Arkla Exploration Co.

ASHLAND OIL, INC.
Post Office Box 391
Ashland, KY 41114
(606) 329-3333
Primary Business: Petroleum, coal,
  chemicals
Chairman: John R. Hall
CEO: John R. Hall
Vice-Chairman: Robert T. McCowan
Senior Vice-President: Paul W.
  Chellgren
Vice-President (Human Resources):
  William Harkins
Revenue: $8.25 billion
Net Worth: $845 million
# of Employees: 32,000

Subsidiaries:
Ashland Pipe Line Co.
Ashland Coal, Inc.
Ashland Development, Inc.

Divisions:
Ashland Chemical Co.
Chemical Systems Div.
Drew Chemical Corp.
Electronic & Lab. Products Div.
Polyester Div.
Ashland Petroleum Co.

Miscellaneous Facts: Incorporated in
  1936 in Kentucky as Ashland Oil &
  Refining Co. Present name adopted in
  1970.

ATLANTIC RICHFIELD CO.
515 S Flower Street
Los Angeles, CA 90071
(213) 486-3511
Primary Business: Petroleum, minerals
  and chemicals
Chairman: Robert O. Anderson
CEO: L. M. Cook
President: L. M. Cook
Vice-Chairman: Ralph F. Cox
Vice-Chairman: J. P. Downer
Personnel Director: Phillip Silcox
Revenue: $25.22 billion
Net Worth: $9.9 million
# of Employees: 37,700

Operating Companies:
Anaconda Minerals Co.
ARCO Alaska, Inc.
ARCO Chemical Co.
ARCO International Oil & Gas Co.
ARCO Exploration & Technology Co.

ARCO Metals Co.
ARCO Oil & Gas Co.
ARCO Petroleum Products Co.
ARCO Pipe Line Co.
ARCO Transportation Co.
Lyondell Petrochemical Co.

Miscellaneous Facts: Incorporated in
  1985 in Delaware as successor to
  company incorporated in 1870 in
  Pennsylvania. Name changed from
  Atlantic Refining Co. to present one
  in 1966.

BAKER INTERNATIONAL CORP.
500 City Parkway
Orange, CA 92668
(714) 634-2333
Primary Business: Oil field tools
Chairman: E. H. Clark, Jr.
CEO: E. H. Clark, Jr.
President: James D. Woods
Executive Vice-President: John F.
  Schaefer
Senior Vice-President: J. J. Shelton
Vice-President (Human Resources):
  Phillip Rice
Revenue: $1.83 billion
Net Worth: $1.6 billion
# of Employees: 22,000

Subsidiary:
Envirotech, Inc.

Miscellaneous Facts: Incorporated in
  1913 in California.

BIG THREE INDUSTRIES, INC.
3535 W 12th Street
Houston, TX 77008
(713) 868-0333
Primary Business: Industrial gases, oil
  field tools
Chairman: Harry K. Smith
CEO: Harry K. Smith
President: Thomas E. Sanos
Co-Chairman: Albert K. Smith
Executive Vice-President (Sales):
  Harold E. Purdom
Personnel Director: Gerald Dowman
Sales: $775.68 million
Net Worth: $566 million
# of Employees: 5,325

Subsidiaries:
Bayou Cogeneration

Big Three Cogeneration
Big Three International
Bowen Tools, Inc.
The Dia-Log Co.
Nowsco Services, Inc.

Divisions:
Industrial Gas Div.
Northern Div.
Ransome Div.
Southern Div.
Tempil Div.

CAMERON IRON WORKS, INC.
Post Office Box 1212
Houston, TX 77251
(713) 939-2211
Primary Business: Pressure-control
  equipment for oil fields manufacturer
Chairman: M. A. Wright
CEO: M. A. Wright
President: P. J. Burguieres
Senior Vice-President: J. D. Deakins
Senior Vice-President: C. B. King
Sales: $515 million
Net Worth: $341 million
# of Employees: 11,070

THE CHARTER CO.
Post Office Box 2017
Jacksonville, FL 32203
(904) 358-4111
Primary Business: Holding company,
  petroleum
Chairman: Raymond K. Mason
CEO: Alexander P. Zechella
President: Alexander P. Zechella
Executive Vice-President: Howard C.
  Serkin
Executive Vice-President: D. Thomas
  Moody
Revenue: $3.7 billion
# of Employees: 4,000

Subsidiaries:
Charter Oil
Charter Marine Fuels, Inc.
Charter Marketing Co.
Riffe Petroleum Co.
New England Petroleum Industries

CHEVRON CORP.
225 Bush Street
San Francisco, CA 94104
(415) 894-7700
Primary Business: Gasoline, jet fuel,
  natural gas
Chairman: G. M. Keller
President: J. R. Grey
Vice-Chairman: D. L. Bower
Vice-Chairman: K. T. Derr
Vice-President (Public Affairs): W. K.
  Morris
Revenue: $29.20 billion
Net Worth: $14.7 billion
# of Employees: 65,000

Subsidiaries:
American Gilsonite Co.
Chandeleur Pipe Line Co.
Chevron Chemical Co.
Ra-Pid-Gro Corp.
Chevron Industries Co.

Divisions:
Chevron Land & Development Co.
Chevron Oil Field Research Co.
Chevron Shale Oil Co.
Chevron Stations, Inc.

Miscellaneous Facts: Operates in more
  than 80 countries. One of the largest
  marketers of petroleum in the U.S.
  One of the largest manufacturers of
  refined products in the U.S.
  Incorporated in 1926 in Delaware as
  Standard Oil Co. of California.
  Present name adopted in 1984.

COASTAL CORP.
9 Greenway Plaza
Houston, TX 77046
(713) 877-1400
Primary Business: Natural gas gathering
Chairman: O. S. Wyatt, Jr.
CEO: O. S. Wyatt, Jr.
President: James R. Paul
Senior Vice-President (Marketing): Dan
  J. Hill
Senior Vice-President (Legal): Bernard
  W. Schrader
Senior Vice-President (Refining): Albin
  W. Smith
Revenue: $6.26 billion
Net Worth: $577 million
# of Employees: 6,661

Subsidiaries:
ANG Coal Gasification Co.
ANR Coal Co.
ANR Western Coal Dev. Co.
Associated Truck Lines
Garrett Freightlines, Inc.
Border Exploration Co.
Derby Refining Co.
Coastal Oil & Gas Corp.
Belcher Co. of New York
Belcher Oil Co.
Coscol Marine Corp.

COMBUSTION ENGINEERING, INC.
900 Long Ridge Road
Stamford, CT 06904
(203) 329-8771
Primary Business: Supplies equipment
  for the oil and gas industry
Chairman: Arthur J. Santry, Jr.
CEO: Charles E. Hugel
President: Charles E. Hugel
Executive Vice-President: George S.
  Kimmel
Vice-President: Dudley C. Mecum
Sales: $3 billion
Net Worth: $795 million
# of Employees: 36,387

Subsidiaries:
Beaumont Forged Products
C-E Air Preheater
C-E Bauer
C-E Invalco
C-E Minerals, Inc.
C-E Raymond
C-E Refactories
C-E Studsvik
C-E Tyler

Miscellaneous Facts: Incorporated in
  1912 in Delaware as the Locomotive
  Superheater Co. Name changed to
  Superheater Co. in 1921, then to
  Combustion Engineering Superheater
  Co. in 1948. Present name adopted in
  1953.

DIAMOND SHAMROCK CORP.
717 N Harwood Street
Dallas, TX 75201
(214) 922-2000
Primary Business: Oil and gas producer
Chairman: W. H. Bricker
CEO: W. H. Bricker

President: J. L. Jackson
Executive Vice-President: C. E. Stewart
Vice-President (Communications): P. A.
  Hesse
Sales: $4.4 billion
Net Worth: $2.7 billion
# of Employees: 12,740

Subsidiary:
Diamond Shamrock Coal Co.

E.I. DUPONT DE NEMOURS & CO.
1007 Market Street
Wilmington, DE 19801
(302) 774-1000
Primary Business: Extraction, refining
  and sale of petroleum
Chairman: Edward G. Jefferson
Department Chairman: Richard E.
  Heckert
Vice-Chairman: Ralph E. Bailey
Sales; $35.91 billion
# of Employees: 154,500

Divisions:
Du Pont Canada, Inc.
Biomedicals Dept.
Caribe Biochemicals, Inc.
Finishes & Fabricated Products
Polymer Products Dept.

Miscellaneous Facts: Trade name "Du
  Pont." One of the largest chemical
  companies in the U.S. Owns three
  country clubs with 18-hole golf courses
  for employees.

ENRON CORP.
Post Office Box 1188
Dallas, TX 77021
(713) 654-6161
Primary Business: Oil exploration
Chairman: K. L. Lay
CEO: K. L. Lay
President: J. M. Seidel
Executive Vice-President: R. LoChiano
Vice-President (Personnel): L. D. Snow
Revenue: $10 billion
Net Worth: $5.8 billion
# of Employees: 11,000

ETHYL CORP.
330 S Fourth Street
Richmond, VA 23219
(804) 788-5000

Primary Business: Antiknock compounds, other additives for petroleum products
Chairman: F. D. Gottwald, Jr.
CEO: F. D. Gottwald, Jr.
President: Bruce C. Gottwald
Vice-President (Health and Environment) Gary L. Ter Haar
Vice-President (Corporate Communications): A. Prescott Rowe
Sales: $1.67 billion
Net Worth: $789 million
# of Employees: 11,000

Subsidiaries:
William L. Bonnell Co., Inc.
Capitol Products Corp.
Elk Horn Coal Corp.
Fiberlux, Inc.
First Colony Life Insurance Co.

EXXON CORP.
1251 Avenue of the Americas
New York, NY 10020
(212) 333-1000
Primary Business: Operating petroleum company through subsidiaries
Chairman: C. C. Garvin, Jr.
CEO: C. C. Garvin, Jr.
President: Lawrence G. Rawl
Vice-President (Public Affairs): S. Stamas
Vice-President (Employee Relations): G. B. McCullough
Vice-President (Human Resources): T. H. Tiedemann, Jr.
Revenue: $90.85 billion
Net Worth: $29 billion
# of Employees: 150,000

Divisions:
Exxon Co. U.S.A.
Exxon International Co.
Exxon Pipeline Co.
Exxon Research & Engineering Co.
Exxon Enterprises
Exxon Mineral Co.

Affiliated Companies:
Esso Eastern, Inc.
Esso Exploration, Inc.
Exxon Nuclear Co.
Gilbarco, Inc.

Miscellaneous Facts: Is the oldest and one of the largest industrial enterprises in the world. From 1973 to 1983, spent over $4 billion on research.

GULF CORP.
Post Office Box 1166
Pittsburgh, PA 15230
(412) 263-5000
Primary Business: Oil and gas production
Chairman: J. E. Lee
CEO: J. E. Lee
President: E. B. Walker III
Vice-President (Human Resources): L. Fernandez, Jr.
Vice-President (Public Affairs): W. E. Moffett
Sales: $28.90 billion
# of Employees: 42,7000

Miscellaneous Facts: Subsidiary of Chevron Corp.

HALLIBURTON CO.
2600 Southland Center
Dallas, TX 75201
(214) 748-7261
Primary Business: Oil field service products
CEO: Thomas H. Cruikshank
President: Thomas H. Cruikshank
Executive Vice-President: Dennis R. Hendrix
Senior Vice-President: Jack W. Miller
Vice-President (Investor Relations): J. G. Nuland
Revenue: $4.79 billion
Net Worth: $2.86 billion
# of Employees: 67,540

Subsidiaries:
Brown & Root, Inc.
Highlands Insurance Co.
Joe D. Hughes, Inc.
Jet Research Center, Inc.
NUS Corp.
Otis Engineering Corp.
Taylor International, Inc.

Divisions:
Freight Master Div.
Halliburton Services Div.
IMCO Services Div.
Vann Systems Div.
Welex Div.

KERR-MCGEE CORP.

Kerr-McGee Center
Oklahoma City, OK 73102
(405) 270-1313
Primary Business: Production and
manufacture of oil, gas
Chairman: F. A. McPherson
CEO: F. A. McPherson
President: J. W. McKenny
Executive Vice-Preident: Marvin K.
Hambrick
Senior Vice-President: Tom J. McDaniel
Human Resources Director: J. N. Fruits
Sales: $3.3 billion
Net Worth: $1.7 billion
# of Employees: 8,351

Subsidiaries:
Benedum-Trees Oil Co.
Kerr-McGee Chemical Corp.
Kerr-McGee Coal Corp.
Cato Oil & Grease Co.
Southwestern Refining Co., Inc.
Triangle Refineries, Inc.
Quivira Mining Co.
Sunning Oils, Ltd.
Transworld Drilling Co.

Miscellaneous Facts: Incorporated in
1932 in Delaware as A & K Petroleum
Co. Present name adopted in 1965.

MCDERMOTT, INC.

1010 Common Street
New Orleans, LA 70112
(504) 587-4411
Primary Business: Energy services
company, oil fields
Chairman: J. E. Cunningham
CEO: J. E. Cunningham
President: R. E. Howson
Vice-President (Employee and Public
Relations): R. E. Wolbert
Executive Vice-President: J. A. Lynott
Revenue: $3.3 billion
Net Worth: $1.2 billion
# of Employees: 35,000

Subsidiaries:
Babcock & Wilcox Co.
Marine Contractors, Inc.

Miscellaneous Facts: Subsidiary of
McDermott International, Inc.,
Republic of Panama. Incorporated in
1946 in Delaware.

MITCHELL ENERGY & DEVELOPMENT CORP.

2001 Timberloch Place
The Woodlands, TX 77380
(713) 363-5500
Primary Business: Natural gas producer
Chairman: George P. Mitchell
CEO: George P. Mitchell
President: George P. Mitchell
Vice-Chairman: Bernard F. Clark
Senior Vice-President: Philip S. Smith
Revenue: $843 million
Net Worth: $575 million
# of Employees: 3,000

MOBIL CORP.

150 E 42nd Street
New York, NY 10017
(212) 883-4242
Primary Business: Holding company,
petroleum and natural gas
Chairman: Rawleigh Warner, Jr.
CEO: Rawleigh Warner, Jr.
President: Allen E. Murray
Vice-President (Public Affairs): Herbert
Schmertz
Vice-President (Exploration): Robert R.
Graves
Personnel Director: R. D. Adams
Revenue: $60.47 billion
Net Worth: $14 billion
# of Employees: 163,100

Subsidiaries:
Mobil Oil Corp.
Mobil Pipe Line Co.
Container Corp. of America
Marcor, Inc.
Montgomery Ward & Co., Inc.
Mobil Chemical Co.
The Superior Oil Co.

Miscellaneous Facts: One of the largest
petroleum companies in the U.S.
Operates in more than 100 countries.
Incorporated in 1882 in New York as
Standard Oil of New York. Present
name adopted in 1966.

NL INDUSTRIES, INC.

1230 Avenue of the Americas
New York, NY 10020
(212) 621-9400
Primary Business: Petroleum service
Chairman: Theodore C. Rogers

CEO: Theodore C. Rogers
President: Theodore C. Rogers
Executive Vice-President: Fred W.
  Montanari
Vice-President: Robert E. Booker, Jr.
Vice-President and General Counsel:
  Robert J. Hurley
Revenue: $1.36 billion
Net Worth: $785 million
# of Employees: 12,800

Divisions:
NL Acme Tool
NL Atlas Bradford
NL Baroid
NL Chemicals
NL ERCO
NL Hycalog
NL McCullough
NL Shaffer
NL Sperry-Sun

OCCIDENTAL PETROLEUM CORP.
10889 Wilshire Boulevard
Los Angeles, CA 90024
(213) 879-1700
Primary Business: Natural gas, crude oil
Chairman: Armand Hammer
CEO: Armand Hammer
President: Ray R. Irani
Vice-President (Public Relations):
  Gordon Reece
Vice-President (Health, Environment
  and Safety): Frank B. Friedman
Vice-President (Employee Relations):
  Ronald H. Asquith
Revenue: $15.58 billion
Net Worth: $3.6 billion
# of Employees: 41,000

Subsidiaries:
Cities Service Co.
IBP, Inc.
Island Creek Corp.
Midcon Corp.
United Energy Resources
UER Overseas Finances N.V.
United Gas Pipe Line Co.
United Overseas Services, Inc.
United Texas Transmission Co.
Sea Robin Pipeline Co.
Occidental Chemical Corp.

Miscellaneous Facts: Incorporated in
  1986 in Delaware.

PACIFIC LIGHTING CORP.
810 Flower Street
Los Angeles, CA 90017
(213) 689-3481
Primary Business: Natural gas
  distribution
Chairman: Paul A. Miller
CEO: Paul A. Miller
President: James R. Ukropina
Vice-Chairman: Joseph R. Rensch
Executive Vice-President: Robert T.
  Bonn
Public Relations Director: Stephen H.
  Baer
Sales: $5.08 billion
Net Worth: $1.5 billion
# of Employees: 11,965

Subsidiaries:
Dual Fuel Systems, Inc.
Pacific Alaska LNG Co.
Pacific Interstate Co.
Pacific Lighting Energy Systems
Pacific Lighting Gas Development Co.
Pacific Real Estate Projects, Inc.
Blackfield Hawaii Corp.
Fredericks Sales, Inc.
Thrifty Corp.

PANHANDLE EASTERN CORP.
3000 Bissonnet Avenue
Houston, TX 77005
(713) 664-3401
Primary Business: Petroleum
  manufacturer
Chairman: Richard L. O'Shields
CEO: R. D. Hunsucker
President: R. D. Hunsucker
Senior Vice-President: Vernon D.
  Rigdon
Personnel Director: Herbert E. Schulze,
  Jr.
Sales: $2.8 billion
Net Worth: $1.6 billion
# of Employees: 5,700

Subsidiaries:
Anadarko Productions Co.
Divilyn Field Drilling Co.
Pan Alaskan Gas Co., Inc.

PENN CENTRAL CORP.
500 Putnam Avenue
Greenwich, CT 06836
(203) 629-5000

Primary Business: Manufactures products for oil telecommunications industry
Chairman: Carl H. Lindner
CEO: Alfred W. Martinelli
President: Alfred W. Martinelli
Senior Executive Vice-President: Herbert S. Winokur
Executive Vice-President: Edward F. Kosnik
Sales: $2.5 billion
Net Worth: $1.8 billion
# of Employees: 31,000

Subsidiaries:
Great Southwest Corp.
Marathon Manufacturing Co.
Solid State Scientific, Inc.
Penn Central Technical Security
Qualcorp, Inc.
Vitro Corp.
Buckeye Gas Products Co.
Gulf Energy Development Co.

Miscellaneous Facts: Incorporated in 1847 in Pennsylvania as Pennsylvania Railroad Co. Name changed to Pennsylvania New York Central Transporting Co. in 1968. Present name adopted in 1978.

PENNZOIL CO.
Post Office Box 2967
Houston, TX 77252
(713) 546-4000
Primary Business: Producer, refiner of petroleum
Chairman: J. Hugh Liedtke
CEO: J. Hugh Liedtke
President: Richard J. Howe
Group Vice-President (Communications): P. L. Manning
Group Vice-President (Mining): Douglas J. Bourne
Revenue: $2.35 billion
Net Worth: $752 million
# of Employees: 7,700

Subsidiaries:
Pennzoil Sulphur Co.

Divisions:
Pennzoil Exploration & Production Co.
Pennzoil International Div.
Pennzoil Products Co.
Penreco
Wolf's Head Oil Co.

Miscellaneous Facts: Famous golfer Arnold Palmer, spokesman. Trademark first appeared in 1916. Company formed in 1963 through consolidation of South Penn Oil Co., Zapata Petroleum Corp. and Stetco Petroleum Corp.

PHILLIPS PETROLEUM CO.
Phillips Building
Bartlesville, OK 74003
(918) 661-6600
Primary Business: Petroleum, chemicals
Chairman: C. J. Silas
CEO: C. J. Silas
President: Glenn A. Cox
Vice-President (Public Affairs): J. Thomas Boyd
Vice-President (Human Resources): W. R. Thomas
Revenue: $15.54 billion
Net Worth: $6.6 billion
# of Employees: 29,600

Subsidiaries:
Alamo Chemical Co.
Applied Automation, Inc.
Catalyst Resources, Inc.
Phillips 66 Companies
Phillips Communications, Inc.
Phillips Fibers Corp.
Phillips Investment Co.
Phillips Natural Gas Co.
Phillips Pipe Line Co.

Miscellaneous Facts: Incorporated in 1917 in Delaware.

PUBLIC SERVICE ELECTRIC & GAS CO.
80 Park Plaza
Newark, NJ 07101
(201) 430-7000
Primary Business: Electricity and natural gas
Chairman: Harold W. Sonn
CEO: Harold W. Sonn
President: Harold W. Sonn
Vice-President (Public Relations): Robert H. Franklin
Vice-President (Human Resources): Charles E. Maginn, Jr.
Vice-President (Nuclear): Corbin A. McNeill, Jr.
Revenue: $4.20 billion
# of Employees: 13,706

Subsidiaries:
Community Energy Alternatives, Inc.
Mulberry Street Urban Renewal Corp.
PSE & G Research Group
Public Service Resources Corp.

QUAKER STATE OIL REFINING CORP.
255 Elm Street
Oil City, PA 16301
(814) 676-7676
Primary Business: Refinery, coal
Chairman: Quentin E. Wood
CEO: Quentin E. Wood
President: Roger A. Markle
Vice-President (Refining): William C. Helsley
Vice-President (Marketing): J. N. Kelley
Revenue: $994.63 million
Net Worth: $311 million
# of Employees: 6,700

Subsidiaries:
Truck-Lite Co., Inc.
Quaker State Minit-Lube, Inc.
The Valley Camp Coal Co.

Miscellaneous Facts: Incorporated in 1931 in Delaware.

SHELL OIL CO.
One Shell Plaza
Houston, TX 77001
(713) 241-6161
Primary Business: Crude and refined oil, natural gas, chemicals
Chairman: L. C. Van Wachem
CEO: John F. Boocout
President: John F. Boocout
Executive Vice-President (Products): Frank H. Richardson
Vice-President (Health, Safety and Environment): Paul F. Deisler, Jr.
Vice-President (Public Affairs): James H. DeNike
Sales: $20.9 billion
Net Worth: $12.5 billion
# of Employees: 35,185

Subsidiary:
Shell Pipe Line Corp.

Miscellaneous Facts: Incorporated in 1922 in Delaware as Shell Union Oil Corp. Present name adopted in 1949. One of the nation's largest chemical manufacturers among U.S. oil companies.

THE STANDARD OIL CO.
200 Public Square
Cleveland, OH 44114
(216) 586-4141
Primary Business: Petroleum, coal
Chairman: R. B. Horton
CEO: R. B. Horton
President: F. E. Mosier
Executive Vice-President: J. C. E. Webster
Vice-President (Human Resources): W. M. Alspaugh
Vice-President (External Affairs): F. G. Giribaldi
Revenue: $13 billion
Net Worth: $8 billion
# of Employees: 30,371

Subsidiaries:
BP Oil Inc.
Old Ben Coal Co.
S. Minerals, Inc.
Kennecott Corp.
Sohio Petroleum Co.
Sohio Pipe Line Co.
Sohio Supply Co.
Standard Alaska Production
Standard Oil Chemical Co.

Miscellaneous Facts: Incorporated in 1870 in Ohio.

SUN COMPANY, INC.
100 Matsonford Road
Radnor, PA 19087
(215) 293-6000
Primary Business: Holding company, petroleum products
Chairman: Theodore A. Burtis
CEO: Robert McClements, Jr.
President: Robert McClements, Jr.
Senior Vice-President (Public Affairs): Harlan T. Snider
Vice-President (Human Resources): Patrick E. Coggins, Jr.
Revenue: $15.40 billion
Net Worth: $5.3 billion
# of Employees: 36,963

Subsidiaries:
Elk River Resources, Inc.
Radnor Corp.

206

Sun Carriers, Inc.
Sun Distributors, Inc.
Sun Exploration & Production Co.
Sun Refining & Marketing Co.

Miscellaneous Facts: Incorporated in
1971 in Pennsylvania.

TENNECO, INC.
Tenneco Building
Houston, TX 77002
(713) 757-2131
Primary Business: Natural gas pipelines,
oil operations
Chairman: J. L. Ketelsen
CEO: J. L. Ketelsen
President: J. P. Diesel
Executive Vice-President: Joe B. Foster
Executive Vice-President: Allen T.
McInnes
Revenue: $15.89 billion
Net Worth: $8.8 billion
# of Employees: 111,090

Subsidiaries:
Tenneco Oil Co.
Tenneco Realty, Inc.
Tenneco Automotive
Tenneco Corp.
Packaging Corp. of America

TESORO PETROLEUM CORP.
8700 Tesoro Drive
San Antonio, TX 78217
(512) 828-8484
Primary Business: Oil and gas
Chairman: Robert V. West, Jr.
CEO: Robert V. West, Jr.
President: Dennis F. Juren
Executive Vice-President: J. P. Schmalz
Senior Vice-President (Refining): John
T. Tagliarino
Revenue: $3.10 billion
Net Worth: $709 million
# of Employees: 2,500

Subsidiaries:
Tesoro Alaska Petroleum Co.
Tesoro Crude Oil Co.
Tesoro Drilling Co.
Tesoro Land & Marine Rental Co.
Tesoro Petroleum Distributing Co.

TEXACO, INC.
2000 Westchester Avenue
White Plains, NY 10650
(914) 253-4000
Primary Business: Oil production,
transportation, refining
Chairman: John K. McKinley
CEO: John K. McKinley
President: Alfred C. DeCrane, Jr.
Vice-Chairman: James W. Kennear
Senior Vice-President and General
Counsel: William C. Weitzel, Jr.
Sales: $40.07 billion
Net Worth: $13.6 billion
# of Employees: 60,330

Subsidiaries:
Getty Oil Co.
Arbuckle Pipe Line Co.
Getty Gas Gathering, Inc.
Vanply, Inc.
Getty Pipeline Co.
Texaco Chemical Corp.
The Harrison Corp.
Texaco Development Corp.
Texaco Indonesia Corp.
The Texas Pipeline Co.

Miscellaneous Facts: Incorporated in
1926 in Texas as the Texas Corp.
Present name adopted in 1959.

TEXAS EASTERN CORP.
Post Office Box 2521
Houston, TX 77052
(713) 759-3131
Primary Business: Petroleum products
Chairman: J. David Bufkin
CEO: J. David Bufkin
President: Dennis R. Hendrix
Vice-Chairman: Henry H. King
Senior Vice-President: Edward Hickam
Vice-President (Personnel): J. E.
Mulligan
Revenue: $6.91 billion
Net Worth: $1.46 billion
# of Employees: 13,500

Subsidiaries:
Eastern Drilling Systems
Grant-Norpac, Inc.
Petrolane, Inc.
Air Drilling Services
Scientific Design Co.
Skyline Oil Co.
Tetco Three, Inc.
Texas Eastern Nuclear, Inc.

UNOCAL CORP.
Post Office Box 7600
Unocal Center
Los Angeles, CA 90051
(213) 977-7600
Primary Business: High technology earth
  resource
Chairman: Fred L. Hartley
CEO: Fred L. Hartley
President: Richard J.Stegemeier
Director, Corporate Information:
  Gordon Dolfie
Vice-President (Human Resources):
  Joseph Byrne
Sales: $11.5 billion
Net Worth: $5.7 billion
# of Employees: 20,664

Subsidiaries:
Unocal Corp.
Molycorp., Inc.

Miscellaneous Facts: Incorporated in
  1983 in Delaware.

VALVOLINE OIL CO.
Post Office Box 14000
Lexington, KY 40512
(606) 268-7777
Primary Business: Motor oil and
  lubricants
President: J. F. Boehm
Senior Vice-President (Marketing): C.
  F. Frey
Senior Vice-President (Sales): John D.
  Barr
Vice-President (Branded Sales): O. D.
  Felty III
# of Employees: 900

Miscellaneous Facts: Division of Ashland
  Oil, Inc.

PACKAGING

BALL CORP.
345 S High Street
Muncie, IN 47302
(317) 747-6100
Primary Business: Glass containers and closures manufacturer
Chairman: John W. Fisher
CEO: Richard M. Ringden
President: Richard M. Ringden
Executive Vice-President: D. E. Emmerson
Vice-President (Human Resources): C. E. Wild
Revenue: $1.05 billion
Net Worth: $295 million
# of Employees: 9,100

Groups:
Glass Container Group
Industrial Products Group
Technical Products Group
Metal Container Group

Miscellaneous Facts: Incorporated in 1922 as Ball Brothers Co.

BEMIS CO., INC.
800 Northstar Center
Minneapolis, MN 55402
(612) 340-6000
Primary Business: Packaging products
Chairman: Edward W. Asplin
CEO: Howard J. Curler
President: Howard J. Curler
Executive Vice-President: John H. Roe
Vice-President (Personnel): Alvin L. Park
Sales: $779 million
Net Worth: $175 million
# of Employees: 8,381

Subsidiaries:
Bemis Machinery Co.
Curwood, Inc.
Luxtour Corp.
Mactac Co.
Mankato Corp.
Peoria Paper Mill

Miscellaneous Facts: Incorporated in 1885 in Missouri as Bemis Bro. Bag Co. Present name adopted in 1965.

BROCKWAY, INC. (NY)
McCullough Avenue
Brockway, PA 15824
(814) 268-3015
Primary Business: Glass and plastic containers
Chairman: John A. Winfield
CEO: John A. Winfield
President: John J. McMackin
Executive Vice-President: Gerald Stecker
Vice-President (Human Resources): J.W. Hysong
Revenue: $963 million
Net Worth: $215 million
# of Employees: 11,500

Subsidiaries:
Brockway Standard, Inc.
Clinton Aero Corp.
Crown Airways, Inc.
Captainer Plastics Corp.

CROWN CORK & SEAL CO.
9300 Ashton Road
Philadelphia, PA 19136
(215) 698-5100
Primary Business: Manufactures cans
Chairman: John F. Connelly
CEO: John F. Connelly
President: William J. Avery
Senior Vice-President: Henry E. Butwel
Personnel Director: H. J. Abrams
Sales: $1.4 billion
Net Worth: $498 million
# of Employees: 12,600

KMI CONTINENTAL, INC.
41 Harbor Plaza
Post Office Box 10129
Stamford, CT 06904
(203) 964-6000
Primary Business: Packaging products and machinery
Chairman: Donald L. Sturm
CEO: Donald L. Sturm
President: Donald L. Sturm
Senior Vice-President: John B. Folts
Senior Vice-President: Robert E. Julian
Vice-President (Law): James H. Cornell

Revenue: $4.82 billion
# of Employees: 55,500

OWENS-ILLINOIS, INC.
One Sea Gate
Toledo, OH 43604
(419) 247-5000
Primary Business: Glass, paper and
plastic containers
Chairman: Robert J. Lanigan
CEO: Robert J. Lanigan
President: Joseph H. Lemieux
Senior Vice-President (Human
Resources): David A. Ward
Vice-President (Communications):
Thomas R. Weiss
Sales: $3.7 billion
Net Worth: $1.56 billion
# of Employees: 44,048

Subsidiaries:
Alliance Mortgage Co.
Prudent Supply
U.S. Cap & Closure, Inc.
Doughtery Bros. Co.
Kontes Glass Co.

Divisions:
Closure Div.
Kimble Div.
Glass Container Group
Forest Products Div.
Libby Glass Div.
Television Products Div.

PREMARK-INTERNATIONAL, INC.
2211 Sanders Road
Northbrook, IL 60062
(312) 498-8000
Primary Business: Plastic food-storage
containers
Chairman: Warren L. Batts
CEO: Warren L. Batts
Senior Vice-President and General
Counsel: John M. Costigan
Vice-President (Communications):
Becky W. Osterberg
Sales: $1.8 billion
# of Employees: 20,000

Operations:
Food Equipment Group
Tupperware
Ralph Wilson Plastics Co.
The West Bend Co.

TEMPLE-INLAND, INC.
Post Office Drawer N
Diboll, TX 75941
(713) 829-5511
Primary Business: Holding company
Chairman: Arthur Temple
CEO: Clifford Grum
President: Clifford Grum
Executive Vice-President: Cleveland G.
Ames
Executive Vice-President: Joe C.
Denman, Jr.
Sales: $1.26 billion

PAPER PRODUCTS

BOISE CASCADE CORP.
One Jefferson Square
Boise, ID 83728
(208) 384-6161
Primary Business: Lumber, plywood, paper products
Chairman: John B. Fery
CEO: John B. Fery
President: Jon H. Miller
Senior Vice-President and General Counsel: John E. Clute
Senior Vice-President: William Bridenbaugh
Director of Communications: Robert B. Hays
Sales: $3.81 billion
Net Worth: $1.4 billion
# of Employees: 28,708

Subsidiaries:
Abiqua Power Co.
Beaver Falls Power Co.
Boise Cascade Credit Corp.
Boise National Leasing, Inc.
Brownville Power Co.
Cascada Stationers, Inc.
Cuban Electric Co.
Lowville & Beaver River Railroad Co.
Normin Mining Co.
Oxford Paper Co.
Sawtooth Commodity Corp.

Miscellaneous Facts: Incorporated in 1931 in Delaware as Boise Payette Lumber Co. Present name adopted in 1957.

BOWATER, INC.
One Parklands Drive
Post Office Box 4012
Darien, CT 06820
(203) 656-7200
Primary Business: Makes newsprint
Chairman: A. P. Gammie
CEO: A. P. Gammie
President: A. P. Gammie
Senior Vice-President: L. E. Culbertson
Senior Vice-President: R. D. McDonough
Chief Personnel Officer: H. D. Chandler
Sales: $887 million
Net Worth: $461 million
# of Employees: 4,200

Subsidiaries:
Bowater Canadian, Ltd.
Bowater Computer Forms
Bowater Foreign Sales Corp.
Catawba Newsprint Co.

Miscellaneous Facts: In 1984, company separated from parent company in the United Kingdom and became independent.

CHAMPION INTERNATIONAL CORP.
One Champion Plaza
Stamford, CT 06921
(203) 358-7000
Primary Business: Fine papers, paper packing
CEO: Andrew C. Sigler
President: Robert F. Longbine
Executive Vice-President: B. Taggart Edwards
Executive Vice-President: William H. Burchfield
Sales: $5.12 billion
Net Worth: $2.4 billion
# of Employees: 58,700

Miscellaneous Facts: Incorporated in 1937 in New York as U.S. Plywood Corp. Present name adopted in 1972.

CONSOLIDATED PAPERS, INC.
231 First Avenue N
Wisconsin Rapids, WI 54494
(715) 422-3111
Primary Business: Paper manufacturer
Chairman: George W. Mead
CEO: George W. Mead
President: L. H. Boling
Vice-President: L. A. Engelhardt
Director, Human Resources: J. B. Casper
Sales: $686 million
Net Worth: $417 million
# of Employees: 4,901

Subsidiaries:
CPI Distribution Center, Inc.

Consolidated Water Power Co.
Cibsiwekd Ciro.
Hotel Mead Corp.
Mead Realty Corp.

CROWN ZELLERBACH CORP.
One Bush Street
San Francisco, CA 94104
(415) 951-5000
Primary Business: Paper, wrappings,
    bags, tissue
Chairman: James Goldsmith
CEO: W. T. Creson
President: W. T. Creson
Senior Vice-President (Public Affairs):
    D. D. Taylor
Vice-Chairman: Roland A. E. Franklin
Personnel Director: Bess Jones
Sales: $3.09 billion
Net Worth: $1.18 billion
# of Employees: 32,000

Divisions:
Business Converting Papers Div.
Eczel Corp.
Chemical Products Div.
Crown Advanced Films
Communications Papers Div.
Pulp Sales Div.
Containerboard Div.
NW Wood Products Div.
Southern Timber & Wood Products Div.
Stationers Distribution Co.
Virginia Paper Co.
Zellerbach Paper Co.

GEORGIA-PACIFIC CORP.
133 Peachtree Street, NE
Atlanta, GA 30309
(404) 521-4000
Primary Business: Plywood and
    structural panels, paper products
Chairman: T. Marshall Hahn, Jr.
CEO: T. Marshall Hahn, Jr.
President: Robert A. Schumacher
Vice-President (Human Resources):
    David W. Reynolds
Vice-President (Sales): Michael B.
    Wilson
Revenue: $6.68 billion
Net Worth: $2.14 billion
# of Employees: 40,000

Subsidiaries:
Ashley, Drew & Northern Railway Co.

Georgia-Pacific International Corp.
National Management, Inc.
St. Croix Pulpwood Co.

Divisions:
Building Products Div.
Chemical Div.
Distribution Div.
Gypsum Div.
International Div.
Northern Paper & Pulp Div.

Miscellaneous Facts: Products include
    Coronet tissue, Hopper printing
    papers. Owns 512 million acres of
    timberland in North America.
    Incorporated in 1927 in Georgia as
    Georgia Harwood Lumber Co. Name
    changed in 1948 to Georgia-Pacific
    Plywood & Lumber Co. Present name
    adopted in 1956.

GREAT NORTHERN NEXOOSA CORP.
75 Prospect Street
Post Office Box 9309
Stamford, CT 06904
(203) 359-4000
Primary Business: Business
    communication papers
Chairman: William R. Laidig
CEO: William R. Laidig
President: William R. Laidig
Vice-Chairman: Peter F. Yacavone
Director, Investor Relations: Stephen
    M. Hill
General Counsel: Joseph F. O'Handley
Sales: $1.87 billion
Net Worth: $962 million
# of Employees: 14,000

Subsidiaries:
Butles Paper Co.
Mail-Well Envelope Co.
Chattahoochee Industrial Railroad
Leaf River Corp.
Makplex Products Co., Inc.
Nekoosa Papers, Inc.

Miscellaneous Facts: Incorporated in
    1898 in Maine as Northern
    Development Co. Present name
    adopted in 1970.

INTERNATIONAL PAPER CO.
77 W 45th Street
New York, NY 10036
(212) 536-6000
Primary Business: Manufacturer of
paper products
Chairman: John A. Georges
CEO: John A. Georges
President: Paul H. O'Neill
Vice-President and General Counsel: J.
P. Melican
Vice-President (Human Resources):
David Oskan
Revenue: $4.71 billion
# of Employees: 33,700

Subsidiaries:
American Central Corp.
Arizona Chemical Co.
GCO Minerals Co.
International Paper Realty Corp.
International Pulp Sales Co.

Divisions:
Bagpak Div.
Custom Packaging Div.
Folding Cartons & Label Div.
U.S. Container Div.
Uniwood Div.
Wood Products Div.

Miscellaneous Facts: Incorporated in
1941 in New York as International
Paper & Power Corp. After merger in
1941, present name adopted.

JAMES RIVER CORP.
Tredegar Street
Richmond, VA 23219
(804) 644-5411
Primary Business: Paper manufacturer
Chairman: Brenton S. Halsey
CEO: Brenton S. Halsey
President: Robert C. Williams
Executive Vice-President: Judd H.
Alexander
Senior Vice-President (Human
Resources): Lawrence S. Morrow
Sales: $2.6 billion
Net Worth: $753 million
# of Employees: 34,500

Subsidiaries:
Communications Papers Business East
Dixie Products Business
Specialty Papers Business

KIMBERLY-CLARK CORP.
Post Office Box 619100
DFW Airport Station
Dallas, TX 75261
(214) 630-1200
Primary Business: Paper products
Chairman: Darwin E. Smith
CEO: Darwin E. Smith
Vice-Chairman: Robert C. Ernest
Vice-Chairman: Marvin F. Gade
Vice-Chairman: Donald R. Hibbert
Senior Vice-President (Personnel
Director): Wayne R. Sanders
Sales: $4.07 billion
Net Worth: $1.74 billion
# of Employees: 36,648

Subsidiaries:
Avent, Inc.
K-C Advertising, Inc.
K-C Aviation, Inc.
Midwest Express Airlines, Inc.
Kimberly-Clark International, S.A.
Kimfibers, Ltd.
Kimtech, Ltd.
Spenco Medical Corp.

Miscellaneous Facts: Incorporated in
1928 in Delaware.

THE MEAD CORP.
Courthouse Plaza, NE
Dayton, OH 45463
(513) 222-6323
Primary Business: Manufacturing from
forest products
Chairman: B. R. Roberts
CEO: B. R. Roberts
President: S. C. Mason
Senior Vice-President (Human
Resources): R. P. Carzoli
Senior Vice-President (Forest Products):
A. D. Correll, Jr.
Vice-President (Corporate
Communications): D. P. Kircher
Revenue: $2.72 billion
Net Worth: $1.03 billion
# of Employees:17,000

Subsidiaries:
Escanaba Land Co.
Escanaba Paper Co.
Mead Containers Europe, Inc.
Mead Data Central, Inc.
Mead Export, Inc.
Mead Panel Board, Inc.

Mead Pump Sales, Inc.
Mead Timber Co.

Miscellaneous Facts: Incorporated in
1930 in Ohio.

POTLATCH CORP.
Post Office Box 3591
San Francisco, CA 94199
(415) 947-5500
Primary Business: Print and business
papers
Chairman: Richard B. Madden
CEO: Richard B. Madden
President: Roderick M. Steele
Senior Vice-President (Public Affairs):
George C. Cheek
Vice-President (Employee Relations): I.
W. Krantz
Vice-President and General Counsel:
Mrs. Francis M. Davis
Sales: $993.91 million
Net Worth: $659 million
# of Employees: 8,354

Subsidiaries:
Brown & Kauffmann, Inc.
Clearwater Commodity Corp.
Duluth & Northeastern Railroad Co.
The Prescott & Northwestern Railroad
Co.
St. Maries River Railroad
Warren & Saline River Railroad Co.

SCOTT PAPER CO.
Scott Plaza
Philadelphia, PA 19113
(215) 522-5000
Primary Business: Home and industrial
paper products
Chairman: Philip E. Lippincott
CEO: Philip E. Lippincott
President: Philip E. Lippincott
Executive Vice-President (Service): J.
Lawrence Shane
Senior Vice-President and General
Counsel: Norman M. Heisman
Vice-President (Timberlands): Stephen
J. Conway
Revenue: $2.85 billion
Net Worth: $1.57 billion
# of Employees: 20,000

Divisions:
Natural Resources Div.

Mountain Tree Farm Co.
Nonwovens Div.
Packaged Products Div.
Scott Paper, International
S.D. Warren Co.

STONE CONTAINER CORP.
360 N Michigan Avenue
Chicago, IL 60601
(312) 346-6600
Primary Business: Containerboard, kraft
paper
Chairman: Roger W. Stone
CEO: Roger W. Stone
President: James E. Frew
Senior Vice-President: Arnold F.
Brookstone
Vice-President (Industrial Relations):
Covington Shackleford
Sales: $1.30 billion
Net Worth: $303 million
# of Employes: 9,950

Divisions:
Containerboard & Paper Div.
Flexible Packaging Div.
Forest Products Div.
Paper Bag & Kraft Paper Div.

Miscellaneous Facts: Incorporated in
1945 in Illinois.

WEYERHAEUSER CO.
Tacoma, WA 98477
(206) 924-2345
Primary Business: Wood products, paper
products
CEO: George H. Weyerhaeuser
President: George H. Weyerhaeuser
Executive Vice-President: Charles W.
Bingham
Vice-President (Timberlands): John
McMahon
Vice-President (Corporate
Communications): William H. Oliver
Revenue: $5.55 billion
Net Worth: $3.2 billion
# of Employees: 38,000

Subsidiaries:
The Babcock Co.
Centennial Homes
Cornerstone Development Co.
Pardee Construction Co.
The Quandrant Corp.

Scarborough Corp.
Trendmaker Homes
Westminster Co.

Miscellaneous Facts: Weyerhaeuser is the largest producer of lumber in the U.S.

WILLAMETTE INDUSTRIES, INC.
1300 SW Fifth Avenue
Portland, OR 97201
(503) 227-5581

Primary Business: Lumber, plywood, paper products
Chairman: William Swindells, Jr.
CEO: William Swindells, Jr.
Executive Vice-President: Felix M. Hammack
Executive Vice-President: C. W. Knodell
Sales: $1.18 billion
Net Worth: $473 million
# of Employees: 8,400

PUBLIC RELATIONS AND ADVERTISING

BURSON-MARSTELLER
230 Park Avenue S
New York, NY 10003
(212) 614-4000
Primary Business: Public relations
  agency
Chairman: Harold Burson
President: James Bowling
Vice-Chairman: Elias Buchwald

CARL BYOIR & ASSOC.
380 Madison Avenue
New York, NY 10017
(212) 986-6100
Primary Business: Public relations
  agency
President: Peter Osgood

Miscellaneous Facts: Subsidiary of
  Foote, Cone & Belding
  Communications, Inc.

**DOYLE DANE BERNBACH GROUP,
  INC.**
437 Madison Avenue
New York, NY 10022
(212) 415-2000
Primary Business: Advertising agency
Chairman: Joseph R. Daly
CEO: Barry E. Loughrane
President: Barry E. Loughrane
Executive Vice-President: Robert G.
  Pfundstein
Vice-President (Personnel): Hal Scott
Sales: $1.15 billion
Net Worth: $40 million
# of Employees: 3,500

Subsidiaries:
Cargill Wilson & Acree, Inc.
Fletcher/Mayo Associates, Inc.
Kallir, Phillips, Ross, Inc.
Milici, Valenti, Smith, Park, Inc.
Millsport, Inc.
Rapp & Collins, Inc.
The Story Tellers, Inc.

**FOOTE, CONE & BELDING
  COMMUNICATIONS, INC.**
101 E Erie Street
Chicago, IL 60611
(312) 751-7000
Primary Business: Advertising agency
Chairman: Norman W. Brown
President: Abbott L. Jones
Senior Vice-President: Charles H.
  Gunderson
Revenue: $287 million
Net Worth: $107 million
# of Employees: 5,800

Subsidiaries:
Albert Frank-Guenther Law, Inc.
Carl Byoir & Assoc.
FCB Advertising, Inc.

**GREYCOM, INC., PUBLIC
  RELATIONS**
777 Third Avenue
New York, NY 10017
(212) 546-2200
Primary Business: Public relations
  service
Chairman: Frances Friedman
President: Frances Friedman
Vice-Chairman: Norman Weissman

Miscellaneous Facts: Subsidiary of Grey
  Advertising, Inc.

HILL & KNOWLTON, INC.
420 Lexington Avenue
New York, NY 10017
(212) 697-5600
Primary Business: Public relations
  agency
CEO: Robert L. Dilenschneider
President: Robert L. Dilenschneider
# of Employees: 1,200

JWT GROUP, INC.
466 Lexington Avenue
New York, NY 10017
(212) 210-7000

Primary Business: Advertising agency
Chairman: Don Johnston
CEO: Don Johnston
Executive Vice-President: Glen A. Dell
Executive Vice-President: Hugh P.
  Connell
Revenue: $569 million
# of Employees: 9,800

Subsidiaries:
J. Walter Thompson Co.
Hill & Knowlton, Inc.
Lord, Geller, Federico & Einstein, Inc.

LEO BURNETT CO., INC.
Prudential Plaza
Chicago, IL 60601
(312) 565-5959
Primary Business: Advertising agency
Chairman: C. R. Kopp
CEO: J. J. Kinsella
President: J. J. Kinsella
Executive Vice-President: N. L. Muse
Executive Vice-President: W. A.
  Wiggins

TED BATES WORLDWIDE, INC.
1515 Broadway
New York, NY 10036
(212) 869-3131
Primary Business: Advertising agency
Chairman: Robert E. Jacoby
CEO: Robert E. Jacoby
Executive Vice-President: Donald M.
  Zuckert
Executive Vice-President: John R.
  Hoywe
# of Employees: 725

YOUNG & RUBICAM, INC.
285 Madison Avenue
New York, NY 10017
(212) 210-3000
Primary Business: Advertising agency
Chairman: Edward N. Ney
CEO: Alexander Kroll
President: Alexander Kroll
Executive Vice-President: Harold
  Burson
# of Employees: 9,000

ACE HARDWARE CORP.
2200 Kensington Court
Oak Brook, IL 60521
(312) 990-6600
Primary Business: Retail hardware
Chairman: Theodore Costoff
President: Lawrence R. Gavin
Vice-Chairman: Gregg Ziegler
Director, Human Resources: Fred J.
  Neer
Sales: $1 billion
Net Worth: $102 million
# of Employees: 2,200

ALLIED STORES CORP.
1114 Avenue of the Americas
New York, NY 10036
(212) 764-2000
Primary Business: Holding company,
  department stores
Chairman: Thomas M. Macioce
CEO: Thomas M. Macioce
President: James A. Walsh
Vice-Chairman: John T. Cullen
Executive Vice-President: Howard E.
  Hassler
Vice-President (Personnel): Susan
  Sharon
Revenue: $3.97 billion
Net Worth: $1.06 billion
# of Employees: 63,800

Principal Department Stores:
Block's
The Bon
Cain-Sloan Co.
Deys
Donaldsons
Herp's

Specialty Shops:
Ann Taylor
Bonwit Teller
Brooks Brothers
Catherin's Stout Shoppe
Garfinckel's
Plymouth Shops

Miscellaneous Facts: Incorporated in
  1928 in Delaware as Hahn
  Department Stores, Inc. Present name
  adopted in 1935.

AMERICAN CAN CO.
American Lane
Greenwich, CT 06836
(203) 552-2000
Primary Business: Packaging, specialty
  retail stores
Chairman: William S. Woodside
President: Francis J. Conner
Executive Vice-President: Alfred E.
  Goldstein
Executive Vice-President: John G. Polk
Director, Corporate Human Resources:
  Patricia M. Geradi
Sales: $3.18 billion
Net Worth: $1.1 billion
# of Employees: 30,000

Subsidiaries:
AC Insurance Co.
Voyager Life Insurance Co.
Transport Life Insurance Co.

Specialty Retailing Groups:
Fingerhut Companies
Figi's, Inc.
Michigan Bulb Co.
Sam Goody, Inc.
Musicland Group

Miscellaneous Facts: Incorporated in
  1901 in New Jersey.

AMES DEPARTMENT STORES, INC.
2418 Main Street
Rocky Hill, CT 06067
(203) 563-8234
Primary Business: Department stores
Chairman: Herbert Gilman
CEO: Herbert Gilman
President: Gerald Kanter
Vice-President (Personnel): Joseph J.
  Penna
Vice-President (Loss Prevention): Henry
  Sobinski
Sales: $821.99 million
Net Worth: $124 million
# of Employees: 7,000

Subsidiaries:
AKD, Inc.
G.C. Murphy Co.
Court House Village Co.
M & L Realty Co., Inc.

Mack Realty Co.
Murphy Development Corp.
Spotsylvania Realty Co.

ASSOCIATED DRY GOODS CORP.
417 Fifth Avenue
New York, NY 10016
(212) 679-8700
Primary Business: Department stores
Chairman: Joseph H. Johnson
CEO: Joseph H. Johnson
President: David P. Williams III
Vice-President (Marketing): Joan S.
  Levan
Vice-President (Personnel): Howard
  Falberg
Vice-President (Operations): Joel Wise
Revenue: $4.10 billion
Net Worth: $985,469 million
# of Employees: 60,000

*Department and Specialty Store
  Divisions:*
L.S. Ayres & Co.
The Denver Dry Goods Co.
Goldwaters
Hahne & Co.
Joseph Horne Co.
Lord & Taylor
Powers Dry Goods Co.
J.W. Robinson Co.
Robinson's of Florida
Sibley, Lindsay & Curr Co.
The Stewart Dry Goods Co.
Sycamore Specialty Stores

Miscellaneous Facts: Incorporated in
  1916 in Virginia as a reorganization of
  the Associated Merchants Co. and
  United Dry Goods Companies.

BATUS, INC.
2000 Citizens Plaza
Louisville, KY 40202
(502) 581-8000
Primary Business: Holding company
Chairman: C. I. McCarty
CEO: H. F. Frigon
President: H. F. Frigon
Vice-President (Human Resources): T.
  G. Hall
Vice-President and General Counsel: D.
  A. Schechter
Vice-President (Public Affairs): J. D.
  Tyson
Sales: $6.02 billion

Net Worth: $1.4 billion
# of Employees: 62,000

Operating Companies:
John Breuner Co.
The Crescent Stores
Frederick & Nelson
Gimbels–East
Ivey's–Carolinas
Kohl's Department Stores
Marshall Field & Co.
Saks Fifth Avenue
Thimbles
Brown & Williamson Tobacco Corp.
Appleton Papers, Inc.

Miscellaneous Facts: Subsidiary of BAT
  Industries.

BEST PRODUCTS CO., INC.
Post Office Box 26303
Richmond, VA 23260
(804) 261-2000
Primary Business: Discount retailer
Chairman: Andrew M. Lewis
CEO: Andrew M. Lewis
President: Robert E. R. Huntley
Vice-President (Corporate
  Communications): Mark M. Murphy
Vice-President (Human Resources):
  Wayne T. Tennent
Revenue: $2.25 billion
Net Worth: $419 million
# of Employees: 18,500

Subsidiaries:
Ashby's, Ltd.
First Land & Development, Inc.
Modern Merchandising, Inc.
Dolgins, Inc.
Great Western Distributing, Inc.
La Belle's of Colorado
Phil Miller, Inc.

BOOK-OF-THE-MONTH CLUB, INC.
485 Lexington Avenue
New York, NY 10017
(212) 867-4300
Primary Business: Retail sale of books
  by mail to subscribers
Chairman: Edward E. Fitzgerald
CEO: Edward E. Fitzgerald
President: Al Silverman
Vice-Chairman: Reginald K. Brack, Jr.

Senior Vice-President and Editor-in-Chief: Gloria Norris
Vice-President (Fulfillment): Leonard Kessler
# of Employees: 700

Miscellaneous Facts: Subsidiary of Time, Inc.

BROWN GROUP, INC.
8400 Maryland Avenue
St. Louis, MO 63105
(314) 854-4000
Primary Business: Maker and retailer of men's, women's and children's footwear
Chairman: B. A. Bridgewater
CEO: B. A. Bridgewater
President: B. A. Bridgewater
Senior Vice-President: Harry E. Rich
Senior Vice-President: Erik R. Risman
Vice-President and General Counsel: Robert D. Pickle
Sales: $1.57 billion
Net Worth: $400 million
# of Employees: 28,000

Subsidiaries:
Wohl Shoe Co.
Linen Center
Cloth World, Inc.
Meis of Illiana, Inc.

Divisions:
Regal Shoe Shops
Brown Shoe Co.

Miscellaneous Facts: Incorporated in 1913 in New York as Brown Shoe Co., Inc. Present name adopted in 1972.

CARSON PIRIE SCOTT & CO.
One S State Street
Chicago, IL 60603
(312) 641-8000
Primary Business: Operates department stores
Chairman: Peter S. Willmott
CEO: Peter S. Willmott
President: Peter S. Willmott
Vice-Chairman: Robert P. Bryant
Vice-Chairman: Dennis S. Bookshester
Vice-President (Human Resources): Bruce R. Rismiller
Revenue: $1.78 billion
Net Worth: $194 million
# of Employees: 21,425

Subsidiaries:
CPS Credit Corp.
CPS Hotel Management Services, Inc.
Carson International, Inc.
Country Seat Stores, Inc.
Dobbs Houses, Inc.
Dobbs Houses Restaurants, Inc.

CARTER HAWLEY HALE STORES, INC.
550 S Flower Street
Los Angeles, CA 90071
(213) 620-0150
Primary Business: Retail stores
Chairman: Phillip M. Hawley
CEO: Phillip M. Hawley
President: Waldo H. Burnside
Executive Vice-President: Arthur L. Crowe
Vice-President: Matthew J. Guglieimo
Personnel Director: Geene Richey
Sales: $3.73 billion
Net Worth: $648 million
# of Employees: 56,000

Subsidiaries:
C.H.H. Holdings, Inc.
C.H.H. Realty, Inc.
Carter Hawley Hale Credit Corp.
Private Business Air Service

Divisions:
Bergdorf Goodman, Inc.
The Broadway
Contempo Casuals
The Emporium Capwell Co.
Neiman-Marcus Co.
Thalhimer Bros, Inc.
Weinstock's

Miscellaneous Facts: Incorporated in 1984 in Delaware as successor to company incorporated in California in 1897.

CIRCUIT CITY STORES, INC.
2040 Thalbro Street
Richmond, VA 23230
(804) 257-4292
Primary Business: Chain of consumer electronic stores
Chairman: Alan L. Wurtzel
CEO: Alan L. Wurtzel
President: Richard Sharp
Vice-Chairman: S. S. Wurtzel

Executive Vice-President: Daniel M. Rexinger
Personnel Director: William Zierden
Sales: $519 million
Net Worth: $89 million
# of Employees: 3,796

Divisions:
Circuit City Div.
Lafayette Div.
Los Angeles Div.

COMPUTERLAND CORP.
2950 Peralta Oaks Court
Oakland, CA 94605
(415) 568-2283
Primary Business: Franchisor of retail computer stores
Chairman: William H. Millard
CEO: William H. Millard
President: Barbara J. Millard
Senior Vice-President (Marketing): Roger Lewis
President (Corporate Affairs Div.): Vin O'Reilly
Sales: $1.3 billion
# of Employees: 1,300

Miscellaneous Facts: Subsidiary of IMS Assoc., Inc.

CONSUMERS DISTRIBUTING CO., LTD.
62 Belfield Road
Rexdale, Ontario Canada M9W 1G2
(416) 245-4900
Primary Business: Sells products through retail catalog showrooms
Chairman: Jack Stupp
CEO: Jack Stupp
President: Michael Haberman
Vice-President (Corporate Service): Gary McCabe
Vice-President (Human Resources): Cliff St. Pierre
Sales: $898.92 million
# of Employees: 2,500

Miscellaneous Facts: Subsidiary of Provigo, Inc.

CROWN BOOKS CORP.
3301 Pennsy Drive
Landover, MD 20785
(301) 772-6000

Primary Business: Operates retail book stores
Co-Chairman: H. H. Haft
CEO: R. M. Haft
President: R. M. Haft
Co-Chairman: L. H. Straus
Vice-President (Personnel): Tom Ksiazek
Sales: $114.44 million
# of Employees: 1,320

DAYTON-HUDSON CORP.
777 Nicollet Mall
Minneapolis, MN 55402
(612) 370-6948
Primary Business: Department stores
Chairman: Kenneth A. Macke
CEO: Kenneth A. Macke
President: Boake A. Sells
Vice-President (Public Relations): Ann H. Barkelew
Vice-President (Law): William E. Harder
Senior Vice-President (Personnel): Edwin H. Wingate
Revenue: $8.79 billion
Net Worth: $1.7 billion
# of Employees: 115,000

Subsidiaries:
B. Dalton Bookseller
Lechmere, Inc.
Mervyn's

Divisions:
Dayton Hudson Department Store Co.
Target Stores

Miscellaneous Facts: Incorporated in 1902 in Minnesota as Dayton Co. In 1967, name changed to Dayton Corp. Present name adopted in 1969.

DILLARD DEPARTMENT STORES, INC.
900 W Capitol
Little Rock, AR 72203
(501) 376-5200
Primary Business: Operates department stores
Chairman: William T. Dillard
CEO: William T. Dillard
President: William Dillard II
Vice-Chairman: E. Ray Kemp
Executive Vice-President: Alex Dillard
Sales: $1.3 billion

Net Worth: $298 million
# of Employees: 12,965

DOLLAR GENERAL CORP.
427 Beech Street
Scottsville, KY 42164
(502) 237-5444
Primary Business: Operates discount
  stores
Chairman: Cal Turner
CEO: Cal Turner, Jr.
President: Cal Turner, Jr.
Executive Vice-President: Steve Turner
Sales: $480 million
Net Worth: $93 million
# of Employees: 3,500

Miscellaneous Facts: Operates 1,080
  franchised discount stores in the
  eastern and southeastern U.S.

ECKERD (JACK) CORP.
8333 Bryan Dairy Road
Clearwater, FL 33518
(813) 397-7461
Primary Business: Retail drug chain
Chairman: Stewart Turley
CEO: Stewart Turley
President: Stewart Turley
Senior Vice-President: John W. Boyle
Vice-President (Distribution): Curt M.
  Neel
Vice-President (Public Affairs): Michael
  Zagorac, Jr.
Revenue: $2.62 billion
# of Employees: 36,000

Divisions:
Eckard Drug Co.
Jack Eckard Drug Co.

EVANS PRODUCTS CO.
6719 Collins Avenue
Miami Beach, FL 33141
(305) 866-7771
Primary Business: Retailer of building
  materials
Chairman: Victor Posner
CEO: Victor Posner
President: Monford A. Orloff
Vice-Chairman: Steven Posner
Vice-President (Corporate Relations):
  Gerald A. Parsons

Vice-President (Human Resources):
  Phillip A. Smalley
Sales: $1.40 billion
Net Worth: $152 million
# of Employees: 13,000

Subsidiaries:
Alamo Enterprises Building Supplies
ATEC Industries, Inc.
Evans Adco, Inc.
Evans Financial Corp.
Lindsley, Inc.
Ferdinand Railroad Co.
Morrison Railway Supply Co.

Divisions:
Glass Fiber Div.
Grossman's
Monon Trailer Div.

FEDCO, INC.
9300 Santa Fe Spring Road
Los Angeles, CA 90670
(213) 946-2511
Primary Business: Department store
CEO: Edward L. Butterworth
President: Edward L. Butterworth
Vice-President: John R. Goodman
Treasurer: Roy L. Olofson
Sales: $500 million
# of Employees: 3,500

FEDERATED DEPARTMENT STORES, INC.
7 W Seventh Street
Cincinnati, OH 45202
(513) 579-7000
Primary Business: Department store
  operations
Chairman: Howard Goldfeder
CEO: Howard Goldfeder
Vice-Chairman: Norman S. Matthews
Executive Vice-President: Bernard S.
  Klayf
Senior Vice-President (Human
  Resources): Avner M. Porat
Public Relations Director: James A.
  Sluzewski
Sales: $9.98 billion
Net Worth: $2.70 billion
# of Employees: 127,700

Divisions:
Abraham & Straus
Bloomingdale's

Bullock's
Burdines
The Children's Place
Filene's
Foley's
Gold Circle
Goldsmith's Department Stores
Lazarus
I. Magnin & Co.
Ralphs
Rich's
Sanger Harris

Miscellaneous Facts: Founded in 1929 by three family-owned department store companies. Filene's in Boston, Abraham and Straus in Brooklyn, New York, and Lazarus in Columbus, Ohio.

GAP, INC.
900 Cherry Avenue
San Bruno, CA 94066
(415) 952-4400
Primary Business: Operates chain of specialty stores
President: Donald G. Fisher
Executive Vice-President: Millard Drexler
Senior Vice-President (Human Resources): John P. Carver
Senior Vice-President and General Counsel: Dexter C. Tight
Sales: $534.13 million
Net Worth: $151 million
# of Employees: 10,600

Subsidiaries:
Banana Republic
Pottery Barn, Inc.

GREAT EARTH INTERNATIONAL, INC.
1801 Parcourt Drive, Suite A
Santa Ana, CA 92701
(714) 541-2823
Primary Business: Franchisor of vitamin stores
Chairman: John R. Gorman
CEO: Patrick Stewart
President: Patrick Stewart
Vice-President: Richard Johnson
Director, Franchise Relations: Steve Anderson
# of Employees: 500

Miscellaneous Facts: Joint venture of Evergood Products Corp.

HARTMAN CORP.
101 N Wacker Drive
Chicago, IL 60606
(312) 372-6300
Primary Business: Men's retail stores
Chairman: Richard P. Hamilton
CEO: Richard P. Hamilton
President: Elbert O. Hand
Senior Vice-Chairman: John R. Meinert
Vice-President (Licensing): Ralph Kaufmann
Vice-President (Human Resources): Sherman D. Rosen
Revenue: $1.13 billion
Net Worth: $332 million
# of Employees: 25,000

Subsidiaries:
Country Miss, Inc.
Gleneagles, Inc.
Kuppenheimer Manu. Co., Inc.
Silverwoods

Divisions:
Hart Schaffner & Marx Clothes
Hickey-Freeman Co., Inc.
Intercontinental Branded Apparel
Johnny Carson Apparel, Inc.
Jaymar-Ruby, Inc.
Whiteville Apparel Corp.

KINNEY SHOE CORP.
233 Broadway
New York, NY 10079
(212) 349-8300
Primary Business: Shoe and apparel retailing
Chairman: H. E. Sells
President: C. I. Anderson
Vice-President (Communications): John Aneser
Vice-President (Personnel): Philip H. Cease
Sales: $1.42 billion
# of Employees: 17,789

Miscellaneous Facts: Division of F. W. Woolworth Co.

K-MART CORP.
3100 W Big Beaver
Troy, MI 48084
(313) 643-1000
Primary Business: Mass merchandiser
Chairman: Bernard M. Fauber
CEO: Bernard M. Fauber
President: Norman G. Milley
Vice-President (Government and Public
Relations): A. Robert Stevenson
Vice-President (Sales and Marketing):
James L. Moser
Senior Vice-President (Corporate
Personnel): Bernard E. Thomas
Sales: $22.42 billion
Net Worth: $3.27 billion
# of Employees: 250,000

Subsidiaries:
K-Mart Insurance Services, Inc.
Bishop Buffets, Inc.
Builders Square, Inc.
Furr's Cafeterias, Inc.
K-Mart Apparel Corp.
Payless Drug Stores
Waldenbooks, Inc.

Divisions:
Designer Depot
Jupiter Div.
K-Mart Stores
Kresge Div.

THE LIMITED, INC.
2 Limited Parkway
Columbus, OH 43230
(614) 475-4000
Primary Business: Operates women's
apparel stores
Chairman: Leslie H. Wexner
President: Leslie H. Wexner
Vice-Chairman: Robert H. Moroskey
Executive Vice-President: Thomas G.
Hopkins
Vice-President (Public Relations):
Alfred S. Dietzel
Sales: $2.4 billion
Net Worth: $404 million
# of Employees: 25,300

Subsidiaries:
ALG, Inc.
Brylane
Henri Bendel
Lane Bryant
Lerner Stores

Limited Express
Limited Stores
Mast Industries
Sizes Unlimited
Victoria's Secret

LONGS DRUG STORES CORP.
141 N Civic Drive
Walnut Creek, CA 94596
(415) 937-1170
Primary Business: Retail drug stores
Chairman: J. M. Long
CEO: R. M. Long
Executive Vice-President: R. A. Scott
Senior Vice-President: R. A. Plomgren
Vice-President (Personnel): Les
Anderson
Sales: $1.5 billion
Net Worth: $290 million
# of Employees: 11,000

Subsidiary:
Long Drug Stores, Inc.

LOWES CO.
Post Office Box 1111
Highway 268 E
North Wilkesboro, NC 28659
(919) 651-4000
Primary Business: Hardware, building
materials
Chairman: Robert Strickland
CEO: L. G. Herring
President: L. G. Herring
Executive Vice-President (Sales):
Wendell R. Emerine
Senior Vice-President: Clayton A.
Griffing
Sales: $2.07 billion
Net Worth: $408 million
# of Employees: 13,317

Miscellaneous Facts: One of the nation's
largest lumber and hardware supply
retailers.

R. H. MACY & CO., INC.
151 W 34th Street
New York, NY 10001
(212) 560-3600
Primary Business: Department stores
Chairman: Edward S. Finkelstein
CEO: Edward S. Finkelstein
President: Mark S. Handler

Senior Vice-President (Personnel): A.
  David Brown
Senior Vice-President (External
  Affairs): Gertrude G. Michelson
Sales: $4.37 billion
Net Worth: $1.17 billion
# of Employees: 49,000

Subsidiaries:
Bay Fair Shopping Center
Brunswick Square
Columbia Mall
The Garden State Plaza Corp.
Kings Plaza Shopping Center
Macy Credit Corp.
Mission Shopping Center
New Park Mall
Quaker Bridge Mall
Sunnyvale Towncenter
South Shore Mall
Valley Fair Shopping Center

Miscellaneous Facts: Incorporated in
  1919 in New York. Business was
  founded by R. H. Macy in 1858.

MARSHALLS, INC.
30 Harvard Mill Square
Post Office Box 1000-34
Wakefield, MA 01880
(617) 721-3001
Primary Business: Clothing, shoes,
  domestic goods
Chairman: Francis C. Rooney, Jr.
President: Frank H. Brenton
Senior Vice-President (Sales): Larry
  Finn
Vice-President (Human Resources):
  Fred Postelle
Sales: $1.20 billion
# of Employees: 15,230

MAY DEPARTMENT STORES CO.
Sixth and Olive Streets
St. Louis, MO 63101
(314) 342-6300
Primary Business: Department stores
Chairman: David C. Farrell
CEO: David C. Farrell
President: Thomas A. Hays
Vice-Chairman: Richard L. Battram
Vice-Chairman: Allan J. Bloostein
Vice-President (Personnel): Andrea
  Moloney
Sales: $5.08 billion

Net Worth: $1.42 billion
# of Employees: 79,000

Subsidiaries:
The May Dept. Stores Credit Co.
May Centers, Inc.
May Dept. Stores International, Inc.
May Merchandising Corp.
Volume Shoe Corp.

Divisions:
Eagle Stamp Co.
Famous-Barr Co.
G. Fox & Co.
Hecht's
Kaufmann's
Mejer & Frank Co.
O'Neil's
Venture Stores, Inc.

Miscellaneous Facts: Incorporated in
  1910 in New York.

MELVILLE CORP.
3000 Westchester Avenue
Harrison, NY 10528
(914) 253-8000
Primary Business: Maker and retailer of
  footwear, apparel
Chairman: Francis C. Rooney, Jr.
CEO: Francis C. Rooney, Jr.
President: Kenneth K. Berland
Executive Vice-President: Richard L.
  Anderson
General Counsel: Arthur V. Richards
Sales: $4.8 billion
Net Worth: $954 million
# of Employees: 73,000

Subsidiaries:
Kay-Bee Toy & Hobby Shops, Inc.
Linens 'N Things, Inc.
Marshalls, Inc.
Melville Realty Co., Inc.
Wilsons House of Suede, Inc.

Divisions:
Chess King
Consumer Value Stores–CUS
Meldisco
Open Country/Vanguard
Thom McAn Shoe Co.

MERCANTILE STORES CO., INC.
1100 N Market Street
Wilmington, DE 19801
(302) 575-1816

Primary Business: Department store chain
Chairman: Leon F. Winbigler
CEO: Leon F. Winbigler
President: James C. Lovell
Vice-President (Operations): Roger Ciskie
Vice-President (Real Estate): Edward J. Sharkey
Director, Personnel: Frank Magennis
Sales: $1.71 billion
Net Worth: $678 million
# of Employees: 16,500

Affiliated Companies:
J. Bacon & Sons
Castner Knott Co.
Gayfers
Glass Block
Hennesys
The Jones Store Co.
Joslins
de Lendrecie's
Lion
McAlpin's
J. B. White

MONTGOMERY WARD & CO., INC.
Montgomery Ward Plaza
Chicago, IL 60671
(312) 467-2000
Primary Business: General merchandising through stores and catalog
CEO: Bernard F. Brennan
President: Bernard F. Brennan
Senior Vice-President (Human Resources): Roy Dillow
Executive Vice-President (Store Operations): William J. McCarthy
Executive Vice-President (Merchandise): Marvin Stern
Sales: $5 billion
# of Employees: 103,000

Subsidiaries:
Montgomery Ward Credit Corp.
Montgomery Ward Life Insurance Co.

Miscellaneous Facts: Subsidiary of Mobil Corp.

MUSICLAND GROUP
7500 Excelsior Boulevard
Minneapolis, MN 55426
(612) 932-7700

Primary Business: Operates music stores
President: Jack W. Eugster

Miscellaneous Facts: Subsidiary of the American Can Co.

NEIMAN MARCUS
Main and Ervay Streets
Dallas, TX 75201
(214) 821-4000
Primary Business: Specialty store
Chairman: Richard C. Marcus
President: Philip Miller
Executive Vice-President (Sales Promotion): Tom Alexander
Senior Vice-President (Personnel): Lawrence Elkin
# of Employees: 3,837

Miscellaneous Facts: Division of Carter Hawley Hale Stores, Inc.

NORDSTROM, INC.
1501 Fifth Avenue
Seattle, WA 98101
(206) 628-2111
Primary Business: Men's, women's and children's apparel
Co-Chairman: Bruce A. Nordstrom
Co-Chairman: John N. Nordstrom
President: James F. Nordstrom
Executive Vice-President: John A. McMillan
Senior Vice-President: Robert E. Bender
Sales: $982.69 million
# of Employees: 14,000

PAY LESS DRUG STORES NORTHWEST, INC.
9275 SW Peyton Lane
Wilsonville, OR 97070
(503) 682-4100
Primary Business: Super drug store
Chairman: Edward B. Hart
CEO: Edward B. Hart
President: Edward B. Hart
Executive Vice-President: Ron Schiff
Senior Vice-President (Pharmacy): Noel Flynn
Senior Vice-President (Finance): Eugene Guinn
Revenue: $852.94 million
# of Employees: 7,000

Miscellaneous Facts: Subsidiary of K-Mart Corp.

PAY 'N SAVE CORP.
1511 Sixth Avenue
Seattle, WA 98101
(206) 938-6500
Primary Business: Operates retail stores (drugs, appliances, etc.)
Chairman: M. Lamont Bean
CEO: M. Lamont Bean
President: E. Ronald Erickson
Vice-Chairman: Calvin Hendricks
Executive Vice-President: Stuart M. Sloan
Vice-President (Personnel): Jim Petitmermet
Sales: $1.22 billion
# of Employees: 10,000

Miscellaneous Facts: Subsidiary of Trump Group, Ltd.

J. C. PENNEY CO., INC.
1301 Avenue of the Americas
New York, NY 10019
(212) 957-4321
Primary Business: Department store and catalog chain
Chairman: William R. Howell
CEO: William R. Howell
President: David F. Miller
Vice-Chairman: Robert B. Gill
Vice-President (Public Affairs): William R. Johnson
Vice-President (Credit): Ted L. Spurlock
Sales: $13.75 billion
Net Worth: $6.5 billion
# of Employees: 180,000

Subsidiaries:
J. C. Penney Financial Corp.
J. C. P. Realty, Inc.
J. C. Penney Credit Services, Inc.
J. C. Penney Europe, Inc.
J. C. Penney Properties, Inc.
J. C. Penney Purchasing Corp.
J. C. Penney Systems Services

Miscellaneous Facts: 73 percent of the employees are women.

THE PEP BOYS
32nd and Allegheny
Philadelphia, PA 19132
(215) 229-9000
Primary Business: Chain stores (auto parts and accessories)
Chairman: Benjamin Strauss
CEO: Benjamin Strauss
President: Benjamin Strauss
Executive Vice-President: Mitchell G. Leibovitz
Executive Vice-President: Scott L. Rosen
Director of Personnel: Thomas Ruggieri
Revenue: $398.35 million
Net Worth: $130 million
# of Employees: 3,700

Miscellaneous Facts: Also known as "Manny, Moe and Jack."

RADIO SHACK
Post Office Box 17180
Fort Worth, TX 76102
(817) 390-3011
Primary Business: Consumer electronics retailer
President: B. Appel

Miscellaneous Facts: Division of Tandy Corp.

RAPID-AMERICA CORP.
888 Seventh Avenue
New York, NY 10106
(212) 621-4500
Primary Business: Operates retail chain stores
Chairman: Meshulam Riklis
CEO: Meshulam Riklis
President: Meshulam Riklis
Vice-Chairman: Harold S. Divine
Executive Vice-President: Daniel J. Manella
Executive Vice-President: Charles L. Jarvine
Sales: $1.9 billion
Net Worth: $109 million
# of Employees: 56,500

Subsidiaries:
McCrory Corp.
TG&Y Stores Co.
J. J. Newberry Co.
McGregor Corp.

Botany "500"
Schenley Industries, Inc.
Tennessee Dickel Distilling Co.
BTK Industries, Inc.
Faberge, Inc.

REVCO D.S., INC.
1925 Enterprise Parkway
Twinsburg, OH 44087
(216) 425-9811
Primary Business: Chain retail drug
   stores
Chairman: Sidney Dworkin
CEO: Sidney Dworkin
President: William B. Edwards
Vice-Chairman: Henry H. Gray
Vice-President (Purchasing): Elliott F.
   Dworkin
Vice-President (Security): Frank D.
   Petruno
Sales: $2.23 billion
Net Worth: $457 million
# of Employees: 20,800

Subsidiary:
Carls Drug Co.

SEARS, ROEBUCK AND CO.
Sears Tower
Chicago, IL 60606
(312) 875-2500
Primary Business: General merchandise,
   retailer, financial services
Chairman: Edward A. Brennan
CEO: Edward A. Brennan
President: Richard M. Jones
Vice-President (Public Affairs): Gene L.
   Harmon
Vice-President (Personnel): William E.
   Sanders
Vice-President and General Counsel:
   Philip M. Knox, Jr.
Revenue: $40.72 billion
Net Worth: $11.8 billion
# of Employees: 458,000

Subsidiaries:
Dean Witter Reynolds, Inc.
Discover Card Services, Inc.
Sears Roebuck Acceptance Corp.

Groups:
Allstate Insurance Companies
Coldwell Banker & Co.
Sears Merchandise Group
Sears World Trade

Miscellaneous Facts: Incorporated in
   1906 in New York.

THE STOP & SHOP COMPANIES, INC.
Post Office Box 369
Boston, MA 02101
(617) 463-7000
Primary Business: Operates chain of
   food stores
Chairman: Sidney R. Rabb
CEO: Avram J. Goldberg
Vice-Chairman: Robert J. Levin
Vice-President (Personnel): Edwin W.
   Barr
Vice-President (Public Affairs): Aileen
   Gorman
Revenue: $3.25 billion
Net Worth: $768 million
# of Employees: 45,000

Divisions:
Almy Stores, Inc.
Bradlees
Stop & Shop Manufacturing Co.
Stop & Shop Supermarkets
Edgars

TANDY CORP.
1800 One Tandy Center
Fort Worth, TX 76102
(817) 390-3700
Primary Business: Consumer electronics
Chairman: John V. Roach
CEO: John V. Roach
President: John V. Roach
Senior Vice-President and Treasurer:
   Charles W. Tindall
Vice-President: George Kuhnreich
Personnel Director: George Berger
Sales: $3.03 billion
Net Worth: $1.3 billion
# of Employees: 36,000

Subsidiaries:
A & A International, Inc.
Lika Corp.
Lika Southwest
O'Sullivan Industries

Divisions:
Computer Div.
Radio Shack
TDP Electronics
Tandy Advanced Products
Tandy Home Computers

Miscellaneous Facts: Company is the largest retailer of consumer electronics in the U.S. 75 percent of Tandy employees participate in the company stock-purchase program.

TARGET STORES
33 S Sixth Street
Post Office Box 1392
Minneapolis, MN 55440
(612) 370-6073
Primary Business: Discount stores
Chairman: Bruce G. Allbright
CEO: Bruce G. Allbright
President: Robert J. Ulrich
Revenue: $3.9 billion
# of Employees: 51,700

Miscellaneous Facts: Subsidiary of Dayton-Hudson Corp.

THOM MCAN SHOE CO.
67 Millbrook Street
Worcester, MA 01606
(617) 791-3811
Primary Business: Men's, women's footwear
President: Larry A. McVey
Senior Vice-President (Sales): Richard A. Ferraioli
Senior Vice-President: William P. Yeager
Sales: $4.55 million

Miscellaneous Facts: Division of Melville Corp.

THRIFT DRUG CO.
615 Alpha Drive
Pittsburgh, PA 15238
(412) 781-5373
Primary Business: Retail drug stores
President: James B. Armor
Senior Vice-President: Robert Hannan
Senior Vice-President: Robert Oberfield
Sales: $652 million
# of Employees: 6,000

Miscellaneous Facts: Subsidiary of J. C. Penney Co., Inc.

THRIFTY CORP.
3424 Wilshire Boulevard
Los Angeles, CA 90010
(213) 251-6000
Primary Business: Retail drug and discount stores
Chairman: Leonard H. Straus
CEO: Leonard H. Straus
President: Richard G. Eils
Senior Vice-President (Buying and Merchandising): Kenneth M. Crosby
Vice-President (Community Relations): Iris M. Hackett
Vice-President (Loss Prevention): Robert E. Gebhardt
Sales: $1.30 billion
# of Employees: 14,000

Miscellaneous Facts: Subsidiary of Pacific Lighting Corp.

TOYS R US, INC.
395 W Passaic Street
Rochelle Park, NJ 07662
(201) 845-5033
Primary Business: Retail toys
Chairman: Charles Lazarus
CEO: Charles Lazarus
President: Norman Ricken
Senior Vice-President (Buying): Ronald Tuchman
Vice-President (Human Resources): Jeffrey S. Wells
Sales: $1.7 billion
Net Worth: $579 million
# of Employees: 18,200

Divisions:
Department Store Div.
Kids "R" Us
Lash-Tamaron Distr.
Real Estate Div.
Toy Div.

WALGREEN CO.
200 Wilmot Road
Deerfield, IL 60015
(312) 940-2500
Primary Business: Drug store chain
Chairman: Charles R. Walgreen III
CEO: Charles R. Walgreen III
President: Fred F. Canning
Executive Vice-President: Charles D. Hunter
Senior Vice-President: Vernon Brunner

Vice-President (Human Resources):
John Rubino
Sales: $3.16 billion
Net Worth: $480 million
# of Employees: 37,000

Subsidiaries:
Fountain Products Corp.
International Travel Service, Inc.
Nutrition Research Laboratories
Walgreen Food Service, Inc.

Miscellaneous Facts: Operates 1,200
stores across the U.S. Incorporated in
1909 in Illinois. Founded by C. R.
Walgreen in 1901.

WAL-MART STORES, INC.
702 SW Eighth Street
Bentonville, AR 72712
(501) 273-4000
Primary Business: Operates retail
discount department stores
Chairman: Sam M. Walton
CEO: Sam M. Walton
President: David D. Glass
Executive Vice-President (Sales): A. L.
Johnson
Vice-President (Pharmacy): Clarence H.
Archer
Vice-President (Personnel): Thomas M.
Coughlin
Revenue: $8.58 billion
Net Worth: $1.27 billion
# of Employees: 104,000

Subsidiaries:
Benton County Publishing Co., Inc.
Mass-Mart, Inc.
Nadco, Inc.
North Arkansas Wholesale Co., Inc.
Wal-Mart Properties, Inc.

Miscellaneous Facts: Subsidiary of
Walton Enterprises, Inc. Operates the
second-largest discount store chain in
the U.S. and is one of the fastest-
growing store operations in the
nation.

F. W. WOOLWORTH CO.
233 Broadway
New York, NY 10279
(212) 553-2000
Primary Business: Retail stores
Chairman: John W. Lynn
CEO: John W. Lynn
President: Harold E. Sells
Vice-President (Public Affairs): Joseph
F. Carroll
Vice-President (Corporate Liaison):
Aubrey C. Lewis
Sales: $5.96 billion
Net Worth: $1.22 billion
# of Employees: 117,200

Subsidiaries:
Holtzman's Little Folk Shop, Inc.
Kinney Shoe Corp.
The Richman Brothers Co.

Miscellaneous Facts: Incorporated in
1911 in New York.

ZAYRE CORP.
Framingham, MA 01701
(617) 620-5000
Chairman: Sumner L. Feldberg
CEO: Maurice Segall
President: Maurice Segall
Honorary Chairman: Max Feldberg
Executive Vice-President: Arthur F.
Loewy
Vice-President (Labor Relations): Irving
Ritz
Revenue: $3.12 billion
Net Worth: $605 million
# of Employees: 26,000

Subsidiaries:
Atlantic Zayre, Inc.
Chicago Trading Corp.
Gaylords National Corp.
Georgia Purchasing, Inc.
New England Trading Corp.

TELECOMMUNICATIONS

ALLTEL CORP.
100 Executive Parkway
Hudson, OH 44236
(216) 650-7000
Primary Business: Holding company,
  telephone utilities
Chairman: Weldon W. Case
CEO: Weldon W. Case
President: Joe T. Ford
Vice-President (Sales): John Farina
Executive Vice-President: Charles W.
  Miller
Vice-President (Human Resources):
  David Stoska
Revenue: $646 million
Net Worth: $460 million
# of Employees: 5,600

Subsidiaries:
Allied Utilities Corp.
Alltel Answering Service, Inc.
Alltel Communications Corp.
Alltel Finance Corp.
Alltel Publishing Corp.
Alltel Service Corp.
Alltel Supply, Inc.
Brookville Telephone Co.
Clymer Telephone Co.
Preston Electric Co.
TUP Properties, Inc.

Miscellaneous Facts: Owns and operates
  28 telephone companies in the U.S.

**AMERICAN INFORMATION
  TECHNOLOGIES CORP.**
30 S Wacker Drive
Chicago, IL 60606
(312) 750-5000
Primary Business: Telecommunications
Chairman: William L. Weiss
CEO: William L. Weiss
President: James J. Howard
Vice-Chairman: William H. Springer
Vice-President (Corporate
  Communications): Leighton L.
  Gilman
Vice-President (Human Resources):
  Martha L. Thornton
Sales: $8.3 billion
# of Employees: 77,500

**AMERICAN TELEPHONE &
  TELEGRAPH CO.**
550 Madison Avenue
New York, NY 10022
(212) 605-5500
Primary Business: Communications
Chairman: Charles L. Brown
President: James E. Olson
Senior Vice-President (Public
  Relations): Edward M. Block
Senior Vice-President (Personnel): H.
  Weston Clarke, Jr.
Senior Vice-President and General
  Counsel: Howard J. Trienens
Revenue: $33.18 billion
Net Worth: $13.7 billion
# of Employees: 365,000

Subsidiaries:
AT & T Bell Laboratories, Inc.
AT & T Communications, Inc.
AT & T Credit Corp.
AT & T Information Systems, Inc.
AT & T International, Inc.
AT & T Resource Management
AT & T Technologies, Inc.
AT & T Nassau Metals Corp.
AT & T Teletype Corp.
American Transtech, Inc.

Miscellaneous Facts: Established in 1885
  as subsidiary of the American Bell
  Telephone Co. Became parent
  company in 1899.

ANIXTER BROS., INC.
4711 Golf Road
Skokie, IL 60076
(312) 677-2600
Primary Business: Supplier for
  telecommunications industry
Chairman: Alan B. Anixter
CEO: Alan B. Anixter
President: John A. Pigott
Vice-Chairman: William R. Anixter
Vice-Chairman: Bruce Van Wagner
Vice-Chairman: James R. Anixter
Revenue: $597 million
# of Employees: 2,700

Miscellaneous Facts: Owns and operates
  79 subsidiaries across the U.S.

AT & T COMMUNICATIONS, INC.
295 N Maple Avenue
Basking Ridge, NJ 07920
(201) 221-2000
Primary Business: Telecommunications
Chairman: Morris Tanenbaum
CEO: Morris Tanenbaum
President: Robert W. Kleinert
Executive Vice-President (External Affairs): Alfred Partoll
Vice-President (Personnel): Robert H. Gaynor
Vice-President and General Counsel: Alfred A. Green

Miscellaneous Facts: Subsidiary of American Telephone & Telegraph Co.

AT & T INFORMATION SYSTEMS, INC.
100 South Gate Parkway
Morristown, NJ 07960
(201) 898-8000
Primary Business: Sale and lease of communications products
Chairman: Charles Marshall
CEO: Charles Marshall
Executive Vice-President: Robert J. Lasale
Vice-President (External Affairs): Harold W. Burlingame
Vice-President (Personnel and Labor Relations): John H. Rufe

Miscellaneous Facts: Subsidiary of American Telephone & Telegraph Co.

BELL TELEPHONE CO. OF PENNSYLVANIA
One Parkway
Philadelphia, PA 19102
(215) 466-9900
Primary Business: Telephone service
President: Gilbert A. Wetzel
Vice-President (External Affairs): James H. Brenneman
Vice-President (Sales): Bruce Gordon
Vice-President and General Counsel: William L. Leonard
Sales: $2.33 billion
# of Employees: 21,000

CENTEL CORP.
O'Hare Plaza
8725 W Higgins Road
Chicago, IL 60631
(312) 399-2500
Primary Business: Telecommunications
Chairman: Robert P. Reuss
CEO: Robert P. Reuss
President: John P. Frazee, Jr.
Vice-Chairman: William G. Mitchell
Vice-President (Human Resources): John N. Brindley
Revenue: $1.32 billion
Net Worth: $845 million
# of Employees: 12,374

Subsidiaries:
Centel Cellular Co.
Centel Communications Co.
Centel Credit Co.

CHESAPEAKE & POTOMAC TELEPHONE CO.
2055 "L" Street, NW
Washington, DC 20036
(202) 392-9900
Primary Business: Telephone service
CEO: Thomas M. Gibbons
President: Thomas M. Gibbons
Vice-President (Operations): Walter S. Daron
Vice-President and General Counsel: Mark J. Mathis
Vice-President: Delano E. Lewis
Total Assets: $892.90 million
# of Employees: 4,531

Miscellaneous Facts: Subsidiary of Bell Atlantic Corp.

COMMUNICATION SATELLITE CORP.
950 L'Enfant Plaza, SW
Washington, DC 20024
(202) 863-6000
Primary Business: Satellite-based communication services
Chairman: Irving Goldstein
CEO: Irving Goldstein
President: Marcel P. Joseph
Executive Vice-President: John L. McLucas
Vice-President (Human Resources): Robert W. Baumann
Revenue: $459 million

Net Worth: $536 million
# of Employees: 3,084

Divisions:
COMSAT General Corp.
Satellite Television Corp.
COMSAT Technology Products, Inc.
INTELSAT Satellite Services

GTE CORP.
One Stamford Forum
Stamford, CT 06901
(203) 965-2000
Primary Business: Owns equity
  securities of telephone operating
  systems
Chairman: Theodore F. Brophy
Senior Vice-President: James L.
  Broadhead
Vice-President (Corporate
  Communications): Edward L.
  MacEwen
Senior Vice-President (Human
  Resources): Bruce Carswell
Vice-President (Quality Services): D.
  Otis Wolkins
Revenue: $14.55 billion
Net Worth: $5.57 billion
# of Employees: 185,000

Subsidiaries:
GTE Financial Corp.
GTE Leasing Corp.

Telephone Operating Group:
GTE Directories Corp.
GTE Mobilnet Inc.
GTE Telecom Inc.

GTE Telephone Companies:
G.T. of California, Florida, Illinois,
  Indiana, Michigan Midwest,
  Northwest, Ohio, Pennsylvania South,
  Southwest, Wisconsin

ILLINOIS BELL TELEPHONE CO.
225 W Randolph Street
Chicago, IL 60606
(312) 727-9411
Primary Business: Telephone service
President: Ormand J. Wade
Vice-President (Finance): Thomas L.
  Cox
Vice-President (Corporate
  Communications): John A. Koten

Vice-President (Human Resources):
  Paul A. Downing
Sales: $2.68 billion
# of Employees: 23,751

Miscellaneous Facts: Subsidiary of
  American Information Technologies
  Corp.

INDIANA BELL TELEPHONE CO.
240 N Meridian Street
Indianapolis, IN 46204
(317) 265-2266
Primary Business: Telephone service
President: Ramon L. Humke
Executive Vice-President: Thomas L.
  Walker
Vice-President (Human Resources):
  Fredric A. Hunn
Vice-President (External Affairs): H.
  Tuck Schulhof
Operating Revenues: $820.02 million
# of Employees: 7,308

Miscellaneous Facts: Subsidiary of
  American Information Technologies
  Corp.

ITT CORP.
320 Park Avenue
New York, NY 10022
(212) 752-6000
Primary Business: Telecommunications
  and electronics
Chairman: Rand Araskog
CEO: Rand Araskog
President: Edmund M. Carpenter
Vice-Chairman: Richard E. Bennett
Senior Vice-President and General
  Counsel: Howard J. Aibel
Revenue: $12.70 billion
Net Worth: $6.5 billion
# of Employees: 283,000

Subsidiaries:
International Standard Electric Corp.
ITT Telecom Products Corp.
ITT Rayonier, Inc.
W. Atlee Burpee Co.
Carbon Industries, Inc.
Federal Electric Corp.
ITT Life Insurance Corp.
Baylock Manufacturing Corp.
Rochester Form Machine
All American Cables & Radio

Miscellaneous Facts: Incorporated in 1968 in Delaware as International Telephone & Telegraph Corp. Present name adopted in 1983.

MCI COMMUNICATIONS CORP.
1133 19th Street, NW
Washington, DC 20036
(202) 872-1600
Primary Business: Long distance, intercity, business and residential telecommunications
Chairman: William G. McGowan
Vice-Chairman: V. Orville Wright
President: Bert C. Roberts, Jr.
Senior Vice-President (Corporate Affairs): Howard C. Crane
Vice-President (Human Resources): John H. Zimmerman
Sales: $25 billion
Net Worth: $1.1 billion
# of Employees: 12,550

Subsidiaries:
MCI Airsignal
MCI Information Services
MCI International
MCI Telecommunications Corp.

MICHIGAN BELL TELEPHONE CO.
444 Michigan Avenue
Detroit, MI 48226
(313) 223-9900
Primary Business: Telephone service
President: William P. Vititoe
Executive Vice-President: David K. Wenger
Vice-President (Personnel): E. Daniel Grady
Vice-President (General Counsel): H. W. Wells
# of Employees: 18,900

Miscellaneous Facts: Subsidiary of American Information Technologies Corp.

MOUNTAIN STATES TELEPHONE & TELEGRAPH CO.
931 14th Street
Denver, CO 80202
(303) 896-2355
Primary Business: Communications services

President: Robert C. Blanz
Executive Vice-President: James F. Maher
Vice-President (Public Relations and Affairs): Stanley J. Boulier
Vice-President (Human Resources): Fred L. Cook
Revenue: $1.70 billion
# of Employees: 31,546

Miscellaneous Facts: Subsidiary of U.S. West, Inc.

NEW ENGLAND TELEPHONE & TELEGRAPH CO.
185 Franklin Street
Boston, MA 02107
(617) 743-9800
Primary Business: Telephone service
President: Gerhard M. Freche
Executive Vice-President (Operations): Frederic V. Salerno
Vice-President (Public Relations): Walter E. Bartlett
Vice-President (Personnel): Peter W. Bertschmann
Revenue: $2.84 billion
# of Employees: 29,600

Miscellaneous Facts: Subsidiary of NYNEX Corp.

NEW JERSEY BELL TELEPHONE CO.
540 Broad Street
Newark, NJ 07102
(201) 649-9900
Primary Business: Telephone service
President: Anton J. Campanella
Vice-President (Operations): Paul D. Loser
Vice-President (Public Affairs): William L. Kirchner, Jr.
Vice-President (Sales): John W. Seazholtz
Sales: $2.53 billion
# of Employees: 20,000

Miscellaneous Facts: Subsidiary of United Telecommunications, Inc.

NEW YORK TELEPHONE CO.
1095 Avenue of the Americas
New York, NY 10036
(212) 395-2121

Primary Business: Telephone communications
CEO: W. C. Ferguson
President: W. C. Ferguson
Vice-President: P. H. Caswell
Vice-President (External Affairs): J. N. Fallon
Vice-President (Personnel): J. W. Stone, Jr.
Sales Range: $6–$7 billion
# of Employees: 62,000

Miscellaneous Facts: Subsidiary of NYNEX Corp.

NORTHWESTERN BELL TELEPHONE CO.
1314 Douglas On The Mall
Omaha, NB 68102
(402) 422-2000
Primary Business: Phone communications
CEO: Richard D. McCormick
President: Thomas F. Madison
Vice-President (Communications Service): Janice D. Stoney
Vice-President and General Counsel: Melvin R. Quinlaw
Vice-President (Human Resources): K. D. Power
Sales: $1.67 billion
# of Employees: 18,400

Miscellaneous Facts: Subsidiary of U.S. West, Inc.

NYNEX CORP.
335 Madison Avenue
New York, NY 10017
(212) 370-7400
Primary Business: Telecommunications
Chairman of the Board: Delbert C. Staley
CEO: Delbert C. Staley
President: Delbert C. Staley
Vice-Chairman: W. G. Burns
Executive Vice-President: J. E. Hennessy
Personnel Director: R. B. Pulling
Sales: $11.2 billion
Net Worth: $8.6 billion
# of Employees: 90,000

Subsidiaries:
NYNEX Business Information Systems Co.

NYNEX Credit Co.
NYNEX Information Resources Co.
NYNEX Material Enterprises Co.
NYNEX Mobile Communications Co.
NYNEX Properties Co.
New England Telephone & Telegraph Co.
New York Telephone Co.
NYNEX Service Co.
NYNEX Development Co.

PACIFIC BELL
140 New Montgomery Street
San Francisco, CA 94105
(415) 542-9000
Primary Business: Communications services
Chairman: Donald E. Guinn
CEO: Theodore J. Saenger
President: Theodore J. Saenger
Vice-Chairman: John E. Hulse
Executive Vice-President (Human Resources): Benton W. Dial
Vice-President (Sales): Alfred I. Boschulte
Revenue: $8 billion
# of Employees: 77,000

Miscellaneous Facts: Subsidiary of Pacific Telesis Group

PACIFIC NORTHWEST BELL TELEPHONE CO.
Bell Plaza
1600 Seventh Street
Seattle, WA 98191
(206) 345-2211
Primary Business: Telephone service
President: Andrew V. Smith
Vice-President (Personnel): Larry L. Wolfard
Vice-President (General Counsel): Bruce B. Samson
Vice-President (External Affairs): Eugene L. Pfeifer
Revenue: $1.63 billion
# of Employees: 15,464

Miscellaneous Facts: Subsidiary of U.S. West, Inc.

PACIFIC TELESIS GROUP

140 New Montgomery Street
San Francisco, CA 94105
(415) 882-8000
Primary Business: Holding company,
  telecommunications
Chairman of the Board: Donald E.
  Guinn
CEO: Donald E. Guinn
President: Donald E. Guinn
Vice-Chairman: Theodore Saenger
Vice-Chairman: Sam Ginn
Executive Vice-President (Human
  Resources): Benton W. Dial
Sales: $8.5 billion
Net Worth: $7.3 billion
# of Employees: 71,488

Subsidiaries:
Pacific Bell
Pacific Bell Directory
Pactel Carital Resources
Pac Tel Corp.
Pac Tel Communications Companies
Pactel Mobile Companies
Nevada Bell

ROLM CORP.

4900 Old Ironsides Drive
Santa Clara, CA 95050
(408) 986-1000
Primary Business: Designs and sells
  business communication systems
CEO: M. Kenneth Oshman
President: M. Kenneth Oshman
Executive Vice-President: Leo J.
  Chamberlain
Vice-President: Walter Loewenstern, Jr.
Vice-President (Business
  Communications Group): Anthony V.
  Carollo, Jr.
Sales: $659.70 million
# of Employees: 8,940

Miscellaneous Facts: Subsidiary of IBM.
  Company has a "Great Place to
  Work" Department to provide
  employees with a better work
  atmosphere. In the middle of its
  corporate headquarters is a recreation
  center complete with pools, sauna,
  tennis courts and more. Each
  employee, after working for the
  company six or more years, can take
  three months off at full pay.

SOUTH CENTRAL BELL TELEPHONE CO.

Post Office Box 771
Birmingham, AL 35201
(205) 321-1000
Primary Business: Communications
  services
CEO: Carl F. Baily
President: Carl F. Baily
Executive Vice-President: John C.
  McPherson, Jr.
Vice-President (Corporate Affairs):
  Howard E. Palmes
Vice-President and General Counsel: W.
  M. Booker, Jr.
Revenue: $4.50 billion
# of Employees: 39,000

SOUTHERN BELL TELEPHONE & TELEGRAPH CO.

675 W Peachtree Street, NE
Atlanta, GA 30303
(404) 529-8611
Primary Business: Telephone
  communications
CEO: B. Franklin Scinner
President: B. Franklin Scinner
Executive Vice-President: Richard K.
  Snelling
Vice-President and General Counsel: J.
  R. Fitzgerald
Revenue: $5.20 billion
# of Employees: 52,911

Miscellaneous Facts: Subsidiary of
  Bellsouth Corp.

SOUTHWESTERN BELL CORP.

One Bell Center
St. Louis, MO 63101
(314) 247-9800
Primary Business: Holding company,
  telecommunications
Chairman: Zane E. Barnes
CEO: Zane E. Barnes
President: Zane E. Barnes
Executive Vice-President: Joe H. Hunt
Vice-President and General Counsel:
  Edgar Mayfield
Vice-President (Public Relations):
  Gerald D. Blatherwick
Revenue: $7.9 billion
Net Worth: $7.3 billion
# of Employees: 71,100

Subsidiaries:
Southwestern Bell Telephone Co.
Southwestern Bell Mobile Systems, Inc.
Southwestern Bell Publications, Inc.
Southwestern Bell Telecommunications,
Inc.

SPERRY CORP.
1290 Avenue of the Americas
New York, NY 10104
(212) 484-4444
Primary Business: Information
processing systems
Chairman: Gerald G. Probst
CEO: Gerald G. Probst
President: Gerald G. Probst
Executive Vice-President: Vincent R.
McLean
Executive Vice-President: Joseph J.
Kroger
Vice-President (Public Affairs): Vincent
Puritano
Revenue: $5.6 billion
Net Worth: $3 billion
# of Employees: 73,447

Groups:
Aerospace and Marine
Defense Products
Information Systems
Sperry New Holland

**UNITED TELECOMMUNICATIONS,
INC.**
2330 Shawnee Mission Parkway
Westwood, KS 66205
(913) 676-3000
Primary Business: Holding company,
telecommunications
Chairman of the Board: Paul H. Henson
CEO: William T. Esrey
President: William T. Esrey
Vice-Chairman: Charles W. Baitey
Vice-Chairman: Robert H. Snedaker
Vice-President (Human Resources):
Thomas A. Benedett
Sales: $3.2 billion
Net Worth: $1.7 billion
# of Employees: 27,415

Subsidiaries:
Carolina Telephone & Telegraph Co.
United Inter-Mountain Telephone Co.
United Telephone Co. of Arkansas
United Telesentinel, Inc.

United Telespectrum, Inc.
United-Sussex Telephone Co.
U.S. Telecom, Inc.
West Jersey Telephone Co.

U.S. POSTAL SERVICE
475 L'Enfant Plaza, SW
Washington, DC 20260
(202) 245-4000
Primary Business: Mail delivery, sale of
stamps, distribution of food stamps
Chairman: John R. McKean
Vice-Chairman: George Camp
Postmaster General: Paul N. Carlin
Chief Postal Inspector: Charles R.
Clauson
General Counsel: Louis A. Cox
Sales: $25.31 billion
# of Employees: 702,123

U.S. WEST, INC.
7000 E Orchard
Englewood, CO 80111
(303) 793-6500
Primary Business: Telecommunications
CEO: Jack A. MacAllister
President: Jack A. MacAllister
Executive Vice-President: Richard D.
McCormick
Director, Public Information: Don A.
Johnson
Revenue: $7.8 billion
Net Worth: $7.6 billion
# of Employees: 65,000

Subsidiaries:
Betawest
Mountain Bell
New Vector Communications
Northwestern Bell
Pacific Northwest Bell
Tei-Co Services
U.S. West District

WESTERN UNION CORP.
One Lake Street
Upper Saddle River, NJ 07458
(201) 825-5000
Primary Business: Communications and
information service
Chairman: Robert S. Leventhal
CEO: Robert S. Leventhal
President: Robert S. Leventhal

Executive Vice-President: Richard C. Hostetler
Vice-President: Graham R. Brown
Revenue: $1.13 billion
Net Worth: $904 million
# of Employees: 13,836

Subsidiaries:
Western Union Data Service Co.
Western Union Electronic Mail
Western Union Realty Corp.
The Western Union Telegraph Co.
Western Union Teleprocessing, Inc.
Western Union Videoconferencing, Inc.

Air Freight

AIRBORNE FREIGHT CORP.
3101 Western Avenue
Seattle, WA 98121
(206) 285-4600
Primary Business: Air freight forwarding
Chairman of the Board: Robert S. Cline
CEO: Robert S. Cline
President: Robert G. Brazier
Executive Vice-President: Kent W.
  Freudenberger
Vice-President (Human Resources): Hal
  D. McClellan
Revenue: $417 million
Net Worth: $76 million
# of Employees: 4,281

Subsidiaries:
Airborne Express, Inc.
Wilmington Air Park, Inc.

EMERY AIR FREIGHT CORP.
Wilton, CT 06897
(203) 762-8601
Primary Business: Air freight forwarding
Chairman: John C. Emery, Jr.
CEO: John C. Emery, Jr.
President: John C. Emery, Jr.
Vice-President (Human Resources):
  Daniel W. Shea
Vice-President (Marketing): Clifford J.
  Stueck
Director, Corporate Communications:
  Robert Sykes
Revenue: $817.79 million
Net Worth: $178 million
# of Employees: 7,400

Subsidiaries:
Emery Asset Management Corp.
Emery Customs Brokers
Emery Distribution Systems, Inc.
Emery Facilities, Inc.
Emery Financial Services, Inc.
Emery Ocean Freight
Mitchell Facilities, Inc.

FEDERAL EXPRESS CORP.
2990 Airways Boulevard
Memphis, TN 38194
(901) 369-3600
Primary Business: Small package air
  express
Chairman of the Board: Frederick W.
  Smith
CEO: Frederick W. Smith
President: Frederick W. Smith
Senior Vice-President and General
  Counsel: Kenneth R. Masterson
Senior Vice-President (Personnel):
  James A. Perkins
Vice-President (Sales): Craig Bell
Sales: $1.43 billion
Net Worth: $717 million
# of Employees: 31,000

THE PITTSTON CO.
Post Office Box 8900
Greenwich, CT 06830
(203) 622-0900
Primary Business: Air freight forwarding
Chairman of the Board: Paul W.
  Douglas
CEO: Paul W. Douglas
President: Paul W. Douglas
Executive Vice-President: Joseph C.
  Farrell
Executive Vice-President: David L.
  Marshall
Revenue: $1.26 billion
# of Employees: 12,000

PUROLATOR COURIER CORP.
131 Morristown Road
Basking Ridge, NJ 07920
(201) 953-6400
Primary Business: Specialized
  transportation of small packages
Chairman: Nicholas F. Brady
CEO: C. Howard Hardesty, Jr.
President: C. Howard Hardesty, Jr.
Senior Vice-President (Human
  Resources): W. Thomas Margetts
Senior Vice-President (U.S. Courier):
  Donald F. Mayer

Revenue: $790.33 million
# of Employees: 20,000

Subsidiaries:
Purolator Products North America
Stant, Inc.
Purolator Courier Corp.

TIGER INTERNATIONAL, INC.
1888 Century Park E
Los Angeles, CA 90067
(213) 552-6300
Primary Business: Holding company
Chairman of the Board: Wayne M.
  Hoffman
CEO: Robert P. Jensen
President: Robert P. Jensen
Vice-President (Taxes): Rolf Bodenburg
Sales: $1.02 billion
Net Worth: $1.9 million
# of Employees: 6,300

Subsidiaries:
The Flying Tiger Line, Inc.
Hall's Motor Transit Co.
Tiger Leasing Group, Inc.
North American Car Corp.
National Equipment Rental, Ltd.

UNITED PARCEL SERVICE OF
  AMERICA, INC.
Greenwich Office Park 5
Greenwich, CT 06830
(203) 622-6000
Primary Business: Specialized
  transportation services
Chairman of the Board: John W. Rogers
CEO: John W. Rogers
Senior Vice-President: John W. Alden
Senior Vice-President
  (Communications): Robert E. Smith
Senior Vice-President (Personnel):
  Donald W. Layden
Sales: $7.67 billion
# of Employees: 150,000

Miscellaneous Facts: Also known as
  "UPS."

Airlines

AIR CAL, INC.
3636 Birch Street
Newport Beach, CA 92660
(714) 752-7000

Primary Business: Air transportation
Chairman of the Board: William Lyon
CEO: William Lyon
President: David A. Banmiller
Vice-President (Passenger Seattle):
  Mike P. Loffman
Vice-President (Personnel): Peter M.
  Deiser
Vice-President (Corporate Public
  Affairs): William R. Bell
Revenue: $303.95 million
Net Worth: $36 million
# of Employees: 2,274

Subsidiary:
Air Cal

AIR CANADA
Place Air Canada
Montreal, Quebec, Canada H221X5
(514) 879-7000
Primary Business: Air transportation
Chairman of the Board: Claude I.
  Taylor
CEO: Pierre J. Jeanniot
President: Pierre J. Jeanniot
Vice-President (Sales and Operations):
  R. W. Linder
Senior Vice-President (Human
  Resources): J. Whitelaw
Vice-President (Government and Public
  Affairs): G. Chiasson
Sales: $1.94 billion
# of Employees: 23,715

ALASKA AIRLINES, INC.
Post Office Box 68900
Seattle, WA 98168
(206) 433-3200
Primary Business: Air transportation
Chairman of the Board: Bruce R.
  Kennedy
CEO: Bruce R. Kennedy
President: Gus Robinson
Senior Vice-President (Public Affairs):
  James A. Johnson
Vice-President (Personnel): Robert H.
  Putman
Revenue: $361.64 million
Net Worth: $109 million
# of Employees: 3,000

Miscellaneous Facts: Subsidiary of
  Alaska Air Group, Inc.

ALLEGIS, INC.
Post Office Box 66919
Chicago, IL 60666
(312) 952-4000
Primary Business: Air transportation
Chairman: Richard J. Ferris
CEO: Richard J. Ferris
President: Richard J. Ferris
Senior Vice-President: John L. Cowan
Senior Vice-President and General
  Counsel: Edward H. Hoenicke
Revenue: $6.38 billion
Net Worth: $1.78 billion
# of Employees: 76,000

Subsidiaries:
United Airlines, Inc.
The Hertz Corp.
Mauna Kea Properties, Inc.
Westin Hotel Co.

AMERICAN AIRLINES, INC.
Post Office Box 619616
Dallas–Fort Worth, TX 75261
(817) 355-1234
Primary Business: Air transportation
Chairman of the Board: Robert L.
  Crandall
President: Robert L. Crandall
Vice-President (Passenger Service):
  William E. Crosby
Vice-President (Corporate
  Communications): Lowell C. Duncan
Vice-President (Employee Relations):
  Charles A. Pasciuto
Revenue: $5.35 billion
# of Employees: 37,500

Miscellaneous Facts: Subsidiary of AMR
  Corp. Began as a collection of many
  small airlines in 1929. Changed name
  from Universal Aviation Corp. to
  American Airlines in 1934. Charles A.
  Lindbergh made first flight for what is
  now A.A. According to the company,
  623 million passengers boarded its
  planes in 1985.

AMR CORP.
Post Office Box 619616
Dallas, TX 75261
(817) 355-1234
Primary Business: Holding company
Chairman: Robert L. Leandall
CEO: Robert L. Leandall
President: Robert L. Leandall
Senior Vice-President: Donald J. Carty
Senior Vice-President and General
  Counsel: Richard A. Lempert
Director of Personnel: J.R. Hickey
Sales: $6.13 billion
Net Worth: $1.6 billion
# of Employees: 46,900

Subsidiaries:
American Airlines
AMR Services Corp.
AMR Energy Corp.
AA Training Corp.
Sky Chefs
Rainbow House

BRANIFF, INC.
7701 Lemmon Avenue
Dallas, TX 75209
(214) 358-6011
Primary Business: Air transportation
Chairman of the Board: J. A. Pritzker
President: Ronald Ridgeway
Senior Vice-President: W. T. Lagow
Senior Vice-President: Jeff Warner
Senior Vice-President: Dale R. States
Sales: $205.47 million
# of Employees: 2,200

CONTINENTAL AIRLINES CORP.
Post Office Box 4607
Houston, TX 77010
(713) 630-5000
Primary Business: Air transportation
Chairman: Frank Lorenzo
CEO: Frank Lorenzo
President: Philip J. Bakes
Vice-Chairman: Howard P. Swanson
Vice-President (Customer Service): Don
  J. Thompson
Revenue: $1.18 billion
# of Employees: 1,500

Miscellaneous Facts: Subsidiary of Texas
  Air Corp.

DELTA AIR LINES, INC.
Hartsfield Atlanta International Airport
Atlanta, GA 30320
(404) 765-2600
Primary Business: Air transportation
CEO: David C. Garrett
President: Ronald W. Allen

Senior Vice-President (Finance): M. O. Galloway
Vice-President (Passenger Service): Rex McGlelland
Vice-President (Personnel): Russell H. Heil
Revenue: $4.68 billion
Net Worth: $1.2 billion
# of Employees: 37,671

EASTERN AIR LINES, INC.
Miami International Airport
Miami, FL 33122
(305) 873-2211
Primary Business: Air transportation
Chairman of the Board: Frank Borman
CEO: Frank Borman
President: Joseph B. Leonard
Senior Vice-President (Communications): Jerry Cosley
Vice-President (Employee Service): Dwain L. Andrews
Revenue: $4.8 billion
Net Worth: $325 million
# of Employees: 37,415

NORTHWEST AIRLINES, INC.
Minneapolis–St. Paul International Airport
St. Paul, MN 55111
(612) 726-2111
Primary Business: Air transportation
CEO: Steven G. Rothmeier
President: Steven G. Rothmeier
Executive Vice-President (Marketing and Sales): T. J. Koors
Vice-President (Personnel): James F. Redeske
Vice-President (Public Relations): William C. Wzen
Revenue: $2.19 billion
# of Employees: 11,000

Miscellaneous Facts: Subsidiary of NWA Inc.

PAN AM CORP.
200 Park Avenue
New York, NY 10166
(212) 880-1234
Primary Business: Holding company
Chairman: L. E. Acker
CEO: L. E. Acker

Vice-Chairman: G. L. Gitner
Vice-Chairman: M. R. Shugrue Jr.
Senior Vice-President: Neil Effman
Senior Vice-President (Corporate Affairs): John M. Lindsey
Revenue: $3.68 billion
Net Worth: $448 million
# of Employees: 24,130

Subsidiaries:
Pan American World Airways, Inc.
Pan-Am World Services, Inc.

PAN AMERICAN WORLD AIRWAYS, INC.
Pan Am Building
New York, NY 10017
(212) 880-1234
Primary Business: International air transportation
Chairman: C. Edward Acker
CEO: C. Edward Acker
President: C. Edward Acker
Vice-President (Corporate Communications): Jeffrey F. Kriendler
Vice-President (Cargo): J. Bruce Gebhardt
Vice-President (Personnel): Robert G. Adams
Revenue: $3.08 billion
# of Employees: 27,700

Miscellaneous Facts: Subsidiary of Pan Am Corp.

PIEDMONT AVIATION, INC.
Smith-Reynolds Airport
Winston-Salem, NC 27156
(919) 767-5100
Primary Business: Airline transportation
CEO: William R. Howard
President: William R. Howard
Senior Vice-President (Marketing): W. G. McGee
Senior Vice-President (Passenger Service): J. L. Martin
Vice-President (Employee Relations): J. B. Wilson
Revenue: $1.28 billion
# of Employees: 12,589

PEOPLE EXPRESS AIRLINES, INC.
North Terminal, Newark International
  Airport
Newark, NJ 07114
(201) 961-2935
Primary Business: Passenger airline
  service
Chairman: D. C. Burr
CEO: D. C. Burr
President: D. C. Burr
Managing Officer: Jim Barrall
Managing Officer: Jack Browning
Revenue: $586.80 million
Net Worth: $190 million
# of Employees: 3,975, including part-
  time

Subsidiaries:
Britt Airways
Frontier Airlines, Inc.

PSA, INC.
3225 N Harbor Drive
San Diego, CA 92101
(714) 574-2100
Primary Business: Holding company
Chairman: John P. Guerin
CEO: Paul C. Barkley
President: Paul C. Barkley
Executive Vice-President: George M.
  Shortley
Senior Vice-President (Operations):
  James W. Sheehan
Personnel Director: Carol Costa
Revenue: $689.72 million
Net Worth: $198 million
# of Employees: 3,900

Subsidiaries:
Airline Training Center
North American Aircraft Finance Corp.
Pacific Aircraft Finance Corp.
Pacific Southwest Airlines
Pacific Southwest Exploration Co.
Pacific Southwest Trading Co.

SOUTHWEST AIRLINES CO.
Post Office Box 37611
Dallas, TX 75235
(214) 353-6100
Primary Business: Airline transportation
Chairman of the Board: Herbert D.
  Kelleher
CEO: Herbert D. Kelleher
President: Herbert D. Kelleher

Executive Vice-President: Robert W.
  Lawles
Vice-President (Personnel): Marcy
  Laroon
Vice-President (In-Flight Service):
  William Q. Miller Jr.
Revenue: $535 million
# of Employees: 4,200

TEXAS AIR CORP.
4040 Capital Bank Plaza
Houston, TX 77002
(713) 658-9588
Primary Business: Airline holding
  company
CEO: F. A. Lorenzo
President: F. A. Lorenzo
Senior Vice-President and General
  Counsel: Charles T. Goolsbee
Vice-President: Clark H. Onstad
Revenue: $1.37 billion
# of Employees: 15,000

Subsidiaries:
CCS Automation Systems, Inc.
Continental Airlines Corp.
Eastern Airlines Corp.
New York Airlines, Inc.

TRANS WORLD AIRLINES, INC.
605 Third Avenue
New York, NY 10158
(212) 692-3000
Primary Business: Air transportation
Chairman: L. E. Smart
President: R. D. Pearson
Senior Vice-President: C. J. Bradshaw
Senior Vice-President: S. G. Long
Vice-President and General Counsel: U.
  V. Hoffmann
Revenue: $3.73 billion
Net Worth: $729 million
# of Employees: 28,400

UNITED AIR LINES, INC.
Post Office Box 66100
Chicago, IL 60666
(312) 952-4000
Primary Business: Air transportation
Chairman: Richard J. Ferris
CEO: Richard J. Ferris
President: James J. Hartigan
Vice-President (In-Flight Service):
  Diane M. Sena

Vice-President (Food Service): John R.
  Costello
Vice-President (Customer Service):
  Barry A. Kotar
Sales: $2.90 billion
# of Employees: 43,806

Miscellaneous Facts: Subsidiary of
  Allegis, Inc.

WESTERN AIR LINES, INC.
Box 92005 World Way Postal
Los Angeles, CA 90009
(213) 646-2345
Primary Business: Air transportation
Chairman: Lawrence H. Lee
CEO: Gerald Grinstein
President: Robin H. H. Wilson
Senior Vice-President (Service): Don L.
  Beck
Vice-President (Flight Operations):
  Duane Bird Gerrard
Vice-President (Corporate Affairs): C.
  F. Van Every
Revenue: $1.18 billion
Net Worth: $240 million
# of Employees: 10,066

Car Rental

AGENCY RENT-A-CAR, INC.
30000 Aurora Road
Solon, OH 44139
(216) 349-1000
Primary Business: Short-term auto
  rentals
Chairman of the Board: S. J. Frankino
President: S. J. Frankino
Executive Vice-President: V. T.
  Garrenton
Vice-President: G. Beard
Vice-President (Personnel): Kelly
  Borchelt
Sales: $87.71 million
Net Worth: $44 million
# of Employees: 1,200

Subsidiaries:
Agency Chrysler-Plymouth, Inc.
Agency Ford, Inc.
Altra Chevrolet
Transautomotive Insurance Co.

AVIS, INC.
900 Old Country Road
Garden City, NY 11530
(516) 222-3000
Primary Business: Car rental and leasing
Chairman of the Board: J. Patrick
  Barrett
President: Joseph V. Vittoria
Senior Vice-President (Sales): James E.
  Collins
Vice-President (Personnel): Donald L.
  Korn
Vice-President (Security): Seth
  Kaminsky
Sales: $1.01 billion
# of Employees: 10,500

Miscellaneous Facts: Subsidiary of
  Beatrice Companies, Inc.

BUDGET RENT-A-CAR CORP.
200 N Michigan Avenue
Chicago, IL 60601
(312) 580-5000
Primary Business: Rent-a-car franchises
CEO: Morris Belzberg
President: Morris Belzberg
# of Employees: 300

Miscellaneous Facts: Subsidiary of
  Transamerica Corp.

GELCO CORP.
One Gelco Drive
Eden Prairie, MN 55344
(612) 828-1000
Primary Business: Leasing and renting
  of cars and truck fleets
Chairman: N. Bud Grossman
CEO: N. Bud Grossman
President: Morton L. Zalk
Executive Vice-President: Michael J.
  Morris
Vice-President (Communications): Elin
  A. Schomaker
Vice-President (Human Resources):
  Charles D. DeVine
Revenue: $1 billion
Net Worth: $222 million
# of Employees: 6,392

Subsidiaries:
Gelco CTI Container Services, Inc.
Gelco Domestic Services
Gelco Truck Leasing

Gelco Fleet Management
Gelco Payment Systems, Inc.
Gelco Rail Services
Gelco Space

THE HERTZ CORP.
660 Madison Avenue
New York, NY 10021
(212) 980-2121
Primary Business: Renting and leasing
automobiles, trucks and equipment
Chairman: Frank A. Olsen
CEO: Frank A. Olsen
Executive Vice-President (Rent-a-Car):
Craig R. Koch
Senior Vice-President (Marketing):
Brian J. Kennedy
Director, Employee Relations:
Jacqueline Bander
Sales: $1.50 billion
# of Employees: 14,000

Subsidiary:
Hertz International, Ltd.

Miscellaneous Facts: Subsidiary of
Allegis, Inc. Company toll-free
consumer number is (800) 654-8212.

NATIONAL CAR RENTAL SYSTEM, INC.
7700 France Avenue
S Minneapolis, MN 55435
(612) 830-2121
Primary Business: Car and truck rental
and leasing
President: Bemiss A. Rolfs
Vice-President (Sales and License):
Henry F. Boubelik
Vice-President (Marketing): Edward W.
Rhodes
Vice-President (Personnel Relations):
Kenneth B. Sanville
Sales: $698 million
# of Employees: 5,000

Miscellaneous Facts: Subsidiary of
Household International, Inc.
Company toll-free number for
emergency road service is (800)
367-6767.

THRIFTY RENT-A-CAR SYSTEM, INC.
4606 S Garnett
Tulsa, OK 74145
(918) 665-3930
Primary Business: Operates rent-a-car
chain
President: William E. Lobeck, Jr.
Executive Vice-President (Sales): James
R. Philton
Vice-President: Robert E. Pendergrass
Sales: $72 million
# of Employees: 165

Miscellaneous Facts: Company is a
division of Thrifting, Inc.

Miscellaneous

ALLIED VAN LINES, INC.
25th Avenue and Roosevelt Road
Broadview, IL 60153
(312) 681-8000
Primary Business: Moving
Chairman of the Board: Dennis I. Mudd
President: Sidney Epstein
Senior Vice-President: Peter P. Mazzetti
Vice-President and General Counsel:
Terry G. Fewell
Revenue: $460 million
# of Employees: 1,042

Subsidiaries:
Allied Airfreight Corp.
Allied Van Lines of Alabama, Inc.
Allied Van Lines of Indiana
Allied Van Lines Terminal Co.

Divisions:
Consumer Products Div.
Household Goods Div.
Special Products Div.
Texas Intrastate Operation

AMERICAN PRESIDENT COMPANIES, LTD.
1800 Harrison Street
Oakland, CA 94612
(415) 272-8000
Primary Business: Steamship line
Chairman of the Board: W. B. Seaton
Executive Vice-President: John Flynn
Executive Vice-President: William B.
Hubbard
Revenue: $950 million

Net Worth: $505 million
# of Employees: 3,000

Subsidiaries:
American President Domestic
  Transportation
American President Lines, Ltd.
American President Real Estate Co.

ATLAS VAN LINES, INC.
1212 St. George Road
Evansville, IN 47703
(812) 424-2222
Primary Business: Transportation
  services
Chairman of the Board: Thomas P.
  Fagan
President: Norman D. Gee
Personnel Director: Patricia Walter
Vice-President (Agency Affairs):
  Michael N. Scavuzzo
Sales: $173.10 million
# of Employees: 457

BEKINS CO.
777 Flowers Street
Glendale, CA 91201
(818) 507-1200
Primary Business: Transportation
Chairman of the Board: Irwin L. Jacobs
President: Thomas E. Epley
Senior Vice-President: Ronald L.
  Hartman
Senior Vice-President: Richard J. Morse
Personnel Director: Joan Curtis
Revenue: $327.50 million
# of Employees: 3,500

Subsidiaries:
Bekins International Lines, Inc.
Bekins Van Lines Co.

Miscellaneous Facts: Subsidiary of
  Minstar, Inc.

BRINK'S INC.
Thorndal Circle
Darien, CT 06820
(203) 655-8781
Primary Business: Armored car service
CEO: Hobart K. Robinson, Jr.
Executive Vice-President: Alfred N.
  Tolan
Vice-President (Security): Edward S.
  Lenehan

Vice-President (Sales): Robert J.
  O'Connell
Revenue: $232.64 million
# of Employees: 6,000

BURLINGTON NORTHERN, INC.
999 Third Avenue
Seattle, WA 98104
(206) 467-3838
Primary Business: Holding company,
  transportation
Chairman of the Board: Richard M.
  Bressler
CEO: Richard M. Bressler
President: Richard M. Bressler
Vice-Chairman: Thomas H. O'Leary
Vice-Chairman: Richard C. Grayson
Senior Vice-President (Human
  Resources): Allan R. Boyce
Revenue: $8.65 billion
Net Worth: $4.1 billion
# of Employees: 45,000

Subsidiaries:
Burlington Northern Motor Carriers,
  Inc.
Burlington Northern Railroad Co.
The El Paso Natural Gas Co.
Glacier Park Co.
Meridian Minerals Co.
Plum Creek Timber Co., Inc.

CAROLINA FREIGHT CARRIERS
CORP.
Post Office Box 697
Cherryville, NC 28021
(704) 435-6811
Primary Business: Motor freight carrier
Chairman of the Board: Kenneth G.
  Younger
CEO: Kenneth G. Younger
President: Kenneth E. Mayhen, Jr.
Executive Vice-President: James R.
  Eaton
Executive Vice-President: Palmer E.
  Huffstetler
Revenue: $373 million
# of Employees: 5,816

Miscellaneous Facts: Subsidiary of
  Carolina Freight Corp.

CHROMALLOY AMERICAN CORP.

120 S Central Avenue
St. Louis, MO 63105
(314) 726-9200
Primary Business: Transportation
Chairman of the Board: Norman E.
  Alexander
CEO: Norman A. Alexander
President: William E. Stevens
Executive Vice-President: Thomas G.
  Barnett
Vice-President (Human Resources):
  Ernest M. Felago
Revenue: $720 million
Net Worth: $268 million
# of Employees: 13,750

Subsidiaries:
Chromalloy Finance Co.
Chromalloy Material Handing
E.D.M. of Texas, Inc.
Precoat Metals
Turbine Aeroservices
Gemoco
Sturm Machine Co., Inc.
Woolley Tool & Manufacturing

CONSOLIDATED FREIGHTWAYS, INC.

3240 Hillview Avenue
Palo Alto, CA 94303
(415) 494-2900
Primary Business: Truck transportation
Chairman of the Board: Raymond F.
  O'Brien
CEO: Raymond F. O'Brien
President: Raymond F. O'Brien
Vice-President: Frank E. Roberts
Executive Vice-President: Donald E.
  Moffitt
Sales: $1.7 billion
Net Worth: $552 million
# of Employees: 18,100

Subsidiaries:
CF Air Freight, Inc.
CF Corp. of Delaware
CF Land Services, Inc.
CF Arrowhead Services

CSX CORP.

701 E Byrd Street
Richmond, VA 23219
(804) 782-1400
Primary Business: Holding company
Chairman: Hays T. Watkins
CEO: Hays T. Watkins
President: A. Paul Funkhouser
Senior Vice-President (Audit): Josiah A.
  Stanley, Jr.
Vice-President (Corporate
  Communications): Edwin E. Edel
General Counsel: Garth E. Griffith
Sales: $7.32 billion
Net Worth: $4.9 billion
# of Employees: 60,900

Subsidiaries:
CSX Beckett Aviation, Inc.
CSX Minerals, Inc.
CSX Resources, Inc.
Chessie Systems Railroad
CSX Hotels, Inc.
Seaboard Coast Line Railroad
Texas Gas Resources Corp.

DRAVO CORP.

One Oliver Plaza
Pittsburgh, PA 15222
(412) 566-3000
Primary Business: Transportation
CEO: Thomas F. Faught, Jr.
President: Thomas F. Faught, Jr.
Executive Vice-President: Philip J. Berg
Senior Vice-President: William S.
  Brown
Vice-President (Communications):
  William P. Stewart
Sales: $845 million
Net Worth: $202 million
# of Employees: 8,000

GREYHOUND CORP.

Greyhound Tower
Phoenix, AZ 85013
(602) 248-4000
Primary Business: Bus transportation
Chairman: John W. Teets
CEO: John W. Teets
President: Frank L. Nageotte
Vice-President (Public Relations):
  Dorothy A. Lozant
Vice-President (Human Resources):
  Paul A. Weber
Revenue: $2.72 billion
Net Worth: $1.14 billion
# of Employees: 33,000

Subsidiaries:
Aircraft Service International, Inc.

The Dial Corp.
Faber Enterprises, Inc.
Glacier Park, Inc.
MCI Acceptance Corp.
Travelers Express Company, Inc.
Universal Coach Parts

KANSAS CITY SOUTHERN INDUSTRIES, INC.
114 N 11th Street
Kansas City, MO 64105
(816) 556-0303
Primary Business: Railroad holding
   company
Chairman of the Board: W. N. Deramus
   III
CEO: W. N. Deramus III
President: L. H. Rowland
Senior Vice-President: Donald L. Graf
Vice-President (Personnel): J. L.
   Deveney
Sales: $474 million
Net Worth: $438 million
# of Employees: 5,015

Subsidiaries:
The American-Coleman Co.
Janus Capital Corp.
Arkansas Western Railway Co.

LEASEWAY TRANSPORTATION CORP.
3700 Park E Drive
Cleveland, OH 44122
(216) 464-3300
Primary Business: Motor truck
   transportation
Chairman of the Board: Gerald C.
   McDonough
CEO: Gerald C. McDonough
President: John C. Dannemiller
Vice-President (Human Resources):
   Robert S. Plantz
Vice-President (Sales and Marketing):
   C. Mark Jones
Manager, Communications: Paul A.
   Napoli
Revenue: $1.4 billion
Net Worth: $341 million
# of Employees: 19,000

Subsidiaries:
AMAC Trucking, Inc.
Atlas Service Co.
Best Transport, Inc.

Boston Deliveries, Inc.
East Alpine Corp.
Gold Star, Inc.
LDF, Inc.
B&D Motor Parts, Inc.
Leaseway Intermodal Co.
A.R. Gundry, Inc.
Yellow Truck Rental, Inc.

LOOMIS CORP.
55 Battery Street
Seattle, WA 98121
(206) 223-4900
Primary Business: Armored car service
Chairman of the Board: Charles W.
   Loomis
President: George A. De Bon
Vice-President (Finance): C. L. Nuzum
# of Employees: 5,000

Miscellaneous Facts: Subsidiary of
   Mayne Nickless, Ltd.

MAYFLOWER GROUP, INC.
9998 N Michigan Road
Carmel, IN 46032
(317) 875-1000
Primary Business: Holding company,
   interstate transportation
Chairman: John B. Smith
CEO: John B. Smith
President: John B. Smith
Senior Vice-President (Corporate
   Communications): Elizabeth O.
   Stevens
Executive Vice-President: Gary L. Light
Personnel Director: Collin K. Kebo
Sales: $580.72 million
Net Worth: $87 million
# of Employees: 2,129

Subsidiaries:
ADI Appliances
Mayflower Transit, Inc.
American Transfer & Storage Co.
Avenue Realty Corp.
Crest-Mayflower International, Inc.
Elder Moving and Storage Co.
Flagship Advertising, Inc.
Gentry Insurance Agency, Inc.
Pilgrim Provisions, Inc.
Rover of Indiana

MINSTAR, INC.
100 S Fifth Street
Suite 2400
Minneapolis, MN 55402
(612) 339-7900
Primary Business: Transportation and
storage
Chairman: Irwin L. Jacobs
President: Walter J. Mahanes
Senior Vice-President: Richard E.
Karkow
Vice-President: James B. Farrell
Vice-President: William A. Munsell
Revenue: $880 million
Net Worth: $233
# of Employees: 13,000

**NATIONAL RAILROAD PASSENGER
CORP.**
400 N Capitol Street
NW Washington, DC 20001
(212) 383-3000
Primary Business: Intercity rail
passenger service
Chairman: W. Graham Clayton, Jr.
President: W. Graham Clayton, Jr.
Group Vice-President (Passenger
Service and Communication): M. L.
Clark Tyler
Vice-President (Sales): James Callery
Vice-President (Personnel): John N.
Stulak
Revenue: $825 million
Net Worth: $194 million
# of Employees: 19,900

Subsidiary:
Chicago Union Station Co.

Miscellaneous Facts: Trade Name
"Amtrak."

NORFOLK SOUTHERN CORP.
One Commercial Place
Norfolk, VA 23510
(804) 629-2600
Primary Business: Railroad
Chairman of the Board: Robert B.
Claytor
CEO: Robert B. Claytor
President: Harold H. Hall
Executive Vice-President: John L. Jones
Vice-President (Public Relations):
Magda A. Ratajski

Net Worth: $4.5 billion
# of Employees: 38,000

Subsidiaries:
N.W. Equipment Corp.
North American Van Lines, Inc.
Chesapeake Western Railway
Airforce Pipeline, Inc.
Southern Railway Co.
Chattanooga Station Co.

Miscellaneous Facts: Operates many
other railroad companies.

NORTH AMERICAN VAN LINES, INC.
5001 U.S. Highway 30 W
Fort Wayne, IN 46801
(219) 429-2511
Primary Business: Transportation
Chairman: Kenneth W. Maxfield
President: Kenneth W. Maxfield
Vice-President: James Longbons
Treasurer: Robert M. Steller
Sales: $655 million
# of Employees: 2,400

Miscellaneous Facts: Subsidiary of
Norfolk Southern Corp.

ROADWAY EXPRESS, INC.
1077 George Boulevard
Arrow, OH 44309
(216) 384-1717
Primary Business: Motor carrier
CEO: J. P. Delaney
Vice-President: Jonathon T. Pavloff
Personnel Director: P. L. Heinzerling

Miscellaneous Facts: Subsidiary of
Roadway Services, Inc.

RYDER SYSTEMS, INC.
3600 NW 82nd Avenue
Miami, FL 33166
(305) 593-3726
Primary Business: Truck leasing and
rental
Chairman of the Board: M. Anthony
Burns
CEO: M. Anthony Burns
President: M. Anthony Burns
Executive Vice-President (Human
Resources): Ronald H. Dunbar
Executive Vice-President (Corporate
Affairs): Daniel K. O'Connell

Revenue: $2.49 billion
Net Worth: $1.67 billion
# of Employees: 27,825

Subsidiaries:
Complete and Transit, Inc.
Delavan Industries, Inc.
Aviall, Inc.
Aviation Sales Corp., Inc.
DPD, Inc.
RPD, Inc.
Ryder Carrier Co.
Ryder Truck Rental, Inc.

SANTA FE SOUTHERN PACIFIC CORP.
2245 Michigan Avenue
Chicago, IL 60604
(312) 427-4900
Primary Business: Holding company
Chairman: John J. Schmidt
CEO: John J. Schmidt
President: Robert D. Keebs
Senior Vice-President (Law): Richard K. Knowlton
Vice-President (Human Resources): C. Ore Davis
Vice-President (Corporate Communications): Frank N. Grossman
Revenue: $6.44 billion
Net Worth: $11 billion
# of Employees: 63,600

Subsidiaries:
The Southern Pacific & Santa Fe Railway
SFSP Fiber Optics
Santa Fe Industries, Inc.
SF Minerals Corp.
Southern Pacific Co.
BLC Corp.
Pacific Fruit Express Co.
Pacific Motor Trucking Co.
Sunset Railway Co.
Sunset Communications Co.
Santa Fe Pacific Lumber Co.
The Commonwealth Plan

SEA-LAND CORP.
10 Parsonage Road
Menlo Park, NJ 08837
(201) 632-2000
Primary Business: Interests in container shipping and other freight

transportation
Chairman: Joseph F. Abely, Jr.
CEO: Joseph F. Abely, Jr.
President: R. Kenneth Johns
Senior Vice-President (Transportation Systems): Jack A. Drobnick
Staff Vice-President (Public Relations): Stanford A. Erickson
Sales: $1.76 billion
Net Worth: $787 million
# of Employees: 9,000

Subsidiary:
Sea-Land Service, Inc.

SOUTHERN PACIFIC TRANSPORTATION CO.
One Market Plaza
San Francisco, CA 94105
(415) 541-1000
Primary Business: Rail transportation
Chairman: Denman K. McNear
CEO: Denman K. McNear
President: Denman K. McNear
Vice-President (Public Relations): L. M. Phelps
Vice-President (Sales): Joseph E. Neal
Vice-President (Real Estate): Stanley A. Sutfin
Sales: $2.17 billion
# of Employees: 25,847

Miscellaneous Facts: Subsidiary of Southern Pacific Co.

THE TEXAS MEXICAN RAILWAY CO.
1200 Washington Street
Laredo, TX 78040
(512) 722-6411
Primary Business: Common carrier
Chairman of the Board: Andres R. Ramos
CEO: Andres R. Ramos
President: C. Howard Darnell, Jr.
Vice-President: Solis Zaragoza III
Sales Manager: Israel Cantu
Revenue: $18.81 million
# of Employees: 347

TRAILWAYS, INC.
1500 Jackson Street
Dallas, TX 75201
(214) 655-7711

Primary Business: Intercity bus lines
Chairman: J. L. Kerigan
CEO: J. L. Kerigan
President: H. J. Lesko
Executive Vice-President: S. W. Griffith
Senior Vice-President: B. A. Robinson
Sales: $350 million
# of Employees: 8,000

Subsidiaries:
Trailways Manufacturing Group
Trailways of New England, Inc.
Trailways Miami, Inc.

Miscellaneous Facts: Subsidiary of
Trailways Corp.

U-HAUL INTERNATIONAL, INC.
2727 N Central Avenue
Phoenix, AZ 85004
(602) 263-6011
Primary Business: Rental services,
trucks, trailers
Chairman: William E. Carty
President: Samuel W. Shoen
Personnel Director: Richard Renckley
Public Relations Director: Paul J. Kelley
Sales: $700 million
# of Employees: 13,000

Miscellaneous Facts: Subsidiary of
Amerco.

UNION PACIFIC CO.
345 Park Avenue
New York, NY 10154
(212) 418-7800
Primary Business: Holding company,
railroad, crude oil
Chairman: William S. Cook
CEO: William S. Cook
President: William S. Cook
Senior Vice-President (External
Affairs): C. L. Eaton
Senior Vice-President (Law): W. J.
McDonald
Vice-President (Corporate Relations):
R. W. Anthony
Revenue: $7.92 million
Net Worth: $4.7 million
# of Employees: 285

Subsidiaries:
Champlin Petroleum Co.
Rocky Mountain Energy Co.
Union Pacific Railroad Co.
Upland Industries Corp.

UNITED VAN LINES, INC.
One United Drive
Fenton, MD 63026
(314) 326-3100
Primary Business: Transportation
Chairman of the Board: Maurice
Greenblatt
CEO: Maurice Greenblatt
President: Robert J. Baer
Vice-Chairman: Gerald P. Stadler
Senior Vice-President: David Hollis

Subsidiaries:
Matlock Trailer Corp.
Transprotection Service Co.
United Leasing, Inc.

VIKING FREIGHT SYSTEM, INC.
3405 Victor Street
Santa Clara, CA 95050
(408) 988-6111
Primary Business: Freight transportation
Chairman: Richard W. Bangham
President: Randolph Bangham
Marketing Director: Dennis Pickering
Personnel Director: Deborah Leddon
Sales: $102.96 million
# of Employees: 2,200

Miscellaneous Facts: One of the largest
fright carriers by truck in California.

THE WILLIAMS COMPANIES
One Williams Center
Tulsa, OK 74102
(918) 588-2000
Primary Business: Owns and operates
common carrier pipeline system
Chairman: Joseph H. Williams
CEO: Joseph H. Williams
President: Joseph H. Williams
Executive Vice-President: D. W. Calvert
Executive Vice-President: Vernon T.
Jones
Senior Vice-President and General
Counsel: C. J. Head
Revenue: $3.17 billion
Net Worth: $1.2 billion
# of Employees: 7,000

Subsidiaries:
AGRICO Chemical Co.
Northwest Central Pipeline Corp.
Northwest Pipeline Corp.
Williams Exploration Co.
Williams Natural Gas Co.

YELLOW CAB CO.
2501 W Lexington Street
Baltimore, MD 21203
(301) 685-1212
Primary Business: Taxicab service
President: George J. Joseph
Vice-President: Mark L. Joseph
Vice-President: Michael Muscalli, Jr.
Sales: $2 million
# of Employees: 400

**YELLOW FREIGHT SYSTEM, INC.,
OF DELAWARE**
10990 Roe Avenue
Box 7563
Overland Park, KS 66204
(913) 345-1020

Primary Business: Holding company,
motor carrier industry
Chairman: George E. Powell, Jr.
President: Raymond A. Stewart, Jr.
Senior Vice-President (Marketing):
Robert W. Burdick
Vice-President (Sales): Newton A.
Graves
Vice-President (Human Resources):
Mike Haughton
Revenue: $1.38 billion
Net Worth: $321 million
# of Employees: 19,500

Subsidiaries:
Freightor Services, Inc.
Har-Bet, Inc.
Northcutt, Inc.
Yellow Freight System, Inc.

APPENDIXES

A: The Top 50 Industrial Companies, According to Sales (Source: Fortune 500)

Company	Sales (in thousands of dollars)
General Motors	$96,371,700
Exxon	86,673,000
Mobil	55,960,000
Ford Motor	52,774,400
International Business Machines	50,056,000
Texaco	46,297,000
Chevron	41,741,905
American Telephone and Telegraph	34,909,500
E.I. du Pont de Nemours	29,483,000
General Electric	28,285,000
Amoco	27,215,000
Atlantic Richfield	22,357,000
Chrysler	21,255,500
Shell Oil	20,309,000
U.S. Steel	18,429,000
United Technologies	15,748,674
Phillips Petroleum	15,676,000
Tenneco	15,400,000
Occidental Petroleum	14,534,400
Sun	13,769,000
Boeing	13,636,000
Procter & Gamble	13,552,000
RJ Reynolds Industries	13,533,000
Standard Oil	13,002,000
ITT	12,714,276
Beatrice	12,595,000
Philip Morris	12,149,000
Dow Chemical	11,537,000
McDonnell Douglas	11,477,000
Rockwell International	11,337,600
Unocal	10,738,000
Westinghouse Electric	10,700,200
Eastman Kodak	10,631,000

Dart & Kraft	9,942,300
Goodyear Tire & Rubber	9,896,700
Lockheed	9,535,000
Allied-Signal	9,115,000
General Foods	9,022,418
Union Carbide	9,003,000
Xerox	8,947,600
Pepsico	8,478,902
General Dynamics	8,410,600
LTV	8,198,800
Coca-Cola	8,138,904
Sara Lee	8,117,206
Ashland Oil	7,891,223
Minnesota Mining & Manufacturing	7,846,000
Amerada Hess	7,653,439
W.R. Grace	7,260,100
Coastal	7,254,300

B: The 50 Most Unusual Businesses in America

While these 50 businesses didn't qualify for the "1,000 Most Important Companies" in America category, I found these firms so interesting that I thought many people might like to contact them.

ADVANCE WORK, LTD.
Post Office Box 1245
Greenwich, CT 06836
(203) 622-9207
President: Janis Hearell

Acts as advisor, and will also completely plan and orchestrate special occasions and large events. Has resources around the world.

**THE AMERICAN MUSEUM OF
HISTORICAL DOCUMENTS**
3601 W Sahara Avenue
Las Vegas, NV 89102
(702) 364-1000
President: Todd M. Avelrod

Company is one of the largest dealers of American historical documents.

BATHROOM JOURNAL
19701 S Miles Road
Cleveland, OH 44128
(216) 662-6969
Publisher: Michael S. Cohen

Company publishes a general-interest magazine designed to be read in the bathroom.

BEEGOTTEN CREATIONS
28 Bonning Court
Spring Valley, NY 10977
President: Lloyd Eckert

Company makes and sells men's maternity clothes.

BINGO SCENCE MAGAZINE
8500 Station Street # 240
Mentor, OH 44060
(216) 255-7858
President: Peter James

Company publishes local bingo
players' guide in different states.

BORING INSTITUTE
Post Office Box 40
Maplewood, NJ 07040
(201) 763-6392
Founder: Alan Caruba

Company published book called
Boring Stuff in 1987. Offers members
information on the boring things in
life.

BRIDAL EXPOS, INC.
510 Montauk Highway
West Islip, NY 11795
(516) 669-1200
President: Bill Heaton
Public Relations: Laura M. Baddish

Company operates the largest
traveling bridal show in the world.

BROADCAST INTERVIEW SOURCE
2500 Wisconsin Avenue NW
Suite 930
Washington, DC 20007
(202) 333-4904
Editor: Mitchell P. Davis

Company publishes a talk show
directory, which lists thousands of
guests for the media.

CAPE ANN ANTIQUES
Post Office Box 3502
Peabody, MA 01960
(617) 777-3011
President: Jed Power

First business specializing in drug
antiques and collectibles.

CELEBRITY DIRT
821 N Pine
Lansing, MI 48906
(517) 372-1026
President: Barry Gibson

Collects and sells packages of dirt
collected from stars' homes.

CONCANNON'S HORSELESS STABLE
2990 Redhill Avenue
Costa Mesa, CA 92626
(714) 549-4913
President: Gary Concannon

One of the largest dealers of pre-
owned Roll-Royce autos. Will pick up
your Rolls in a semi truck, clean it,
and repair or restore it.

CYCLE EXPRESS
102 Orange Avenue
Long Beach, CA 90802
(213) 432-0474
President: Judy Greenstein

Offers services for the business
executive, which include petting,
hugging and feeding your dog when
you leave town.

DEBIT ONE, THE MOBILE BOOKKEEPING SERVICE
3433-5 S Campbell
Springfield, MO 65807
(800) 331-2491
President: Jack Dunn

Bookkeeping service that comes to
your business. Has office that travels.

DENISE AUSTIN FITNESS SYSTEMS
60 W Ninth Street
New York, NY 10011
(212) 475-4001
President: Kevin R. Weaver

Provides fitness and exercise programs
for people who use video display
terminals (that is, computers).

DIENER INDUSTRIES, INC.
20257 Prairie Street
Chatsworth, CA 91311
(818) 886-7800
President: Murray Garrett

Is one of the largest manufacturers of custom-designed erasers in the world.

DOVE, INC.
12711 Ventura Boulevard, Suite 250
Studio City, CA 91604
(818) 762-6662
President: Michael Viner

Company is one of the largest producers of audio cassettes in the country.

FIDDLER ON THE ROOF
7850 Alabama Boulevard
Canoga Park, CA 91304
(818) 884-8935
Owner: Russ Gardner

Company specializes in chimney sweeping.

FUTREX
1510 Andalusia
Venice, CA 90291
(213) 392-4836
President: Jody Dikoff
Senior Consultant: Joseph Dikoff

Futrex is a patent consulting company. Clients with inventions are advised on what to do and how to get product produced.

THE INCREDIBLE MACHINE
17922 Skypark Circle, Suite 6
Irvine, CA 92714
(714) 261-9395
President: Frank Geyer

Company specializes in computer-engraved gifts.

INKY DINKY, INC.
Post Office Box 1699
Newport Beach, CA 92663
(714) 722-6291
President: Al Newman

Publishes baby books for cats and dogs.

JACKSON-MITCHELL, INC.
Post Office Box 5425
Santa Barbara, CA 93108
(805) 565-1538
CEO: Robert Jackson

Produces Meyenberg Goat Milk. Products include evaporated, powdered and fresh ultrapasteurized goat milk.

LETTERDIAL
Post Office Box 241532
Los Angeles, CA 90024
(213) 216-6800
President: James A. Novack

Company uses phone prefixes and area codes to make personalized phone numbers.

M.A. SCALE MODELS
3074 Gibraltar Avenue
Costa Mesa, CA 92626
(714) 641-1453
Owner: Mike Arensdorf

Company builds small scale models. Specializes in metal race car kits.

MERRY MAIDS, INC.
11117 Mill Valley Road
Omaha, NE 68154
(800) 345-5535
President: Thomas G. Guy

One of the largest home cleaning companies in the U.S. The company offers many different cleaning programs for consumers to choose from.

METER ADVERTISING CORP.
17 Battery Place
New York, NY 10004
(213) 422-8888
President: Len Butler

Places advertising on parking meters.

METRO BUSINESS CONSULTANTS, INC.
2425 S Progress Drive
Salt Lake City, UT 84119
(801) 973-7600
President: Lloyd Peterson

Marketers of the first microwave popcorn vending machine.

MURDER MYSTERY WEEKENDS
3650 Clark Avenue, Penthouse E
Burbank, CA 91505
(818) 842-3407
President: Margo Morrison
Vice-President: Keith O'Leary

Company sells and plans murder mystery parties for groups.

NATIONAL SURVIVAL GAMES
Box 1439
New London, NH 03257
(412) 935-7460
President: Robert Gurnsey
Director, Public Relations: Debra Dion

Sells equipment for an air-gun game that is the adult version of "Capture the Flag." They also organize corporate functions for the game.

NEW PIG CORP.
2614 18th Street
Altoona, PA 16601
(800) HOT-DOGS
President and Co-Founder: Donald L. Beaver, Jr.
Secretary, Treasurer and Co-Founder: Bernard E. Stapelfeld

Manufactures tubular absorbent socks, used to contain and absorb industrial fluid leaks.

NEWSMAKER INTERVIEWS
439 S La Cienega #219
Los Angeles, CA 90048
President: Arthur Levine

Publishes a newsletter that is sent to major radio stations indicating who is available for interviews.

O'MALLEYS FLOWER, INC.
16303 Ventura Boulevard
Sherman Oaks, CA 91403
(818) 990-3631
President: Allen Yabko

A flower shop that also sells gourmet food baskets, Crabtree & Evelyn soaps, fresh coffee beans, teddy bears, balloons and more.

PETS ARE INN
125 Sixth Street, Suite 950
Minneapolis, MN 55402
(800) 248-7387
President: Harry Sanders-Greenberg

A special inn for pets that is far more luxurious than a kennel.

PORTA-BOTE-INTERNATIONAL
1074 Independence Avenue
Mountain View, CA 94043
(415) 961-5334
President: Alex R. Kaye

Makes porta-botes that fold to four inches flat and can strap onto a car like a surfboard. They are available in 8-, 10-, and 12-foot models.

PREMIER LUXURY LINERS, INC.
15303 Ventura Boulevard, 9th Floor
Sherman Oaks, CA 91403
(818) 998-6558
Executive Coordinator: William R. Robeson

Provides limousines with bulletproof glass, bodyguard service, safety tire bands, tailpipe protection and much more.

PRIMITIVE TECHNOLOGIES, INC.
34 Judson Lane
Bethlehem, CT 06751
(203) 266-7322
President: Jeff Kalin

Company makes replicas of Native American tools and shelters using authentic methods and materials.

PRO CREATIONS MATERNITY
   LEASEWEAR
Post Office Box 22253
Milwaukee, OR 97222
(503) 659-4020
President: Donna Smith

Leases maternity clothes designed especially for pregnant professionals.

RAINBOW RIDGE
Box 190
Kapaau, Hawaii 96755
(808) 961-2114
Owner: John Broussard

Company sells an address list of women worldwide who are looking for a perfect mate.

S&H MOTIVATION
5999 Butterfield Road
Hillside, IL 60162
(312) 449-4900
President: William Weller

Company sells motivation programs that help improve the productivity of people.

SOLMAR CORP.
625 W Katella Avenue, Suite 5
Orange, CA 92667
(714) 538-0881
President: R. B. Grubbs

Company cultures, packages, and distributes bacterial formulations that eat waste products, reducing sludge and controlling odors.

SPECIAL RESPONSE CORP.
Post Office Box 541
Hunt Valley, MD 21030
(301) 494-1900
President: Colonel W. T. Travens, Jr.

Controls the use of drugs and alcohol in the work place.

SPORTSCASTER CAMPS OF
   AMERICA
405 Vista Grande
Newport Beach, CA 92660
(714) 760-3131
Director and Founder: Roy Englebreght

A camp that anyone can attend to get a basic education in the sports broadcasting business.

STEVE'S DETAILING
1545 Newport Boulevard
Costa Mesa, CA 92629
(714) 631-6900
President: Steve Marchese

Called a "Health Spa For Your Car." Uses cotton swabs, popsicle sticks and toothbrushes for special cleaning of your car.

STORK NEWS
6537 Raeford Road, #104
Fayetteville, NC 28304
(918) 868-3065
President: Chyrl Young

Rents eight-foot storks with personalized bundle hanging from mouth. Unique gifts available announcing new arrivals.

TANK GOODNESS
40 Skokie Boulevard, #30
Northbrook, IL 60062
(312) 498-4620
President: Betty Hoeffner

Designs and maintains aquariums and provides a wide range of aquarium-related services.

TRANS-TIME, INC.
10208 Pearmain Street
Oakland, CA 94603
(415) 639-1955
President: Art Quaife

Places people in cryonic suspension
capsules after death in hopes of one
day bringing them back to life.

ULTIMATE ISSUES
2265 Westwood Boulevard, Suite 312
Los Angeles, CA 90067
(213) 558-3958
Publisher: Dennis Prager

Company publishes a quarterly
newsletter on the great issues of our
time, from the existence of God to the
immorality of pacifism.

VIDEO PITCH
14003 Palaway Way, Suite 310
Marina Del Ray, CA 90292
(213) 821-7725
President: George M. Marlowe

Puts together new business pitches on
video for advertising agencies.

VOICINGS PUBLICATION, INC.
Post Office Box 3102
Margate, NJ 08437
(609) 645-9393
President: Jim Colaianni

Writes and publishes *Sunday Sermons,*
which is a weekly publication of
complete homilies for use by the
clergy.

WOMEN AT LARGE
704 S Seventh Avenue
Yakima, WA 98908
(509) 965-0115
Co-Founder: Sharlyne Powell
Co-Founder: Sharon McConnell

Provides a fitness program that helps
renew self-esteem in large ladies.

WORLDWIDE TELEVISION NEWS
1995 Broadway
New York, NY 10023
(212) 362-4440
President: Kenneth A. Coyte

One of the world's leading news
services. Shoots such unusual activities
as camel wrestling in Turkey, a 105-
year-old lady on her first parachute
jump, people racing downhill on pink
elephants in val d'Isere and more.

10 Largest Commercial Banks
(Source: Fortune 500)

Company	Assets (in thousands of dollars)
Citicorp	$173,597,000
BankAmerica Corp.	118,541,125
Chase Manhattan Corp.	87,685,442
Manufacturers Hanover Corp.	76,525,769
J. P. Morgan & Co., Inc.	69,375,000
Chemical New York Corp.	56,990,174
Security Pacific Corp.	53,503,239
Bankers Trust New York Corp.	50,581,041
First Interstate Bancorp	48,991,038
First Chicago Corp.	38,892,506

10 Largest Life Insurance Companies
(Source: Fortune 500)

Company	Assets, 1985 (in thousands of dollars)
Prudential	$91,139,140
Metropolitan	76,494,165
Equitable Life Assurance	47,989,964
Aetna Life	37,889,119
New York Life	27,977,512
John Hancock Mutual	26,256,393
Travelers	25,571,766
Teachers Insurance & Annuity	23,159,057
Connecticut General Life	22,245,808
Northwestern Mutual	17,897,884

Top 25 Retailing Companies
(Source: Fortune 500)

Company	Sales, 1985 (in thousands of dollars)
Sears Roebuck	$40,715,300
K-Mart	22,420,002
Safeway Stores	19,650,542
Kroger	17,123,531
American Stores	13,889,528
J. C. Penney	13,747,000
Southland	12,719,241
Federated Department Stores	9,978,027
Lucky Stores	9,382,282
Dayton-Hudson	8,793,372
Household International	8,685,500
Wal-Mart Stores	8,580,910
Winn-Dixie Stores	7,774,480
F. W. Woolworth	5,958,000
BATUS	5,881,408
Great Atlantic & Pacific Tea Co.	5,878,286
Montgomery Ward	5,388,000
Supermarkets General	5,122,633
May Department Stores	5,079,900
Albertson's	5,060,265
Melville	4,805,380
Associated Dry Goods	4,385,019
R. H. Macy	4,368,386
Wickes Companies	4,362,454
Marriott	4,317,900

10 Largest Transportation Companies
(Source: Fortune 500)

Company	Operating Revenues, 1985 (in thousands of dollars)
Burlington Northern	$8,650,927
United Parcel Service	7,686,719
CSX	7,320,000
Santa Fe Southern Pacific	6,438,000
UAL	6,383,405
AMR	6,131,028
Eastern Air Lines	4,815,070
Delta Air Lines	4,684,115
Norfolk Southern	3,825,077
Trans World Airlines	3,725,418

The Most (and Least) Admired Companies in America

According to *Fortune* magazine, IBM has lost its most-admired company status this past year. Merck came up from the number-five spot to bump IBM out.

Fortune magazine polled 8,200 financial analysts and executives to rate 300 companies in eight areas of reputation, including financial resources, quality of management and quality of products, among others.

The most admired companies are:

Merck, pharmaceuticals
Liz Claiborne, apparel
Boeing, aerospace
J. P. Morgan, banking
Rubbermaid, rubber and plastic
Shell Oil, petroleum
IBM, office equipment, computers
Johnson & Johnson, pharmaceuticals
Dow Jones, publishing
Herman Miller, furniture

The least admired companies are:
LTV, metals
BankAmerica, banking
American Motors, motor vehicles
Financial Corp. of America, thrifts
Manville, building materials
Bethlehem Steel, metals
Pan Am, transportation
Union Carbide, chemicals
Manhattan Industries, apparel
Trans World Airlines, transportation

INDEX

Limited, 224
Lionel, 190
Lipton, 143
Litton, 26
Liz Claiborne, 32
Lockheed, 26
Loews, 184
Lone Star, 85
Longs Drugs, 224
Loomis, 248
Lorimar, 115
Lowes, 224
LTV, 196
Lucky, 127
L'Eggs, 32

M&M/Mars, 151
Mack, 38
Macy, 224
Magic Chef, 89
Malt o Meal, 144
Manor Care, 160
Manufacturers Hanover, 50
Manville, 86
Marantz, 113
Marcus, 132
Marmon, 196
Marriott, 185
Marsh & McLennan, 175
Marshalls, 225
Martin Marietta, 27
Marvel, 70
Mary Kay, 100
Maserati, 38
Master Lock, 103
Mastercraft, 181
Matsushita Electric, 113
Mattel, 190
Max Factor, 100
May Dept. Stores, 225
Mayflower, 248
Maytag, 90
MCA, 116
McCormick, 144
McCullogh, 103
McDermott, 203
McDonald's, 131
McDonnell Douglas, 26
McGraw, 70
MCI, 234
McIchenny, 144
Mc Kesson, 156
MCorp, 175
Mead, 213
Melville, 225
Memorex, 81
Mennen, 100
Mercant, 225
Merck, 156
Meredith, 71
Merle Norman, 101
Merrill Lynch, 120

Metromedia, 65
Metropol, 175
MGM/UA, 116
Michigan Bell, 234
Midas, 42
Miles, 157
Miller, 52
Milton Bradley, 190
Minnetonka, 101
Minnesota Mining, 60
Minstar, 249
Mitchell Energy, 203
Mitsubishi, 38
Mobil, 203
Monfort of Colorado, 144
Monsanto, 61
Montgomery Ward, 226
Moore Business, 166
Morgan, J.P., 50
Morton Salt, 144
Morton Thiokol, 61
Motel, 185
Mother's, 151
Motorola, 110
Mountain States, 234
Mrs. Fields, 145
Mrs. Paul's, 145
Mrs. Smith's, 145
MTV, 116
Munsingwear, 32
Musicland, 226

Nabisco, 145
Nalco, 61
Nalley's, 152
National Car Rental, 245
National Convenience, 123
National Distillors, 61
National Intergroup, 196
National Med, 161
National Railroad, 249
National Service, 62
National Steel, 196
Navistar, 38
NBC, 66
NCR, 78
Neiman Marcus, 226
Nestle, 145
Neutrogena, 101
New England T&T, 234
New York Stock Ex, 120
News America, 71
Newsweek, 71
Nike, 34
Nikon, 188
N.J. Bell Telephone, 234
NL Industries, 203
Nordstrom, 226
Norfolk, 249
North American Philips, 110
North American Van, 249
Northrop, 27

Northwest Bell, 235
Northwestern Mutual, 176
Northwest Airlines, 242
Norton, 167
Norwest, 176
Nucor, 197
Nutrasweet, 146
NYNEX, 235
N.Y. Life, 176
N.Y. Telephone, 234
N.Y. Times, 71

Occidental, 204
Ocean Spray, 53
Oldsmobile, 39
Olin, 62
Olympic, 167
Oneida, 96
Ore-Ida, 146
Orion, 116
Oscar Meyer, 146
Oshmans, 181
Outboard Motors, 181
Owens-Corning, 86
Owens Ill, 210
Oxford, 33
O'Brien, 167

Pabst, 53
Paccar, 39
Pacific Bell, 235
Pacific Gas, 106
Pacific Light, 204
Pacific North Bell, 235
Pacific Telesis, 236
Paine Webber, 121
Pan Am, 242
Pan American, 242
Panasonic, 114
Panhandle, 204
Paper Mate, 103
Paramount, 117
Parker, 104
Parker Hannifin, 165
Payless, 226
Pay'N'Save, 227
Penn Central, 204
Pennwalt, 62
Pennzoil, 205
Penthouse, 72
People Express, 243
Pep Boys, 227
Pepperidge Farms, 146
Pepsico, 55
Perkin-Elmer, 111
Peter Paul, 152
Pfizer, 157
PG&E, 106
Philip Morris, 57
Phillips, 205
Phillips-Van Husen, 33
Piedmont, 242